HEATHER'S

HERBS IN THE GARDEN

HERBS IN THE GARDEN

Allen Paterson

Director of the Royal Botanical Gardens, Hamilton, Ontario

TVSSILAGO   Roßhůb.

COLTSFOOT (Fuchs, 1542)

J.M. Dent & Sons Ltd
London   Melbourne

First published 1985
Copyright © Allen Paterson 1985

All rights reserved. No part of this
publication may be reproduced, stored
in a retrieval system, or transmitted,
in any form or by any means, electronic,
mechanical, photocopying, recording or
otherwise, without the prior permission
of J. M. Dent & Sons Ltd

Phototypeset in 10½ on 12½pt Linotron Trump Medieval by
The Word Factory, Rossendale, Lancashire
Printed in Great Britain by
Richard Clay (The Chaucer Press) plc for
J.M. Dent & Sons Ltd
33 Welbeck Street, London W1M 8LX

British Library Cataloguing in Publication Data

Paterson, Allen
  Herbs in the garden.
  1. Herb gardening
  I. Title
  635'.7   SB351.H5
ISBN 0–460–04520–2

CONTENTS

LIST OF COLOUR PLATES

Between pages 180 and 181

Illustrations by Roger Mould
from the author's original plans and sketches

vii

FOR MARK

INTRODUCTION

For a dozen years, from the late fifties, I had the good fortune to share a little house for weeks at a time on the western edge of Provence. It belonged to the beneficent aunt of the friends with whom I travelled. There were fig trees, cypresses, pomegranates, a couple of acres of vines whose crops went to the local *cave cooperative*. An un-cultivated area and the vineyard edge sprouted the weeds of the surrounding garigue. These were green at Easter when the vines were nothing but gnarled stumps. By the summer holidays the roles were reversed: the vineyard became an illustration to a bacchanalian revel while the native plants had dwindled to sun-soaked skeletons. Only a twiggy plant or two of fennel had the ability to call up the swallowtail butterflies, which obviously kept them in mind as prospective larva-fodder.

But every step sent up new scents from that parched ground; every plant, it seemed, was aromatic. Excursions into the surrounding limestone hills confirmed this impression: it was a flora composed of sages, thymes, lavenders, rosemary, calamint, oregano, fennel and rue. The rest seemed hardly to count at all.

A further decade, with at least annual trips to Greece, followed to emphasize that the visual delights of the Mediterranean flora were at least equalled by those of the nose, and, by the very slightest extension, the palate. For this is a flora upon which civilisations have been built and have flourished. The 'glory that was Greece' and the 'grandeur that was Rome' were based upon it: plants for shelter, for clothing, for food and for medicine, for religion and even for aesthetic pleasure.

Growing these plants in maritime Hampshire (on heavy clay, with mixed success) and in Thamesside Oxfordshire, where a sandy river terrace provided happier homes, helped to demonstrate their ornamental garden potential. Here it was often seen that the sun-loving Mediterraneans, in spite of occasional winter injury, made finer plants than did their drought-ridden, goat-browsed relations at home.

Eight years at the historic Chelsea Physic Garden provided the perfect place for discovering the further potential of herbs. With an ideal climate and soil, Chelsea had, since 1973, maintained an even earlier herbal tradition and the plants within it. It is not surprising therefore that the Physic Garden is frequently referred to in the following pages.

Equally it is suitable, in deciding which of the early texts to use for a general reference to the plants' medicinal uses that I should choose one based upon that Apothecaries' Garden. Joseph Miller was himself an Apothecary and published in 1722 'Botanicum Officinale; or a Compendious Herbal: Giving An Account of all such PLANTS as are now used in the Practice of Physick with their Descriptions and Virtues'. After a fulsome dedication to Sir Hans Sloane, Miller begins a disarming preface which could well apply today:

'The great Number of Books already extant upon the same subject, may perhaps, at first view, make this Work appear superfluous . . .'.

Joseph Miller (not to be confused with Philip Miller who became, as Sloane's protege, Gardener at Chelsea also in 1722) is an ideal source. He comes at the end of what might be called the age of acceptance herbalism. The mystery of Gerard and the alchemical nonsense of Culpeper are purged. He is dispassionate where the later 'Sir' John Hill is merely an opportunist. Miller coolly writes the sense of his time and makes an admirable guide: Elizabeth Blackwell lifted it almost verbatim to go with her illustrations for *A Curious Herbal* (1733).

This present book, however, is concerned with herbalism only as a herbal use justifies a plant for inclusion into the category of herb as an adjunct to the social history of plants and planting. Its real concern is with herbs as garden plants, in 'herb gardens' or in any other association because they are attractive to our senses.

Therefore it becomes desirable to extend the range by including herbs from other climes and countries which either can be grown outside here or, conveniently, used as pot specimens. By Joseph Miller's time many North American plants had reached Chelsea and were being used by the Apothecaries. A search of mainly nineteenth-century Shaker records shows that, based upon the native people's knowledge, many more suitable species are worthy of inclusion in today's herbal garden scene.

By the mid nineteenth century in the west interest in plant-based medicine had declined drastically and for a hundred years the famous plant collectors, Hooker, Sargent, Wilson, Kingdon Ward and Rock searched out plants of value only to the ornamental garden. Their field of discovery was the Orient where a strong herbal tradition existed. It still does and working herbal gardens can be found in Kyoto and Hokkaido in Japan and Lushan and Hong Kong in China. Thus many of these oriental plants were brought back to embellish western gardens. We are used to seeing them as ornamentals: here a number revert to their native roles as legitimate herbs. It must be emphasized that my major source, 'A Barefoot Doctors Manual', is a current text which avoids the inevitable quaintness of Joseph Miller.

What, then, has been brought together is a collection of plants from the temperate world which in their original or adopted homes, man has harnessed for his 'use and delight'. Thus they are considered as plants having more than one reason for their being grown. Accepted herbs which are visually dull, such as chickweed and wall pellitory, are omitted as are conch grass and green ground elder which only the most foolhardy would consciously cultivate. So too are pretty plants such as the semi-parasite eyebrights which are virtually impossible to please in the garden. Figwort and a few others get in by the skin of their teeth.

There is a further thread in suggesting garden uses for these plants which is to demonstrate, in spite of general belief to the contrary, that ornamental herb gardens are a recent invention. Indeed, of all garden trends, other than those based upon modern technology, enthusiasm for herb gardens is one of the most recent. Certainly, as is shown, our concept of the genre hardly predates the beginning of this century. Not surprisingly therefore with so little practice behind us, there is still much scope in the greater use of *Herbs in the Garden*. Hence this book and hence with some slight validity I might continue to quote from Joseph Miller's preface 'but I can assure the Reader, that no ambition of becoming an Author had an Influence with me and that nothing could have engaged me herein, but the instances of some Friends, who have in a very pressing Manner importuned me to it (for) few were willing to give themselves the Trouble to read over so many Authors as were necessary to a full Accomplishment therein. . . .'

To be honest, in this case the importunity has been on the other foot and I am most grateful for the help and assistance generously afforded by a number of invaluable people. Dr Brent Elliott, Lindley Librarian, led me to the Parkinson Society and other nineteenth-century movements; Susan Vutz and James Hart of the University of California, Berkeley provided information on Gertrude Jekyll's essays in herb gardening; Jane Gelder in London and Shirley DePaul in Canada between them typed my text; Ina Vrugtman, librarian at Royal Botanical Gardens, Hamilton was always to hand for reference checks. I thank too owners of herb gardens which over the years have been an interest and spur to further discoveries.

Finally, as is not uncommon in such credit lists, I thank my wife, Penelope, not merely with the conventional gratitude for forbearance but much more constructively for compiling most of the *herbs in the house* section and in doing so producing all the delicious recipes shown here and lots of others beside. They gave two happy herbal summers and are in place, we hope, for many more.

J. M. Dent and I would like to thank the trustees of the Chelsea Physic Garden for their kind permission to reproduce the map on p.24.

Allen Paterson
Royal Botanical Gardens,
Hamilton, Ontario, Canada.

examples of herbs / categories

longevity of herbs

I

Origins of Herbs: Herbs and Man

Herbs may be defined as plants which are of use to man in a number of specific ways – as culinary aids, as medicines, for perfumery, cosmetics and even as poisons; dye-plants too can logically be included. They are generally not the source of any major plant product such as timber, staple foods or textiles. No, their role is seldom life-supporting but life-enhancing, and as such this second category is almost as important as the first. In the words of the Herb Society of America they are 'for use and for delight'.

Such a definition of herbs needs to be clearly separated from that used in botany where a herb is a plant which is herbaceous – that is, one which dies down in periods of inclement weather (excessively hot summers or hard winters) to a resting organ of some sort. In the case of annual plants this may be the seed which is shed in autumn and germinates the following spring, or, in warmer climates, shed in late spring to germinate with the autumn rains. Or the resting organ can be a subterranean bulb, corm, tuber or root-stock of some kind usually associated with food storage. Botanically, therefore, a herb cannot be a shrubby or woody species. Yet sweet bay, rosemary, lavender and so on are perfectly good shrubs and are included amongst the most basic of herbs.

Thus in the colloquial sense there are herb representatives of all perennation forms – annuals (nasturtium, basil), biennials (parsley, borage), perennials (origano, horse-radish), shrubs (rosemary, sage), and trees (sweet bay, elder). They may be small and bushy, spreading or climbing; brilliant in flower or quietly elegant in leaf; interesting in shape or unusual in fruit. They may be so easy to grow as to be positively invasive or conversely needing all the wiles of the most green-fingered. They may require moisture or perfect drainage; sun or shade.

Such a rapid survey, apparently including much of the plant kingdom, serves to indicate the diversity of potential which herbs offer in the garden as part of the visual scene. How each is subsequently to be used – to make an *omelette aux fines herbes* live up to its name or to poison wolves (wolfsbane must have done a good job in Britain, for there are none of these creatures left wild outside of a zoo) – is a further decision: that there is this further choice is the essence of 'herb-ness'. All herbs have, as it were, dual nationality.

It must be admitted, of course, that in some cases the visual has to take second place to the actual utilitarian, or to an association or historical connection which adds so much to the plant concerned. A really good garden is not made up merely of that which pleases the eye but of a combination of effects and qualities which satisfies all the senses. It will appeal to the head as well as to the heart.

Herbs have a particularly strong suit in such a context. Their history is seen to stretch back into the very dawn of man's emergence from being a hunter-gatherer into a sophisticated cultivator. The value associated with each and the changing uses through the centuries add much to the pleasure to be obtained from them today. It is possible to appreciate them almost as palimpsests, reading what is still just visible in the lower layers.

From the narrow point of view of garden decoration, for example, few would grow mandrake – pleasant though the flowers are, like a cluster of upward-facing campanula bells at ground level in late February, and despite the unusual clutch of pheasant-egg-sized fruit in June. This is because its name has entered the vocabulary as an inevitable part of medical quackery with the marvellous reputation of being able to kill, by uttering a death-dealing shriek, anyone who is foolish enough to wrench it from the ground. Such rumours, of course, were put about by early Greek herbalists who operated what might be called a mandrake closed shop, its use as an effective early anaesthetic making it highly valued and not to be considered lightly. It is still used homoeopathically.

It can be seen from this example (and many others could be cited) that herbs exist culturally as well as *horticulturally*, in our minds as well as in our gardens. It should not surprise us that the growing of herbs epitomizes gardens of earlier times. Even without documentation it is entirely reasonable to suppose that members of settled communities, even up to 10,000 years ago, would attempt to transplant from the wild those plants which were known to be of use to them. Such an attempt was, initially, no doubt entirely utilitarian: it was simpler, safer and altogether more convenient to grow accepted pot herbs or medicinal plants near to hand. Subsequently, conscious arrangement of these plants with the addition, perhaps, of brightly coloured flowers chosen from the wild because they *were* bright sees the dawn of gardening as we know it. That there are garden myths linked with images of paradise in the folklore of so many races indicates how long ago that dawn was.

It is easy today to overlook the problems of the early cultivators and indeed those well into our Christian era. Problems, not merely of cultivation – they are always with us – but of identification, of dissemination of ideas, of attempts at naming and at classification. Until it is possible to refer to something *by name* it has no existence beyond that of itself. Similarly until some form of conceptual group-forming is done no classification is possible.

Obviously at first, as in primitive tribes today, knowledge passed on was purely by word of mouth – folklore in the basic sense of that phrase – with all the dangers of misconstruction and uncertain facts which that implies. But with the advent of a written language, however simple, some of these dangers receded. It is significant then that the earliest written material referring to plants is of herbs. These were the plants at the very core of the culture concerned, in its religion, its magic and its medicine: these three are inextricably linked. By the third millennium BC, parallel cultures in China and Egypt possessed a sophisticated plant-based medicinal tradition which had begun to be written down.

Few of the original sources have come down to us – Egyptian medical prescriptions on papyri dating from about 1800 BC and Assyrian tablets of the seventh century BC record 250 drugs made from plants based upon earlier Sumerian traditions and practices as old as those of Egypt.

As we near the classical world of Ancient Greece and Rome we meet writings on herbs and herbalism which comprised almost the full corpus of medical knowledge until the seventeenth century of the Christian era. Thus Theophrastus, a friend and pupil of Aristotle and contemporary of Plato, lists over 500 plants in his two works *Historia plantarum*, and *De causis plantarum*. These date from the third century BC. In AD 60 Dioscorides listed 600 plants and very soon afterwards the elder Pliny (soon to die in the famous AD 79 eruption of Vesuvius which overwhelmed Pompeii and Herculaneum) listed over 1000 in his *Historia naturalis*.

These writings show a decided change of emphasis in tone and in content. There are still references to religion and the gods, yet clearly independent questioning minds are at work. These are the roots of scientific thinking, the bases of botany. The period also can be seen as developing a literature of gardening, of grouping plants not just for their utilitarian virtues but because they appealed to the aesthetic sense of cultivated men now living in a relatively balanced and sophisticated society. Gardening as an art form is clearly not suited to an insecure world: full appreciation of floral form and colour is inhibited by looking over the shoulder for potential trouble (I am reminded of those hilarious South of France village activities, the *Course au Libre*, where in an arena the protagonists have, amongst other things, to add up a long column of figures on a blackboard while behind a young and frisky bull is being encouraged to behave badly by members of the opposing team).

Yet, in many cases – if not most – the plants grown ornamentally were also those which today we should classify as herbs. There are two reasons for this overlap. One is that the clear separation of the utilitarian from the aesthetic which is so much a part of modern life (and not only in the garden) did not then exist. The second is that the ancients were not confused by the incredible profusion of plants now known to us: these are initially a product of much more recent periods of exploration and colonial expansion subsequently compounded by the art of the hybridist.

No, gardens of the classical world comprised mainly indigenous species or those which over slow centuries had gradually infiltrated from farther east with the movement of learning. And the most desirable local plants, of course, evolutionary products of hot dry Mediterranean or Middle Eastern hillsides, are the aromatic denizens of herb gardens today.

In any attempt to trace the links between today's world and that of classical Rome in relation to art such as architecture, artifacts or wall-painting, and science we are apt to be presented with too definite a polarity: on the one hand the fall of the Roman Empire (in Gibbon's resounding phrase), on the other a sudden Renaissance of classical knowledge. The intervening thousand years are, it might be thought, as the hymn has it, 'like an evening gone'.

But this is obviously not so. Though the hierartic splendour of Imperial Rome disappeared so utterly that the ruins of its buildings were later thought to have been built and peopled by giants (and would perhaps have had to be invented by Piranesi had they not survived); and though centralized formal learning may seem to have died, the land and most of its population survived. And the bases of any human survival are those of food, medicaments, shelter and clothing. For which, even with flocks and herds decimated or driven off, the plants remain.

Thus even without formal lists of species grown throughout the so-called Dark Ages (and so described, surely, by later commentators who failed to see the light that those, then existing, lived by), there can be no doubt of a continuity of plant-knowledge and plant-use.

Obviously for Romanized provincials on the colder northern fringes of the Empire things were more difficult. A visit today to the restored Roman palace garden at Fishbourne near Chichester in Sussex makes the point. So many of the plants in our herb gardens today are of Mediterranean origin, and accidental neglect or a series of cold winters plays havoc with rosemary or lavender or sweet bay. And communications with Rome having been broken, replacements became unavailable, and there was no convenient garden centre down the road. After this it does not need many years to pass before a generation is born which knows nothing of such plants; word of mouth or even written material is of no use if the relevant plants are not available. In such a situation two particular things become lost: knowledge of plants' utilitarian roles which may have been the product of hundreds of years of trial and error, and secondly the appreciation of such plants in the context of the garden as part of the accepted cultural scene. And, of course, with a reversal from safety to insecurity men's efforts are concentrated upon survival: the life-enhancers give way to the solely life-supporters.

But fortunately for the progress of civilization, although Rome's imperial power was broken the majority of its citizens were not on the cold northern fringes described above but lived in areas where so many of the classic herb plants were native and hence always available to replace those lost in cultivation – an activity which in these parts was anyway less vulnerable to inclement weather. Thus we see the simple gardening of the Greek and Latin races continuing, probably without much change.

Other aspects can be cited to indicate that these post-Roman, pre-Renaissance 500 years were not a desert of plant-knowledge and plant-appreciation. On the one hand the apparently inexorable extension of Islam along the North African coast and, by the end of the seventh century AD, into Spain, appeared disastrous to Christendom. Yet as Arab scholars and physicians continued the Greek tradition and combined it with that of the main centres of the Arab world further east, this amalgam spread with conquest.

On the other hand much of the more formal part of the Roman tradition, neglected by the populace in favour of folklore, was maintained in monastic institutions throughout Europe. Here, indeed, relative security could be ensured so that the cultivation of plants useful to man and others for the glory of God continued. In this way the Christian Church can be seen as a facilitator both in maintaining tradition and (although apt to be morbidly afraid of heresy and schism) in promoting new learning.

Always, however, dissemination of ideas remained difficult. There were only two ways: by word of mouth or through laboriously, if beautifully, hand-written treatises available to the few, of whom even fewer could read. The invention of the printing press in the mid-fifteenth century is perhaps the greatest technological breakthrough of our era: no aspect of European life was unaffected, particularly the cultivation of plants, because herbals were amongst the very first books to be printed. This, above anything, indicates the importance accorded to plants.

At last therefore it is possible for us today to have direct contact with the herbs and herb growing of historical times. The methods by which they were grown and the types of gardens which they embellished will be considered in a later chapter. It might be better now to examine the origins of the plants themselves whose continuity of cultivation it has been possible to trace unbroken, if in periods somewhat tenuously, for around 10,000 years. This contact with the remotest beginnings of man's gardening past is one of the perennial fascinations of herb growing.

The ecology of herbs

Ecology as a branch of biology may be defined as 'the study of an organism in its habitat'. It arose as a science in response to the realization that while it is possible to discover much about, say antelopes or anemones in zoos or gardens we learn much more, and often very different things, by studying them in their natural environment. Because, of course, every organism is particularly designed to fit in with that environment. Such an essential fact need cause no dissent between fundamentalist belief in individual creation and acceptance of continuous evolutionary progress; it is sufficient here to recognize rapport – habitat and organism are one.

But we are concerned, obviously, with the artificial, with the cultivation of plants away from their natural habitat. This is why, if cultivation is to be successful from an aesthetic as well as a technical point of view, knowledge of their homes as well as the herbs themselves is highly desirable. It also adds greatly to the interest.

It is a continual source of surprise to consider that for the most part herbs, with a history of cultivation as long as any plants known to man, are still those same plants that were grown by our remotest ancestors, while most modern staple food crops and many of today's ornamentals would have been unrecognizable to people living even a few hundred years ago.

A single well-known herb example will make the point. Rosemary (*Rosmarinus officinalis*) is described in exact botanical detail in Volume 3 of *Flora Europaea* (CUP, 1972). The account ends, by referring to habitat and distribution:

> Dry scrub. Mediterranean region, extending to Portugal and NW Spain; cultivated elsewhere for ornament and its aromatic oil.

Then follows a list of seventeen countries where rosemary grows wild, from the Azores in the far west and the Russian Crimea in the east, to Crete and Malta in the south and Switzerland and Albania in the north: in longtitude beyond the strict bounds of the 'Middle Sea' and with a 10° latitude range between 35° and 45°N.

In cultivation in Britain, although not proof against the hardest winters, rosemary grows even in Scotland, artificially adding another 10° to its range. Yet wherever it is seen, on the wildest Grecian hillside or in the most sophisticated garden it is most obviously the same plant. Of course there are variants – slight differences in leaf shape or colour, in habit or even in flower-colour, with pink or white not unknown. Gardeners eagerly compete for such forms; they come and go and still we are left with the typical species in its 'Dry scrub, Mediterranean region . . .'. The merest whiff of a crushed leaf immediately evokes an authentic 'beaker full of the warm south' to use Keats' effective phrase.

Again, in earlier authorities rosemary maintains its obvious existence, without the doubt that so often mars plant inquiry in the classic texts. Leonhard Fuchs's *De Historia Stirpium Commentarii* of 1542 carries an immediately recognizable folio-sized illustration labelled *Rosmarinus* and descriptions of its virtues.

Fifty years later the woodcut is more formal in the *Herball* by John Gerard, but his description, despite its Elizabethan language, can hardly be bettered today. The plant is brought straight to the mind's eye:

> Rosemarie is a woodie shrub, growing oftentimes to the height of three or fower cubits, especially when it is set by a wall. It consisteth of slender brittle branches whereon do grow verie many long leaves, narrow, somwhat hard, of a

quicke spicie taste, whitish underneath, and of a full
greene colour above, or in the upperside, with a pleasant,
sweete strong smell, among which come foorth little flowers of a whitish blew colour: the seed is blackish: the roots
are tough and woodie.

In 1629 John Parkinson's famous *Paradisi in Sole, Paradisus Terrestris* – a punning allusion to his own name 'Park in sun's earthly
paradise' repeats (as Gerard does before him) the then conventional
medicinal virtues and uses but is more evocative of seventeenth
century cultivation of the plant:

> *Our* [my italics] ordinary Rosemary groweth in Spain and
> Provence of France and in others of those hot countryes,
> neere the sea side. It will not abide (unless kept in stoves)
> in many places in Germany, Denmarke and those colder
> countries. And in some extreame hard winters, it hath
> well neere perished here in England with us, at the least in
> many places: but by slipping it is usually, and yearly en-
> creased, to replenish any garden.

By the eighteenth century herbals no longer had to be all things to
all men and Philip Miller's great *Dictionary of Gardening* is able to
instruct us as well as any book (including this one) today. The
Dictionary ran to eight editions in Miller's lifetime. Here in the
eighth edition of 1767 he writes of rosemary:

> These plants grow plentifully in the southern parts of
> France, in Spain and Italy, where, upon dry rocky soils near
> the sea, they thrive prodigiously and perfume the air, so as
> to be smelt at a great distance from the land; but notwith-
> standing they are produced in warm countries, yet they are
> hardy enough to bear the cold of our ordinary winters very
> well in the open air, provided they are planted upon a poor,
> dry, gravelly soil, on which they will endure the cold
> much better than on a richer soil, where the plants will
> grow more vigorously in summer, and so be more subject
> to injury from frost, and they will not have so strong an
> aromatic scent as those upon a dry barren soil.

Clearly the literature of rosemary is extensive. It refers to an exotic
plant that has been cherished and cultivated for its quiet beauty in
the garden, its scent, its aromatic oil which was extracted by
distillation as long ago as the 1330s, and for a dozen uses in medicine in herbalism and in the kitchen.

As a low shrub in the wild, rosemary is a typical member of the *maquis* (or *garique* or, in Greece, the *phrygana*) flora. This association is a combination of generally small or medium sized shrubs with, in their shelter, an understory of herbaceous plants of several main types. These include woolly-leaved salvias or mulleins with close-to-the-ground rosettes of leaves followed by tall early summer spikes of flowers; bulbs or corms such as tulips, crocuses and sternbergias; terrestrial orchids with underground tubers. Most of these are potentially pretty mouthfuls for browsing animals and so usually grow in the protection of woody shrubs. The shrubs in turn protect themselves in two main ways: by reducing their leaves to spines, which also reduces water-loss on hot dry hillsides, and by secreting unpalatable pungent oils or, in the case of the spurges, the white, poisonous latex.

While these aromatic oils may put feeding animals off they are just the attributes that we find attractive and they provide a main reason for growing the plants which possess them. They also provide the reason why these are plants to be added only in small quantities to more bulky foods as flavourings and explain why even the herd of goats working across an area only nibbles at these plants.

While visual resemblances (macro- or microscopic) have traditionally been the main aids to classifying plants, it is also possible to find clear botanical (and hence evolutionary) relationships between them through their chemical constituents. Thus it is not surprising that many plants in the same family as our classic example of rosemary share its property of possessing an essential oil. This family is the Labiatae, in turn a classic herb family. It includes all the herbs which, with rosemary, immediately come to mind – lavenders, mints, savories, marjorams, thymes, sages. All, it will be noticed, are referred to in the plural: all are Mediterraneans, evocative of their home with their scented leaves, and their tight narrow-foliaged greyness. They are evocative too of old-fashioned English gardens which perfectly provide the conditions – as far as northern gardens can – which make such plants feel at home. These are essentially protection from cold winds for the top growth, perfect drainage at the root and full sun for both. Only mints are moisture lovers. All these conditions are exactly what Philip Miller was recommending 250 years ago.

It is worth pursuing the inquiry into this family so especially represented in the herb garden. Out of around 300 garden herbs almost forty are labiates; only the Umbelliferae can approach this – such as parsley, caraway, coriander, chervil. Otherwise plants with herbal uses in the kitchen, in the pharmacy or just in the mind of Gerard or Culpeper are strewn amongst the full gamut of plant families.

The Labiatae also, although cosmopolitan with over 3000 species spread among 170 to 180 genera (depending more upon the authorities consulted than the plants, for botanists may also be classified: into 'splitters' or 'lumpers'), is centred upon the Mediterranean. Hence again the herb garden dependence upon this area.

Of the forty labiate herbs only three (lemon verbena and bergamot, native to South and North America respectively, and the basils originally from India) do not grow wild in some or all of those countries with a Mediterranean coastline. Half of them are also members of the British flora, though only by adoption: it is significant that the length of time they have been in cultivation with us is reflected by winter savory, hyssop and wall germander having become naturalized on old walls of Beaulieu Abbey in Hampshire and elsewhere. How convenient for the plants that, as the Dissolution deprived the Abbey herb garden of its monkish gardeners, so too was the fabric of the great building deprived of its masons; thus providing, in its decay, perfect homes for these sun-loving subshrubs.

It will be noted that of those labiates which occur in both southern and northern Europe – and by definition in between as well – a few such as white harehound and catmint are clearly southerners existing on the geographical and climatic limit of their range. Our commoner native herb-labiates, on the other hand, such as the mints, self-heal and bugle, really are northerners and become plants of wooded uplands as they go south. Such a distribution provides an invaluable group of plants which will flourish in those shadier parts of the herb garden which are bound to exist in any formally enclosed design.

Fortunately for garden use, a second great family of herbs has less of a strong preference for the sunny side of the street: these are the umbellifers. The Umbelliferae, like the Labiatae, are largely a hardy northern hemisphere family of herbaceous plants. There are, of course, exceptions. Both families have southern hemisphere members, both have shrubs and members in the tropics but the general description holds true. Both have around 3000 species divided into some 200 genera. Both are groups which were recognized as such in pre-Linnaean times as their names indicate. It will be noticed in passing that almost all plant families have names with an '-aceae' ending built upon that of the 'type genus' eg.

Ranunculus – Ranunculaceae, *Papaver* – Papaveraceae, *Rosa* –
Rosaceae. These two herb families are among only a half-dozen
that are permitted to retain old forms of family names, which
indicates again the interest taken in them from early times; they
predate the rules.

The great majority of umbellifers are immediately recognizable, though paradoxically their individual flowers are too small to
make any impression upon anyone without a lens. The name picks
out the essential umbrella-rib pattern of the flower heads. Thus the
cow parsleys and all their friends are obvious umbellifers, as are
other common garden plants which only the improvident ever see
attaining that stage. Carrot, parsnip and celery are usually con-
sumed long before they flower.

Botanical classification developing with knowledge is, as has
already been said, a method of attempting to bring order out of the
chaos of diversity and multiplicity of form. And with modern
techniques in microscopy added to the less sophisticated observations of the past the classification works wells. The ancient
texts, however, classify in another way, according to the use or
properties of the plants. That worked equally well in a simpler age
and remains valid in the traditional herb garden where plants are
still often grouped in this way. Botanical relationships were overtly
disregarded – though they often shine through in a bed of herbs –
just as they are now in all but botanic gardens, whose role is
especially to make that point. There, in the order beds, all the
umbellifers will be put together to demonstrate diversity of form
within a single family. In a herb garden, put into beds according to
their use, they show dramatic differences in their interest and value
to man. It is significant that such a traditional arrangement
emphasizes extreme diversity in chemical content.

Thus the three umbellifers already mentioned were classic pot
herbs – where much or all of the plant can be used for food. So good
were they that selection and subsequent breeding has taken them
into the category of vegetables proper. In their wild forms, however,
they retain a herb garden place, although the closely related lovage
remains firmly in the pot herb class, for while one of the very best
soups is made with the leaves, the plant has been surprisingly
untouched by the selector: it is still the wild plant that we grow.

The next group of umbellifers illustrates the expected role of
herbs, that of flavouring. These have essential or volatile oils
whose aroma is especially brought out by warmth, so that they
affect other ingredients eaten or cooked with them. This group
includes dill and angelica, caraway and coriander, fennel and –

most ubiquitous of herbs – parsley. With or without the floral umbel signature, the pattern of their fern-like leaves begins to indicate a recognizable relationship.

Such visual similarities, however, are apt to be a snare. No doubt to our earliest ancestors this was learnt the hard way – by trial and fatal error. Even in modern times, as was reported in the papers only a few years ago, two campers died having collected and eaten roots of hemlock water dropwort. In flower and leaf a very typical umbellifer, in effect deadly. A number of umbellifers contain alkaloids like this, all highly poisonous to man. Hemlock proper is the best known from having been used to put Socrates to death in 399 BC; less well known is that for centuries it was used to treat epilepsy and other neurological disorders, though this is no longer done.

In spite of the fact that hemlock and certain other umbellifers are known to possess poisonous properties, they are still not infrequently grown in the type of herb garden where the plants are grouped according to use. They can be collected together with other officinal plants to illustrate our forebears' dependence upon the plant kingdom for most of their medicinal needs. Alternatively a separate bed of known poisonous species can be an important part of a herb garden attempting to be as comprehensive as possible.

It has not been fully explained why plants secrete substances such as these poisonous alkaloids. The defence mechanism idea, which applies to the aromatic oils, seems not to apply here and it appears that the secreted substances may be merely by-products of the plants' metabolism; whatever the reason for their presence it is of perennial fascination that closely related plants can be of such diverse significance to man.

A third herb family demonstrates this even more clearly. This is the Solanaceae, whose members include a staple food crop of much of the world's population – the potato (but not if the tubers are permitted to green in light: then a conventionally poisonous alkaloid develops which causes deaths every year). It includes delicious fruit – tomatoes, sweet peppers and aubergines. It includes spices, the burning hot chili peppers and several drug plants of historical or current importance, sometimes indeed of both. Mandrake in the former category has already been mentioned, thorn apple is in the latter. True deadly nightshade (*Atropa belladonna*) spans the centuries.

This is a plant often confused with the related but utterly different woody or black nightshades, both *Solanum* species, and it can be taken as the epitome of medicinal herbs. The French *Grand*

Herbier of 1504 contains the earliest description of its use, but as this is almost at the dawn of printing it is inconceivable that it was unknown to earlier, less lettered, ages.

The Latin name is beautifully evocative. Atropos, it will be recalled, was the third of the Fates of Greek mythology. A man's birth was controlled by Clotho; Lachesis determined the pattern of his life, while Atropos is always shown as a black-draped hag flourishing the scissors with which she cuts his lifeline. The connection with the deadly properties of *Atropa* is only too clear. The specific epithet *belladonna* has a lighter touch and refers to a sixteenth- and seventeenth-century practice in Italy and Spain of women putting distilled atropa water into their eyes. It dilated the pupil to a huge and lustrous size. No doubt it impaired vision somewhat but perhaps indicates again the excesses demanded of her votaries by the current goddess of Beauty.

Today *Atropa* is grown commerically for its medicinally valuable alkaloids, hyoscyamine and atropine: the latter of course is still used for pupil-dilation but to facilitate clinical examination rather than the merely cosmetic.

But should this plant be in the garden? As an unconsidered specimen, certainly not: a half-dozen of its shining berries, visually as inviting as the black cherries they resemble, will kill a child. Even the taste, pleasantly bland, gives no hint of danger. Yet in a herb collection concerned with education at any level *Atropa belladonna* is bound to appear. Suitable labels and warnings may well be necessary and this is discussed further in Chapter 3.

The example of deadly nightshade is an important one and serves to demonstrate yet again the hold that herbs have upon us at a whole range of levels – the broadly cultural, including aspects of social history, the medicinal, both orthodox and folk medicine, and the botanical impinging upon ecology, taxonomy and physiology. Lastly, but in the context of this book most importantly, there are the horticultural considerations of choice of species, effective cultivation and aesthetic arrangement. With such long tradition which reaches back, as has already been shown, into earliest times, it is difficult if not impossible for us to be unaffected by it, consciously or unconsciously when we plan the use of herbs in our own gardens. Success today is perhaps most likely to be built upon success in the past. This does not mean that fresh approaches are not possible, but like that mythical beast which confusingly looked back as well as forward we probably neglect the past at our peril. The next chapter seeks to trace herbs in the garden from early times.

2

HERBS AND HERITAGE

Herbs are so linked in our literature with times past that it is inevitable that we should search those more or less distant periods for hints or clues which remain valid for the design of herb gardens today. If we imagine the expected traditional herb garden (though this is by no means the only way of growing herbs, as this book is concerned to show) it would be an area relatively small in size, walled or hedged around. In it would be a regular arrangement of beds, sometimes raised, sometimes sunken. Sometimes there would be arbours or bowers covered with climbers or shrubs, apparently trained to behave as such, the enclosing walls or fences offering further positions for these same plants. How close is this expectation to the actual early patterns? Indeed, what early patterns? To what period, or periods, do we turn for help?

Though it has been asserted that cultivation of herbs goes back to man's earliest horticultural activities, as a convenient addition to and development from collecting samples from the wild, such beginnings are hardly garden-making – though perhaps not far removed from the little plot outside a lot of kitchen doors today.

Of course initially there were no distinct 'herb gardens' as separate from any other type of garden; all gardens were 'herb gardens'. All gardens grew medicinal and culinary herbs, with ornamental herbs often preserved for their abnormality (such as striped leaves) and bush fruits and dye-plants would also be grown here. These were the *only* plants that were grown in gardens.

But actual garden plans available to us from the distant past are lamentably few. There are the Pharaohs' tomb paintings and papyri which elegantly depict gardens in the somewhat confusing convention of two and a half millennia ago where every aspect faces the viewer. Palms are clearly differentiated from cypresses but little else is offered to the plantsman. Moving on in time, the younger Pliny's literary powers and love for his gardens have made it possible to draw conjectural plans and make elaborate models of such a Roman patrician's villa in the first century AD. Pliny's use of formal hedging is well supported by the recent and continuing excavation and recreation *in situ* of the third-century contemporary Roman palace at Fishbourne in Sussex. Earlier excavations at Pompeii and Herculaneum give further details of the smaller courtyards within the villa complex, or of Roman town gardens. Our ideas are greatly helped by surviving wall-paintings depicting such gardens in their heyday. But actual arrangements of plants elude us.

It is clear from lists compiled by Theophrastus, Dioscorides and others that given collections of herbs were grown. Moving well into the Christian era, it is also demonstrated by the list of plants which Charlemagne ordered should be grown in the imperial lands by every city of the Holy Roman Empire. The decree dates from his coronation in AD 800 and names eighty-nine plants.

In a recent book, *Medieval Gardens*, John Harvey describes the Charlemagne list and discusses its origin. Throughout his book Mr Harvey is at pains to trace the threads of ornamental gardening in his period to the mid-sixteenth century and finds it significant that the two plants which head the decree are ornamentals, the lily (*Lilium candidum*) and roses (in the plural). Neither were of great medicinal value or economic importance at the time but were presumably important in the symbolism of the Church and used in its decoration, for although the Empire's title was later to fall into disrepute, at this stage it was both Holy and Blessed by Rome, if centered on Aachen.

This significant list can be divided into categories. There are nuts, including almond and walnut; fruits, including quince, medlar and fig; salads, such as parsley and alexanders; pot herbs including mint and savory while 'physical' herbs have savory, fennel, poppy and rosemary etc. While this is a perfectly logical grouping it is but one of several arrangements possible: *all* the plants here picked out from the divisions have or had at the time clear herbal uses, including even the lily and the roses. It seems just as probable that the list, drawn up by a monk, brought together plants which, while not yet *crops* in the agricultural sense, were produced on a garden scale and were of use. In other words they are herbs in the full use of the word: that many were and are considered beautiful as well is the sort of bounty that churchmen in that age would have expected. This we, in a less religious age, are delighted to discover and rashly presume it to be fortuitous. How they were to be grown and arranged at that time is not discussed.

No search for early herb gardens could possibly omit the Church, inheritor and preserver of classical learning as well as, in erratic periods of liberalism and enlightenment, the initiator of new learning. Ironically, for two or three hundred years each side of the millennium the two great rival religions of Christianity and Islam were virtually the only sources of an ongoing Western civilization.

Islam had two European footholds, in Sicily and, much more importantly, in Spain where an enviable culture was vigorously pursued. Its effect upon northern Europe was greater than it is generally given credit for. Equally, the compressing eye of history is apt to forget that much of Spain was Moorish, and Islamic for 600 years – as if Britain had been French since the Renaissance. How different the course of garden design would have been in that case!

Spain, Islamic then, with its filigree threads of connection with the distant East, insinuates into the thoughts, ideas, and innovations of gardens as much as in other areas of learning.

Many of the greatest Moorish gardens in Spain at, for example, Medina Azahara near Córdoba and at Toledo no longer exist, while those of the well-known Alhambra and the Generalife at Grenada are restorations. Yet their architectural surroundings remain intact and sufficiently magnificent for us to gain a clear idea of what there must have been. Courtyards, their ground plans patterned Persian-carpet-like with geometric flower beds, pools and water-courses, were meant not only to be enjoyed from within, but to be looked down upon from above. Surrounding windows and frequently a central pavilion offered various points of view. Though grander, in essence such a plan is not greatly different from patrician medieval gardens throughout Europe. Both John Harvey and Teresa McLean, in her *Medieval English Gardens*, refer to and describe from the somewhat thin records available – tantalizing glimpses through the mists of time – the enclosed royal herb gardens in Britain as at Windsor Castle and Clarendon Palace, near Salisbury, Wiltshire, in the thirteenth century. At Clarendon the herb garden made for Henry III's Queen is noted as being paved in 1247.

But perhaps it is generally not to the gardens of the great we should look for herb gardens except that through dynastic inter-marriage, royal gifts and interchange of courtiers and men of letters they can be considered as entrepôts with styles, fashions and knowledge as the commodities traded.

To return to the Christian Church might be more profitable, if only because, before the birth of printed books, this is where almost all literature had its base and where for centuries records were relatively safe from pillage and loss.

A remarkable survival exists in the well-documented plan pre-served at the Abbey of St Gall in Switzerland, near Lake Constance. This dates, amazingly, from around AD 820–830 and, as Ms

McLean says: 'It is a diagram of an ideal, not of an actual foundation and it amounts to an extended, Christianized, edition of a Roman villa estate with a wealth of gardens.' The plan shows in great detail how a major religious institution should be laid out according to the Rule of St Benedict as a self-contained and self-sufficient community. It thus has farms, orchards and gardens. Next to the physician's house is a square infirmary garden. The sixteen beds are each labelled with their herbal occupant. Mr Harvey also discusses St Gall and lists the plants as 'Kidney bean', savory, rose, horse mint, cumin, lovage, fennel, tansy or costmary, lily, sage, rue, flag iris, pennyroyal, fenugreek, mint and rosemary. Translation leaves some room for discussion, however.

Some way off is the kitchen garden whose eighteen narrow beds, again in two ranks, hold onions, garlic, leeks, shallots, celery, parsley, coriander, chervil, dill, lettuce, poppy, savory, radishes, parsnip, carrot, colewort (cabbage), beet and black cumin (*Nigella sativa*). With only a few exceptions the plants grown in the kitchen garden can equally be considered 'herbs' as those in the infirmarian's garden. Such difference of site seems to indicate the main emphasis of use – not necessarily any exclusiveness of, say, rosemary to the infirmary or poppy to the kitchen. Savory, it will be noted, is common to both gardens: Mr Harvey suggests that the infirmary garden might hold winter savory, and summer savory might be with the pot herbs in the kitchen garden.

The quantity of herbs grown in medieval times frequently seems to move them into the category of crops. For the Royal Palace at Rotherhithe in 1354 14 lbs of parsley seed (cost 5s 10d), 12 lbs onion seed, and 72 lbs of hyssop are recorded. Twenty years later the Bishop of Ely's garden in Holborn had in store 32 lbs of parsley seed (rapidly losing viability one would think) and 8 lbs each of hyssop, savory and leek seed. But to quote Ms McLean again: 'Herbs had a culinary importance that is hard for us to grasp because we have been able to supplement our starch with a whole range of different foods and tastes. They are no longer the redemptive kitchen force they once were'. However, as so much modern food becomes more and more homogenized, that necessary 'redemptive force' takes on a new importance.

As time goes on the available references begin to include a greater diversity of herbs. Alexander Neckham, foster brother to Richard Coeur de Lion, as a foremost scientist of his age, listed 140 species then grown in the late-twelfth century. Though identification of some of his plants is open to discussion it certainly includes such exotics as mandrake, acanthus and pomegranate.

Neckham's is also the first reference to the growing of borage in
Britain. By 1327 its seeds were sufficiently available to be
bought, with those of savory, chervil and violet, by the gardener
at the Abbot of Westminster's country palace of Neyte in
Middlesex.

While gardeners of the nobility, princes of the Church, and
most great monastic houses clearly worked on large areas, thus
extending the knowledge and range of plants grown, a different
pattern was followed by the Carthusian order. Members of
Charterhouses shared only their religious devotions and lived
almost as a community of solitary hermits, each with his separate
cell. Each cell had a small walled garden within which personal
predilections of vegetables and herbs – should they be considered
separately – flowers and fruit could be followed. Ground plans only
remain to us, as at Mount Grace Priory, Yorkshire, for instance.
Such small-scale, individual, contemplative gardening, though of
course like the rest killed in Britain at the Dissolution in the 1530s,
seems closer to us today than the grander and inevitably better-
documented forms of Benedictine houses.

The formal plans of St Gall are not vastly different in essence
from kitchen gardens today – or perhaps they are especially close to
the large establishments of great country houses of a century ago
when, similarly, a whole community was fed from them. Nor do
they differ greatly from the lay-out of the early physic or botanic
gardens. They are all, ultimately, gardens cultivated for their produce but this does not mean that aesthetic considerations are
absent, merely that they are secondary to the main aim.

The search for early productive herb garden patterns, then,
begins literally to take shape: enclosed areas holding a pattern of
regular beds in which plants are grown that are accepted as herbs.
But continued search for gardens with more overtly ornamental
aims throughout the Middle Ages is necessary. Verbal descriptions,
then as now, are open to various interpretations but fortunately
pictures show either a type of garden which exists or one which is
considered, at the time of painting, to be an ideal.

Dutch paintings of the fifteenth century can be considered the
height of northern Mediterranean pictorial art, already strongly
affected by Renaissance ideals welling northwards from Italy.
Ravishing pictures by Jan van Eyck, Roger van der Weyden and
Hans Memling with books of hours and illustrated calendars by
lesser masters often show gardens as background to the main
theme. The subjects, whether religious or depicting contemporary
life as led by royalty and nobles, are invariably staged in a castle or

palace. Still the gardens are the ageless geometric plots – sometimes raised, sometimes flat and set in grass or gravel.

On other occasions the enclosed gardens are as devoid of design as the most banal suburban front garden today – a central bit of grass with a narrow flower border all round, though the more imaginative will train roses or other climbers on the surrounding fence. The charm, the beauty, comes, it must be admitted, from the mastery of the painting and the depiction of elegantly caparisoned people, dead and dust these 500 years. Horticulturally, the one aspect of real delight is the fact that their gardeners had no access to selective herbicides and that the grass is studded with daisies, wild strawberries and dandelions. Such 'flowery meads' are today being again encouraged under the aegis of meadow gardening: this is both sensible and delightful but not of particular relevance to the herb garden search.

While, in most cases, northern gardens offer little design to excite us there is no doubt – if the paintings can be taken as guides – that there was strong interest and appreciation in the simple beauty of wild plants. Here is our real connection with times past, here the real continuum, because there is never a plant depicted in plot or flowery mead that is not a herb, medicinal or culinary, flavouring or food. Equally we can relate to them because with few exceptions those plants have not been changed over the intervening centuries. Only parsley has been accorded the Western plant breeders' attention; only curly parsley would give a reincarnated medieval any problems with identification. Fortunately his nose and his taste buds would tell him. 'French parsley' remains visually unchanged.

If early northern gardens offer plants without design, those in the south tend to the opposite: design without plants. Indications of the *giardino segreto* show vine-covered arbours and walks but the emphasis seems to lie, not surprisingly, with the need for shade from a hot southern sun. Native evergreens – bay, cypress and pines – are used for this same reason but also as architectural components in the design, clipped into buttressed hedges, cones and obelisks. Where there are 'flower'-beds their outlines are frequently etched, equally architecturally, with low clipped shrubs and the spaces filled similarly with plants of contrasting texture. In other words they are elementary knot gardens, patterns on the ground.

Garden history, however, is both a relatively new science and one whose sources are easily blotted out. The seminal work on Italian gardens by the late Georgina Masson (and described in her book of that name) would appear to show that the architectural was

the main, if not only, emphasis of gardens of the Italian renaissance. Not long before her death Miss Masson lamented to the
present author that archival sources did exist which, though she
knew she had no time to explore, she was sure would extend our
knowledge of actual plant use at this time. Such research is still in
progress through other scholars.

Fortunately, although *Italian Gardens* is concerned with
gardens of the great (and great gardens, not necessarily the same
thing) because those are the most likely to have survived, there are
descriptions of domestic gardens of interest to us. At the Villa
Capponi above Florence 'is that rare jewel, a Tuscan garden of the
second half of the sixteenth century preserved in all its original
charm. . . . When on the 7th of February 1572, Gino Capponi
bought a small house with a tower on the steep road leading up to
the Pian de Giullari, his choice may well have been influenced by
the superb view it enjoyed over the city. . . .'

Miss Masson describes two small enclosed gardens at the Villa
Capponi, either of which could be a pattern for an ideal herb garden
today, leaving the choice of plants, as always, to the current owner.
'At the Western end of the terrace [is] the little walled garden
room . . . with its flower-filled box parterres, gurgling wall fountain
and battlemented walls festooned with roses and wisteria. This
little room is probably the most enchanting example of the Italian
giardino segreto in existence. The hot sun beating down into this
enclosed space distils a veritable bouquet of flower scents mingled
with the spicy tang of the cypresses, whose dark spires frame the
rolling panorama of the Tuscan landscape.'

There is no doubt that this is the pattern we have been seeking:
enclosure, warmth, aromatic scents, water. Just as the English
landscape school turned to idealized views of the Roman campagna
for inspiration to embellish great estates in the eighteenth century,
so for herb gardens we look similarly south, coveting a kind climate
which encourages civilized enjoyment of life outdoors and makes
possible the cultivation of a wide range of lovely plants.

The English garden designer, Cecil Pinsent worked on the
lower terraces at the Villa Capponi in 1930 but there is no reason to
believe he changed this upper garden. Though that garden may
exemplify an early ideal its particular virtues of design and planting
in combination seem elsewhere (transience of gardens being kept in
mind) to develop separate lives. The architectural component
grows from simple knots to the complexity of the vast Versailles-
type *parterres de broderie* of the seventeenth and early-eighteenth
centuries in which plants were entirely subservient to patterns, to

the extent that the former became actually unnecessary and replaced by coloured earths and broken bricks.

Mr Harvey stated in his *Medieval Gardens* that 'we do know
that as early as 1494 "a knot in a garden, called a mase" (maze) was
an understood commonplace'. This claim is not easy to substan-
tiate and it is not until the sixteenth century that knots and knot
gardens took on the impetus which fashion demanded. Then one
might look down upon knot gardens from the windows of a new
Elizabethan house or up at the plaster strap-work on the ceiling in
the great parlour. Only position and material differ. Though outlined in box, thrift, hyssop, thyme or *Teucrium chamaedrys* and
filled in with santolina and, it is presumed, with flowering plants
on occasion, these are not true herb gardens. They do offer us,
however, a further dimension to apply to herb garden design today,
rather as a stage design sets the scene for a period play. Simple
forms are easily contrived, or Elizabethan and Jacobean pattern
books (see page 91) such as William Lawson's *Countrie House-
wife's Garden* of 1617 can be consulted. Miles Hadfield's *A History
of British Gardening* reproduces a page of this.

Early herbals and the rise of botanic gardens

In 1548 William Turner, the 'Father of English Botany', published
*The Names of Herbs in Greek, Latin, English, Dutch and French,
with the Common Names that Herbaries and Apothecaries Use*. In
this are the first written records in English of the extensions to the
herb gardener's palette with which this present book is concerned.
Chinese lantern, southernwood or lad's love, peony and summer
jasmine are typical innovations. In 1562 Turner's *New Herball* was
published and twenty-five years later came Gerard's perennially
popular *Herball* with further plants, hitherto unknown in England,
being described. There is no doubt that Gerard was a great
plagiarist, using descriptions and woodcuts from earlier, mainly
continental, sources; but he was also a keen gardener and actually
experimented with the growing of potato (successfully) and ginger
(unsuccessfully) for the first time in Britain in his own garden in
Holborn. Culpeper's *Herball* of 1649 linked herbs with astrology
and upheld the medieval Doctrine of Signatures, a system of
natural healing based on the premise that 'like cures like': thus
plants with red flowers are good for the blood, plants with liver-
shaped leaves are good for the liver, and so on.

With Turner, with Gerard, and especially with John Parkinson, whose *Paradisi in Sole, Paradisus Terrestris* of 1629 describes around 1000 garden plants, we reach plantsmen who seem to speak directly to us across the centuries. Perhaps because they use the language of Shakespeare rather than that of Chaucer the relationship becomes possible: there is also very little doubt what plants are being referred to, even though they pre-date Linnaean binomials by 150 years.

Every gardening writer knows today that it is professional suicide to attempt to describe plants he has never grown, or at least seen. That John Gerard departed from this cardinal rule, with accounts of vegetable sheep and barnacle goose trees, has cast doubts on some of his other, more acceptable sections. But from the mid-sixteenth century intending writers began to use not only their own gardens and plants, as did Gerard, but invaluable reference collections in the newly developing physic or botanic gardens. Those of Pisa and Padua date from the 1540s, set up to support schools of medicine at their respective universities and are the first in a famous line which continues to the present.

It was clearly desirable for practitioners of medicine, at a time when the incipient science was based almost entirely upon plants, to be able to recognize plant species used to treat the sick. The difference in effect on a patient, for instance, between woody nightshade, black nightshade and deadly nightshade was then, as now, dramatic and only too permanent. Illustrations in the herbals generally available were often poor and of little help. The marvellous folio plates in Leonhard Fuchs's *De historia stirpium* of 1542 some of which appear on the half-title pages of this book, are shining exceptions.

Hence the botanic garden pattern quickly spread throughout Europe – to Florence, Bologna, Montpellier, Leiden, Paris and, in 1621, to Oxford. The Oxford Physic Garden (it changed officially to Botanic Garden only in the nineteenth century) was founded by Henry Danvers, Earl of Danby. For, 'He, being minded to become a benefactor to the University, determined to begin and finish a place where learning, especially the faculty of medicine might be improved'. The magnificent Danby Gateway, which completed the garden's enwalling, was built in 1632–1633 by Nicholas Stone, Inigo Jones' master mason. It is significant, as an indication of how such a garden should be regarded, that Dr Clayton, the first Regius Professor of Physic at Oxford, commented on 'the furnishing and enriching whereof with all usefull and delightfull plants'.

England's second such establishment was the Chelsea Physic Garden, founded by the Society of Apothecaries in 1673. Though walled round less grandly and in red brick rather than the golden stone of Oxford, in the eighteenth century it became far more nationally central to the development of gardens and gardening. From 1722 to 1771 it was in the care of Philip Miller, whom Linnaeus referred to as *Hortulanorum Princeps*, and who, as Peter Collinson said, 'raised the reputation of the Chelsea garden so much that it excels all the gardens of Europe for its amazing variety of plants of all orders and classes and from all climates as I survey with wonder and delight this 19th July 1764'.

Because the Physic Garden remained in the care of the apothecaries until 1899 and has changed little in this present century, it can be used as a typical example of such early gardens whose *raison d'être* was, as their very names make clear, the growing of herbs. Yet it is equally important to remember firstly that the word 'herb' was a broadly inclusive one and that the terms 'physic garden' and 'botanic garden' were synonymous. (At Chelsea an existing stone in the east wall is dated 1684 and reads *Giardino Botanico Chelsieano*.)

Philip Miller's incumbency was a period of extraordinary activity as Peter Collinson took pains to record. Sir Hans Sloane was the Garden's patron and its virtual refounder, having passed the freehold he owned as Lord of the Manor of Chelsea to the apothecaries in perpetuity in 1722 'on condition that it be for ever kept up and maintained by the company as a Physick Garden'. In 1733 Sloane was also responsible for the erection of the fine new building in 'Wrennaissance' style which combined the roles of greenhouse, orangery, library and administrative centre.

The period is well documented, though one laments the lack of Miller's own papers which disappeared at his death, through whose hand it is not known. But his great folio *Gardeners' Dictionary*, whose first edition came out in 1732, and his *Gardeners' Calendar* (1734) describe plants and their cultivation in minute detail and in entirely practical terms.

The garden was a source for a number of other publications: Philip Miller himself and Isaac Rand, an apothecary, both produced annotated lists of the 'physical plants'; Joseph Miller's (no relation to Philip) *Botanicum Officinale* of 1722 has been used in this present book as a source of eighteenth-century herbal use and lore. It also was the source of most of the text of Elizabeth Blackwell's more famous *A Curious Herbal* (1733). Mrs Blackwell took a house in adjoining Swan Walk and drew and painted her folio illustrations directly from plants in the garden. A much more accomplished artist, Georg Dionysius Ehret, also depicted many plants from its collection.

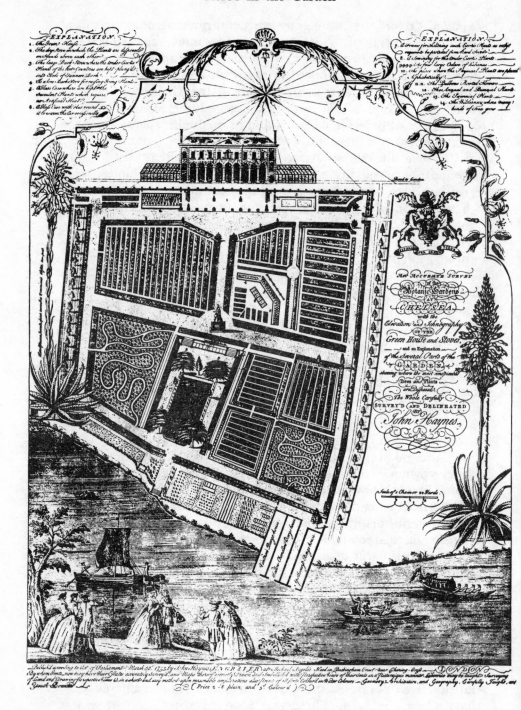

The Botanic Gardens at Chelsea, 1753

To support this mass of written and illustrative material the eighteenth-century Physic Garden has two interesting plans. One, undated, is by Charles Oakley, who also designed and built Sloane's greenhouse: it seems likely to have been drawn in 1732, though more as Oakley thought it should look rather than how it actually did.

The second is dated 30 March 1753. Its elegantly written legend declares it to be 'An accurate survey of the Botanic Gardens at Chelsea, the Whole carefully Survey'd and Delineated by John Haynes'. The small print adds 'Price 2/6d plain and 5s colour'd'.

The legend, referring to numbers on the plan, reads:

1 The Greenhouse
2 The Dry Stove
3 The Large Bark Stove
4 A low Bark Stove for raising young plants
5 A glass case for succulents
6 A glass case with a flue
7 A frame for sheltering such exotic plants as only require to be protected from hard frost
8 A seminary for the tender exotic plants
9 The four large Cedars of Lebanon
10 The place where the physical plants are placed alphabetically
11 The bulbous rooted plants
12 The annual and biennial plants
13 The perennial plants
14 The wilderness where many kinds of trees grow

From Haynes's map it is clear that Philip Miller's Chelsea Physic Garden was a working garden laid out to facilitate research and observation: for use but also for delight, as the writings of many visitors show from John Evelyn onwards. Two-thirds of the 3½ acres is down to long narrow beds to facilitate cultivation and ease of approach. Two 'wilderness' areas hold woody plants and those which could not satisfactorily be classified. A large central pool and the surrounding high walls offer further diversity of habitat and in a strip of ground between the river and the south wall is a nursery, the most protected spot in a garden renowned for its warmth. (It still is: in December 1976 the author gathered 7 lbs of ripe olives from an aged tree in the garden, an extraordinary feat for the latitude. In November 1983 kiwi fruit and pomegranates were harvested.)

Early plates of the circular walled garden at Pisa show central ornamental knots, but at Chelsea, though a few urns stand outside, the ornament and the delight comes from its multiplicity of plants, old and new, common and used for centuries, rare and with unknown potential. It might almost pre-date V. Sackville-West's dictum that gardens should have the maximum formality of design with maximum informality of planting. The succeeding editions of the *Gardeners' Dictionary* indicate Philip Miller's broad and developing interests in the diversity of plants that might be legitimately grown in such a garden, and how they might best be cultivated.

That diversity, and the open mind which welcomed the unknown, is well illustrated by the story of Madagascar periwinkle which came to Chelsea in 1754 unknown and unnamed from the *Jardin des Plantes* in Paris (Madagascar then being a French colony). Refusing the new-fangled Linnaean Binomial system, Miller named it *Vinca foliis oblongis tubo flore integerrimis caulo ramoso fruticoso*. Passed on to Linnaeus it became simply *Vinca rosea*. This is the plant which, following exhaustive research into its alkaloid properties two centuries later, has become one of the most important treatments for leukemia and Hodgkin's disease. The potential of herbs for man's use is of continual extension.

Chelsea, then, through its books and its plans – and the fact it is still there with much of its lay-out and even more of its atmosphere intact – offers much to the search for herb garden style. On the site of Miller's 'place where the physical plants are grown alphabetically' the present herb garden, formed around an enormous bay tree, groups plants according to their uses – culinary herbs, historic medicinals, current drug plants, dye-plants, species used in perfumery and so on. It forms a useful pattern for a herb garden of today where the role is predominantly educational yet where, in a highly concentrated space, the sensual effect is also of importance. There is a nice link with the distant past: a record exists (quoted by Mavis Batey: in *Oxford Gardens*) at Lincoln College, Oxford, of a payment 500 years ago 'for mendying the seat under the bay-tree'. The same could be needed today at Chelsea.

Herb gardens in the eighteenth and nineteenth centuries

In the half-century centred upon 1750, Chelsea, with Philip Miller at the helm, was at its apogee of fame with perhaps the most comprehensive collection of plants in the Western world. Other 'curious gardeners', in the complimentary eighteenth-century sense of the phrase, in that period had fine and fascinating collections – Peter Collinson, quoted above; Dr Fothergill; The Princess Augusta, mother of King George III; Lord Petre. Royalty, aristocrats, rich merchants with contacts in the colonies, all were interested in what new plants those colonies could offer.

Sadly our knowledge of how they used those plants ornamentally is still not great: for instance, though from the time of the Tradescants, the two famous plant hunters from the previous century, the North American herbs continued to reach Britain in increasing numbers, their arrangement in the garden scene is something of a mystery. One reason for this is that the great change of taste from French formalism to the English landscape garden was taking place at the same time. This was a revolution in attitudes which encompassed every art form, every philosophy, every writer: treatises, polemics, poems and novels poured out discussing the freeing of the garden from the shackles of the past. The early-eighteenth-century practitioner William Kent 'leaped the fences', according to Horace Walpole, 'and saw that all Nature was a garden'.

Yet, while the convoluted parterres banished flowering plants because of their unfortunate but natural propensity to grow irregularly, the new style which brought the park to the very walls of the house had equally little place for them. Flowers joined vegetables and herbs in walled kitchen gardens out of sight of the naturalistic, if not natural, landscapes seen from the house. Here the pattern of planting within the walls followed the eminently successful pattern of the botanic or physic gardens, where ease of cultivation and convenience of close observation were combined.

It is perhaps surprising that the craze for medieval models in architectural forms – the lighthearted Gothick of Walpole's eighteenth-century Strawberry Hill and the heavily serious ecclesiastical Gothic of the nineteenth century – did not attempt to put the buildings into a suitably archaic landscaped context. Garden history has come very late upon the scene, so late indeed that, because of the very mutability of plants and planting, re-creators of an earlier style have not very much to go upon.

However, there are exceptions to the fashionable flower-lessness of the eighteenth century. One great estate, Nuneham Courtenay, just five miles south of Oxford, illustrates the odd ambivalence between the high-handed actions of the fashionable 'improving' landowner and the cottage garden tradition. While Nuneham is very well documented and hence is easily discussed,

neither its village nor its garden flowers may be quite as unique as
is usually claimed.

It is a strange story. In the early 1760s the new 'seat' of the first
Earl of Harcourt, built on a commanding bluff overlooking the
Thames, was finished. It was (and is, though somewhat altered) a
severe, Palladian villa of perfect proportions standing like a
classical temple in its apparently natural, yet utterly contrived
landscape.

To make its setting as Italianately perfect as possible it was
decided that the only way to extend the prospects to the north was
to knock down the Domesday village which clustered too near the
great house. In 1764 even the medieval church was removed and
replaced by a dramatic Greco-Roman temple to serve both as
garden feature and village church.

It was this village removal which Goldsmith turned into his
epic poem 'The Deserted Village':

Sweet Auburn, fairest Village of the plain . . .
Thus fares the land by luxury betrayed . . .
The mournful peasant leads his humble band
And while he sinks, without one arm to save,
The country blooms – a garden and a grave.

In the poem the poor peasants are forced from their village, their
land and their country: in fact at Nuneham the distance was little
more than a mile to a new, model village, planned as regularly as
the Palladian house, especially built for them at the edge of the
park. Each red brick cottage had (and has) a considerable garden,
some of a half-acre or so.

Such an amount of ground, however necessary to supplement
meagre agricultural wages of the time, was by no means always
available to eighteenth-century peasants. Cultivation and improvement, for economy and beauty, was actively encouraged by the
second Earl of Harcourt, who succeeded his father in 1777, the
latter having fallen down a well on the old village site when trying
to rescue the spaniel which had preceded him.

The story of the second Earl relates in two ways to the growing
of what, even then, were considered old-fashioned plants. On the
one hand his tenantry were presented with awards of merit for
worthiness in work (an M was displayed in the cottagers' windows),
of which commendable cottage gardening was a part; on the other,
he developed a 'secret garden' of his own to the north of the great
house. There, behind a screen of trees and shrubs, he developed
what was probably the first *planned* informal flower garden in the

Western World. Now being restored, Mason's Garden (as it was called) was the product of a mixture of literary associations and eighteenth-century sensibility.

The Chaurcerian *Romaunt of the Rose*, Ariosto's *Orlando Furioso*, Marvell and Milton were evoked, combined with a current cult of the perfection of Nature. Jean-Jacques Rousseau (who actually stayed, at the invitation of the Earl, in the village) became the presiding deity. Paul Sandby's charming watercolour of the scene shows a floral miscellany of hollyhocks, lilies, sunflowers edged with clipped santolina, box or teucrium, while honeysuckles and roses clamber about the trees. It is all, in one sense, a full century before its time and Nuneham can be seen to provide a continuity of growing old-fashioned flowers and herbs as ornamental plants in a sophisticated planned garden. It is a link between John Parkinson and William Robinson, being halfway between them in time.

Thus, in the context of herbs and herb gardens, we see again that the thread of continuity is in the individual plants which, virtually untouched by the plant breeders, would be immediately recognized by reincarnations of gardeners from all times past. Throughout the ages they have been grown by peer and peasant alike, though in situations as different as the extensive stillroom of the great house is from the humble cottage kitchen where they were subsequently put to use.

Then, late in the nineteenth century, appeared a trend in gardens whose effects are still very much a part of the way in which we look at plants today. As will be shown, it was related to other avant-garde artistic movements which were gathering strength at the time; that its acceptance and development have progressed for a century indicates its strength.

William Robinson's *The English Flower Garden* was first published in 1883: edition followed edition at a rate to be the envy of every garden writer before and since. As a fierce diatribe against what Robinson saw as the artificiality of Victorian carpet bedding and ju-jube-clipped shrubberies, *The English Flower Garden* gained the adherence of Gertrude Jekyll, whose own numerous books kept up the crusade. It is easy both to over-simplify and to exaggerate the Robinson-Jekyll axis: the importance here lies in two particular facets. These are the acceptance of plants, particularly herbaceous plants, as things of beauty in their own right and in their use in mutually complementary combinations.

The following sentence of Addison's written for his *Spectator* article of 1712 is so often quoted as one of the earliest shots in the English landscape war: 'I cannot but fancy that an orchard in flower is not infinitely preferable to all the little labyrinths in the most finished parterre'. It is strange that it led to such flowerlessness. It is separated by two hundred years from Miss Jekyll's pronouncement that 'the duty we owe to our gardens is to [develop] a state of mind and artistic conscience that will not tolerate bad or careless combinations or any misuse of plants'.

While Victorian architectural historicity and mock medievalism made little attempt to plant gardens in period, the same was not true of Miss Jekyll's gardens. But the model was a very different one. This was the discovery of an aesthetically acceptable vernacular tradition in the fifteenth- to seventeenth-century yeoman's house of south-east England, often fallen by disrepair to the category of a cottage by the late-nineteenth-century. Yet it often retained a bit of ground in which a tumble of flowers and vegetables, fruit bushes and apple trees grew in happy profusion. Seen through the eyes of artists such as Helen Allingham and Myles Birkett Foster the 1890s became the golden age of the cottage garden in which pretty pinafored children smile sweetly from a bower of hollyhocks and honeysuckle.

With Edwin Lutyens as architectural collaborator, Gertrude Jekyll turned this picturesque idyll into a highly sophisticated reality. The vernacular motifs of old Sussex farmhouses were adapted to produce houses which today we would consider rather grand, the miscellany of plants each side of the garden path became intricately planned borders, equally grand. The combination has radically changed our way of looking at plants and gardens. The early decade of this century was a period in which new hardy plants flooded in from plant collectors abroad and from nurserymen selecting and breeding new cultivars. All tended to broaden the garden designer's palette, yet in sensitive hands the base of the cottage garden tradition was maintained.

Thus the simple, uncontrived, old-fashioned flowers – Miller's plants, Parkinson's plants, Gerard's plants – were re-established in the planned ornamental garden. That so many of them are herbs, in the broad sense, makes this sequence of events important in tracing the trends towards today's renewed interest in such plants.

Vistas and long borders were often a part of Gertrude Jekyll's plans, so too was the division of the garden into a series of interconnecting 'rooms' rather like the enfilade of salons and chambers in a great country house. Like them, furnishing and colour-schemes differed in their progression.

It is perhaps therefore surprising that Gertrude Jekyll, the most influential garden designer of the last 100 years, offers relatively little to the specific herb garden scene. A sketch does exist for a little herb patch for Knebworth House in Hertfordshire in 1907, showing a quincunx of small circular beds with a tumble of permanent herbs in each. Clearly the effect, with its lavender, sage, southernwood and roses, but no annuals or biennials, was not intended as a comprehensive herb garden. Existing records indicate a full decade before Miss Jekyll produced another herb garden design. This was in 1917 for Col. and Mrs Lyle at Barrington Court, Somerset, and here the 'typical' herb garden at last appears. An area 100 feet by 30 feet is enclosed by 10-foot high walls on three sides and a yew hedge on the fourth. Within, are eight rectangular beds, each 14 by 8 feet (an area the size of many complete herb gardens today). The range of plants is small but they are used on the large scale that the monumentality of the garden demands. Thus one bed requires a dozen feet of 'chervil sown, 18 thyme, 3 lavender, 18 pink pinks'. Other beds also combine a couple of culinary herbs with cottage garden flowers such as mignonette, *Campanula persicifolia* and white phlox. Roses ('Zephyrin Drouhin' and 'Jersey Beauty') jasmine and honeysuckle drape the walls.

The small number of species used reflects the fact that at Barrington Court so much else is planned that here the simple statement of a scented summer spot is all that is required. That some of the plants are in fact culinary herbs is rather by the way.

For Boveridge Park, Cranborne, a smaller plan exists dated March 1920, and for Burningfold (December 1923) a design which is clearly for kitchen use. Here, a 40 by 20-foot plot has lavender hedges on two sides. There are two clumps of fennel, a long line of parsley, 10 feet of tarragon: 14 herbs in all. No indications are made of successional planting and it seems that Miss Jekyll made no further essays into this specific field. It has been left to her successors to do so.

Despite her lack of herb garden designs, Miss Jekyll's influence naturally extended to all herb gardens planned after her time.

Writing in *The Education of a Gardener* (1962), Russell Page asserts: 'I can think of few English gardens made in the last fifty years which do not bear the mark of [Gertrude Jekyll's] teaching, whether in the arrangement of a flower border [or] the almost habitual association of certain plants . . .'

So many gardens could be used to support this claim: Hidcote Manor in Gloucestershire, Great Dixter in Sussex, Sissinghurst Castle in Kent. Only at the last is there a herb garden proper, but at all of them herbs are used – to provide scent, for grey foliage, for their flowers, in so many of their garden rooms. The connection with that ideal sixteenth-century garden room at the Villa Capponi immediately comes to mind.

Thus it can be shown that Jekyll and Lutyens observed, in the nick of time, the remnants of an English country garden tradition and revitalized it; their distillations, as Russell Page indicates, are an accepted, if not always recognized, part of our present garden scene. Other vestiges of that pre-industrial world, like guttering candles, could then still be glimpsed and their images recorded for posterity. Gwen Raverat recalls in *Period Piece* a Christmas visit to a Darwin uncle in Hampshire in 1899 when mummers came to the house; her cousin Ralph Vaughan Williams' folk song suites reflect and extended Cecil Sharpe's contemporary researches. Folklore, folk traditions, country crafts, all were being rescued from the oblivion which by the end of the First World War was all but complete. Such emergency work in the realms of old garden plants has a parallel today (no less in the nick of time): the National Council for the Conservation of Plants and Gardens, set up in 1980, has county groups one of whose roles is to search out good garden plants which are no longer in commerce but which, it is hoped, still lurk under some unconsidered gooseberry bush.

As always, it is easy to exaggerate the effect of certain individuals upon any trends in art and it would be a mistake to see Miss Jekyll and her work as an act of spontaneous creation, especially during the lifetime of Charles Darwin. In fact she was following lines set in the mid-nineteenth century by Ruskin and William Morris. We must remember that Miss Jekyll, who in many ways seems so close to us in time, was born in 1843: the Victorian age had a further fifty-eight years to run. The idealism of the Pre-Raphaelites led to William Morris's Arts and Crafts Movement with its emphasis on traditional workmanship and traditional methods. Certainly this is a part of Miss Jekyll's own Munstead Wood to which she refers again and again.

While, through her, it is possible to talk of a 'Surrey School' of vernacular architecture and gardening to match, it is equally valid to look at a post-William Morris 'Cotswold School'. Again, it is easy to forget how many of today's smart and tidy, visited-to-death Cotswold villages were but a tumble of tired cottages at the turn of this century. Even many of their lovely manor houses were in sad decline. William Morris founded the Society for the Preservation of Ancient Buildings in 1877. Neglect through periods of agricultural depression had brought fine buildings to the brink of ruin but at the same time it had also preserved them, and the plants in their gardens, until, just in time, they could be appreciated, rescued and restored.

In the context of the Arts and Crafts Movement many herbs became popular in surprising ways. Some practitioners returned to plant-based dyes for their 'aesthetic' clothes: more lasting have been the motifs of William Morris prints and wallpapers in which marigold, honeysuckle, corncockle and chrysanthemums continue to cover acres of wall throughout the western world.

Following Morris' Kelmscott Press, Ernest Gimson, the furniture designer and maker, and other craftsmen-artists began to work in the Cotswolds. The lichen-covered limestone of cottage walls, the mossy Stonesfield slates on the roofs, or a clump or two of houseleek on the porch, the 'Welcome-home-husband-however-drunk-you-be' as named in the *Flora of the British Isles* (Clapham, Tutin and Warburg, 1951), all combined into a late Victorian vision of pre-industrial perfection of which herbs were a part. It was shattered by the cataclysm of the 'War to end all wars'.

It now becomes possible to see the 1920s and 1930s as the period when the growing and cultivation of herbs began to develop as a new interest in its own right, both in Britain and America. Though the fact should not be exaggerated it is significant that it is in Britain and America where Miss Jekyll's garden dicta had the greatest effect: though in northern France there are a couple of fine Jekyll gardens, the French connection is not great. It is also noticeable that most European countries had maintained a peasant tradition of which the collection and use of wild herbs was still a normal part of life while the French bourgeois *potager* always included herbs for culinary use. There herbs needed no Renaissance.

The herb tradition in America

The American situation adds a further dimension. Just as aspects of New England vocabulary and figures of speech maintain the language of the seventeenth-century founding fathers, so there are remnants, sufficiently clear for authentic recreations to be possible, of herbal use in garden and kitchen, in stillroom and in chemist's shop. Over three centuries the settlers had brought seeds and plants from the 'old country' (not by any means only the British Isles), they adopted native plants used by the native peoples and in doing so revitalized a herbal tradition which in industrial northern Europe was in decline. The distances and isolation of the new country necessarily maintained it. The Puritan ethic which lay at the root of much early colonial thought was led to reassert itself, as industrialization and 'civilizing influences' softened the pioneer spirit. Religious sects seeking again the simple life sprang up, tending to move westward but, wherever they settled, a pattern of subsistence farming became an inevitable part of life, at least at first. It meant a return to plants of the garden and of the wild woods and fields, and to herbs.

continued on P36

Such a sect were the Shakers which grew from tiny beginnings when Ann Lee and eight followers embarked at Liverpool in May 1774 for New York, first settling in Albany, New York State. By the mid 1800s the sect's members numbered six or seven thousand. Because of their avowed intent to keep separate where possible from 'the world' they had to be relatively self-sufficient and this self-sufficiency extended quickly to medicine. Soon home medicaments from introduced or local plant species developed into the Shakers' predominant method of support. They became one of America's main suppliers of medicinal and culinary herbs and soon expanded to the production of seeds as well. The obligatory Shaker journals record this. One kept in 1848 by William Charles Brackett listed orders for the following: motherwort, peppermint, spearmint, thoroughwort, catnip, pennyroyal, thyme, butternut, henbane, saffron, boneset, white root, dandelion, bloodroot, spikenard root, belladonna, elder flower, lobelia, wintergreen, solomon seal, scullcap, comfrey root, blackberry bark and root, sage, wormwood, southernwood, blue cardinal flower, bittersweet, marshmallow, tansy, thyme, hyssop, lemon balm, slipper elm, horehound, foxglove, summer savory, bugle, sweet marjoram, lettuce, sweet fern, rue, ground ivy, chamomile flower, double tansy, dwarf elder-root, liverwort, skunk cabbage root, angelica seed, burdock root, pleurisy root, mugwort, coltsfoot, male fern root, buckthorn berries, bayberry bark, smallage, cranesbill, stramonium, frostwort, sweet flagroot, moldavian balm, goldthread, poppy flowers, poppy seed, poppy capsules, mullein, cleavers, cohosh root, yarrow, thorn apple, mayweed, coriander seed, elecampane, hemlock and oak barks, mandrake root, cranberry bark, caraway seed, and many others.

The big orders were placed in the fall between October and December and again in the spring from March to the end of May. Smaller orders came in and were filled monthly during the year. Two catalogues had been issued by 1835, and there was now as much business as the Shakers could handle. One hundred and thirty herbs and 25 other items were sold to 22 agents, 10 doctors, and 14 'individual purchasers'. Those orders went to Albany, Utica, Hudson, New York City, several hospitals in Philadelphia, and some even further afield. Two hundred pounds of material was shipped to an agent, A. Thompson, in San Francisco, California. The bill was $184.36 and $6.00 for freight. On 4 November, 1857, one of the largest orders to be filled from the settlement at Watervliet went to Butler and McCullock, Liverpool, England. It was comprised of garden seeds and herbs, and the total cost including 'freight, carriage and custom house charges' amounted to $175.46. The herbs sent were basil, sage, lavender, rue, mandrake, lobelia, mint, lemon and Moldavian balm, vervain, and poppy seed. The garden seeds were short top scushot radish, scarlet turnip, white winter Spanish onion, black Spanish onion, white flat Dutch turnip, rutabaga, round spinach, Richley spinach, early oxheart cabbage, early York cabbage, cauliflowers, and 'purple' eggplant.

Very often the order book also recorded observations about the plant being sent. When filling a large order in 1832 for 'Hemlock plant' (*Conium maculatum*), the clerk noted: 'Grows high, 6 feet'. The brother keeping the book, William C. Brackett, also noted of *Conium maculatum*: 'Good to ease pain in open cancer which it does more powerfully than opium. Produces sweat and urine, but this plant is so very poisonous that it is imprudent to eat. It ought not to be administered by those unskilled in medicine.' He also gives the 'dose of the leaves in powder and extract' and concludes, 'great care ought to be taken to distinguish this plant from water hemlock for the latter is a deadly poison'. The account books throughout show a constant concern for accuracy and a professional knowledge of the material being handled.

Medicinal veracity and diversity of herbs used are the keynote of Shaker herbalism. Such diversity adds greatly to the range of fine garden plants which, through their publications, it is valid to add to the herb gardener's palette today.

Shaker records emphasize the point which has been clearly emerging through this narrative, that the ornamental, aesthetic, herb garden was unknown. It would indeed have been considered unnecessary and against Shaker beliefs:

> In the fine gardens were rows of tansy, horehound, feverfew, thyme, marjoram, marigold, foxglove, dandelion, boneset, numerous mints, roses and lavender. . . . The sisters went gathering in the wild berry-tea, pennyroyal and catnip for teas, poke berries for ink and sundry roots and herbs for poultices and steeps. The neatly kept rows of red roses with no thought of their beauty and fragrance were raised to be converted into delicate rosewater. . . .

(C. Piercy, *The Valley of God's Pleasure*, 1951)

This passage shows the typical division of the herb industry: important plants grown in rows on a field scale, others collected in the wild. All accounts surprise by the size of production. A report in the *American Journal of Pharmacy* (Vol 18, No 24, American Pharmaceutical Association, Washington DC) of 1852 describes a visit to the Shaker settlement of New Lebanon, New York, which existed from 1787 to 1947. The 'Chief Trustee, Edward Fowler' is quoted:

> It is about fifty years since our Society first originated as a trade in this country the business of cultivating and preparing medicinal plants for the supply and convenience of apothecaries and druggists. . . . We believe the quantity of botanical remedies used in this country, particularly of indigenous plants, has doubled in less than that time.
>
> There are now probably occupied at physic gardens in different branches of our Society, nearly 200 acres, of which about 50 are at our village. As we find a variety of soils are necessary to the perfect production of the different plants we have taken advantage of our farms and distributed our gardens accordingly . . . Of indigenous plants we collect about 200 varieties and purchase from the South, and West, and from Europe some 30 or 40 others, many of which are not recognized in the pharmacopaeoia, or the dispensatories, but which are called for in domestic practice and abundantly used.'

The Shakers' probity and industry made them particularly fit to fill the role of, it might be said, 'Apothecaries, by appointment to the whole North American Continent'. This they were for much of the nineteenth century. But trends in medicine away from their plant-based nostrums coincided with the Shakers' own decline in numbers (their strict laws regarding chastity did not increase their popularity in a less religious age). Thus they have now moved into history.

This emphasis has been laid upon the American Shaker experience because it carries into our own century the archetypal herbal tradition and brings together its threefold strands of collection in the wild, the setting up of botanic or physic gardens for study and the cultivation of the rarer plants, and field-scale herb production.

Shaker village declined
John Parkinson's books
sources & written
referon
herbis?
uses
37

The ornamental herb garden in this century

As the diversity of herbs in use and cultivation was sliding into decline in Shaker America, interest in them – at least in some of them – began to revive in England. The search for a valid architectural style for the Victorian age led designers to adapt motifs and ideas from almost every earlier age. Only the classical orders, so much a part of the previous century against which its successor was reacting, were rejected. Thus churches, banks, mansions and villas were erected in a bewildering array of styles, Gothic, Romanesque, Tudor, Elizabethan. A few were even Tudorbethan.

Not surprisingly some of those who sought historical exactitude in their new-old houses looked for help in creating suitably 'period' gardens to match. An interest in 'old-fashioned flowers' began to be prominent in the 1860s. Hollyhocks, sunflowers, pinks, 'old-fashioned' roses were associated with clipped beasts, balls and obelisks in yew or box (many existing topiary gardens, presumed to be truly ancient, date from this period).

The search for early models led to a renewed interest in sixteenth-and-seventeenth century herbals and a Parkinson Society flourished in the 1890s. John Parkinson's *Paradisus* and *Theatrum Botanicum* were amongst the most important of such texts. Significantly too, that seminal work on early gardens by Alicia Amherst, *A History of Gardening in England*, was first published in 1895. But still, at the end of the century, no new herb garden had yet been planned and planted. Nor, it must be remembered, did any such garden remain from an earlier time. The style, if indeed there had ever been one, was apparently lost.

However, all was in place for its creation, if not re-creation: plant-lore had been researched in the herbals, the plants themselves had been rescued from cottage gardens and, in 1901, came Reginald Blomfield's *The Formal Garden* which offered thoughts on suitable architectural frames. Some owners of truly historic houses made efforts to put them into a setting which would emphasize their period: the analogy with re-setting historic jewels for the same reason is inescapable. The example of Broughton Castle in Oxfordshire has all the elements of the 'old-fashioned' garden. Developed by Lady Gordon Lennox in the early 1900s, it had borders of herbaceous plants, topiary shapes with even a sun dial cut in yew and, at last, a separate herb garden. If there is any doubt of this latter, long-sought-for fact, it is utterly dispelled at the garden's entrance, where spelled out in santolina are the words 'Ye olde herb garden'.

Miss Jekyll's designs for herb gardens at Knebworth House, Barrington Court, Boveridge Park and Burningfold (p. 31) have already been mentioned and were produced between 1907 and 1923.

Between the wars the enthusiasm and knowledge of Eleanour Sinclair Rohde (1881–1950) extended the renaissance of herb growing much further into a new genre of ornamental herb gardening. Distillations of her wide reading from primary and secondary sources emerged in several books. *Old English Gardening Books* (1924), *Old English Herbals* (1922) and *Rose Recipes* (1936) treated these then somewhat esoteric subjects in a popular but serious style for the general reader.

Her thoughts on the practical use of plants are especially clear in *Gardens of Delight* (1934), where historic herbs are often put to new and visually attractive uses. Many of these ideas have become a part of the common currency of gardens in the succeeding half-century. So it is surprising today to read in Miss Rohde's *The Story of the Garden* (1932), discussing John Parkinson's seventeenth-century contribution to the evolution of gardening, that:

> From his garden of pleasant flowers he leads us to the kitchen garden, full not only of 'vegetables' as we understand the term, of strawberries, cucumbers and pompions, but also a vast number of herbs in daily use, many of them never seen in modern gardens. Besides the familiar thyme, balm, savory, mint, majoram, and parsley, there are clary, costmary, pennyroyal, fennel, borage, bugloss, tansy, burnet, blessed thistle, marigolds, arrach, rue, patience, angelica, chives, sorrel, smallage, bloodwort, dill, chervil, succory, purslane, tarragon, rocket, mustard, skirrets, rampion, liquorice and caraway.

Few of these are today in the 'never seen' category.

The final chapter in *The Story of the Garden* was written by a founder member of the Garden Club of America, Mrs Frances King; it has a short passage highly significant in this search for the original of the ornamental herb garden. This Mission House in Stockbridge, Massachusetts, was built in 1739 (pre-dating the Shakers by half a century) and was the first house of substance in that town. It was restored as a museum in the 1920s and its garden laid out to match. The plain clap-board façade is enlivened by a very grand front door case capped with a curved broken pediment. Mrs King describes the Mission House garden:

It is close to the street and near one side of the lot. Between it and the highway is a small fenced-in herb garden. Behind the house is a little yard with woodshed, (weaving-room and garage), well and well-sweep and grape-arbour. Still further on is the caretaker's house, where once the barnyard would have been. Between street, house and barn is the old-fashioned garden with its straight walk lined with fruit trees and flower borders, its vegetable plots, bush fruits, and casual rose bushes and beds of striped grass.

This garden of the Mission House is not a restoration but a recreating of an early American garden as it was supposed to exist. We have no actual authorities to turn to for such gardens, but must build on what we think those gardens were.

The success of the Mission House and renewed interest in America's early years led to many such re-creations throughout the eastern States. Further south the Garden Club of Virginia was founded in 1920, a banding together of a few garden clubs formed in the decade before. The Club soon became concerned with the decay of important homes and gardens dating back into the earliest years of the Commonwealth of Virginia. The first in a line of major restorations it supported was at the fine Tidewater House, Kenmore, which had been the home of George Washington's sister Betty.

Here, in Virginia, from the late 1920s, and until today, significant buildings have been selected by the Garden Club for grounds and garden restoration. Funded by an annual Garden Week when dozens of historic gardens are opened to the public and by the proceeds from a descriptive guide book, these restorations are monuments to painstaking research.

Seventeenth- and eighteenth-century American gardens are invariably formal in effect with box-edged parterres, brick-paved walks leading to charming little gazebos (which may in fact turn out to be the 'necessary house'). 'Parterre' however is too grand and daunting a term for what, even at the Governor's Palace at Williamsburg, is a series of charming garden rooms on a domestic scale. They hold a diversity of plants: ornamental natives, florists' flowers of the period, such as hyacinths, tulips and daffodils and inevitably those herbs which can be incorporated into a regulated scheme – rosemary, lavender, santolina and germander.

The culmination of the American passion for restoration is Colonial Williamsburg itself where an entire town has been rebuilt from great Governor's Palace to Apothecary's Shop. Throughout the nineteenth and early twentieth centuries Williamsburg had degenerated sadly from its period of political and social importance when it was the capital of Virginia from 1679 to 1781. The elegance of architecture and the other visual arts during that time is legendary; in America, Williamsburg was a byword.

Work began in 1927 to restore existing buildings in the city core and to rebuild, on archaeologically excavated foundations, those which had disappeared. Similarly careful research made replacement of the houses' gardens possible. Today Williamsburg's early eighteenth-century architectural beauty is enhanced by its trees, squares and gardens, large and small. All are 'in period' with the typical Virginian components described above – simple formality of walks, box-bordered beds, and a restrained palette of 'authentic' plants.

Box, or boxwood as it is known in America, though a seventeenth-century importation from Europe, is the *eminence verte* of almost every garden. The little 'Suffruticosa' form is tightly clipped as low formal edgings, or is allowed to tumble out over the grass plots; the typical *Buxus sempervirens* makes high green walls, architectural bastions and topiary shapes. Left alone it develops great billowing heaps like green thunder-clouds fallen to earth.

The room-like enclosure of so many colonial Williamsburg gardens, both large and small, gave the impression of being herb gardens even when, in most cases, that role is not a conscious intention. The point is, of course, that broad extension of the word 'herb' in pre-industrial societies which made most garden plants literal grist to the herbalists' mill and, conversely, flowers to that of the ornamental gardener. Here with such plants and planting we see an interrelation of house and garden, of use and of delight, which is the hallmark of civilized domesticity.

This is the American contribution to both garden design and garden history, a domestic form almost utterly lost in Britain from which it had apparently originally come. It provides a firm foundation on which to base a herb garden ethic today.

Again, then, the 1930s can be seen to be the meeting place, on both sides of the Atlantic, of interests which has led to the present passion for herbs. Belief that modern medicine was throwing out proven remedies of the past led to the formation in England of the Society of Herbalists by Hilda Leyel and from it the Culpeper shops as retail outlets (the first was opened on St Valentine's Day 1927 in Baker Street, London; they still flourish and the Society is now the

Herb Society, a non-profit organization which serves more than medicinal interests). In 1933 the Herb Society of America was founded: its semi-centennial year, under a Canadian President, has been celebrated across the continent.

In 1931 came the publication of the two-volume *A Modern Herbal* by Mrs Grieve ('M Grieve FRHS Herb Expert and Consultant', as she appears on the flyleaf of her later *Culinary Herbs and Condiments*) and edited by Mrs. Leyel *A Modern Herbal* can be seen as a milestone in the renaissance of herb interest and of herbalism as acceptable alternative medicine. Early texts were scoured, documented and used but also the author was concerned to be known, in spite of an apparent hankering after the Doctrine of Signatures, as the practical grower and user of herbs that indeed she was, having a herb farm and school at Chalfont St Peter.

As so often, the time was ripe for this renaissance: the First World War had encouraged the use of herbal aids in the treatment of those hideously maimed in body and mind who emerged from the trenches. Increasing research into plant substances reinforced that use. So too did the financial economies necessary only too soon in a beleagured island during the Second World War.

Fortunately, to move into happier times, it has been the modern opportunities for foreign travel taken by countless people that have been a spur to a much more general interest in herbs at least from a culinary point of view. The British tourist abroad is not always the figure of fun, insisting upon his cuppa and fish and chips: French, Spanish, Italian and Greek cooking, enjoyed on holiday, has been recognized as being dependent on herbs. Why could they not be grown at home? They could, and often were.

Any trend in gardens has to be supported by the availability of those plants which are considered suitable for it, whether it be tropical annuals by the vanload for carpet bedding or specimen trees for an arboretum. In the 1930s intending herb growers soon were able to be supplied by a range of plants, the lack of which Miss Rohde had complained about only a year or two earlier, from nurseries such as the Seal Herb Farm, in Kent. This was begun by Dorothy Hewer in 1925 and continued by Margaret Brownlow, both significant names in the world of herbs, although the farm no longer exists.

It is suitable therefore that at nearby Sissinghurst Castle V. Sackville-West should have planted a herb garden that is now, under the care of the National Trust, one of the best known in the world. It is also one of the most beautiful. As with Sissinghurst's other garden rooms – here literally planted above the foundations of the ghostly rooms of this vast Elizabethan mansion – it combines great artistic sensitivity of planting with rigidly cerebral formality of design.

Reference to Sissinghurst brings us full circle, for this great house was in its heyday in the time of Gerard and Parkinson, when its population was like that of a small town that had to be relatively self-supporting. What would grow was grown. Here again, like the famous Sissinghurst rose which the Nicholsons found surviving in the ruins when they bought the Castle, the herb garden plants themselves are the real link with that age. Though now in careful graduations of colour and height, form and mass, they are the same tansy and tarragon, sage and sorrel, that the garden's first makers grew in their simple clumps or rows. They offer their unchanged virtues to us today.

3

HERBS IN GARDEN DESIGN TODAY

As has already been shown by a brief discussion of the ecology of herbs, a diversity of habitat indicates a parallel diversity of form. It has also been emphasized that the definition of a herb is clearly one of human convenience and refers to plants of some sort of use to man and by man. Although, therefore, in some cases, the definition reflects botanical relationship as well (the herb-important families of Labiatae, Umbelliferae, Solanaceae and Compositae), what makes these families hold together in our minds is their essential herb-ness. And that in turn is what, most often, makes them hold together in the garden.

Effective grouping of plants is dependent upon a number of factors, but practical aspects must always take first place. However clever one might be in the arrangement of shape, texture, form and colour, for instance, it is a vain exercise if the plants are not equally suited to the site in which they are to show off the planter's artistry, and to the conditions provided. These may be conditions determined by soil-type, aspect, exposure or microclimate, all of which in combination will affect the ability of the plants to succeed as living organisms.

Knowledge of the needs of plants is obviously a first requirement and this is most clearly supported by knowledge of their original homes. The geographical spread of plants on a well-stocked rock garden may span the world – Switzerland, Iran, China and Chile – but they will all be upland plants adapted by evolution to somewhat similar conditions. Because of this they will also have a visual affinity of scale and shape.

Similarly a natural association may be reproduced in the garden with an equal atmosphere of 'rightness' occurring. A Scots pine for instance backs a group of silver birches with a tumble of ling or Scotch heather at their feet. The sensitive gardener will maintain that rightness by adding only exotics from similar conditions – a clump of yellow azaleas perhaps and *Cyperus pendulus* in front. The effect obtained (and of course the permutations are endless) should surprise and delight the viewer, but while the delight in the scene will continue, initial feeling of the surprise will turn to one of 'but of course' – that what is seen is 'right'.

Such ecological rightness is easily available to us by the association of Mediterranean herbs in a hot sheltered corner: lavenders, sages, rosemary and borage building up a picture of complementary colours and shapes, which is compounded by their scent. But here the marvelling inevitability is underlined by a cultural (as distinct from a *horti*cultural) sense of what is right. These are plants which have been put together ever since gardeners gardened and hence maintain their association even for those who have never seen the original southern habitat.

So strong, indeed, is the herb connection, so long have herbs been grown together, that it is possible to transcend (if not ignore) the ecological because of the strength of the cultural. Such a discussion may seem unnecessarily academic but it does help to explain their effect and, I believe, to extend the ways in which herbs can be used effectively in the garden. Because we see a plant differently in different associations doing different jobs, the same plant can possess a whole range of roles even in the same garden. This is particularly true of herbs.

Rosemary again is the epitome: it may be clipped into a formal pyramid near a severely classical front door (so long as it is not facing north), it can tumble over the edge of a retaining wall or lean through the balusters of a formal terrace, it can join a heap of herbs or a group of old-fashioned roses, it can be grand or it can be simple. It can even make mutton taste like lamb. What more can be expected or any plant? The point is worth labouring – that many herbs have a diversity of roles and that they will be seen in many guises in and out of the herb garden proper.

Thus while different gardeners, responding to their personal predilections and their very different gardening opportunities, will choose to grow a wide range of legitimate herbs, most will consider a near-to-hand basic collection as the centre of their herb gardening. Development from this provides the diversity that is possible, from window box to large-scale landscape, providing in turn pleasures to excite taste, scent, sight and touch – all but one of the senses. Only sound needs further contrivance; water falling into water or the noise, like a summer shower heard through drawn curtains, of shivering aspen leaves.

This combination of pleasures is almost entirely dependent upon living plants, wild species or near species which, as has been mentioned, have evolved their every part over time to be efficient in the struggle for species survival. The Biblical injunction to 'consider the lilies of the field' gives a false impression with its emphasis that 'they toil not, neither do they spin'. For toil indeed they do, to exist and to attain perfection, a perfection which is not to flatter the eye of the beholder (unless it be the eye of a pollinating insect), but for survival.

Herb growing, therefore, to be fully effective and to give the greatest pleasure must be based upon the needs of the plants themselves. A charming site, perfectly laid paths, or impeccable edgings are pretty pointless if the reason for their existence, the plant inhabitants, are poor. To cultivate implies not just a physical activity which turns soil or hoes off weeds, it also implies a search after excellence. We cultivate our intellect as well as our plots. Books on gardening are apt to hover disconcertingly between offering simple advice to the new house owner and garden novice and attempting at the same time to divert the *cognoscenti*. This is nowhere more difficult than in the obligatory section concerned with 'cultivation'.

Thus it seems here to be sensible, rather than repeating *ad nauseam* the 'rules of thumb' for a range of green fingers from emerald to near black, to look at the problem of successful cultivation and in turn design from the plants' point of view. If we accept, as we must, that these are efficient organisms in their own right then, as cultivators searching after success, apparently all we have to do is to reproduce as fully as possible the herbs' original home. In some ways we can even improve upon it: competition from other local plant species can be reduced (weeding), physical danger from browsing herbivores obviated (fencing), certain vagaries of weather ameliorated (watering). Further examples are not difficult to find, yet still we must return to each plant's original way of life and try either to emulate it or find an acceptable alternative. This book discusses some 400 different plant species; their designation by man as herbs holds them together conceptually but their habits and habitats vary enormously. What becomes necessary is to group them into cultivational as well as visually agreeable categories. These have several concerns. One is basic perennation habit – that is whether the plant is an annual like chervil, which can go through at least a couple of life cycles, seed back to seed, in one calendar year; or a woody perennial like sweet bay, which as an evergreen tree may survive a century or more. Many herbs are herbaceous perennials whose life cycle is between those two extremes.

Climate is another vital factor in which endemic plants from any given region becomes adapted, not only to extremes of heat and

cold but also to seasonal sequence. In the context of most of the
classic herbs the equally classic Mediterranean climate is decisive
in the organization of their distinctive pattern of growth. We all
remember the classroom chore of chanting its clichés: 'warm wet
winters and hot dry summers'. Then we coloured, on a barely
visible outline map of the world, those areas which enjoyed it: the
shores of the Middle Sea itself in Europe, plus Asia and Africa,
Southern California, South Africa and parts of Australia (the nasty
know-alls added a little bit of Chile). Later, more succinctly, one
learned from observation and from texts that a Mediterranean climate is one where olives will grow.

It never ceases to surprise that those other areas of climatic
synonymy have produced virtually no herbs nor indeed any major
food-plants for man's use. That the Mediterranean area itself is so
rich in life-supporting and life-enhancing plant species made it a
natural base for developing cultures: the 'Glory that was Greece'
may be famed for philosophy and the cultivation of men's minds
but it was made possible by the cultivation of plants. It is
significant that in none of those other 'Mediterranean' areas did
native peoples succeed in building up a lasting culture.

What should now be considered is the effect upon an endemic
flora of such a climatic pattern. This is a chicken and egg situation,
of course, for the climate has in part made the endemic flora. Each
perennation habit has to deal with the problems (eg. of restricted
and very seasonal rainfall) and potentialities (lack of very cold
periods) in its own way. Our garden use of them depends upon
these factors.

In the wild the annuals, such as chervil, calendula, borage,
coriander and henbane – to take examples from each use-category
of herbs – generally germinate in autumn with the first of the
season's rains. With copious winter moisture and in temperatures
that permit cell division the seedlings continue to develop so that
in five gentle months they are ready for the rapidly warming spring.
The pressure is now on. In a few weeks they thrust up flower-heads
and give their brief but spectacular display. By April seed is ripe on
plants at sea level and the summer sleep begins.

The same species, however, can often be found at greater
altitudes where the olives do not appear, beyond, in other words,
the felicity of the Mediterranean climate. These behave as more
northern species have to, germinating in early spring and going
through a quick life cycle before, even there, summer sun dries
them up. Such natural adaptability provides a permutation of use at
home which self-sown seedlings often demonstrate well. So on a

light soil in open, sunny positions herb annuals can be sown in early
October and though they may stay at the cotyledon (seed leaf) stage
and look appallingly vulnerable throughout our winter, in most
years they will more than survive. In spring robust plants soon build
up which flower in late May or June.

There is then time for a second late sowing, not on the same
spot but in some rotation, even if a somewhat haphazard one, to
develop by autumn. Only annual herbs from which seed is the
desideratum are unlikely to give two perfectly acceptable crops in
this way.

If young leaves are required a planned extension of this pattern
is adapted which follows the behaviour of our own emphemeral
weeds. We are all conscious that young groundsel and chickweed
plants as well as those in flower can be found, unless one is a
particularly tidy gardener, on every day of the year. They have
obviously germinated at different times to provide these enviably
successful overlapping generations. Four sowings of chervil or
parsley (though strictly a biennial) in, say, April, June, August and
October will ensure, unless deep winter snow intervenes, that not a
day in the year is parsley-less.

It should be emphasized that such marvellous adaptability is
not, of course, for all annual herbs: the basils, for example, are truly
tropical and if even shown the outside air before June – and a warm
June at that – are apt to turn very sullen and the merest suggestion of
an autumn frost literally stops them dead in their tracks.

Mediterranean perennials have their own but similar way of
dealing with their home climate. Growth sometimes begins in
late autumn or certainly early spring, again in order to get through
their life cycles and back to the safety of subterranean resting
organs, the bulbs, corms, tubers and rhizomes of the glossy autumn catalogues, before summer heat makes soft leaves above
ground impossible to support with the water available. The recipe
for successful garlic growing, which without this background
knowledge of Mediterranean ecology seems illogical and very
strange, demonstrates it nicely. Traditionally our garlic cloves are
planted on the shortest day of the year and are harvested on the
longest – and it works.

This is obviously an almost complete reversal of normal
northern garden habits but is essential for that crop: centuries of
cultivation have not changed its pattern one little bit. It behaves as if
it were still living in its original home, like a lone Victorian explorer
dressing for dinner in the depths of darkest Africa.

In the garden there is a very clear visual effect of this behaviour:

a herb garden is apt, unless careful thought is given to the matter, to start to look tired and passé from mid-summer on. The over-wintered annuals and most of the herbaceous perennials have, according to their own lights, done their job and are ready for a well-earned rest – out of sight. Over-emphasis on such plants, therefore, gives all herbs a bad press and wastes an important part of the garden for half the year.

The third major perennation habit group provides the answer. Shrubby plants deal with their inclement weather problems differently. In northern climates the usual answer is to go de-ciduous: take back into the body of the plant all the re-useable elements from the leaves and get rid of the rest as an insupportable encumbrance. Then start again next spring, when conditions be-come more favourable, with a burst of new growth. The brilliance of that spring green is one of the great excitements of the changing seasons in temperate climes.

Winter in the Mediterranean region proper, as has already been shown, is not the problem. But summer is, with its great heat, almost no atmospheric humidity and not much available soil mois-ture either. Summer leaf-drop seems not to be a general answer but instead adaptations to the foliage to prevent water loss are many and various. These adaptations give a very special look to the important herb shrubs – the lavenders, sages, curry-plants and rosemaries.

Leaves are usually long and narrow, often rolled inwards longitudinally to protect the stomata (the pores, which permit gaseous exchange and hence loss of water vapour). Grey or even white felting made up of dense hairs does a similar job and the pale colours also reflect some sun-heat. The whole plant is usually tight and domed in habit (though rosemary is a strangely straggling exception), which helps to maintain an individually more humid microclimate.

The evergreen and evergrey herb shrubs then are invaluable garden plants, in or out of the herb garden proper, for their dis-tinctive growth pattern, for their unusual leaf colours and their architectural permanence. They also flower, often spectacularly, and they are marvellously aromatic. They are, after all, the archetypal herbs of history and the solid base of herb gardening today.

All of these perennation forms and individual aerial adaptations, then, have ultimately developed in response to summer heat and drought. Except for the short-lived annuals which just use the winter-moist upper layer of soil, roots are long, woody and questing. They have to be. But reciprocally they are impatient of an excess of wetness, especially throughout a cold northern winter. As gardeners we can easily improve on the nutrient quality of their home soils but this is positively harmful if drainage is not perfect.

The light soils of our chalk and limestone uplands are ideal for herb gardening, being very much like a lot of the soils from around the Mediterranean. This is something of a comfort for those who garden on chalk and who, in the past, were apt to be made to feel positively inferior through not being able to grow rhododendrons. The reciprocal cannot quite be claimed, for though lime is relished by most herbs it is not essential: any decent light soil is happily accepted.

It should be made clear, however, that a re-creation of the soil poverty of the *maquis* is not the aim, but efficient growing of its most beautiful or useful plants. For while their needs must be satisfied there is no doubt that like other organisms, human or otherwise, which live on short commons they will accept a less rigorous life with pleasure. Our gardens often hold finer specimens than can be found in the wild.

In meeting the one great need of good drainage for herbs, a major herb garden design feature then becomes possible, in its many permutations. This is the raised bed. Often seen as a typical part of modern patio designs, it is also a continuing link with utilitarian gardens right back into classical times.

The moment that early Renaissance painting moves the Madonna from a gold-leaf background into the real world, she is invariably shown in a garden whose central plots are raised and borders along the walls are similarly elevated above the flowery mead. The splendid fifteenth-century Burgundian series, *Les Très Riches Heures du Duc de Berry*, show the same wherever gardens are depicted. Tudor and Elizabethan knot gardens are equally clear. Any fear that this could well be mere artistic convention like the halo around the Madonna's head is nicely dispelled by the 'potager' plate in Diderot's *Encyclopédie* (under Agriculture, significantly). The date is close to that of the Chelsea Physic Garden map of 1753, already discussed, and it shows a number of raised areas of various sizes.

Particularly helpful is Diderot's illustration of a simple method of keeping soil above the path level: bed-length planks, laid longitudinally, are attached to vertical stakes on their inside which protrude a foot or so below them. This makes an edging unit which, obviously, can be moved from plot to plot as a simple rotation of crops for convenience proceeds (chemical nutrient needs not at that time being understood).

Diderot has been used as a pattern for some of the American colonial garden re-creations discussed earlier where utilitarian emphases are to be made in country situations less sophisticated than those in urban Williamsburg. The important point here is the cultivational importance of raised beds, their adaptability in modern garden design combined with historic use.

Wooden plank edges are still valid on the Diderot pattern but it is essential that the timber be 'tanalized' or similarly pressure-treated with preservative for a reasonably long life.

Low single plank edges of this type are valuable also to maintain bed-form when the surrounding paths are of gravel or merely of seasonally tamped earth. On a bigger scale heavier timbers are used, as is often seen in wood-rich countries, but here the method is probably beyond most pockets unless a source of good quality railway sleepers can be tapped. These form excellent modules but because of their almost monumental scale need careful arrangement and sophisticated use. A relatively economical method is to lay one or two sleepers on edge, giving a 4-inch wide wall 9 or 18 inches high, on top of which another is laid flat to form a broad coping, giving a final 13 or 22-inch height. Sleepers can be drilled and assembled with iron rods or the Diderot method can be adapted. In all cases where wood is used bed corners look infinitely better if the constructional material is mitred (a considerable labour with railway sleepers) rather than merely butted together.

Other edgings can be even more permanent and will depend upon availability. They should, however, relate whenever possible to other constructional materials in the vicinity. Too many different materials give a feeling of restlessness at variance with the herb garden ideal. A garden which uses the house walls as part of its scene needs the same brick or stone for at least part of raised bed walls to provide a linking motif. It could appear as coping, as corner quoins or just as bands in the path pattern. Even stucco can be repeated by a cement skin over a cinderblock (breezeblock) construction.

Away from existing buildings no precedent is set and hence choice is more open. Still, however, paths and bed edges should have some consciously planned connection. On those enviable light, warm, early soils no more than a forming edge is required: wood again, old tiles or slates on a small scale or bricks can be employed. These are always best laid with a flat-topped finish. The dogs-tooth, saw-edge pattern, though possibly justifiable as cottage garden vernacular, maddeningly lets soil through onto the paths. The impression is close to that of Victorian cottage net curtains: an interesting survival but not one to be lived behind today.

For raised beds proper, or for retaining walls, bricks, granite sets or natural stone are of course ideal and price is apt to be the deciding factor. Ease of availability therefore becomes crucial because cost of carriage can kill an otherwise possible project. Reconstituted stone, in stone-like colours – *not* the tutti-frutti confections that are only too often on offer – can also be good. Indeed any building material, used with taste and laid with care, can do the job, as diverse as flagstones set vertically one-third deep into the soil or rows of wine bottles set in cement, bottom outwards, and finished with a flat coping stone.

Such a coping is almost always desirable to protect the wall beneath, to provide a seat and to give a finish to the bed. Heights of beds obviously will vary according to need from a couple of inches to 2 or 3 feet. Combinations of heights in any one design can build up a fine architectural pattern which the interesting shapes of the permanent herb shrubs complement perfectly.

Their position, in the centre or the edge of the bed, greatly alters the visual effect. One forgets that a sage or curry plant, which on the flat makes a typical regular hummock, will tumble over a retaining wall in an entirely unexpected way. Again, we normally look down on these plants: when presented at near-eye level we see them very differently. And as aromatic herbs, of course, growing them nearer the nose is entirely sensible.

The potential of raised beds, therefore, will be seen to extend far beyond the original basically cultivational reason for their existence and moves into the full design of the garden where their construction and planting gives a new garden, in particular, a rapid impression of permanence and of maturity. The plants, after all, are immediately twice their normal height.

The point has been repeated about the naturally early-season growth of Mediterranean herbs and of their going to rest soon after mid-summer. With annuals there is, as has been shown, the possibility of arranging overlapping or at least successional generations by careful planning. A few perennials such as sweet cicely, lovage or cardoon (an acceptable herb garden associate or pot herb) will both extend their visual effect and culinary usefulness if cut to the ground in, say, late June. A liquid feed and copious watering will bring about fine lush leaves to last right into autumn. Any of the comfreys and *Artemisia ludoviciana* will take this apparently heartless treatment, and sorrel behaves similarly if cut back as early as the end of May

By no means all herbs, of course, are adapted to that mild winter/hot summer pattern – though they are in the majority. There are a number from harsher regimes, northern European natives whose growth sequence relates to a different type of climate. Here, winter temperatures are such as to inhibit growth which thus naturally begins in spring and uses the whole summer season. Exceptions are woodlanders which have to get on with their life cycles very quickly before the closing tree canopy makes efficient photosynthesis impossible, and biennials such as carrot and angelica whose over-wintering food stores make rapid early summer flower and fruit possible.

This same pattern is followed by a number of herbs from North America. These can be early spring woodland natives such as the exquisite bloodroot (*Sanguinaria*) and hepatica whose uses were well known to the native peoples long before European colonists appeared on the scene. They can also be summer and autumn flowering plants. Aromatic bergamot, *Liatris spicata* and cardinal flower are well-known plants of old country borders as well as valid inhabitants of the herb garden.

Much of Japan and China also offer summer plants for our needs. Information now available about traditional Chinese medicine shows that utilization of its native flora greatly exceeds the Western tradition of plant use. That it still continues throughout the country contemporary travellers can testify. Many of the plants are not unknown to us; on the contrary, collected over the last two centuries they have become well-loved, established members of our ornamental gardens. Thus *Hamamelis mollis*, *Pyracantha* and *Magnolia liliiflora* take up a herbal legitimacy which is not generally realized. We may well not use them, and this book is certainly not advocating home medication without professional orthodox or alternative medical advice, but they add an important dimension to *Herbs in the Garden*.

Such a broadly based herb garden not only maintains its beauty and diversity throughout the year but serves to demonstrate the amazing dependency of man upon the world of plants.

A further aspect which encourages the use of herbs from cooler regions of the world is that concerned with herb garden planning. Any garden based on the traditional model of a series of beds formally arranged within a walled or hedged enclosure obviously contains beds facing each point of the compass. The sun-loving Mediterraneans are naturally placed in the south, southeast or southwest facing beds. Formal mirror image plans demand balanced planting and here, though some of the Mediterraneans will take half-shade on light soil, the northerners not only come into their own but succeed better as well.

Here we find the mints, alchemillas, some of the alliums and Christmas rose, for example, and above them elder and viburnum on soil which does not dry out in summer. These shaded borders will also grow at least some of the waterside herbs – sweet flag and *Iris versicolor*, golden meadowsweet and variegated figwort. A pool will be needed for the real aquatics, waterlily and bogbean.

This concept extends well beyond the area of ground consciously designated 'herb garden' into other parts of the garden with their own names and expected plant associations. In each, ornamental herbs can have their place and hold their own with conventional inhabitants whose only claim to fame is their beauty: an analogy with vapid court favourites might be made. Thus we can consider dual roles in these other garden areas.

The visual effect of a sun-loving herb bed is so dependent upon the grey and white-felted Mediterranean xerophytes that the same spot designed as a grey border can hardly exist without many of the same plants: where would a grey border be without lavender, santolina and helichrysum, to name but three of the many possible? Elsewhere, though less immediately obvious, the shady courtyard with a fine specimen of *Mahonia japonica* underplanted with trilliums and sweet woodruff is in fact associating the herbs of three cultures. The warm terrace holds Chinese gooseberry, scented leaved pelargoniums and lemon verbena and hence combines herbs of three continents. Similarly the herbaceous border and shrub borders have their own particular herbal associations.

The next chapter offers details of this potential by examining a number of very different herb gardens.

HERB GARDENS FROM LANDSCAPE TO WINDOW BOX

❧

This chapter sets out to demonstrate practically a diversity of herb garden types from large and complicated designs to small simple plots. The suggestions should not be copied slavishly but used as bases for individual needs and sites. A few of them do actually exist, but having been designed for a specific set of circumstances they do not, unlike good wine, necessarily travel well. Thus each is a subject for discussion. Vernacular names are used in the plans for those for whom Latin binomials would not give an immediate visual picture.

The formal or classic herb garden

It seems sensible, as many factors are common to all – factors of cultivations and plant needs – to begin with a garden of some comprehensiveness. It can be called a classic herb garden; it is certainly the expected herb garden, though, as has been shown in the chapter on the historical development of gardens, it is truly twentieth century in its design and conception, for there is really no classic herb garden. Be that as it may, it is concerned to provide a number of pleasures and facilities. At one level it is an educational garden with a comprehensive collection of mainly old world herbs, most of which have been cultivated since the time of Dioscorides and Theophrastus. The half dozen or so exotics – aloe, agave, rose geranium, bergamot, nasturtium, American mandrake and Madagascar periwinkle – are an addition to that original classical collection, but have been a part of it for at least 200 years.

The arrangement, as with any garden, is concerned with two basic facets: to accommodate the plants happily as regards cultivational needs, plus those of ease of viewing and accessibility. It is always frustrating to be able to glimpse a plant only at a distance at the back of some deep border when it cries out for close appreciation of flower or scent. In the herb garden the 'hands-on' requirement is even greater and thus ease of access is vital. This need has its dangers in that the path to bed ratio can be unpleasantly high, especially if many visitors are to be catered for. Here the situation is dealt with by varying path width in tune with expected traffic and by permitting plants to spill out of their bed enclosures. Without grass paths no harm is done.

The main north-south axis has a width of 6½ feet while side paths reduce to 5 feet and an access strip of half that lies at the back of the long borders. This last is particularly important for maintenance as the garden is enclosed by hedges. Yew needs only an annual cut but this, done in August when the herbaceous growth is at its most luxuriant, needs space, and plants coming to its very foot can get badly damaged in the operation. Obviously this utilitarian strip is also valuable for access to the herbs themselves and gives a space where roots of hedge and herb are not in direct competition.

It can be seen that in the arrangement of the herbs themselves several factors have been kept in mind and, as far as possible, in balance. Firstly, though gardens are for plants they are also for people: owner or keen plantsman will always visit but others may at first fail to see the point of this comprehensive collection. Thus here, on the principle of Chinese boxes, or Russian dolls, is a garden within a garden within a garden. Its centre is a small restful water garden with seats facing the pool. This in turn is raised 18 inches (for metric measures see plan scale) and has a coping wide enough for at least temporary sitting, where scents of sweet flag and bogbean can be enjoyed and goldfish watched, darting beneath the lily pads.

The water garden becomes extended into a formal scented garden by the inclusion of its four corner beds, solid blocks of purple and variegated sage contained by low, clipped bands of grey-green *Santolina* 'Edward Bowles'. Foliage of all of these is available throughout the year to be crushed in the hand. In corners by the seats, where feet do not continually tread (for none of them will take much wear), camomile, pennyroyal and Corsican mint give further scents. In June rich perfume wafts from the corner bushes of the apothecary's rose and from its striped sport 'Rosa Mundi'.

Vertical emphasis is provided by the four obelisks of bay set in pairs on the main walk and by four matching terracotta pots. Here they are stated as containing aloes and agaves for herbal use but the scented theme would be better maintained if these were exchanged for rose geranium and others of its scented leaved type, *Pelargonium tomentosum* or *P.* 'Lady Plymouth'. Lemon verbena and pineapple sage are equally suitable pot plants.

To the scented garden are added the 'long borders' and four small

FORMAL HERB GARDEN

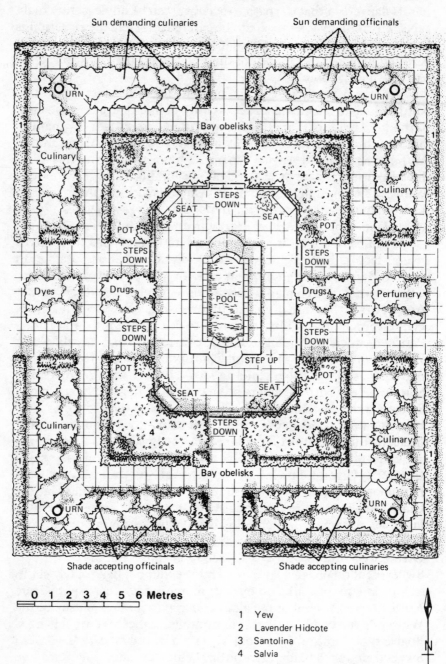

Sun demanding culinaries

Sun demanding officinals

URN

URN

1

1

Culinary

Culinary

Bay obelisks

3

4

4

3

SEAT

STEPS DOWN

STEPS DOWN

SEAT

2

POT

POT

STEPS DOWN

STEPS DOWN

Dyes

Drugs

POOL

Drugs

Perfumery

STEPS DOWN

STEPS DOWN

POT

POT

STEP UP

3

4

SEAT

SEAT

4

3

Culinary

2

Culinary

STEPS DOWN

1

1

URN

2

2

URN

Bay obelisks

Shade accepting officinals

Shade accepting culinaries

0 1 2 3 4 5 6 **Metres**

1   Yew
2   Lavender Hidcote
3   Santolina
4   Salvia

N

The Formal Herb Garden

S. W. Corner
Culinaries
Alecost
Chives
Garlic
Lovage
Spearmint
Parsley
French sorrel
Garden thyme
Lemon thyme

Shade Accepting Officinals
Aconite
Butcher's broom
Bistort
Columbine
Lungwort
Male fern
Meadowsweet
Mezereon
Peony
Stinking iris
Lady's mantle (urn)

S. E. Corner
Culinaries
Angelica
Fenugreek
Parsley
Welsh onion
Alexanders
Sorrel
Sweet Cicely
Horeseradish (variegated)
Nasturtium dwarf (urn)

Balm
Chervil
Fennel
Lovage
Peppermint
Eau de cologne mint
Ginger mint
Parsley
Salad Burnet

Centre E.
Perfumery
Clary
Jasmine
Damask rose
Orris root
Sweet woodruff

Drugs
Autumn crocus
Deadly nightshade
Lily of the valley
Opium poppy
Thorn apple

Pool
White water lily
Bogbean
Sweet flag

N. W. Corner

Culinaries

Angelica
Aniseed
Caraway
Dill
Fennel
Parsley
Rosemary
Rose geranium (urn)
Apothecary's rose

Nasturtium
Pot marjoram
Sweet marjoram
Oregano
Summer savory
Winter savory
Sage
Rosemary

N. E. Corner

Sun Demanding Officinals

Pot marjoram
Sweet marjoram
Nasturtium
Artichoke
Bear's breech
Birthwort
Bergamot
Cowslip
Larkspur
Marigold
Wormwood

Culinaries

Tarragon
Basil
Bush basil
Borage
Chives
Juniper
Parsley
Saffron
Rosemary, prostrate (urn)

Centre W.

Dyes

Dyers alkanet
Dyers greenweed
Madder
Woad
Lady's bedstraw

Drugs

American mandrake
Castor oil
Foxglove
Henbane
Madagascar periwinkle

Centre Pots

Aloe   Agave

near-square beds on the east-west access, all within the yew hedges. These bring the whole concept together as a full-scale herb garden. Over 100 herbs in every category of life-enhancers are grown. But, as these plants are 'for use and for delight', they are carefully segregated; the culinary herbs from the officinals (official or historic medicinal herbs), the dye-plants from those of import-ance today as modern drug-producers. The problem of providing suitable sites in one relatively small area for such a diverse population is solved by addressing the related problem (if such it be) or finding suitable inhabitants for the north-facing or south-facing borders respectively. Antipodean readers now turn the page upside down, and reverse the plants.

. Thus the north and south borders are shared equally, but di-vided clearly by paths, between plants of the apothecary's shop and plants of the kitchen. The latter are given particular emphasis in this plan by taking up the whole east and west borders. Each herb garden maker has to decide on a particular emphasis: here it was considered that culinary herbs have a greater practical use today. As the A-Z section in this book shows, most of them have or had 'official' status as well so that any apparent imbalance is less than areas of ground so used would seem to indicate. And from the practical point of safety it is wise to arrange things so that *some* of the culinaries can be used medicinally rather than that *some* of the medicinals can be used culinarily.

For this same reason the ten modern drug plants shown, pro-ducers of poisonous alkaloids or glycosides, are rigorously kept to a pair of separate beds. Of these, as has been explained elsewhere, only deadly nightshade is a real hazard because of its delicious-looking and pleasant tasting but potentially lethal berries. Again, individual choice has to be exercised if it is to be grown. The present writer leans towards doing so in a comprehensive and educationally orientated herb garden where labelling is impecc-able: facts learnt in this way can then be related to meeting this and other such plants in the wild. Hysterical damning of all plants known to contain elements toxic to man does no good at all: indeed, if followed it is surprising what a large number of well-loved plants from lily of the valley to snowdrops would be excluded from garden use.

It has been shown in the chapter discussing the preponderance of Mediterranean plants in our herb gardens that growth pattern naturally starts early in the year and is apt to have passed its peak by late July. At least three months of major garden enjoyment are yet to come, so it is important to resow the short-lived plants as

soon as the first clump is past its best. But, though keeping within
the use-categories, it is wise to replace each with a different plant:
overwintering chervil with basil, parsley with borage, coriander
(fruits having been collected to turn a pedestrian ratatouille into
food fit for a latter-day Lucullus) with autumn-sown pot marigold.

Such successional cultivations maintain the ongoing nature of
an interesting garden. Meanwhile, of course, shrubby plants and
especially the tender things like rose geranium continue to increase
in size and beauty throughout the year. If no hard frost intervenes
great bushes of the latter can exist into November and indeed
pineapple sage is apt not to flower at all until well into autumn. The
point that cannot be overemphasized is the twelve-month nature of
a comprehensive herb garden where living plants are available every
day of the year. Even under snow the formal bones, yew and lavender
cotton hedges, the walks and bed patterns, maintain the visual
interest that is so desirable in a garden.

The terrace herb garden

In such a place as the 'classic' herb garden, enclosed as it is, it would
be possible to disregard periods of lesser attraction. In the next
example, however, that proviso fails to apply. Here is a south-facing
terrace which, being in view of the windows of the house and having
immediate access from it, it always in sight. The word terrace is
valid for any area, from a grand balustraded place of parade with a
great panorama of distant countryside, to a little sheltered corner
where tea or drinks can be taken out of sight of neighbours who,
hopefully, have got their own bit of room outdoors.

Its convenience to the house – though from drawing-room
rather than kitchen – makes herb availability good sense. Its aspect
and position giving maximum sun combined with shelter from cold
north winds provides a perfect home for so many of the most visually
attractive herbs. Here they are employed as the main furnishing
material for an area that is continually in use: scents from their
flowers and aromatic leaves are particularly valuable. Here, what
one can refer to as 'herb associates', that is actual botanical relatives,
ecological compatriots or just visual complements, are also a logical
part of the scene.

What is suggested, then, in this plan is a 'roofless extension' to a
semi-detached house. It is a common enough site after all. The
shared garden wall, with a short return, extends the width of the
terrace just 15 feet. The terrace length is 27 feet plus and thus this

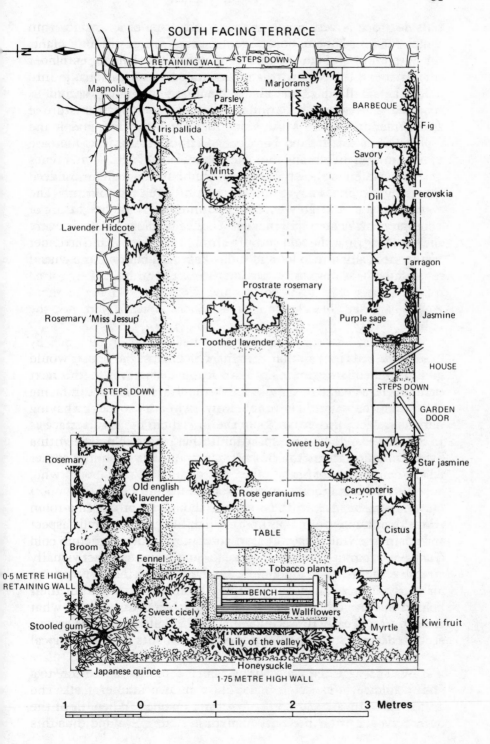

SOUTH FACING TERRACE

N

RETAINING WALL — STEPS DOWN

Magnolia

Parsley

Marjorams

BARBEQUE

Fig

Iris pallida

Savory

Mints

Dill

Perovskia

Lavender Hidcote

Tarragon

Prostrate rosemary

Purple sage

Jasmine

Rosemary 'Miss Jessup'

Toothed lavender

HOUSE

STEPS DOWN

STEPS DOWN

GARDEN DOOR

Sweet bay

Rosemary

Star jasmine

Old english lavender

Rose geraniums

Caryopteris

Cistus

Broom

Fennel

TABLE

Tobacco plants

0·5 METRE HIGH RETAINING WALL

BENCH

Sweet cicely

Wallflowers

Stooled gum

Myrtle

Kiwi fruit

Lily of the valley

Honeysuckle

Japanese quince

1·75 METRE HIGH WALL

1   0   1   2   3 Metres

outside space is very much the size and shape of an inside room which the ever-hopeful house agents are apt to describe as 'suitable for entertaining'. Plant furniture, in the form of herbs, is placed mainly round the edge with a few containers as occasional pieces, able, like small tables and chairs indoors, to be moved around as required. The only conventional furniture shown *in situ* is a fine teak garden seat with its low, stone-topped table in front and, in the far corner, a small fixed barbecue. Further stackable chairs and tables are brought out and removed as required.

The garden is shown as having been built on a site most conveniently sloping away from the house. Thus its southern and western edges inevitably become retaining walls the height of the necessary pair of steps (15 inches). To give further contour interest the border against the house could also be raised above terrace level by the same amount so long as soil is kept well below damp-course level. Such beds obviously provide the excellent drainage required for the plants it is intended to grow. Conversely, many of them would be a sensible choice even if a herb context were not the point.

On a flat site something of the effect could be obtained by raising the beds by a similar amount which, from the house, would give an immediately more enclosed feeling. Wherever the shrubby herbs such as lavender, santolina, rosemary and others are grown in these elevated spots they tumble forward in a most engaging manner, just as they do over rocks in their southern *maquis* home. Put in near the edge they leave space for further plants behind them and excellent associations can be built up in the way described in the chapter on ecology of herbs.

Both garden and house walls have been fully used to support climbing herbs. *Actinidia chinensis* (occasional producer of kiwi fruit, for which its cross-pollinating pair is necessary) and fig provide dramatic leaf-shapes and, in good years, worthwhile crops of fruit. Star jasmine (*Trachelospermum*) and white summer jasmine combine to throw out a delicious fragrance on to the late summer air. Early Dutch honeysuckle underplanted with lily of the valley behind the seat give earlier pleasures. Many spots are available for the addition of early flowering bulbs. While daffodil has, as the A-Z section describes, a marginal herbal validity, it is not necessary to be too rigidly purist in such a garden and various narcissi, tulips and hyacinths can be used with Brompton stocks, forget-me-nots and wallflowers. These all make marvellous container plants and give to the terrace a gay, spring, cottage garden air. When they have been removed from the pots (conversely bulbs planted 8 inches deep in the beds should be left alone) their place can be taken by rose geraniums, basils and other tender things in late May or June. Other containers hold tender permanent herbs such as toothed lavender and prostrate rosemary and, in this small area where every inch matters, three different mints. In summer the latter stand permanently in big saucers of water. They are thus encouraged to give of their best while their natural aggressiveness is discouraged.

Further herbs proper surround the corner barbecue unit: to gather them with one hand and sprinkle onto the steaks with the other while not needing to move a foot is an enviable conversational gambit. Personally, it seems to me that kitchens are a more satisfactory invention.

The terrace is framed on one side by the exquisite white-flowered *Magnolia denudata* and, on the east, a gum tree. A couple of the most reliably hardy species offer very different effects. *Eucalyptus niphophila* is the snow gum from the mountains of New South Wales and makes a most elegant small evergreen tree with green and white mottled bark. Growth is relatively slow. *E. gunnii* on the other hand will rush up to 50 feet in less than ten years but here can be cut down – stooled like a big blackcurrant – every two years to give a 10-foot high cloud of blue-grey foliage, aromatic and invaluable for cutting for indoor arrangements.

Thus in this important part of the garden, the most immediately available part, plants have been arranged in an interesting diversity of form for year-round interest, brilliance of colour in spring when it gives special pleasure and, during summer when outdoor living is most possible, a combination of delicious scents and sights. Throughout the year, and this is the point of the whole selection, there are fresh herbs for almost every culinary occasion.

Herbs in the shady courtyard

Houses that enjoy warm, sunny back gardens very often have shady entrance fronts. If the house is well designed this is no disadvantage as one naturally moves through a hall into the sunny rooms beyond. Nonetheless a welcoming and interesting entrance is required. Careful choice of plants is vital in this north-facing situation, for there is no point in trying to make plants which insist upon sun succeed in a shady site. On the contrary, the shade, the higher humidity, even if the soil is very well drained, and the shelter from drying winds all combine to create a potential to be fulfilled, not a problem to surmount.

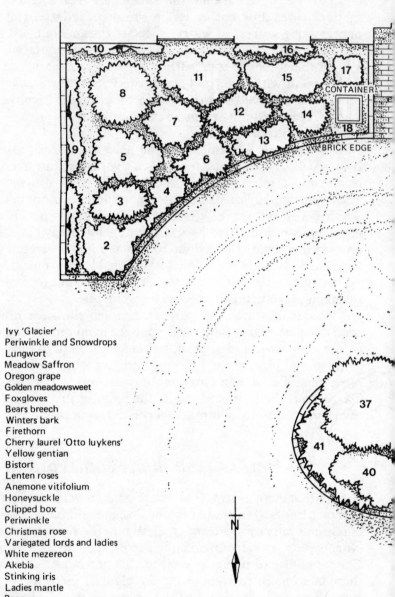

A NORTH FACING ENTRANCE

1   Ivy 'Glacier'
2   Periwinkle and Snowdrops
3   Lungwort
4   Meadow Saffron
5   Oregon grape
6   Golden meadowsweet
7   Foxgloves
8   Bears breech
9   Winters bark
10   Firethorn
11   Cherry laurel 'Otto luykens'
12   Yellow gentian
13   Bistort
14   Lenten roses
15   Anemone vitifolium
16   Honeysuckle
17   Clipped box
18   Periwinkle
19   Christmas rose
20   Variegated lords and ladies
21   White mezereon
22   Akebia
23   Stinking iris
24   Ladies mantle
25   Peony
26   Trillium and Golden feverfew

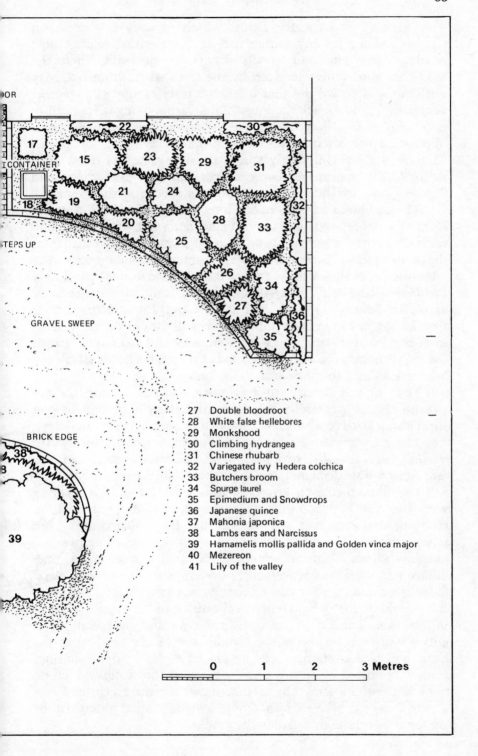

OR

17

CONTAINER

18

STEPS UP

15

22

23

29

30

31

32

19

21

24

20

28

33

25

26

34

27

36

35

GRAVEL SWEEP

BRICK EDGE

38

39

27 Double bloodroot
28 White false hellebores
29 Monkshood
30 Climbing hydrangea
31 Chinese rhubarb
32 Variegated ivy Hedera colchica
33 Butchers broom
34 Spurge laurel
35 Epimedium and Snowdrops
36 Japanese quince
37 Mahonia japonica
38 Lambs ears and Narcissus
39 Hamamelis mollis pallida and Golden vinca major
40 Mezereon
41 Lily of the valley

0   1   2   3 Metres

Thinking ecologically again, which is always wise when choosing plants for any garden site, such a position relates most nearly to woodland and woodland edges in the wild. There the shade and protection are given by the trees which from late May until autumn crowd together in such a leafy canopy as to permit very little light to reach the forest floor. Plants living there need to get on with their life cycles early in the year before growth becomes impossible (this discussion is taken further in my *Plants for Shade*). Thus they are mainly early spring flowering, just as many sun-loving Mediterraneans, and others like them, though in response to different circumstances, disappear out of sight during the summer.

The deciduous forest flora of China, Europe and North America seem to have been well used for medicinal herbs by native peoples and early settlers, the latter usually building upon knowledge gleaned from the former, though it seems much less a habitat for culinary herbs. The huge number of Shaker herbs collected in the wild relates very closely to this woodland flora. A similar folk tradition is still in existence today as Judith Bolyard in *Medicinal Plants and Home Remedies of Appalachia*, has so recently shown. This still uses medicinally herbs from the forested border between Kentucky and Georgia which in Europe are merely considered just good garden plants for visual effect — box elder, kalmia, staghorn sumach, and so on.

Thus in this formal entrance with its pair of wing-like enclosing beds is a carefully balanced miscellany of perennials and shrubs almost all of which have or had documented medicinal uses. The one exception is Lenten rose, Christmas rose's close cousin (*Helleborus orientalis*), which could be replaced if exactitude is the aim but it is a shade plant *par excellence* and difficult to resist.

The floral display is strongest in late winter and early spring with the true hellebores just mentioned, snowdrops, bloodroot, trilliums and lungwort. But an autumn flush also comes from false-hellebores (*Veratrum*), monkshood, Japanese anemones and meadow saffron. Summer emphasis is mainly upon grand, lush foliage providing a cool welcome to visitors on the hottest days. Guarding the door are a pair of clipped box trees, taking the place that would normally be given, in a sunnier spot, to sweet bay. This, in fact, would still do quite well in the warmer areas and, if not grown elsewhere in the garden, could be tried. By the first step a further pair of containers can be placed to hold bright summer annuals followed by spring bulbs (*not* crocus nor tulips which do not open without sun). On balance, however, the green theme of strong foliage is better retained here leaving vibrant colours to be the feature of the sunny gardens beyond.

As always the walls of this site are fully furnished with interesting climbers and wall shrubs. Variegated ivies give winter brightness, Japanese quince and *Akebia* early spring flower, to be followed by *Hydrangea petiolaris* and firethorn. Winter's bark, *Drimys winteri*, is a more unusual choice and one not for the coldest areas. But in general one can expect the narrow evergreen leaves, milk white on their undersides, to give a fine year-round effect with the bonus of heads of strange cream-coloured flowers in April and May in most years.

The central circle within the gravel sweep is planned as a winter garden for it gets a little sun being further from the house. The two predominant plants are valuable at all seasons and hence fully deserve such a site. *Mahonia japonica*, listed in Chinese medical treatises, is for westerners one of the most desirable of garden ornamentals and one which it is almost impossible to overpraise. Eventually a broad 6-foot high bush of dramatic whorls of evergreen leaves, it carries in their centres lax shuttlecock sprays of flowers looking and smelling like pale yellow lilies of the valley and doing so from October to April inclusive. Here above it, cheating the herb theme only slightly (see A-Z section), is Chinese witch hazel with its golden, spidery, scented flowers in the first few weeks of the year. Summer foliage and gentle autumn colour is also attractive. A clump of *Acanthus* (bear's breech) beneath adds a further foliage dimension for summer effect and, as this disappears to nothing from October on, it is underplanted with early spring bulbs, snowdrops, aconites and *Narcissus* 'February Gold'.

While perfectly valid in maintaining a herbal theme the gently green entrance court offers nothing to most herb enthusiasts who, quite rightly, consider the culinary herbs of particular merit. They are, after all, for personal and often immediate use. It has been shown how many can be a part of a comprehensive herb garden and also of a warm terrace. In both cases however they are there as part of a broader need, for demonstration in the one case, for decoration in the other. Three forms of culinary herb gardens are now discussed whose size can be varied depending on the need – how much, say, thyme does your kitchen require in a year? – and on the garden space available.

Cook's Collection 1. A kitchen door herb bed.

Here nothing is more than a few steps away from the cooking pot, and although the whole area covers only 5 square yards (or metres), it contains the dozen and a half herbs that no good cook would wish to be without and which are in fact the full compass of most cook

KITCHEN DOOR HERB GARDEN

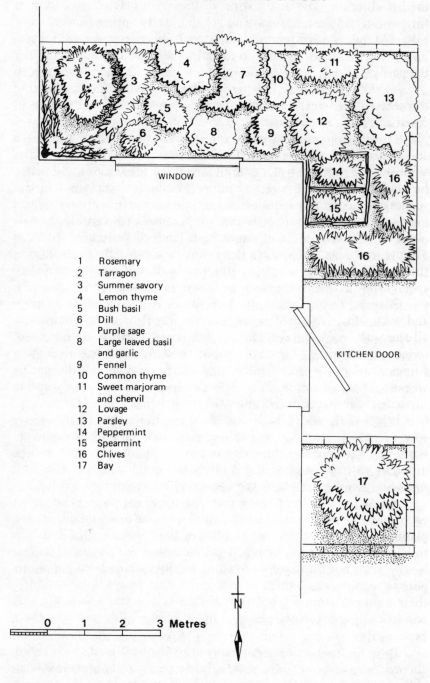

1   Rosemary
2   Tarragon
3   Summer savory
4   Lemon thyme
5   Bush basil
6   Dill
7   Purple sage
8   Large leaved basil
    and garlic
9   Fennel
10 Common thyme
11 Sweet marjoram
    and chervil
12 Lovage
13 Parsley
14 Peppermint
15 Spearmint
16 Chives
17 Bay

WINDOW

KITCHEN DOOR

0   1   2   3 Metres

N

book recommendations. The kitchen door opens to the west and the little border, only 3 feet wide, begins with this aspect and then turns south for just 10 feet. It is backed by the house to north and east. Thus it is warm and protected. A brick edging raises it a few inches over which the front line plants can tumble and steal a bit of the path.

As always, some of the plants are above ground and available throughout the year. These are the shrubs – thymes, sage, and rosemary. Here, because there is so little space and an untrimmed plant could cover half of it, the rosemary is planted in the corner and treated as a wall plant with its branches pinned back at right angles. This method was commonly recommended in early times for the highly prized gold and silver rosemaries: perhaps had the suggestion been more carefully followed these delicately variegated forms might be less rare today. In such a warm spot rosemary will often be in flower by late February and it is ideal in cold gardens. Though not much rosemary is needed in the kitchen it is so distinctive as to be sorely missed if not to hand and hence it earns its special spot. It is a lovely basis for dining-table posies.

Chives, though obviously not shrubby, can, in mild winters and with some care in what is cut over, give green tips for almost all the year. A cloche would help. Similarly, parsley sown at least twice – both in the big patch shown and where a spare spot becomes available – gives fresh leaves for all but the coldest winter weeks. At this time chervil, sown as soon as the first frost has carried off the sweet marjoram, can well produce a little garnishing. It is better still, having fully harvested the marjoram for drying, to sow in mid-September or even earlier; this ensures good overwintering chervil as a fine alternative in appearance and subtly different in flavour from the more usual parsley. *Omelettes aux fines herbes* are believed by the *cognoscenti* to prefer it.

A further couple of spare feet provides two more clear crops each year. Garlic cloves, the individual sections of a whole bulb, are planted 3 inches deep in mid December and these are usually ready to harvest in mid June which is just the moment to plant out the basil plants. For the last two or three weeks, having been bought in pots as seedlings a couple of inches high, these have been watching their summer home-to-be from the safety of the warm kitchen window sill above, until the weather should really live up to their expectations.

Two distinct mints, peppermint and spearmint, have been chosen but applemint or eau de cologne mint could replace one or both depending on personal choice. The important points to note

are that they are given the shadiest spot available in the lea of a 4-
foot high clump of lovage and that both have a square foot or so
enclosed by roofing slates pushed three-quarters of their length into
the soil to keep the rhizomes from roving.

Only one herb uses further ground and this is a bush of sweet
bay. It could take the form of a plant in a big pot or half barrel, or a
specimen planted and trimmed like a bastion to protect the back
door from the north east wind whizzing round from the front of the
house. In either case the single plant will give enough bay leaves for
the biggest family and provide a screen for the dustbin as well.

With care in feeding and watering when necessary, in the
removal of dead leaves, in re-sowing the moment an inch of ground
becomes free, this utilitarian border will always look attractive, not
least because it is doing a job and doing it well. But it is possible,
while keeping to the basic Cook's Collection, to make it even more
of a garden feature.

Cook's Collection 2. A herb-wheel.

On a small scale a herb-wheel is a practical possibility, if something of a gimmick. Here an old cart-wheel is laid flat upon an area
of suitable soil and each radiating gap between the spokes is filled
with a single herb. An ornamental pot of sweet bay or rose
geranium stands on the hub.

It must be admitted, however, that wooden cart-wheels have
moved into the realm of collectors' items and used thus are likely
to rot away in a few years. Nonetheless the principle of such a
shape has much to commend it to separate the herbs, and if the
'spokes' are extended to the width of small paths they provide ease
of maintenance and access. Moreover, in designing a herb-wheel for
a specific site and for particular needs, different interspoke com-
partments for a wider range of herbs can be arranged. The spaces, of
course, need not be the same: as one always needs infinitely more
parsley than, say, summer savory.

Materials for delineating the wheel can vary: the outside circle
is best outlined with a something whose unit size is small so that
gaps at each meeting place are minimal. Bricks are suitable, therefore, and even better are granite setts. Many of the modern modular
paving blocks are also good. Where possible the same material
should continue inwards to compose the spokes and the hub. Such
an architectural pattern can take its place within a paved terrace or
in an area of gravel.

Far cheaper to construct is a herb-wheel cut out of lawn with
the spoke edges maintained by 4-inch high tanalized boards kept

A TEN-SPOKE HERB WHEEL

A Rosemary
B Parsley
C Tarragon
D Garlic followed
  by Basil
E Dill
F Chervil
G Lovage
H Chives
I Sage
J Sweet marjoram
K Mint
L Summer savory
M Winter savory
N Thymes
O Fennel
P Sorrel

1 0 1 2 Metres

A HERBAL CHEQUER BOARD

1,5,24 and 28 Bay obelisks
10 and 15 Lavender cotton
14 and 19 Santolina chamaecyparissus

1 0 1 2 3 4 Metres

vertical with pegs just as Diderot shows in the entry discussed above (p50). As the spoke is not only for delineation but also for access it needs to be filled. On this scale grass is too laboursome to cut but camomile on really light soil, or pennyroyal if heavier, could do the job. Less romantic but more practical is the sort of fine bark-chips sold for mulching. A band of this material between lawn and herbs is also desirable onto which they can spread without killing the grass.

In the sketch the standard herbs are used: chives act as an edging for the lovage segment, as does sweet marjoram for sage and sorrel for fennel. Again, chervil and garlic are employed as successional crops with dill and basil respectively. A clipped rosemary makes the central feature, the upright form 'Miss Jessup' being the obvious choice, though even here a 4-foot high metal stake is desirable to maintain a formal column. It is soon lost in foliage. Alternatives to rosemary in this position are sweet bay, a tub of rose, or other scented leaved, geraniums. A sundial or other statuary feature would also be appropriate.

Cook's Collection 3. A chequer board.

An extension to the herb-wheel concept is the chequer board. In its basic form this is a paved area in which the hard material acts as the black squares of a chequer board and the herbs become the alternate white ones. Within the formal pattern there is unlimited scope in size and shape. The chequer can be a square of just eight planted and eight plain squares or a quincunx of five planted and four plain within a band of hard material. A pair of such beds with a central path offers a convenient and interesting site for ten favourite herbs.

The chequer board described here is bigger with twenty-eight open squares, each a yard or metre square in area. It is surrounded by a low hedge of Hidcote lavender which, after it has flowered and the flowers have been harvested for sachets and pot pourri, is clipped to make a formal frame. At the north end the hedge encloses a south-facing seat backed by a border of scented summer flowers, such as nicotianas, night-scented stock, mignonette, sweet williams and old-fashioned roses. The seat could be within a honeysuckle-swathed canopy – a simple open-sided garden house in fact – in which case, of course, the backing lavender would have to be replaced by a shade tolerant plant such as box.

Within the chequer pattern squares 1 and 5, 24 and 28 hold clipped sweet bay obelisks and the formality is continued with numbers 10 and 15 holding grey-green 'Edward Bowles' lavender cotton and 14 and 19 the tight grey type (*Santolina chamaecyparissus*). These are clipped into half-cubes, their sides slightly battered inwards as they rise. Again the variations on this theme of herb-topiary are legion; it would not be difficult to suggest a living chess board with a few well-placed clipped box pawns (keen chess players would take the point that box-wood is a traditional material for turned-wood pieces) but kings and queens, bishops and knights would be less easy to train – and more than a little absurd.

Two dozen squares remain for herb planting, each traditionally kept to one species. The essentials, such as parsley and chives could well appear twice and complementary but distinct plants like golden thyme and lemon thyme could share a square. The chequer pattern is particularly useful in maintaining a collection of forms of a particular genus close together for comparison but fully separate to avoid confusion. The thymes are a particularly interesting group and this whole chequer garden could be put down to distinct wild species and garden cultivars. At least half could be planted with mints if slates or some such barrier were pushed down the side of each square to keep them apart.

While the chequer board appears a highly regimented method of herb growing, the natural exuberance and habit of those plants not used as architectural accents makes the summer appearance anything but rigid. Indeed this combination and juxtaposition of a mass of well grown plants tumbling out of a formal frame is especially attractive. The plan here shows a garden designed for a completely flat site but it should be emphasized that on a slope a cut and fill operation can be considered on either main axis. The chequer would then appear terraced with retaining walls of the requisite height at A-B (west-facing) or C-D (south-facing); steps would be necessary at the obvious spots for access.

Herbs in the ornamental border

Since Miss Jekyll, as we are rather erroneously led to believe, invented the classic English herbaceous border at the turn of this century, its once accepted place in every garden has somewhat declined. This has been particularly because of the expectation that such features are impossibly labour intensive. Certainly the huge borders of great country house gardens which still exist can be so described, especially if some of Gertrude Jekyll's recommendations which obviate seasonal gaps are followed to the letter. She wrote, it

EARLY SUMMER : WHITE BORDER

0   1   2   3 Metres

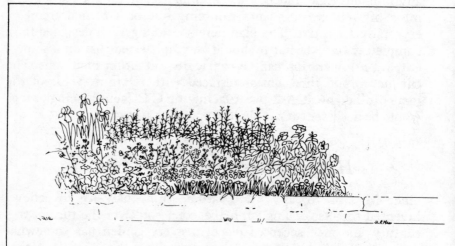

EARLY SUMMER : PINKS,PURPLES AND GREY

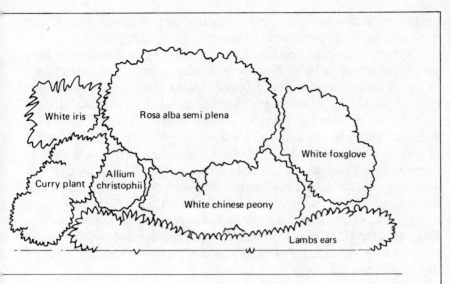

White iris

Rosa alba semi plena

White foxglove

Curry plant

Allium christophii

White chinese peony

Lambs ears

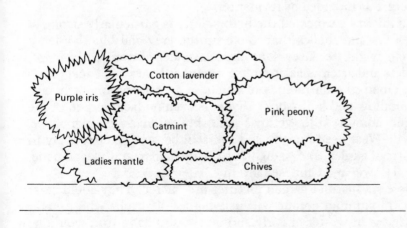

Purple iris

Cotton lavender

Pink peony

Catmint

Ladies mantle

Chives

will be remembered, for a more leisured age: leisured, that is, for the owner, not the squads of gardeners employed by him.

Yet the summer border of permanent plants remains a vital part of our gardens, helped by a few shrubs underplanted with bulbs and perhaps annuals as well. In other words it is a mixed border for general furnishing effect made up of plant associations which provide along the border's length garden pictures at their best at different parts of the season. Looking carefully at original Jekyll plans one notices that this was often done. Big clumps of lavender, santolina, Jerusalem sage and shrub roses were used with monkshoods, peonies, hollyhocks and so on. All these plants and a host of others with which Miss Jekyll and William Robinson began to re-populate gardens a hundred years ago are, of course, herbs. They are also the cottage garden flowers, the old-fashioned flowers rescued from fashionable neglect in the nick of time and brought into sophisticated design.

Thus it is not difficult to justify in both traditional and Jekyllian terms the use of herbs in the ornamental garden. Indeed, they have hardly left it; only the common knowledge of their once-common use has been forgotten. Here, therefore are a few plant associations, groups of herbs which compose garden pictures of beauty: that they can in many cases be evocative of old-fashioned cottage gardens is dependent upon their setting. While frame is not as important as content it does help the viewer to 'see' the picture as intended by its planter.

As might be expected the herb palette is particularly strong in the colours and shades that make up the grey and blue border, a Jekyllian favourite. Grey santolina, lavender cotton, curry plant, lavenders and artemisias provide permanent bones and background to the cloud-like harmonies of Japanese anemones, monkshoods, marshmallow and hollyhocks. There is even no lack, either, of the stronger colours, the yellows and hot orange-reds which V. Sackville-West used bravely and can still be seen so effectively in her cottage garden at Sissinghurst Castle: tansy and elecampane, cardinal flower and Chinese lantern.

Here six distinct garden pictures are offered. They could exist as bays of summer colour within a border of shrubs whose main flowering is in winter or early spring: the shrubs in turn would be underplanted with spring bulbs or low ground cover so that at all times of the year the area is of interest while at certain times it comes particularly alive. Equally, these suggested associations can be a part of a mixed or predominantly herbaceous border. They hold together because of their carefully considered effects of colour, season, size and scale but also in this context because of their herbal connotations and uses.

The two early summer groups (p. 74) can stand alone or could easily be linked together by a bush of rosemary at the back and clumps of white and pink lavender in the foreground tumbling forward over the path. Even after their June glory is over there is interest in shape and foliage.

One is of the soft and cloud-like harmonies already mentioned, the other a classic white border grouping of old-fashioned rose of York, white peonies and spires of white foxgloves and brilliant white-leaved curry plant. The heads of ornamental onion, *Allium christophii*, though opening pale lavender, soon go dry and pale like bleached molecular diagrams. The foxgloves are, of course, strictly biennial and those plants which flower must be expected to die. If taken out immediately a quick sowing of white opium poppy is possible *in situ* or, to avoid a late summer gap, a few pots of white-flowered Madagascar periwinkle can be put out. As soon as they are cut by frost, reserve foxgloves seedling to take their place for next year.

The summer foliage group (p. 78) uses as background two trees which are pruned back to encourage development of their most dramatic leaves. The eucalyptus gives a great cloud of blue circular 'evergreen' foliage if cut to the ground every other spring. Tree of Heaven, on the other hand, is pruned annually back to a basal couple of buds of last year's growth (thus the stump increases by about 6 inches a year) and these buds produce 6 to 8-foot high stems with yard long, almost palm-like, leaves of great beauty.

Globe artichokes and Chinese rhubarb give fountains of grey and green foliage respectively and, in front, is acanthus and asphodel with the biggest elecampane, *Inula magnifica*. The whole effect is spendidly bold. Only one problem looms large, and this literally: is one to allow the fine flower spikes of inula, acanthus, rhubarb and artichoke for their statuesque effect or should they be sacrificed at an early stage for the production of even bigger and better leaves? A personal decision.

A high summer association (p. 78) is composed of warm reds, from cardinal flower, cone flower (*Echinacea*), deep red clove scented carnations and love-lies-bleeding, whose plush-like tassels hang forward as if ready to summon a bevy of Victorian parlour maids to bring out the tea. Purple sage gives a solid base and plume poppy a framing cloud of brown-pink froth beyond.

Depending upon the year the greys, blues and pinks of the early autumn group can start to smoulder gently in August, as the grey-

SUMMER LONG : STRONG FOLIAGE

0　　　　1　　　　2　　　　3 **Metres**

HIGH SUMMER : HOT COLOURS

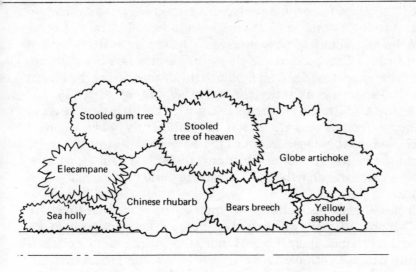

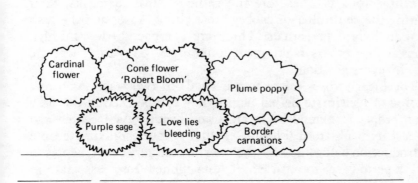

leaved *Caryopteris* opens its misty-blue spikes. *Perovskia* and, in front, the bowls of meadow saffron soon follow. The taller things, monkshood, snakeroot, with its creamy spikes, and anemones can last well into October and the chrysanthemums last even later to close the year just as *Mahonia japonica* in another part of the garden (described above) opens its first flowers to herald another (p. 82).

As the A–Z list shows, the diversity of herbal plants, in form and texture, in colour and in season, is sufficiently wide for such associations as those just described to be repeated in almost infinite permutations. Individual predilections, individual gardens and the variety of sites within will now use them to build up personal garden pictures.

It has already been shown in some of the plans that there are roses which legitimately belong to the herb garden: the apothecary's rose and its striped sport 'Rosa Mundi', the white rose of York and the pink damask both used for attar and rose water production. All have a herbal lineage of centuries. Visually they are also lovely plants, if rather fleeting in their flowering period; June is their month. This is the time when all the 'old-fashioned' roses are at their best in a tumble of gentle, though often rich, colours. Pink is the centre of their spectrum darkening through crimson to thunder-purple and, in the other direction, through every progressively paling shade of blush to white. There are single flowers, heraldically perfect: double flowers are so full of petals that they take on a strange hot cross bun quartered form. In all scent is delicious: in some it is compounded by an aromatic 'moss' on calyx and foot-stalks or even by scented foliage. These are the gallicas, albas, damasks, their offspring the centifolias or cabbage roses, moss roses and the lush Victorian hybrid perpetuals. There are compact little yard-high bushes, while others make great fountains of growth. There are plants for every position.

These early roses relate to our needs in two ways. As direct offspring of legitimate herbal plants they can be used in the herb garden proper to extend its interest and beauty. As accepted and well-researched historical forms – actual year or approximate time of introduction being known – they can be used very conveniently to evoke a period feel to a garden. 'Old-fashioned' roses associate in turn with the other early summer cottage garden plants which have also been shown to possess historic herbal attributes. Spires of foxgloves and larkspurs exactly repeat the rose's colours but architecturally add a vertical dimension.

Flag irises, too, belong here, every soft shade in the lavender/purple range being on call. *Iris pallida* is particularly desirable because its blue-grey foliage fans maintain their effect much longer than the usual germanica hybrids. With them come peonies, which again possess all the colours of the old-fashioned roses and whose robust habit can appear as bushy as the smaller gallicas.

At their feet pinks and carnations, stocks and alliums (whose flowers often smell sweet however oniony the leaves) add to this living pot pourri. More scents come from sages, lavenders and artemisias which pick up the greyness of *Rosa alba* foliage.

But which to use of the dozens of old-fashioned roses still in the lists, with their haunting names of otherwise forgotten beauties and lost places? The following dozen offer variety of form and colour and a sequence of memories of times past, a very evocation of the old-fashioned gardens of the mind.

'Tuscany Superb' is probably one of the oldest garden roses still in cultivation: this is perhaps the velvet rose of Gerard's 1597 *Herball* description. It is a much more upright bush than most gallicas.

The damask roses seem to be hybrids of *Rosa gallica* and another species and have been in England since the early 1500s. Gerard lists two sorts. One has already been mentioned, *R. × damascena trigintipetala*, the Balkan producer of attar of roses. This needs a warmer summer than we can usually give it to get a good show of the loose but lovely pink flowers. 'Madame Hardy' of 1832 exquisitely represents the group with flat white flowers made up of masses of overlapping petals around the green button eye.

In addition to the fine scent of the usual centifolia or cabbage roses their strange variants, the moss roses, add a further dimension. It is said that Philip Miller of the Chelsea Physic Garden introduced the first 'Old Pink Moss' in 1727 from Holland. 'William Lobb' is a mid-nineteenth-century development with flowers of a marvellous vinous purple though is better renowned for this than its moss which needs searching for.

A name like 'Souvenir de la Malmaison' consciously carries memories of the Empress Joséphine's great rose garden, though the Empress had died nearly thirty years before this lovely rose was introduced in 1843. As a Bourbon rose it possesses some of the remontancy of the China rose and hence its wide blush flowers with their alluring scent are produced off and on all summer long. If there is only room for one 'old-fashioned' rose, perhaps this is it. In the same group of Bourbon roses is the thornless 'Zéphirine Drouhin' which grows into a tall lax bush: it looks well as a pillar, loosely trained. Its warm, dusky pink flowers have a delicious perfume: planted along a wire or netting line Zéphirine makes a

EARLY AUTUMN : SOFT SHADES OF GREY FOLIAGE

0   1   2   3 **Metres**

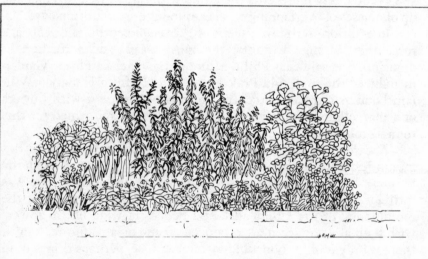

SPRING : SEASONAL FLOWERS AROUND OLD ROSEMARY BUSH

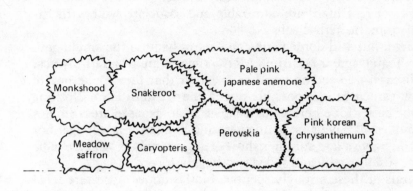

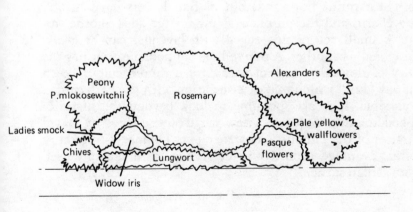

lovely high hedge or screen for a herb garden. This role can be filled by several good roses. On a small scale the Scots burnet roses, only a couple of feet high, are admirable and associate well with the typical aromatic herb shrubs.

Larger but still domed and compact in habit is the single pink rugosa 'Frau Dagmar Hastrup'. All the rugosas are wonderfully pest (and disease) free and so weather resistant that they make one of the few garden hedges possible out in the Western Isles. Nothing could be better for a herb garden screen in an exposed area. Singles and doubles all have a ravishing perfume: the latter last longer but the former give a late summer show of great rosy hips which can be used for rose-hip jelly and added to other conserves.

Petals of these strongly scented 'old-fashioned' roses are ideal for pot pourris and hence fully earn their herb garden place. There are two reasons for apparently extolling the historic roses at the expense of the moderns, beyond the old-fashioned, cottage garden atmosphere connection. Firstly, they are apt to be less prone to the ills which demand today a whole battery of sprays and dusts to combat them: these are not wanted on the herbs around and beneath. Secondly, the emphasis by rose-breeders in this century has been on colour (it has always been an emphasis; the twentieth century has just been dramatically more successful) to the point that many of the remarkable shades obtained must be kept in solitary confinement if they are not to shriek at all comers. These are not right for herb garden associations.

There are, of course, shining exceptions. 'Rosemary Rose' is a pretty bright carmine floribunda but its flat flowers have an old-fashioned charm and the purplish young foliage adds another dimension. A small bed of this edged with lavender can be a joy: 'Fragrant Cloud' is another. A marvellous pot pourri rose it has the prodigality of flower we expect today yet a muted colour (keen rosarians say 'dull') which makes association with the herb garden palette possible. It is also possible to look beyond the historic/modern bedding rose divide to a new range of roses bred by David Austin (raiser of the famous 'Constance Spry') whose 'Canterbury Tales' offer advantages from both sides. They can be happily used in the herb garden scene.

The herbal window box

Not everyone has a garden, nor indeed wants one: after all every operation so far described demands a certain amount of physical labour and rather more of time. But there are many people in each of those categories who would like fresh herbs for kitchen use and it is fortunate that for both non-gardeners and anti-gardeners a herbal *multum in parvo* is possible. There are few keen cooks who have not cherished a pot of parsley or chives on the kitchen window sill during their bed-sitter days or later to see them through a bad winter. With care and planning it is possible to extend this most basic of herb growing into a satisfactory and culinarily rewarding experience.

The first thing to emphasize is that, in spite of the self-derogatory phrase 'Oh, I've only got a window box', to grow herbs well in such conditions is more, not less, difficult than in the open garden. People who have a green-fingered success here can move on to almost anything. On the other hand, this is not to suggest that window box herb gardening is riven with problems; merely that plants growing in a small volume of soil in the necessarily exposed position of a window sill experience an unnatural habitat which needs rather specialized attention.

As with a full-sized ground level herb garden, aspect of the site to be used is important. From the point of view of convenience the kitchen window or windows are the most important and, so long as they get sun for at least half of the day, they will provide a happy home for most of the desirable herbs. North-facing window sills will not be warm enough for the tropical basils, and not very good for most of the Mediterraneans. Mint, parsley, chives and chervil will do perfectly well and, if no other spot is available, thyme and sage will manage happily enough. Obviously if more than one aspect is available a fuller range of herbs can be grown.

Window boxes can be bought ready-made in a variety of materials or they can be easily constructed from sheets of marine plywood. Bespoke boxes have the advantage of being exactly the length and width of the sill. If they are big enough and it is intended to grow herbs all the year round in a cold position, lining the boxes with polystyrene gives some root protection from rapid freezing and thawing. It also prolongs the life of the wood. It is most usual to sit the boxes directly on the window sill: support is assured to take the weight and the plants are immediately to hand. Conventional outward-opening casement windows however make this impossible: either the box is swept off the sill or the plants are difficult to get to. It thus becomes necessary to support window boxes on brackets attached to the wall below the sill.

Even where there are sash windows (which might have been especially invented to encourage window box gardening) the below-sill bracket has the advantage in that from inside the house only the plants and not several inches of box as well are seen. This gives a far more pleasant outlook.

While the herbs can be grown directly in the compost in the box there are advantages to growing them in clay flower pots of rim diameter just less than that of the box. They are then plunged into the box compost (or merely peat), further insulating the roots against extremes of heat and cold and drought. Other advantages are that aggresssive mints are contained and that replacements can be grown elsewhere inside on a rotational basis. Seeds of quick growing summer annuals, such as nasturtium can be pushed into gaps between the pots if space exists. Window box gardening insists on the use of every square inch.

There is not much scope for arrangement yet a close juxtaposition of herb foliage textures always looks attractive. The large culinary herbs such as fennel and lovage will need to be kept to the sides: shrubs like sage, savory or even rosemary can well take centre-stage because they will tumble naturally outwards and hang out down the box front. Any shoots growing too vertically or too vigorously can be the first to go into the pot.

The basic ideas applicable to window boxes can be extended to any available area above ground; irrevocably concreted courtyards, balconies, the space behind the parapet of innumerable Georgian houses that can be reached from a skylight or dormer and flat roofs. Roof gardens, of course, can be of considerable size and complexity.

In all cases the plants are being grown in conditions that need more cultural attention than in the open garden but the larger the container the less damage there is from the restricted root-run. All the sites suggested are apt to be of close visual importance so that the appearance of the growing container itself is equally important. Obviously it is desirable that significantly placed individual pots or tubs should be agreeable to look at: for intensive herb production, however, it is more sensible to organize the effect of a raised bed. This could actually be such a bed or merely a formal frame into which the containerized herbs – in tins, pots, boxes – can be arranged with only their herbs in sight.

Some sort of similar system is desirable for 'grobags': these sealed plastic sacks of lightweight compost are excellent for restricted site gardening but the colours with which they are printed, though no doubt considered desirable as a selling factor while still in the shop, are not a pleasure on the drawing-room balcony. Sitting in low bottomless boxes with coping edges they become an architectural aid rather than a visual embarrassment. Different levels can easily by contrived and contrasting régimes for the different groups of herbs arranged. A small volume of 'soil' can produce really worthwhile crops of herbs.

Herbs indoors

It is not a far cry from containerized plants on roof or balcony to herb growing indoors. Indeed, as has already been mentioned, many of the outside containerized plants will have been started inside. Of the basic plant requirements, which must be kept in balance – warmth, water, air, nutrients and light – it is the latter which can be the most difficult to provide, especially during the winter. Our normal dwelling house temperatures, in combination with warm, moist soil at the roots, have the potential to promote good out-of-season growth. Without adequate light, however, shoots become thin and etiolated, leaves are small and, most importantly in herbs, aromatic qualities decline dramatically as the photosynthetic process, the trigger to all chemical development within the plant, works at a low rate.

For the dozen winter weeks with worst availability of parsley and mint and chives, three or four pots of each are best prepared in early October. Summer-sown parsley plants and mature clumps of the others are potted into a light compost, watered well and left outside in a sheltered spot for a month or so. Half a dozen parsley plants in an 8-inch pot is about right. The shock of the move causes the bigger outside leaves to wilt and these are best pinched off (washed, chopped and frozen in ice cubes they in turn give winter use).

The pots are now brought in. One of each comes into the kitchen window sill where within a fortnight useable fresh foliage is being produced. The others are kept marginally moist on cooler sills – in the spare bedrooms, for instance – to be well watered when brought down to replace those picked bare. These in turn can be returned upstairs to recover and give a second, though much smaller, crop later, or to be completely discarded. Such a simple system ensures fresh garnishing throughout the winter months.

In colder climates than Britain it becomes necessary to over-winter some of the bigger herbs indoors. It is not an uncommon sight to find fine bushes of rosemary in full flower in eastern Canadian homes – where they are not kept at the Florida-like temperatures many humans consider necessary – and which are stood out in summer just as rose geranium or lemon verbena are. Winter savory, purple and variegated sages often need to be similarly treated there. Unlike chives or mint, these plants from the garden do not transplant or pot up happily and if such shrubby things are required for continuing pot culture they are best obtained from nurseries or rooted *de novo* from cuttings early during the previous season.

Once indoors the important thing is to keep a balance between air temperature and moisture at the root and all the while providing plenty of light. As always, relating conditions available to the plant's original habitat gives the answer to any query about basic cultivation. Such knowledge also provides a lead into methods of winter herb production in cold climates which have been a part of commercial nursery practice for years.

In the home fluorescent strips or bulbs are hung above the plant bench to give supplemental or complete illumination requirements, depending on the position chosen. In North America the usual place is in a heated basement or utility room, giving interest to the usual array of washing machines, central heating boilers, tumble dryers and sinks. More elegant units for living room use are commonly available but are apt to display more poinsettias than parsley.

A simple utility room system consists of a narrow bench 4 feet by 18 inches over which is suspended a parallel pair of 40 watt fluorescent tubes within a reflector unit. Though horticultural tubes are available especially to provide the violet/blue and orange/red part of the visible light spectrum, a pair – consisting of one each of ordinary cool-white and warm-white tubes – is suitable for general use. They are also far cheaper.

The light unit needs to be variable in its height so that it can be adjusted to hang at the optimum level of 12 inches to 18 inches above the tops of the growing plants. In this way, with twelve to sixteen hours daily illumination, fresh herbs are easily obtained throughout the winter in an otherwise darkened room. I have enjoyed fresh basil in January from such a bench, constituting something of a *tour de force* by my hostess, while the temperature stood at −10°F (−24°C) outside.

If, however, this indoor herb plot is by a window, so long as suitable growing temperatures are provided, the lights need only be on from 4 pm to 10 pm to transform winter daylight into the long summer days required. If no extra heat is required (in, for example, a centrally heated bathroom, another good spot) the cost of running such a light garden is very small, the tubes using less power than bulbs of similar wattage: extending its use as a spring propagator can cover those costs.

Herbs and Hydroponics

While it is initially simpler to grow herbs indoors in the traditional manner of soil in pots – though even that tradition has moved imperceptibly through carefully composed John Innes composts to light-weight peat-based media – a hydroponic or soilless-culture system has great advantages for the high-rise horticulturist in flat or apartment.

Simply, an inert aggregate material such as sand, gravel or haydite (a burnt shale resembling small pebbles) is used for root support while plant nutrients are supplied directly in solution. Any non-toxic waterproof container may contain the hydroponic unit. As nutrients are much more easily available to the plants in this way than in the garden, root systems are unusually compact and hence plants can be planted closer together: growth is faster and crop yields are more consistent. Add to these facts the cleanness and convenience of hydroponic systems and the infrequency of hand-watering through the use of reservoirs, and the virtues become clear.

On the sort of light garden bench described above plastic trays are ideal receptacles. In the double potting method nutrient solution is poured into central sunken clay flower pots from which it diffuses into the aggregate in which they sit, plunged to their rims. An 18-inch or 2-foot square tray will manage on a central reservoir pot; longer trays will need two or more.

An alternative system is to use two stacked trays. The lower one holds the nutrient solution which absorbent wicks, hanging from the aggregate in the upper tray and poking through its base, soak up for the plants. Again trays can be chosen to fit the illuminated bench area. The wicks, incidentally, are simply made from strips of super-annuated nylon stockings.

Specimen woody herbs – rosemary, myrtle, sweet bay and so on – are also easily cultivated, so long as the other essentials of light and warmth are provided, in individual hydrophonic containers. These are available commercially and normally expect to be furnished with *Monstera, Philodendron* or some other denizen of deep, dark jungles. The herbs have much more use but cannot take, even for a short time, the dark corners the forest plants accept. The basic system is similar: a container of aggregate within another of nutrient solution. There is the added sophistication of a nutrient level indicator to ensure, firstly, that the container does not run dry and, equally important and the reason for all these dual container systems, to ensure it is not overfull. Though it is apt to be forgotten, plant roots need oxygen as much as their leaves do, which is why

THREE SYSTEMS OF HYDROPONIC CULTURE SUITABLE FOR HERBS

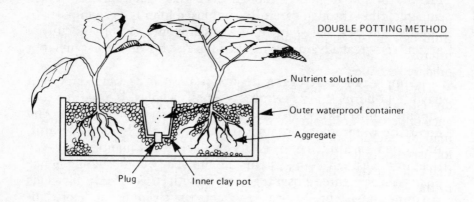

DOUBLE POTTING METHOD

Nutrient solution

Outer waterproof container

Aggregate

Plug

Inner clay pot

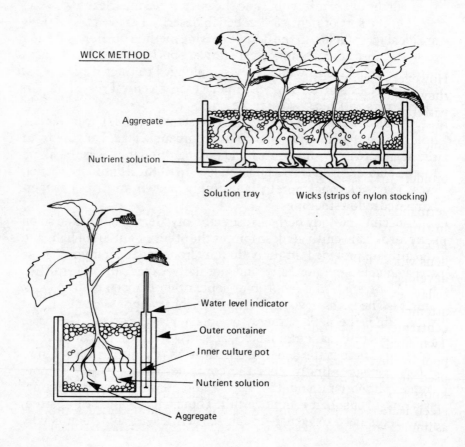

WICK METHOD

Aggregate

Nutrient solution

Solution tray

Wicks (strips of nylon stocking)

Water level indicator

Outer container

Inner culture pot

Nutrient solution

Aggregate

over-watering (or protracted flooding outside) is much more damaging than temporary drought.

Recipes for nutrient solutions are many but they must contain not only the major elements needed for plant growth – nitrogen, phosphorus and potassium – but a further dozen of trace elements from calcium to zinc which are also required in varying, usually microscopic amounts: it is therefore best to accept a commercially prepared product.

In the foregoing discussions of herb gardens in all their possible diversity there has been the general acceptance that the natural exuberance of herbs is desirable. Here are plants which have lived alongside man for thousands of years and which he has made a part of his culture, for use and for delight; yet in the main they are still the same plants that colonize the hillsides on which he first collected them. Certainly in the garden some, like the mints, need a wary eye lest they overwhelm their gentler neighbours, yet this habit is a part of their character. We would not have it any other way: nor indeed would they.

A pattern of herbs

However, several of the herb shrubs are so amenable to doing as they are told that for centuries they have been used to make formal patterns on the ground. This use, as has already been described in the inquiry into the origins of herb gardens, was at its most fashionable in England in Tudor and Elizabethan times. The patterns chosen could equally be seen then on ceiling plaster-work or embroidery for bed hangings and even clothes.

Outdoors, low clipped hedges of santolina, box, and shrubby germander are woven together into patterns to make knot gardens. In times past, as we can see from the plates from du Cerceau (*Les Plus Excellents Bâtiments de France*, 1576) there were great gardens whose terraces were covered in convoluted knots. From these developed the great *parterres de broderie* of Versailles. Their use today, except where a re-creation of an historic garden is being attempted, is greatly reduced. Typically knots are designed as the centrepiece of a broadly-based herb garden to evoke an earlier age. Two small square knots could take the place, for example, of the pool in the first garden plan on page 56. In just this way are they used at the Brooklyn Botanic Garden in New York. These two knots are typical of the genre with their bands of different evergreen leaf colour interlacing and going over and under each other, as if made of ribbons on a richly-worked Elizabethan bed coverlet.

A SIMPLE KNOT GARDEN

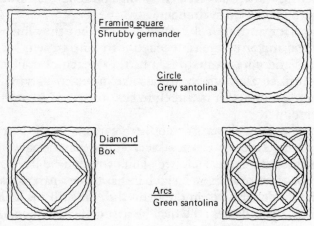

Framing square
Shrubby germander

Circle
Grey santolina

Diamond
Box

Arcs
Green santolina

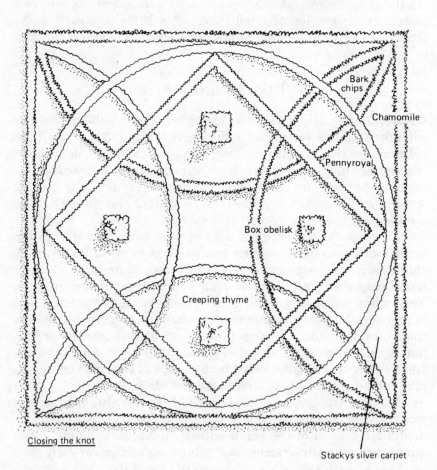

Bark
chips

Chamomile

Pennyroyal

Box obelisk

Creeping thyme

Closing the knot

Stackys silver carpet

At Brooklyn the gaps between the bands are filled with white marble chips, black coal pebbles and broken clay flower pot crocks to emphasize the bands. These knots are therefore in the straight tradition of the seventeenth century but can also be seen to be on the way down the slippery slope that led then to the excesses of parterres which almost entirely dispensed with plants. While the soil of narrow gaps a few inches wide between different hedge ribbons are best covered with an inert material, more open spaces deserve ground cover plants to complement or contrast with the ribbons: pennyroyal and chamomile are admirable and, if coloured foliage is required, Stachys 'Silver Carpet' or forms of bugle – purple, variegated or tricoloured – are available. Choice must depend, not only on aesthetic requirements but also upon the soil and aspect preferences of the plants themselves: fortunately, as is demonstrated in the A–Z section of this book, there are plants for every place. In the past when the knot was fully planted it was said to be closed.

In constructing knots, either as part of a herb garden or as a feature in their own right, it is essential that the basic geometry is exact. As the hedges grow from narrow tapes to broad ribbons mistakes will become ever more apparent. If sited within paving, no further edging is required. If in grass or loose gravel, an initial frame of bricks, setts or timber is a first necessity. Within it the patterns are delineated in arcs using two sticks and a length of cord to act as a pair of compasses and a simply constructed 3–4–5 triangle to ensure right angles. Lines are marked with sand or lime.

Brooklyn's most successful knot is made up of a circle within the framing square whose corners are joined by arcs. A diamond (or second square turned 90°) lies within the circle. Each of the three components is planted in a different hedge. In existing paving, being able to plant the frame offers a further textural line. Similarly, as mentioned above, use of ground cover plants gives yet more interest. The natural temptation to fill the gaps with bright summer annuals is probably best avoided. Certainly few would be 'in period' and transitory brilliance would detract from the pattern. But violets, Johnny jump up-type pansies and small spring bulbs do not come amiss. If the smaller, narrower gaps require an inert cover an organic mulch, peat or the more lasting bark chips are both suitable.

Vertical emphasis can be obtained by adding trained box or sweet bay specimens: narrow obelisks or spirals are best. Equally, an inanimate ornament can do this same job of giving height to an otherwise intentionally flat scene.

Ornaments in the herb garden

This brings me to the last section of herb gardens from landscape to window box. So often, in the attempt to re-create a feeling of times past, herb gardens and even quite small herb beds are the chosen site for pieces of statuary, pots and tubs, sundials and bird baths (though our ancestors' interest in wild birds was entirely concerned with their eradication as competitors for the not over-abundant food: buying bird seed would have seemed like lunacy). There is no doubt that a well-chosen piece or two, well-sited, does add to the scene. But those two provisos must be kept rigorously.

The important roles are as a centre-piece or as an eye-catcher at the end or a turning-point of a path. The object needs to be big enough to make its point without unduly dominating the scene. Choice is less difficult if one is rich for there are several well-known firms dealing in original garden ornaments, pillaged from the past. Without a deep pocket, however, things are not impossible. Reproductions of eighteenth-century urns and other objects in reconstituted stone or even fibre-glass can be very good and a spray with liquid manure encourages algae to soften their newness. One must remember, of course, that the closer an object is seen, as in a herb garden, the better its quality has to be. Those statues on the pediment of St Peter's in Rome, for instance, do not get the same attention as the fountains below.

Unfortunately, statues, sundials and bird baths on general sale at garden centres are apt to lean heavily toward the visually banal, often with soap opera captions to match about 'the kisses of sun for pardon' and gardens being 'lovesome things' – in fact the whole gamut of what has been admirably described as 'Godwottery'. Without doubt well-deserved sundials are fun as well as being beautiful: a reproduction of the famous Thomas Tompion (he of the seventeenth-century clocks) gnomon sundial can be seen near the Orangery at Kew. Also intriguing is the type which is known as an armillary sphere. This is in the form of a skeletal globe with three or more interlaced rings and a shadow-forming arrow: again it is mounted on a column or baluster.

A further snare is the almost obligatory motto carved on the base. Usually a variation on the *Tempus Fugit* theme, perhaps the best was suggested by Hilaire Belloc at Cranborne Manor:

> I am a sundial and I make a botch
> Of what is done far better by a watch

Whatever is inscribed (or avoided) the important thing is that, sun willing, sundials should work. Thus they need to be made for the latitude in which they are to be set up and also correctly aligned.

Economical anthropomorphic statuary is probably an impossibility. Snow White, her seven dwarfs and a family of related gnomes are best left in Disneyland, whence they came.

Perhaps, as so often, a lesson should be learned from Sissinghurst: there the fine herb garden has a relatively low-key centrepiece. This is a shallow container planted with houseleeks, of interest throughout the year: it marks the centre architecturally, it extends the range, it makes its point. Nothing more is required.

5

THE YEAR IN THE HERB GARDEN

❦

Herb Gardens: Planting and Maintenance

Making a garden can be said to be like engaging in marriage: it is expected to be of lasting duration and, during that time, though needing a certain amount of attention here and there, to give great pleasure and satisfaction. Making a herb garden, as a consciously desgined feature can use that same analogy. As King James' prayerbook exhorts us, it 'is not by any to be enterprised, not taken in hand, inadvisedly or wantonly. . . . but discreetly, advisedly, soberly . . .'. Those resounding seventeenth-century phrases lack some of the enthusiasm that both prospective life-partners or garden makers usually profess. But the sentiments advise care and continuity, with which few would quarrel.

The planning of a selection of herb gardens has already been discussed in some detail: a variant of one or another, tailored to size as necessary for each individual site, will provide the personally bespoke arrangement required. We now move on to cultivation, the hands-on side of things.

This chapter can happily be skipped by practised gardeners as it deals with some of the basic aspects of growing plants and these, within the parameters set evolutionary by their original habitats, are similar for all groups. This fact is seen as a continual thread running through *Herbs in the Garden*, as it legitimately should through any gardening text, for any readership.

The five desiderata needed for plant growth – air, light, warmth, water and nutrients, have also been mentioned, especially in the context of their regulation in the contrived situation of window box or house. In the open garden, beyond climate and its more transient aspect the weather, the herb garden's soil is the most important factor for success. What plants require from the soil in which they sit is simply listed below:

1 Adequate moisture especially in the growing season.
2 Adequate air at the plants' roots and thus:

3 Efficient drainage especially in winter and early spring.

4 Adequate warmth at the plants' roots.

5 Adequate plant food (nutrients) in solution throughout the growing season.

6 A suitable chemical balance between extreme soil acidity and alkalinity.

A moment's thought will make it clear that all these factors are closely interlinked. Only with adequate moisture can there be sufficient food: though it be applied by the bucketful plants cannot eat it as a solid. Only with efficient drainage can there be air at the roots and early spring warmth: poorly drained soils are cold soils. Adequate nutrients are available only if there is a chemical balance: excess at either end of the pH scale locks up elements necessary for good growth.

In a good garden soil there are no problems. There is that marvellous material which so many garden books used to insist as essential: that 'deep, rich loam, well-drained yet retentive of moisture' in which parsnips grow a metre long without a blemish. But we don't all have it: indeed the chances are against the fact and we need to make the best of what we have.

It is best to consider the moisture first. A soggy clay only a few inches below the surface becomes obvious by getting out a spade and digging a hole. Water lying on the surface is likely to indicate the same fact but this could, especially in a new garden with the house-builders hardly out of sight, be caused by heavy machinery compacting the surface. In both cases basic cultivation will help but in the case of impervious clay it merely takes the water a little lower to the layer that the spade cannot reach.

Any intended herb garden site with such a soil has only two alternatives apart from moving to another district. One is to insert drainage pipes to conduct water right away; the other is to build upwards. The raised bed, which has already been recommended as a fine design feature, takes on this other vital role. Within it an improved rooting medium can be more easily formed. In general, heavy soil can be helped by the addition, before any permanent planting is done, of grit or coarse sand mixed in with any organic plant material available. All soils are improved by such humus and a major role of the cultivator is to maintain a high humus level. It is continually being oxidized and as it rots away it releases plant nutrients which the herbs take up in the soil water. Humus not only 'opens' a heavy soil to assist drainage but also acts as a sponge on light soils, holding moisture for plant's use. On soils that are not already derived from chalk or limestone, an initial dressing of hydrated lime also helps drainage by chemically causing the microscopic clay particles to combine together. Liming must not be overdone, however, and soil testing may be necessary to ensure this.

In general light soils, limy or sandy and acid, are acceptable to the majority of herbs but finer specimens and much more productive crops are produced if, again, rotted compost is applied annually (see 'The Year in the Herb Garden', below). Of the shrubby herbs which are expected permanently to furnish the scene, the culinary sages do less well on sandy soils and need frequent re-propagation there.

Light soils are typically poor in plant foods simply because, as rotting humus and decomposing organic materials release the elements, they are dissolved in the readily drained soil water and hence are quickly lost. Heavier soils possess more nutrients to begin with and lose them less readily. Decisions on whether or not to use fertilizer and how much obviously depends upon the soil type concerned.

Probably every herb garden benefits from a spring dressing of a fertilizer which releases its nutrients over a long period to the permanent plants. A quick-acting fertilizer should be worked into areas as they are prepared for seed sowing or for new spring planting, the aim being to stimulate rapid root development. It is to be hoped that the soil is not so deficient in one of the vital trace elements as to need especial attention and fortunately in most situations regular addition of a humus source provides what is necessary. Similarly for the major nitrogen, phosphorus and potassium elements compound fertilizers are available which provide a balanced diet.

Many keen herb growers are also dedicated 'organic gardeners' holding strongly to the belief that man-made inorganic fertilizers are incompatible with the production of high-quality herbs and vegetables. Others assert that as plants can only take up their foods as basic elements in solution, the source of say, nitrogen, may as well be sodium nitrate as fish-meal. There is no easy answer, if indeed there is one at all, to this dichotomy; there are advantages on both sides. It is better to be practical rather than prejudiced and base plants' needs upon the physical state of the soil by the use of as much bulky organic material – compost, manure, spent hops and so on – as possible and use concentrated fertilizers, whether of organic or inorganic origin as occasional boosts. They are, in any case, expensive.

Cost is always a consideration in the making of a new garden and though the plants themselves are a relatively small part of it, it is sad so often to see this vital aspect of the whole being scrimped. To be successful, a garden must have the feeling of profuseness, a great cornucopia overflowing with the riches of the earth, encouraged and controlled by the maker. This is very true with herbs: we want a prodigality of parsley, a mass of marjoram, a tumble of tarragon and all the other alliterative superlatives.

Forward planning is the main aid to profusion without penury. Planted at (6 inches) centres, edgings of box and thyme or hedges for knots of santolina and germander use up large numbers. It is best to set aside a bit of vegetable plot for a couple of years ahead of any large herb garden planting. Here the intended collection can be assembled, purchased perennials grown for bulking up by division and rows of shrub cuttings inserted. Some nurseries provide rooted cuttings at a very reasonable rate if bought in bulk for growing on.

The other great advantage of this system is that the construction of the herb garden site, its levelling, possible drainage paths, raised beds and so on, can proceed in an orderly unrushed fashion. If this is done over a winter period it is best (though natural impatience makes it difficult) to leave permanent planting for at least the summer season. On good soil the area can be used for a jolly display of hardy annuals of which many can be the annual herbs planned for next year's finished garden – pot marigolds, summer savory, larkspur, mignonette. All will be finished by the end of August which gives early autumn as the perfect time for soil preparation. A month for this – the digging in of compost and soil settling – and then in October while the soil is still warm one can begin the planting of all the things which are quietly waiting further down the garden or beyond the hedge.

In this way, with the plants only a few minutes out of the ground, in planting conditions of one's own choosing, unaffected by the nursery man's broader concerns – he does have other customers, after all – and the vagaries of the post, one can expect 100 per cent success.

Where a soil needs special building up and where organic material is not available it is better to use the first summer for a couple of rapid crops of mustard, annual lupins or rye-grass as 'green manure'. Seed is broadcast in spring ($\frac{1}{8}$, $\frac{1}{2}$, or 2 ounces per square yard respectively) and just before growth reaches maturity it is trampled and dug in. A second batch can be sown immediately. The herb garden is then planted the following April on the now humus-rich ground: again at a time when weather and soil conditions are right. Such spring planting is desirable in cold areas or indeed elsewhere if for any reason the work has to be delayed to beyond Christmas: Mediterraneans in particular resent root disturbance in cold weather.

The planting season can, of course, be extended in both directions if there is no root disturbance, if, in other words, plants are grown on in containers until needed. In the garden situation this has great potential but it must be remembered that one's developing stock will need much greater care. Potted in good compost, the pots plunged to their rims in rows in the ground or in beds of peat or bark-chips and given automatic watering, the results will reach the optimum. It all returns to the decision to plan ahead if a major garden feature is to be developed and those cautious words from the King James' Prayer Book observed.

While in their nursery position and the collection is being built up it is essential that effective labelling is maintained: aluminium, Hartley-type labels, attached to 18-inch high metal stakes or robust wires are the best. In a block of plants the labelling system must be constant with each label standing in front of its line or part line of plants: a front to back and left to right pattern is wise. It will be a matter of personal choice or even of memory whether such labels transfer with their plants to the permanent garden. So long as a labelled plan is kept for reference it obviously looks better without them. If they read crosswise then they should be taken off their stakes and be pushed in ahead of the nearest plant of any group. Further considerations appear if the garden is to be for demonstration or educational use: then there must be clearly visible generic and specific names, and common name and country of origin should read horizontally. If the label is large enough, family name and herbal use can be added. Without the huge expense of an engraving machine, an embossed tape system is easy and effective and personal preparation of the labels is a wonderful aid to learning the names. Hand-held machines cost only a few pounds or dollars and the range of tape colours and widths permits colour-coding of herbal types.

Gathering the Garden Together

Whether the materials for a new herb planting are entirely bought in for speed of effect or, as suggested above, gradually accumulated in advance, it will always be necessary to do some on-going propagation. Young and vigorous plants look so much better than tired old clumps and provide better herbs for kitchen use. With the annuals, of course, there is no alternative. In general herb propagation presents few difficulties and is best considered by method.

Seed. Most plants, whether they are the humblest little weeds (as are some herbs) or great trees (as are others) can be propagated by seed. Only some hybrids, whose flowers are sterile, and selected garden forms, whose especially desired characters are not carried into the seeds, have to be propagated in other ways. The time to reach maturity, however, is apt to determine whether this method or another is actually employed. Again, for annuals it is the only way. As with all the brilliant summer bedding plants, herbal annuals can be conveniently divided into hardy or half-hardy types. The former can resist many degrees of frost even in their infant stages, while the latter will take none. It all depends upon their country of origin.

Thus, as has already been described, marigold, love-in-a-mist or chervil can be sown at any time of the year and will move into growth and maturity as weather permits: summer savory or nasturtium must have a warm season directly ahead. Whatever the season the technique is the same: soil must be sufficiently dry (the humus will have helped this) so that when cultivated the lumps break down into particles not much bigger than the seeds that are to be sown. To do this each area is forked over and then raked, this is the classic 'fine tilth' of the textbooks. The addition of a couple of ounces of a complete fertilizer each square yard, such as National Growmore or Bonemeal is beneficial.

While the whole patch to be filled with the chosen plant can be scattered with broad-cast seed, it is better to scratch out shallow V-shaped drills barely ½-inch deep, 6 inches apart and sow thinly as if in parallel vegetable rows. Germinating seedlings all look very much the same: those that come up in lines are apt to be those one has sown: the rest are weeds and can be removed at once. Like vegetables, seedlings of most herbs should be thinned to 3 inches and again, this time using those pulled out in the kitchen, to 5 or 6 inches. Well developed individuals are more productive over a long period than stunted dwarfs struggling for space. The intention, and hopefully the fact, is so to cover all the ground with growth that weeds which germinate later are at such a disadvantage that they never become a problem. In a new garden in order to avoid weeding, where the perennials and the shrubs have not yet joined up, it is sensible to cover bare ground between them with a 2-inch deep loose organic mulch such as peat, bark chips or well-rotted compost. As it rots the humus level of the soil is maintained as a bonus.

Basils, and sweet or pot marjorams are a couple of the few important culinary herbs grown as tender annuals and though they too can be sown outside, when all danger of frost is passed and the soil has sufficiently warmed up, there is not much of a growing season left. Thus they need to be treated like most of our common summer bedding plants. As large numbers are not required it is sensible to concentrate on producing a dozen or so good individual specimens which, when planted out, go straight ahead without a check.

Seed is sown indoors in shallow pots of light seed compost (best bought, not much is needed) as shown in the sketch. A minimum night temperature of 65°F (18°C) is needed: care must be taken so that the compost does not dry out and for the first signs of germination, when darkening paper and then glass coverings are removed to encourage strong compact seedlings. As they develop their first true leaf, or before if sown so thickly that they quickly touch, the strongest seedlings are transferred to small pots of rich compost. Three are dibbled into each in a triangle and will grow as one: death of one or two will not affect the final effect.

Actual sowing time depends upon when the required temperatures can be maintained and the date when it is expected to plant out. Generally the end of March is soon enough with eight weeks to planting time. The whole potful is planted as one to avoid root disturbance.

This same process can be used for all the biennials, perennials, and shrubs for which seed can be obtained, remembering that named garden forms are unlikely to come true to type. The great advantage of course is that from a pinch of seed large numbers can be quickly built up in a couple of years. As with annuals these groups can be sown under glass in early spring or outside in a nursery bed rather later. Again they must be spaced out in pots or in the ground to permit proper development. Care with watering and weeding is obvious, especially in vulnerable early stages.

Even though the named lavenders – 'Hidcote', 'Munstead' and so on – are easily grown from seed and are relatively constant, it is better, especially for the herb garden hedging plants, to raise them clonally: that is in a vegetative fashion from known and desirable parents which, in similar conditions, their offspring will exactly resemble. Fortunately all the herbs used as garden dividers or as knot garden patterns are very easily rooted from cuttings. Several methods are possible. If starting from scratch with the intention of producing one's own herbal hedges for which several hundred plants may be quickly required, something of a pick-a-back pattern will be necessary.

If greenhouse space is available a few bought stock plants are potted in March. Warm, moist conditions soon encourage young shoots which, 3 inches long, are taken as cuttings and put into a mist bed or closed propagating case. Rooting is rapid and these in turn are pinched back and can provide tips, while the stock plants have growth again, for further cuttings in a few weeks. As they root the cuttings are potted, gradually weaned in cooler conditions and planted in nursery rows outside.

Obviously this sort of production time is not for every one. It is simpler to designate a small protected area, just a few feet square as a herb nursery, both to bulk up plants for a new garden and as an on-going resource for an established one. Soil is improved by the addition of peat and grit. Here the perennials can be sown in early May and also cuttings of the shrubs inserted in September. Again, starting from scratch, a few plants can be bought in spring: care will encourage good growth and the current season's shoots 3 to 6 inches in length (depending on species) are taken off, the lower leaves removed, and then firmed, two-thirds of their length into the soil a few inches apart. They are watered and then covered with cloches or a plastic tunnel. In a dry autumn further watering may be necessary but often nothing more need be done until the covers are removed the following April; some earlier ventilation when mild will have helped the transition. The result will be rows of young lavenders, santolinas and sages all ready for their permanent herb garden positions after a further season of growth.

Some perennials can also be propagated by taking cuttings of their first 2 or 3 inches of spring growth and treating them as if they were soft-wood shrub cuttings. More usual and completely foolproof is to increase this group by simple division. Bought plants may well be big enough to pull apart into pieces, each with a couple of buds and some fibrous roots. These would do little for immediate herb garden effect but a season in the nursery bed returns them to the original size and thus, with foresight, a 200 or 300 per cent increase or even more can be produced.

If some perennials can be propagated by cuttings as if they were shrubs, so reciprocally some shrubs can be divided as if they were herbaceous perennials. Twiggy plants of box and lavender are lifted in spring and replanted a few inches deeper. In autumn these 'dropped' plants will have rooted up the stems and can be pulled apart and lined out in a nursery bed. Again, as for cuttings, winter protection by cloche or plastic tunnel will extend the growing season at both ends of winter and produce better plants more quickly.

It is worth repeating that few herbs present much difficulty in propagation: the important thing is to decide what is likely to be required and to plan ahead suitably. Slight overproduction is not a mistake. Extra herbs in a nursery bed can be shorn to ground level for use without affecting a possibly attractive association in the herb garden proper. Equally, spare herbs used as gifts have a wonderful effect upon one's circle of friends.

Now follows a ready reminder of seasonal activities in the herb garden. Obviously it will vary according to each year's weather cycle in order for example, that soil texture is not impaired by cultivations when wet or that plants are not harmed by planting in frosty soil. But in general the pattern remains relatively constant. The gardening year is determined by the growth behaviour of living organisms; it is not concerned with a man-made calendar nor festivals of the church. Here therefore, regardless of these things the herb garden year begins at what is normally taken to be its end. Yet this, as has already been shown, is the most logical time to start in all but the coldest areas.

Herb gardening through the year

October The best time, in all but the coldest areas, for herb garden installation. Low shrubs are planted 9 inches apart for hedges, 18 inches apart in threes to make quick dominant features. Herbaceous herbs are planted in threes, fives or sevens, 9 inches to 18 inches apart depending upon their ultimate size. On light soils hardy annuals are still sown, early in the month, in drills 6 inches apart. In established gardens these, such as chervil and marigold, will take the place of basils and marjorams removed. Marjoram is potted and brought indoors. Tender herbs in containers are moved into protected spots.

Harvest last coriander and other seeds.

November Planting can continue throughout the month, so long as the soil remains unfrozen and in a workable condition. Parsley and mint potted for winter use. Tender herbs brought in before more than a degree or two of frost is experienced: prune back and reduce watering to encourage winter rest.

Tender herbs planted out are cut half down, piled over with dry leaves kept in place with a bit of wire netting pegged down. They might survive a mild winter.

A cloche is put over a clump of chervil to keep growth moving.

Another covers Christmas rose to prevent splashes on the opening flowers.

December As herbaceous perennials' and annuals' top growth dies for the winter it can be removed to the compost and the garden 'tucked up for the winter'. It is better to maintain a continuous interest: dead growth which falls soggily on to shrubs is cleared away but anything which stays erect is left to protect. More protective material – sacking, dry leaves, straw or bracken is kept to hand in case of really hard weather. In cold areas terracotta pots or stone ornaments wrapped round: sweet bay trees in pots are brought to protected corners.

Fresh herbs gathered to stuff the Christmas bird.

January The quietest month. A watching brief is kept. Protect tender herbs as necessary. Plan any changes or additions to the herb garden. Order seeds for spring sowing. Scour the seed lists and specialist plant lists for new varieties which might be of interest.

February Continue to rotate those pots of parsley or whatever is expected to produce fresh leaves in the kitchen, with the others resting in cooler rooms. Sow indoors, at the end of the month, the marjorams and other tender herbs which have not been over-wintered as adult plants. As days lengthen the latter should be watered if space is available for their early development. Branches are pruned back to strong young shoots as they appear.

In the garden continue to check that dead and decaying herbaceous growth has not fallen over shrubs.

March Outside all herbaceous or dead annual growth is cleared away, the ground forked over and a light dressing of bone meal added. If the ground is dry enough the first outdoor sowings are made of parsley, dill, summer savory and other hardy annuals and biennials. A cloche over the important spots a week before sowing helps to raise the soil temperature and dry it. Further sowings indoors as necessary.

Receive orders from nurseries for direct planting or lining out in kitchen garden. Gradually uncover tender plants outside and look for hopeful signs of life.

April The middle of the month is soon enough to sow basil for early June planting – and then only if a winter night temperature of 65°F (18°C) can be maintained.

Outside things are moving well. Rosemary is in flower and it is now possible to prune back branches of any shrubs which have suffered in the winter, to strong young shoots. This is the main month for sowing outdoors as soon as soil conditions permit.

May Growth of herbaceous plants is elongating quickly. Germinating annuals will need thinning. Plants known to be weak are kept erect with twigs pushed in amongst them. Perennials may also need support with brushwood around the clump. Effectively done, none should be visible when plants attain full size.

Tender and half-hardy plants are now hardened off in a cold frame or under a warm wall. Watch must be kept for a sudden late frost. Basil is especially susceptible. Move container specimens into bigger pots or top-dress with new compost.

June All planting is now completed. Plants are joining up so that little further weeding will be needed. Many plants are reaching their peak of perfection. Angelica is harvested for preserving. Biennials such as foxglove, Brompton stocks and wallflowers are sown outdoors in nursery rows. Rogue clumps of flowers showing undesirable variation (eg. purple honesty or blue borage where white is wanted). Santolina hedges get first cut if flowers are not required and formality is to be maintained. Other low hedges and topiary shapes are clipped as necessary. Regularly water and feed pot plants.

July The earlier annuals and biennials are beginning to go over. Seeds are collected if required for autumn or next spring sowing. They are dried, cleaned and carefully labelled. Tarragon, at its best, is preserved in salt. All herbs now begin to produce prodigally: begin to note necessary changes for autumn execution.

Cuttings are taken of tender shrubs as spare shoots become available. Gather lavender and rose petals for pot pourri.

August Preserve many herbs for winter use in freezer or as dried sachets. Continue collection of leaves and flowers for sachets and pot pourri. Continue to root cuttings of geraniums and other tender plants. Further seeds are collected for next spring.

A second clipping of low formal hedges. Surrounding yew hedges get their annual cut.

September By mid-month basil is taken up and leaves preserved. Sowings of overwintering annuals begin to take the place of crops finished. Soil is lightly forked and fertilized. Coriander seed harvested for winter use. Cuttings are lined out in a nursery bed under cloches or polythene tunnels for ultimate hedge renewal. Order new herbs from nursery for autumn or spring planting.

Seasonal associations in the Herb Garden

1   Late winter/early spring
    A collection of greens: *Daphne laureola, Arum italicum* 'Pictum', *Iris foetidissima, Helleborus foetidus*

2   First flowers, February
    Asarum europaeum, snowdrops, *Daphne mezereum* 'Album'

3   Late spring
    Berberis thunbergii, 'Atropurpurea', *Artemisia* 'Lambrook Silver', wallflowers; marigolds follow.

4   Early summer
    Old-fashioned roses, hollyhocks. Old clove carnations in front. *Eryngium giganteum, Asphodeline lutea, Salvia sclarea, Iris pallida*
    Biennials
    White borage, white honesty, white foxgloves

5   Low ground cover
    Sempervivums, thymes, carlina, camomile

6   Mid-summer
    Ceanothus 'Gloire de Versailles', lavenders and catmint *Althaea officinalis, Lilium candidum*, pale opium poppy, purple fennel, scarlet bergamot, *Inula magnifica*

    Late summer
    Perovskia atriplicifolia 'Blue Spire', *Helichrysum italicum*, monkshood.

6

HERBS IN THE HOUSE

❦

The highly effective motto of the Herb Society of America 'for use and for delight' has already been mentioned. Perhaps we can see the delight more clearly in the garden, while the use takes place indoors. Probably they are not to be separated, for further delight certainly arrives with the effective use of herbs. What is especially satisfactory is the use of herbs we have grown ourselves from seed, from cuttings or from young bought plants (there is no shame in buying basil seedlings with three or four pairs of leaves; it is a brute to get going at the start of a cool northern summer).

And in the kitchen, which is by far the major emphasis of this chapter, to have fresh herbs literally at hand makes all the difference to the dish being prepared. Not only are dried herbs, for the most part, only pale reflections of the original plants – the moisture being dispelled seems to take much of the flavour with it – but the fact that the herbs are available *now*, at this moment, encourages their use. It is a dedicated cook who will attempt to search out a given herb for a certain dish; and where, indeed, is it to be found? Better to start the other way around.

Enjoyable use of herbs in the kitchen encourages further use; that success breeds success is as true here as anywhere and the fact that new recipes call for new herbs encourages us in turn to grow them. There is no doubt that our much more mobile population, both within this country and to places abroad, has broadened our national culinary tastes enormously. Not only have the 'big four' herbs of British kitchens – parsley, sage, thyme and mint – been supplemented by many other species – but their own application has also been greatly extended.

In this country, mint, for example, is virtually synonymous with mint sauce; this causes great confusion to dedicated wine lovers who would like a good claret with their roast lamb but find the vinegar in the sauce to be an unkind competition (made with half a glass of the wine, the result is less worrying). But mint, though known to all in this way, is much more pervasive a part of

Middle Eastern cooking than it is here. The flavour in the wonderfully cooling summer salad Tsatsiki (see page 123) of cucumber and yoghurt is typical.

Other garden herbs, grown here for centuries have literally lost ground while remaining highly significant in other cuisines. Dill and coriander are two such. The former is particularly important in Scandinavia and Germany while coriander is vital to much northern Indian and Arabic cooking. It is perhaps significant in the context of dried herbs that while the leaves of both dill and coriander are widely used when fresh, only their seeds are used dry; those of coriander then have a completely different flavour and hence very different applications.

Some herbs, only recently a part of our garden flora, have particularly strong national affinities; one thinks of oregano in Italy, the related dittany in Crete and of tarragon in France. There the impression is apt to be given that a summer passed without a *poulet a l'estragon* being eaten is a summer wasted. That these herbs have not been common with us is, in the case of tarragon, because the true *Artemisia dracunculus* is neither easy to obtain, nor to keep once found. It is very sad that the so-called Russian tarragon (*A.dracunculoides*) has every appearance of the other with none of its flavour. It is a great usurper.

Origano, on the other hand, is a common wild plant of the chalklands, but though agreeably aromatic has little of the authentic Mediterranean pungency. This is the only example of a dried import being preferable to the fresh home-grown article. Dried tarragon, incidentally, is most disappointing.

Herbs straight from the garden have their primary function of flavouring but, coming not far behind, is the visual effect within a dish (Green Herb Paté is a fine example, page 124) and that of garnishing. This does not stop at a tired and timid sprig of parsley, the same bit being used, one often fears, again and again in down-market restaurants. (If everyone would only eat their parsley all might be well!) Chopped parsley, chives, dill, tarragon and so on sprinkled on soups, and salads add immeasurably to sight and to savour.

Though some associations of herb and dish have a peculiar rightness, sanctified by age and convention (mint and tarragon have already been cited, sage with pork and basil with tomatoes are others) this should not restrict their use. On the contrary, experimentation and serendipity should be encouraged; presumably that is how a cuisine advances. Students of English Literature will recall a classic example of culinary accident in Charles Lamb's essay on the invention of roast pork.

While, as is being continually emphasized, herbs plucked as the omelette butter is melting in the pan are *sans-pareil*, councils of perfection cannot always be kept. The weekend cottager (not customarily a subject for sorrow) may well not grow herbs both in the town and the country; fortunately fresh herbs picked and stored in airtight containers in the refrigerator will keep for a couple of weeks. This is much better than a pretty bunch in water on the kitchen window sill which is apt quickly to rot at the base and stink most unpleasantly.

What is important (and herbs *are* important) is that one's favourites are available when they are required; happy memories and good intentions are neither of them enough.

The particular emphasis in this book has been to stress the role of herbal plants as a part of the modern garden scene. To do so it has attempted first to search out the origin of the plants and their uses in early garden styles. The basic fact that emerges is, of course, that today's herb gardens, however apparently evocative of times past, are in fact just what they are – today's gardens, twentieth-century concepts built upon delightful myths.

Beyond the ornamental garden role, of course, is the usefulness of herbs which has been employed here as a sort of obbligato around the main theme. Of those uses only one is given any real importance, that of flavouring in cooking. This is intentional because it represents a modern application of these ancient plants, as do our current herb garden designs.

While it is possible to repeat medieval recipes, it has to be accepted that few have much attraction for us today. Today's cuisine, with the availability of fresh materials at all times, has the potential to be better for most people than it was in the past, however romantic that past may appear. Cooking is a living, developing part of a culture. Already many nineteenth-century dishes have lost their appeal while others have been borrowed or adopted, from an ever more accessible world. Attitudes have altered dramatically: I have in my possession a wholly grisly text which my father brought back from the East called *The Anglo–Chinese Cookbook*. Written in the 1920s it has not a word about the delightful range of Chinese cooking with which we have suddenly become acquainted. On the contrary, it is a conventional English roast meat and boiled pudding manual: with it goes a separate Chinese translation so that one could point out to one's Chinese cook just what one wanted for dinner. Just like home: no wonder the Empire declined!

It is often forgotten how quickly a new ingredient becomes so much a part of kitchen use that its lack cannot be comprehended. Cooking anything 'Provençal' today immediately indicates the use of tomatoes and often sweet peppers. Both emerged as important ingredients only in the last century: already they *mean* Provençal.

Thus the often used analogy of herbs being an unbroken thread which links us to the past should, to really illuminate the situation, be extended. Herbs are strands in the weft of the material of civilization: time is the warp. In culinary terms the cloth begins coarsely and the herbs have not merely to flavour but to disguise. Today the material has greater sophistication and herbal use obviously has to match it.

This analogy, however, must not be done to death. Other herbal uses remain remarkably unaltered by time. Though these uses may well have been generally superseded by later discoveries and inventions, the original method remains. Thus there are innumerable applications.

At the life-enhancing level (one of the herb definitions cited) herbal recipes are available as cosmetics, in bath oils and soaps and of course in perfumery. A number of plants provide, in association with suitable mordants, effective dyes. Such natural colourings have enjoyed a considerable renaissance in recent years as the interest in and renewal of hand-made arts and crafts have gained momentum in all parts of the country.

There have been rediscoveries of ancient herbal uses, which have shown that modern technology does not have answers to man's needs. Lady Meade-Featherstonehaugh's renovation of historic hangings and other fabrics at Uppark by the use of soapwort is a classic example.

Above all, of course, there has been the increase of herbal use as alternative medicine; alternative, that is, to the dominance of orthodox 'chemical' medicine. Stuart (*Encyclopedia of Herbs and Herbalism*, 1979) gives the surprising figures for the USA that within medicines prescribed in 1968, 3 per cent contained crude herbs. This figure represents some 41 million items. Methods differ in the medicinal use of herbs from the ingestion of simple infusions – teas and tisanes for colds and passing indispositions – to highly involved diagnosis and treatment. Homoeopathy is one form of herbalism with many adherents; here herbs are prepared to form tinctures in which the active ingredients are used in infinitesimally small amounts.

In parallel with various schools of herbalism (methods explicable or not, and does this matter if sick patients are helped psychologically or physically?) orthodox medicine and drug firms are taking a much more serious interest in medical use of plants. Not only are Western traditional herbs being screened for adoption for modern needs but so too are plants which are considered of medical importance by native peoples all over the world. Such intelligent inquiry is a direct extension of William Withering's eighteenth-century willingness to take seriously a local foxglove recipe for alleviation of dropsy: digitalin and knowledge of the cardiac glycocides eventually followed. Further examples can be cited from every country. Areas which have maintained a strong herbal tradition to the present day, when modern methods of laboratory enquiry can study the effects, have much to offer to the open minded.

China is the prime example which is why the *Barefoot Doctor's Manual* has provided me with such an extension to the usual herb garden palette. More reverence for the past and economics of the present combined with proven efficacy has ensured that the traditional baby has not been thrown out with the fashionable bath water.

From these very general observations it will be realized that herb-based medicine is a highly complicated subject. The old term 'simples' gives a wholly false impression. Local herbs may be simple to collect but the chemical effect of one organism – the plant, on another – the patient, may be very complex indeed. Home medication, except in the case of a few basic teas and tisanes, is to be treated with the greatest care. It has no place in the present book.

This chapter about herbs in the home therefore is consciously restricted. It suggests some culinary treats and it reminds of simple methods of extending herbal fragrances from summer into winter. Even if all else is initially neglected, the happy euphoria produced by the elderflower champagne (p. 139) could well be sufficient to encourage the most intransigent to try to extend their normal culinary range, and the herbs will help all the way.

At the end of the chapter is a range of recipes which claim to be neither esoteric nor extensive. However it is hoped they will encourage the pleasures of the kitchen by employing what is grown in the garden. All the recipes emphasize fresh herbs from plants grown by oneself and the adjective is assumed in every case unless stated to the contrary. They are a personal selection, all enjoyed by *this* family, in *this* kitchen. It must be stressed that, as there are whole books written about cooking with herbs this short selection can do no more than scratch the surface of what is possible. All good cookery writers agree that most savoury dishes and a few sweet ones are improved, sometimes beyond recognition, by the use of suitable herbs.

Herbs for later use

Storage and subsequent use

It has been stated again and again that the whole point of herb growing is to have an unlimited supply of fresh herbs for kitchen use. Chapter 5 discusses ways of extending the garden's direct contribution; fortunately the usual English climate provides a number of evergreen shrubs which are available every day of the year – rosemary, winter savory, thyme and bay. A really light kitchen window sill can hold a large pot of overwintering marjoram (*Origanum marjorana*), and a succession of parsley plants lifted from outside and moved progressively indoors from cold greenhouse, or porch or garage window.

But there are winter needs beyond this which summer's bounty can supply. There are a number of methods for the preserving of herbs available to us and these used in combination can see even the most herbophile cook through into spring.

A deep-freezer makes both possible and worthwhile the storage of those herbs with tender leaves and delicate flavours, such as basil, chives and chervil, which are quite ruined by conventional drying. Even tarragon emerges with some of its strange liquorice bouquet intact. A personal prejudice, however, maintains that tarragon is a treat for its season, like the first new potatoes and peas, which is unrepeatable at other times except as a pale evocation.

But if they are to be preserved there are two main methods. The herbs are picked in their prime of growth and there is a concentration of essential oil in the early part of the day (Bulgarians at Kazanlik are up at dawn to pluck their damask roses for attar before the sun gets high and hot). This is clearly a summer morning job. Nothing could be pleasanter. The leaf-sprays are washed, patted dry with kitchen paper and laid on trays in the freezer. Next day they are brittle, fit for crumbling and pouring into air-tight pots to be kept in a basket at the top; once they leave this sort of continental shelf and sink into the darker depths summer can come again before they surface. Hence, presumably, the title of *deep* freezer. Legible labelling, as for anything cast into the maw of a freezer – and memories are dreadfully short – is vital.

A second method, collecting and cleaning the herbs as before, is then to chop them up, moisten with sufficient water or light stock and pack them into ice-cube trays. These are popped out next day and moved into strong freezer bags. In the same way combinations of herbs can be prepared (parsley, marjoram, thyme and a bayleaf (uncut) to act as bouquets garni for adding to soups and stews, or as sachets ready to be made up into herb butters when thawed and drained (see recipes page 132). Frozen tablespoonfuls of mixed parsley, tarragon, chives and chervil make immediate material for *omelettes aux fines herbes*.

When needed, the crumbled dry-frozen herbs are used, as are those frozen in ice cubes, as if they were fresh. They are indeed a remarkably satisfactory substitute. Often they do not need defrosting first; though for quickly fried dishes such as omelettes they will – a spot of boiling water is sufficient to melt the bond and begin to release that authentic aroma which makes the work worthwhile.

Drying herbs, as has been suggested, is the classic method of extending these plants' uses and availability into the winter period. But it does this at the cost of some flavour lost by all herbs. Even thyme and rosemary, though still pungent are not quite what they were straight off the bush. Tarragon, when dried, just smells of hay. Fortunately there is another method of preservation which really does preserve the flavours of the two herbs most difficult to evoke out of season. It is surprisingly little known.

Tarragon is picked at the height of its vigour in mid-summer, leaves are stripped from the woody stems and whizzed up in a food processor. They are then combined with a similar quantity of coarse sea salt and packed into an air-tight jar to be used as required.

A similar method is used for basil where again the dried material has little connection with the fresh herb. Here, after the same preparation, the aroma-holding substance is light olive oil and the basil oil jar is kept in the bottom of the refrigerator. No doubt there is an application here for more effective culinary herb preservation.

Without use of a deep-freezer, or even the back of a big ice-tray compartment in a conventional refrigerator, several other herbs can be air dried with success for winter use. Dried herbs are better than no herbs. But sadly it must be admitted that the softer, more delicate leaves lose much of their savour; tarragon has already been mentioned, basil renounces its unique pepperiness and becomes, once cooked, almost indistinguishable from old, tired mint.

Ironically the woody herbs, rosemary, thyme, savory (both

summer and winter) and bay, which anyway are available from the
garden at any time, dry best. Nonetheless there is convenience in
having some on a warm kitchen shelf rather than having to plunge
out on a winter's night with a torch – a true test of devotion to the
cause. Also, prettily packed, these herbs make admirable gifts to
benighted city-dwellers without their own plants; Christmas presents dealt with in July.

Such is their strength of flavour that most of the umbellifers
dry reasonably well; fennel and dill are best, with parsley and
chervil following behind. Drying herbs is a simple enough process
but the results vary with the year; this is likely to be the result of
the difference in the aromatic oil content from year to year as much
as technique (home-grown oregano dried with every care is not a
patch on that snatched in passing from a Grecian hillside and left
on the hotel balcony till it is time reluctantly to return home; no
souvenir from the smartest tourist-trap boutique can be half so
evocative).

As for freezing, the herbs are best collected in the morning
before the sun has gathered strength. The small-leaved woody types
are best snipped off in sprigs while the rest are gathered leaf by leaf.
Fennel leaves should be left on the stems at this stage. The material
is lightly washed and patted dry with absorbent kitchen paper and
the object is now to air-dry it as quickly and evenly as possible;
upon this depends the final result.

In good weather the herbs are tied in small bunches and hung
in a well-ventilated dust-free area away from bright light. Others
are put together as bouquets garni; two sprigs each of parsley and
thyme, one of marjoram or oregano and a bay leaf. Tied while fresh
they hold together well; when dry they become impossibly brittle.

Alternatively the herbs are laid in single layers on trays in the
airing cupboard, above the stove or even in the oven at its lowest
setting (a cool Aga is ideal) and 30°C (90°F) should not be exceeded
for the first twenty-four hours. During this time the herbs are
turned once or twice, the temperature is now slightly reduced and
drying should be complete in three to five days. The final effect
should be of herbs brittle but still green and, of course, aromatic. If
they go brown the chances are that they are overdone; all virtue
dispersed.

Subsequent storage is of prime importance; though it can be
agreeable to give a Provençal air to the kitchen with strings of garlic
and onions and bunches of herbs, the latter are best considered
primarily as decoration. The essential oils are destroyed by light,
time, heat and moisture and thus herbs carefully dried are stored in

airtight containers, well labelled and in the dark. The conventional little row of kitchen herbs and spice jars can be filled from the stored source as they become empty, not, for obvious reasons, merely topped up. Equally, therefore, it is seldom practicable to store dried herbs on the stem (except the bouquets garni in their own wide-necked jar). The leaves are crumbled off but are best not powdered to dust. It is worthwhile keeping stalks of parsley, fennel and dill; recipes frequently call for the first-named and the latter are used with grilled fish to marvellous effect. Because of the annual variation in home-cured herbs it is not wise to be dogmatic about quantities necessary in cooking. Generally, half or less the quantities given for fresh herbs are recommended for their dried surrogate. Thus a tablespoon of fresh chopped herbs that is right for most recipes is reduced to a teaspoon of coarsely chopped dried herbs and a half teaspoon of finely ground dried herbs. The highly aromatic, woody herbs and bouquets garni are usually added at the start of the preparation of a dish and frequently removed before serving. More delicate herbs are naturally added towards the end and in their dried state are helped by soaking in a spot of warm (not boiling) water for ten minutes and then drained before adding to soufflés, salads, etc.

Finally it should be emphasized that dried herbs are seldom worth keeping into a second year and the moment their replacements are certain they should be discarded.

Summer Scents Throughout The Year

One of the pleasures of an old house, dearly loved and lived in for generations, is that distant scent which seems to be compounded of woodsmoke, furniture polish and lavender. It is as if the ambience has distilled these fragrances and held them in the air like motes of dust caught in the sudden sunbeam through a lattice window. Today's furniture polish, though not that spray-on stuff, and woodsmoke, though modern stoves let out less than the old open grates, are no less aromatic than they used to be; any household happy to spend a little more time in living can still enjoy these simple pleasures.

Lavender, too, is as delicious to us as it was to the Elizabethans and equally easily used indoors. One good reason for showing a lot of lavender in the herb garden plans above is to ensure, not only a fine garden show, but plenty to cut for household use as well.

Ideally, lavender heads should be gathered as soon as all

flowers on the spike are open. But it does shorten the garden display and not a lot seems to be lost by waiting until a couple of weeks later. By then, too, the spikes are beginning to dry naturally. They are cut, hung in bunches in a warm dark place and within a month the heads can be crumbled off the stalks.

Left in an open bowl on the hall chest or at the turn of the stair, the lavender gives an evocation of summer past and is there for enjoyment every time the contents are stirred. Obviously the scent decreases over the months but even without replenishment a distant breath is discernable for years. Obviously the most satisfactory method is to enclose the newly-rubbed lavender in airtight containers and replace old for new two or three times during the year. In this way even the residents notice without a personal stir at the bowls as they pass: otherwise one becomes so used to its presence that the all-pervading scent is only perceived by visitors. Casting the old lavender on the fire in the evening gives a further moment of pure pleasure.

Though the simplest to use, lavender is by no means the only summer flower to take its scent into the months ahead. Such essential oils are found in many plants, most of which earn their designation as herbs because of those oils. They are the flavouring agents. Distilled or extracted in other ways, they produce the bases for the best of scents and perfumes, held in oils or alcohol. Though there are certain household methods possible to produce these, it must be recognized that the time-demanding intricacies of the still room have had to be left behind: they were anyway only the prerogatives of great houses each with a staff to match. It is necessary now to work on a smaller scale through a combination of home-produced natural materials and commercial additives. Thus is pot pourri made, a collection of essential-oil-bearing materials. Different species concentrate their oils in different parts of the plant. Most culinary herbs seem to have theirs in the leaves: such as basil, mints, balm or thymes. Oils of roses and camomile are concentrated in the flowers while cinnamon and sandalwood (in the tropics) are in the bark. Such bark oils can be discerned in the hardy *Magnolia salicifolia* and sassafras. Other plants such as lavender and rosemary seem to possess the scent everywhere though its strength and actual aroma varies from leaf and bark to flower. The genus *Citrus* is perhaps the most miraculously endowed with delicious and utterly different dried scents from bark, leaf, flower and fruit. Orange and lemon peels are valuable additions to pot pourri.

Thus any dried combination of such plants can produce a pot

pourri to take its place on the hall-chest, inside little muslin bags for linen cupboards or even, it is suggested as an entirely modern use, to be kept in a bag in the car to sooth shattered traffic-jam nerves.

Garden herbs to be so used are collected when at their peak of growth. This is simple enough with aromatic leaves. Roses pose the same problem as lavender: unlike the Bulgarian growers of damask roses for commercial attar of rose production, it is unlikely that one can bear to pick roses at dawn on the day they open. On the other hand they cannot be left till they fall. Thus one must move into a just-before-dead-heading situation which keeps the rose beds looking wonderfully tidy. The petals of the most scented varieties – all the old-fashioned types and moderns such as 'Fragrant Cloud' – are spread on trays in a dark warm place, such as an attic, for a week or less until fully dry and stored in plastic bags in the dark. It is expected that some of the original colour should be retained.

By the end of summer, therefore, one will have a number of containers of dried materials which can then be mixed together as required and displayed in the usual way. By themselves, however, scents will be rather distant and the use of a fixative is highly desirable. Orris root, the powdered dried rhizome of *Iris florentina*, or gum benzoin are the most usual.

To these a few drops of commercial flower oils are added: rose oil or rose geranium oil, eau de cologne or a proprietory pot pourri blend are all suitable. Proportions of all the ingredients is very much a personal choice. The following is a typical recipe:

> *10 fl oz/1420 ml of mixed dried*
> *flower and leaves*
> *1 tablespoon powdered orris root*
> *1 teaspoon mixed powdered spices:*
> *cinnamon,nutmeg, allspice*
> *a few drops of selected oil or oils*

These ingredients are mixed in a bowl until well combined. Left in open bowls, again the discernable scent diminishes. Pot pourri containers are best covered and the lid removed on special occasions when guests are expected, or merely for personal pleasure as it occurs to one to raise the cover.

Years ago is was usual to carry a bowl of pot pourri into the drawing room of an evening and uncover it by the fire, the warmth bringing out the scent more noticeably. Nothing could be more agreeable today than to bring one in on the after dinner coffee tray as a civilized ending to the day.

RECIPE SECTION

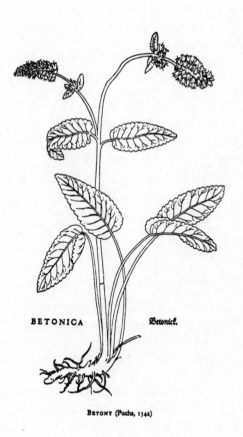

BETONICA   *Betonick.*

BETONY (Fuchs, 1542)

SOUPS AND STARTERS

COURGETTE SOUP

Quite one of the best ways to use up the embarrassing excess of
courgettes (zucchini) which some seasons kindly provide, and a
good way to preserve them for winter use. Instead of marjoram add
double the amount of parsley and this makes a very different soup,
equally delicious.

serves 4–6 *2 oz/50g butter or margarine*
4 medium-sized onions, sliced
2 lb/1 kg courgettes, trimmed and sliced
2½ pt/1.5 l chicken stock
2 teaspoons fresh marjoram
a little flour
salt and pepper

Soften the onion in the melted butter or margarine. Stir in a little
flour and cook for a minute. Add the stock gradually, stirring well.
Then add the courgettes and the marjoram, seasoning to taste, and
simmer gently for 20–30 minutes. Liquidize or sieve the soup and
serve hot, or chilled.

LOVAGE SOUP

Here is one of the best summer soups; worthy of a Glyndebourne
interval picnic for which this family has often used it: as often, that
is, as tickets could be afforded.

serves 4 *2 onions, finely chopped*
1 oz/25g butter
2 tablespoons lovage, chopped
1 oz/25g flour
1 pt/600 ml chicken stock
salt and pepper
½ pt/300 ml milk

Sauté the onions in the butter until soft. Add the lovage and cook
for a couple of minutes. Gradually add the flour and then the stock.
Season to taste and simmer for 20 minutes. Liquidize or press
through a sieve. Add the milk and reheat. It is equally good chilled.

CARROT SOUP

A chopped bunch of herbs added at the last moment to a rich soup, already flavoured with aromatic, orangy coriander seeds.

serves 4–6
    2 oz/50g butter or margarine
    2 onions, sliced
    6 medium-sized carrots, sliced
    2 teaspoons coriander seeds
    salt and pepper
    2 teaspoons flour
    2½ pt/1.5 l chicken stock
    3 tablespoons of mixed chopped herbs (parsley,
        chives, chervil, thyme)

Melt the butter in a pan and add the onion, carrots and crushed coriander seeds (a garlic press prevents them flying all over the kitchen). Add salt and pepper to taste. Cook for a few minutes. Stir in the flour and then gradually mix in the stock. Bring to the boil and simmer for 20 minutes or so (or cook in a pressure cooker for 7 minutes). Liquidize in a blender or press through a sieve. Add the herbs just before serving. Serve hot but beware overcooking as carrot soup burns like little else.

CALLY'S ARGENTINE DIP

An unusual and wholly delicious dip, it is also excellent for rather special picnic sandwiches.

    4 oz/100g butter
    6 oz/150g sugar
    ½ pt/300 ml vinegar
    ¼ pt/150 ml double cream
    3 teaspoons dry mustard
    1 teaspoon salt
    3 beaten eggs
    8 oz/200g grated cheddar cheese
    1 green pepper, finely chopped
    1 red pepper, finely chopped
    1 teaspoon each basil and tarragon, chopped

Mix all the ingredients together and cook gently in a double boiler for about 45 minutes, stirring occasionally. It should by then be thick. Put the mixture in a blender and 'whizz' it for a few seconds. Cool thoroughly before serving. It can be kept for up to two weeks in a refrigerator.

Tzatziki or Yoghurt Salad

A delicious cooling dip on the hottest day.

> *1 pt/600 ml yoghurt*
> *1 medium-sized cucumber, peeled and cut in small*
> *cubes*
> *a few mint leaves, coarsely chopped*
> *salt*
> *a little paprika*

Add the cucumber and the mint leaves to the yoghurt. Season to taste and serve very cold, garnished with a little paprika.

Avocado Salad

When to offer halves of really big avocados would be hinting at extravagance this is an interesting alternative.

serves 4
> *1 large avocado*
> *1–2 medium-sized tomatoes*
> *¼ pt/150 ml mayonnaise or aioli*
> *1–2 tablespoons dill, chopped*
> *4 crisp lettuce leaves*

Carefully peel the skin off the avocado and cut it into four rings, slipping each ring carefully off the stone. Place a lettuce leaf on each plate and put an avocado ring on top. Peel and quarter the tomatoes, and place them in the rings. Spoon over the mayonnaise and sprinkle with the chopped dill and a little seasoning. If this is not going to be served immediately brush the avocado slices with lemon juice to prevent discolouration.

Green Herb Pâté

This is an extremely rich dish to precede a simple main course.

serves 10
2 lb/1 kg courgettes
2 oz/50g butter
4 eggs
½ pt/300 ml whipping cream
2 tablespoons chopped mixed herbs (mint, chervil,
* tarragon)*
salt and pepper
pinch of cayenne pepper
a little cream and some sprigs of fresh herbs to
* garnish.*

Grate the courgettes and sprinkle with salt and leave in a sieve to drain; rinse in cold water, dry, and then cook in the melted butter till soft. Leave to cool. Mix the beaten eggs and cream and add the courgettes, herbs and seasoning. Put the mixture into a lined and greased 3 pt or 1.5 l loaf tin and place in a heated oven 350°F/ 180°C/gas mark 4. Put a tin of water at the base of the oven for humidity and cook for 1 hour, or until the pâté is firm. Leave to cool and then turn out. Whip the remaining cream and decorate the top of the pâté with this and a few herbs.

Cream Cheese Roll With Herbs

Served on toast or cut into thin rounds to moisten steaks, fish or vegetables, or added to hot pasta, this is a marvellous evocation of the herb garden.

4 oz/100g cream cheese
2 oz/50g butter
1 clove garlic, crushed
1 dessertspoon dry vermouth
salt and pepper
2 tablespoons mixed chopped herbs (parsley,
* chives, basil)*

Cream all the ingredients together. Quickly shape into a roll and place it in greaseproof paper. Keep in the fridge until required.

AUBERGINE SOUFFLÉ

Like avocado, aubergine has moved from being an exotic fruit to a fashionable colour. One not only eats it but wears it. Here is one of the best aubergine (egg plant) recipes.

serves 4
1 large aubergine, diced
1 large onion, sliced
8 oz/225g breadcrumbs
¼ pt/150 ml good tomato sauce, or 2 tomatoes
  chopped (see p. 133)
4 eggs
4 oz/100g grated cheese
salt and pepper
2 teaspoons oregano

Sprinkle the aubergine with salt and let it drain in a sieve for one hour. Rinse, pat dry and fry in oil till soft. Add the onion, breadcrumbs, salt and pepper, oregano and the tomato sauce or chopped tomatoes. Separate the eggs and add the yolks to the aubergine mixture and stir in well. Beat the whites till firm and fold into the mixture. Place in a buttered soufflé dish and sprinkle with the grated cheese. Cook for 30–40 minutes at 350°F/180°C/gas mark 4 and serve at once.

KIRKCALDY MUSSELS

Scrubbing mussel shells to the perfection needed for moules marinière and opening them live for grilling are both laboursome occupations. This is an excellent alternative.

serves 6
4 dozen mussels
2 eggs, beaten
2 tablespoons fine oatmeal
1 large handful parsley, chopped
freshly ground pepper

Wash the mussels well in several changes of water, pull out the beards. Add them to a little boiling water in a large pan and cook till all the shells open (any that do not must be discarded). Remove mussels from shells and mix with the eggs and a little milk, the parsley, pepper and oatmeal. Fry quickly, as for an omelette, and serve on hot toast garnished with parsley. The de-shelled mussels can be kept refrigerated for up to 24 hours.

VEGETABLES

Several common vegetables, normally merely boiled and served as an accompaniment to meat, develop a life of their own with suitable herbs.

BRUSSEL SPROUTS AND CARAWAY SEEDS

serves 4–6
1 lb/½ kg Brussel sprouts
2 oz/50g butter
2 tablespoons lemon juice
1 tablespoon caraway seeds
2 oz/50g fine breadcrumbs
2 oz/50g grated cheese

Cook the sprouts for about 10 minutes in boiling salted water until *just tender*. Drain well and place in a shallow dish. Melt the butter and add to it the lemon juice and caraway seeds. Pour this over the Brussel sprouts. Mix the breadcrumbs and the cheese together. Sprinkle on the top and brown under a hot grill.

CARROTS AND JUNIPER

serves 4–6
10 medium-sized carrots, peeled and cut into thick slices
4 tablespoons wine vinegar
1 teaspoon sugar
1 onion, finely sliced
6–10 juniper berries, crushed

Place the carrots in a pan and just cover them with cold water. Add the rest of the ingredients and season with salt and pepper. Stir occasionally while cooking until the carrots are soft and the liquid reduced. Can be served hot or cold.

Ratatouille

This traditional Provençal vegetable stew is one of the pleasures of the summer garden. It freezes extremely well.

serves 4–6
2 medium aubergines, sliced
2 tablespoons olive oil
2 onions, sliced
2 cloves garlic, crushed
2 peppers, cut small
6 ripe tomatoes, peeled and sliced
salt and pepper
2 teaspoons coriander seeds
chopped parsley or basil to garnish

Slice the aubergines and put in a colander sprinkled with salt to drain for 30 minutes. Rinse and pat dry. Heat the oil and cook the onions gently without browning them for 10 minutes. Add the aubergines and the peppers. Cover the pan and cook for 30–40 minutes. Then add the tomatoes, garlic and coriander seeds. (They can be slightly crushed in a garlic press to release more of their delicious orange flavour). Season well and cook for a further 20 minutes. Serve hot or cold with a garnish of chopped parsley or basil.

Baked Tomatoes

serves 6
6 tomatoes, halved
5 mushrooms, sliced
1 tablespoon olive oil
2 teaspoons chopped herbs (parsley, chives, basil)
1 clove garlic, crushed
seasoning
a little Parmesan cheese

Combine ingredients together and spoon on top of the halved tomatoes. Bake for 15 minutes in a moderate oven, or grill until brown.

MAIN DISHES

MARINADES

Marinades have two prime roles. To ensure that the meat will be tender when cooked – the difference is remarkable – and to provide a herbal flavour which adds greatly to the dish. Marinading meat to be used as kebabs is obligatory but the method is also useful for chops and larger cuts.

Cover the meat with the marinade and leave for a few hours, preferably longer, turning occasionally. In warm weather it should be kept in the fridge.

Marinades can be made up in advance and frozen. These must be kept in airtight plastic containers to contain the strong flavours which can otherwise be absorbed by adjacent foods.

MARINADE FOR LAMB

For a leg of lamb weighing about 4 lb/2 kg

> *½ pt/300 ml red wine*
> *2–3 onions, sliced*
> *1 large carrot, sliced*
> *1 tablespoon fresh mint leaves, chopped*
> *2 teaspoons oregano*
> *2 cloves garlic, crushed*
> *a small bunch of parsley, chopped*
> *½ teaspoon powdered cloves*
> *salt and freshly ground black pepper*
> *1 teaspoon grated lemon peel*
> *2–3 teaspoons lemon juice*

Mix all the ingredients together well. Pour the marinade over the meat and cover and leave for 12–24 hours in the refrigerator, turning occasionally. Take out the lamb and drain off the marinade, reserving it for later. Roast the meat allowing 40 minutes per lb/ ½ kg at 350°F/180°C/gas mark 4. 30 minutes before the end of the cooking time pour the fat off the meat and pour over the marinade. When ready to serve, remove the meat from the pan and keep warm. Reheat the marinade and serve as sauce.

COOKED MARINADE FOR BEEF

¼ pt/150 ml olive oil
1 onion, 1 carrot, ½ stick of celery, sliced
¼ pt/150 ml red wine
1 bay leaf
2 tablespoons chopped mixed herbs (thyme,
  rosemary, marjoram, parsley)
2 cloves garlic, crushed
salt
4 black peppercorns

Cook the onion, carrot and celery in the oil for a few minutes. Add the rest of the ingredients and simmer for about 20 minutes. Cool and pour over the beef. The meat could also be cooked in this.

MINT MARINADE FOR CHICKEN OR LAMB

4 tablespoons olive oil
1 clove garlic, crushed
½ pt/300 ml white wine
1 tablespoon mint leaves, finely chopped
1 teaspoon basil, finely chopped
1 tablespoon parsley, finely chopped
salt and pepper
pinch of sugar

Combine all the ingredients together and pour over the meat.

CHICKEN PARMESAN

serves 4–6
1 chicken, cut into serving portions
4 oz/100g butter, melted
8 oz/225g breadcrumbs, finely crushed
2 oz/50g Parmesan cheese, grated
2 oz/50g parsley, chopped
1 oz/25g oregano
1 clove garlic, crushed

Dip each piece of chicken in the melted butter. Put the rest of the ingredients in a polythene bag and shake the chicken pieces one at a time in the mixture until evenly covered. Place in a shallow baking tin and cook for 35–45 minutes in a moderate oven, or until browned and cooked through. Do not turn them while cooking.

MINT AND SAGE POT-ROAST PORK

serves 4

a piece pork, any cut, about 2 lb-1 kg
a handful of fresh sage leaves
1–2 sprigs mint
4 tablespoons water
2 tablespoons oil
2–3 rashers bacon
3–5 cloves garlic
salt and pepper to taste

Fry the bacon and then add the pork to the pan and brown well on all sides, adding a little more fat if necessary. Place the pork in a casserole and add the oil, water, sage and mint leaves, salt and pepper and the whole cloves of garlic. Cover and cook over a low heat for 3–4 hours until the meat is tender, adding more liquid during the cooking time if necessary.

SOUTH SEA ISLAND PORK

serves 6

1½ lb/750g lean pork
1 tablespoon seasoned flour
2 tablespoons oil
rind of 1 orange, cut in thin strips
juice of 2 oranges
¾ pt/450 ml stock
2 tablespoons cream
8 oz/200g peas
2 tablespoons flaked almonds
1 teaspoon fresh ginger, chopped
1 teaspoon oregano
chopped parsley to garnish

Cut the pork into cubes. Toss the meat in the seasoned flour, to which the ginger has been added. Fry a little at a time in the hot oil until browned. Place in a casserole with the orange rind, juice, stock and oregano. Cook gently, either in a moderate oven or on the top of the cooker for 1–1½ hours. Add the peas and cook for a further 30 minutes. Just before serving stir in the cream and the almonds. Heat gently (do not allow to boil) and serve sprinkled with chopped parsley. (The initial cooking, before the addition of the peas, can be done the day before).

PRESSED SALMON, OR TROUT, WITH DILL

There is no better way of enabling the efforts of an only moderately successful angler to be enjoyed by the whole family.

serves 6   *2 lb/1 kg whole fresh trout or salmon*
as a starter *1 large bunch fresh dill*
             2 tablespoons mixed chopped parsley and chives
             2 tablespoons brown sugar
             2 tablespoons salt
             1 teaspoon freshly ground black pepper

Clean the fish, split it lengthways and remove all the bones. Dry well. Place a layer of dill in the bottom of a deep dish and lay half the fish, skin side down, on this. Cover evenly with the mixed parsley and chives, sugar, salt and pepper and some chopped dill. Place the other half of the fish on top, skin side up, and cover with more dill. Cover with foil and a plate or board. On this put a weight of at least 4 lbs (2 kilos) and leave it for 2–4 days in the bottom of the fridge. When ready to serve remove the dill covering and lift the fish out of the 'marinade'. Place skin side down and slice very thinly like smoked salmon.

HERB BUTTERS, SAUCES AND STUFFING

HERB BUTTERS

Basil butter

> 4 basil leaves
> 1 clove garlic, crushed
> 1 oz/25g butter

Chop the basil finely and add the crushed garlic and softened butter. Season. Serve with grilled meat.

Fennel or Parsley butter

> 2 teaspoons fennel or parsley, finely chopped
> 1 oz/25g butter
> a little lemon juice

Add the fennel or parsley to the butter and mix the lemon juice in well. Serve with vegetables or fish.

Garlic butter

> 4 oz/100g butter
> 2 cloves garlic, crushed
> 1 tablespoon parsley, finely chopped
> a little lemon juice

Cream together until well blended. Store covered in the fridge until required. Can be used with meat, fish, vegetables and on hot French bread.

Tarragon butter

> 4 oz/100g butter
> a little grated lemon peel and juice
> freshly ground black pepper
> 1 tablespoon tarragon, finely chopped

Cream together. Store covered until required. Use with grilled beef, and chicken.

Sauces

Pesto

> 1 large bunch basil
> 2–3 cloves garlic, peeled
> 1 oz/25g walnuts or pine nuts
> 2 fl. oz/75 ml olive oil
> 1 oz/25g Parmesan cheese

Combine the basil, garlic, nuts and cheese in a food processor or grinder, or pound them in a mortar to a fine paste, and gradually add in the olive oil. Excellent served with fresh pasta or grilled fish, or a spoonful will flavour a vegetable soup.

Tomato sauce

> 1 lb/450g ripe tomatoes, skinned and roughly
>   chopped
> a little olive oil and butter
> salt and pepper
> ½ teaspoon sugar
> 1 teaspoon basil, chopped

Cook the tomatoes in the oil and butter for a few minutes. Add the rest of the ingredients and cook for a further few minutes. Press through a nylon sieve. This purée can be used for flavouring soups or stews, filling omelettes, or thinned with a little red wine or stock for a tomato sauce.

Sorrel sauce

> a handful of sorrel leaves
> 1 oz/25g butter
> 4 tablespoons chicken stock
> ¼ pt/150 ml single cream
> salt and pepper

Wash and chop the sorrel finely and cook briefly in the melted butter. Gradually add the cream and the stock, stirring well. Season to taste. This, of course, can also be used as a basis for soup which becomes a treat in its own right. Fresh sorrel is one of the earliest of herbs to grow freely.

Sauce for seafood

½ pt/300 ml mayonnaise
2 tablespoons tomato ketchup
1 teaspoon tabasco or Worcester sauce
3 tablespoons olive oil
1 tablespoon wine vinegar
2 level tablespoons onion, finely grated
2 tablespoons parsley, finely chopped
1 tablespoon tarragon, chopped
6 tablespoons whipped cream
salt and pepper
pinch of cayenne pepper
1–2 tablespoons olives, chopped

Blend all the ingredients together and chill for 1–2 hours. Excellent with seafood, especially crab which could be mixed in with the sauce before serving with lettuce and tomatoes. Piled into avocado rings the effect is dramatic and most delicious.

STUFFING

*Stuffing for
turkey*

1 lb/450g breadcrumbs
4 oz/100g butter
grated rind of 1 lemon and a little lemon juice
4 tablespoons parsley, finely chopped
2 teaspoons mixed lemon thyme and marjoram,
    chopped
2 eggs, beaten

Mix all the ingredients thoroughly together. This simple herb-laden stuffing is equally good for chicken or capon. (The amount is suitable for a bird about 8–12 lb/4–6 kg.) It can also be spread on chops before grilling. It stores well in the freezer for up to three weeks.

PUDDINGS

Mint Sorbet

serves 4–6

1 bunch of mint of different sorts
¼ pt/150 ml water
juice of 1 lemon
4 oz/100g castor sugar
2 egg whites

Boil the sugar and water for 5 minutes and cool. Remove the mint leaves from the stalks and put them in the liquidizer with the syrup. Blend well and put the mixture through a nylon sieve. Add the strained lemon juice and freeze till just beginning to harden. Return it to the blender and blend well. Fold in the stiffly beaten egg whites and return to the freezer in an airtight box. Take it out of the freezer about 15 minutes before serving.

Rose Geranium Cream

This makes one of the most delicious of all puddings and, as rose geranium has to be brought indoors in winter, fresh leaves are available throughout the year.

½ pt/300 ml cream
8 oz/225g cream cheese
3 tablespoons sugar
3 sweet-scented geranium leaves

Add the sugar and the geranium leaves to the cream and heat very gently without boiling until the cream is completely heated through. Leave to cool and then stir in the cream cheese and leave in the fridge covered overnight. Remove the leaves before serving and mix the cream thoroughly to make it smooth. Serve with slightly acid fruit such as blackberries.

HERB BREADS

Dill Loaf

3 teaspoons dried yeast
4 tablespoons warm water
½ pt/300 ml sour cream
1 oz/25g butter
1 teaspoon sugar
2 teaspoons dill seed or green dill
2 teaspoons onion powder
2 teaspoons salt
1 egg
1½ lb/675g flour

Stir the yeast into the warm water and sugar and let it stand for 20 minutes. Warm the sour cream slightly with the butter, add to the yeast mixture. Beat in the dill seed, onion powder, salt and the egg. Stir this into the flour and knead well, the dough should be smooth. Cover with a plastic bag and put in a warm place to rise for 1–2 hours. Punch down and place in loaf tin and leave to rise again for about one hour. If left uncovered brush the top with water. Bake for 30–40 minutes at 350°F/180°C/gas mark 4. This mixture could also be shaped into rolls and then the cooking time reduced to 20 minutes. Freezes well.

Herb Bread Rolls

3 teaspoons dried yeast
1 tablespoon sugar
3 lb/1.35 kg flour, half white and half wholewheat
1½ pt/900 ml warm water
3 teaspoons salt
6 tablespoons melted butter
3 eggs
2 teaspoons each thyme and parsley, finely
*   chopped*
1 teaspoon celery seed

Mix the flour, herbs and salt in a large bowl and leave in a warm place. Dissolve the yeast in 3 tablespoons of warm water and stir in the sugar, leave it to rise for 10–20 minutes. Break the eggs and slightly beat them. Stir the yeast mixture, the melted butter and the eggs into the flour and add the water. When well mixed either knead the dough on a floured board or in a 'mixer' until the dough is smooth and satiny, adding more flour if necessary. Place in a greased bowl in a warm place, cover with a damp cloth or a plastic bag and leave until double the size, about 2 hours. Then punch the dough down and shape into rolls and place on a greased baking sheet. Brush with melted butter or milk and leave, again in a warm place, until double the size, about 1–2 hours. Bake at 400°F/200°C/gas mark 6 for 10–15 minutes. These rolls freeze well. Makes about 50 rolls.

Quick Welsh Rarebit

This mixture can be wrapped and kept in the fridge for use. The toasted cheese can be topped with a poached egg, grilled bacon, tomatoes or fried mushrooms.

serves 4

2 oz/50g butter
8 oz/225g finely grated cheddar cheese
2 level teaspoons English mustard (made up)
ground black pepper and a pinch of cayenne
4 tablespoons milk
2 teaspoons dill seed
4 slices bread

Cream the butter and then beat in the other ingredients. Toast one side of the bread only, trim off the crusts and spread the mixture thickly on the untoasted side. Brown under the grill.

Herb Vinegars

Most culinary herbs can be added to white wine vinegar and used in salad dressings, marinades, chutneys and pickles. Tarragon, mint, thyme and basil are all used in this way. Steep a sprig of a chosen herb in a little vinegar and add salt, mustard and a little oil and leave it for several hours before using as part of a salad dressing.

Vinegars for storing

Use about 1 pt/600 ml of vinegar to 8 tablespoons of slightly crushed or chopped herbs of one's choice; pour the warmed vinegar onto the herbs and place in a covered non-metallic container for 10 to 14 days in a warm place. Steeping time will vary with the intensity of the herb but after this time test for strength of flavour and if sufficient strain the vinegar. The liquid is then brought to the boil and poured into sterilized bottles. A few leafy sprigs or blossoms can be added too as decoration. Seal well with non-metallic caps and store in a cool place, in the dark if coloured vinegars are to remain bright.

Herbal Teas or Tisanes

The fresh or dried leaves of herbs have been popular for centuries for making teas or tisanes or to flavour regular teas. They are served hot or iced during or at the end of a meal to aid digestion. Many people now wishing to avoid caffeine dependence are replacing traditional tea and coffee with herbal drinks. Suitable herbs are prepared the same way as conventional tea. 1 teaspoon per cup of boiling water, covered and allowed to stand for 10 minutes before straining. Honey or sugar is added to taste, or lemon if a more tart flavour is preferred. Rosemary, mint, savory, camomile, rose geranium and lime flowers are some of the most frequently enjoyed.

Herb Wines

Herb wines have been consciously omitted from these recipes, but not only because of the very specific techniques required to get them right; there are books which provide excellent instruction. Fond memories of Great Aunt Clara's Cowslip Wine of incredible potency and the famous occasion when the Vicar fell down the front steps are apt to exaggerate alcoholic content, as well as the local incumbent's innocence: cowslips anyway ought never today to be gathered in the prodigal way they once were.

Nonetheless there are good herb-based wines if one can give the care required. Dandelion flowers, mulberry fruit (beautiful but somewhat emetic) and parsley can all be delicious. They can also be disgusting so are best left to those willing to devote time to their preparation and patience to their maturity. Thus the only alcoholic product offered here is Elder Flower Champagne. It is simple to make and quick to become drinkable; one of the treats of summer.

ELDER FLOWER CHAMPAGNE

1 lb/450g sugar
8 pints/14 l hot water
2 tablespoons vinegar
juice of 2 lemons
8 elder flower heads. (These must be chosen as
the florets open and before they develop the
feline fragrance of middle age.)

Put the sugar in a large plastic container and pour on the water. Stir until dissolved and add the vinegar and lemon juice. Leave to cool and then add the elder flower heads. Leave to steep for 24 hours.

Strain and pour into screw-top bottles such as strong cider flagons (but tonic bottles suffice). Store in a cool place for 8–10 days, when the champagne is ready for drinking. Care must be taken on opening the bottles as it can become not only effervescent but indeed explosive. This effect can be reduced if the bottle to be opened is well cooled in the refrigerator first.

After 8–10 days the bottle-tops should be unscrewed to release some gas and then retightened if the champagne is to be drunk at a later date. It is best kept for a maximum of 3–4 months but bottles forgotten in the cellar have still been good a year later.

FURTHER HINTS FOR HERBOPHILES

Coriander leaves chopped and sprinkled on stews, curries, fish dishes.

Fennel sliced raw into fish dishes.

French beans finished with chopped fresh *basil* leaves.

Young *nasturtium* leaves or flowers chopped into salads.

Cold potato salad with French dressing, a few sliced anchovies, chopped *chervil* or *parsley* and a little red wine mixed in with the diced potato.

Chopped *dill* added to cucumber soup.

Chives and *chervil* chopped and added to lettuce soup before serving.

Summer savory added to Jerusalem artichoke recipe helps reduce their explosive after effects. This has to be dried as the crops do not otherwise overlap.

Tomato sauce with chopped fresh *basil* and a few chopped anchovies used as the liquid for a soufflé.

Sorrel purée added to vegetable dishes or into an omelette.

Marinades made up with fresh herbs and frozen for use during the rest of the year. Well sealed and labelled jars facilitate easy identification.

Small trout cooked in a little water and on a bed of *mint* for 5 minutes and served cold.

When making crabapple jelly a leaf of *rose geranium* placed in the base of each jar before adding the jelly and sealing.

Parsley eaten with dishes containing garlic helps reduce the latter's after effects.

Juniper berries when marinading and then cooking hare or rabbit.

Herbs of one's choice added to the fat when frying croûtons.

For summer salad potatoes, when still warm from cooking, sprinkle with French dressing and *dill* seed, and serve warm or cold.

Fresh or even dried *bouquets garni* in preparation of stock. Vital for flavour and also for the smell of the kitchen when there seems to have been an excess of cooking.

Combine *oregano* and *basil* as herbal flavouring to green pepper soup.

Mussels opened live topped with a knob of *parsley* and *shallot* butter and grilled for three minutes.

3 tablespoons of chopped *mixed herbs* to ½ pint/300 ml of single cream and 3 eggs makes a quiche filling

A teaspoon each of chopped *thyme, parsley* and *chives* gently cooked with a pound of mushrooms.

Chopped *chives* added to diced hot beetroot.

Simple spaghetti dishes are enlivened by freshly gathered, chopped *parsley, chives, tarragon* and *oregano.*

A TO Z CATALOGUE OF HERBS

ISATIS
SATIVA

WOAD (Fuchs, 1542)

ACANTHUS MOLLIS BEAR'S BREECH

There are few herbaceous plants which offer so striking a pattern. That the leaves provided the motif for the carved decoration of letters on Corinthian columns is well known and it is this architectural attribute that makes this plant so beautiful in the herb garden, though its herbal use, even in early times, was not very important. The leaves were applied to burns rather as, no doubt, we still search for a dock leaf when stung by nettles. But why the common name of bear's breech?

From deeply rooting crowns the foliage unfurls like a huge cut-leaved hart's-tongue fern; a deep shining green. Even without flower the plant would earn its keep and in half-shade this has to suffice. But in full sun the 5 to 6-foot high flower-spikes shoot up packed with pink and white flowers. Individually these are somewhat foxglove-like, pink-tinged with white lips, held in a prickly calyx. The shape and texture of the spike remains effective in the garden scene long after the actual flowers are over.

As a plant from the western Mediterranean area, adapted to and enjoying heat and a quality of light that more northern climates cannot provide, *Acanthus* is understandably erratic in flower production. Yet, on the Scottish Solway coast it has become naturalized and flowers with abandon. Perhaps the perfect drainage of the sandy soil is significant.

Less effective in leaf is *Acanthus longifolius* (of gardens: botanically this is *A. balcanicus* or *A. hungaricus* – the last a nonsense name as it is not native to Hungary), but it is certainly a better plant for flower. Mr Christopher Lloyd says that it 'flowers abundantly in every site and season'. Almost equally free is *A. spinosus* from the eastern Mediterranean. Forms vary in the prickliness of the clumps of upright leaves, which, as with all acanthuses, are elegantly reflexed towards the tip.

As with *A. mollis*, if flowers are required, these are plants for full sun in well-drained spots where, when really happy, they can become almost invasive. They look marvellous in containers which prevent any such problem.

The flower spikes are excellent in winter arrangements but should be picked and dried when the flowers are newly opened if the needle-sharp bracts are not to be shed later indoors. Bare feet will quickly discover if this is so.

ACHILLEA MILLEFOLIUM MILFOIL, YARROW

Yarrow, milfoil, woundwort, carpenter's weed – the mere existence of this number (and doubtless others) of its common names indicates interest in this native plant. A noxious weed of any grass patch with pretensions to lawn status, it is nonetheless perfectly easy to keep in bounds when grown as a normal herbaceous plant in the herb garden.

The two last names indicate aspects of its herbal use and few plants have wider application, from alleviating colds and toothache to dysentery and coronary thrombosis.

The usual wild plant carries flat heads of tiny dull white flowers above its typically elegant and feathery dark leaves. Tinges of pink are not uncommon and more distinctive forms have been recorded and collected since John Gerard in the sixteenth century: 'Cerise Queen' and 'Fire King' are both good. The more desirable change in flower colour does not detract from herbal use.

Where the latter is of less significance it is valid to use hybrids of yarrow in the herb garden such as *Achillea* × *taygetea* and its lovely form 'Moonshine'. The feathery foliage is maintained but is grey-green, a perfect foil for the pale yellow heads. These plants associate well with pinks and purple-leaved sage and purple fennel. All flower throughout summer at a height of a couple of feet.

ACHILLEA PTARMICA SNEEZEWORT

Sneezewort, says Joseph Miller, in his *Botanicum Officinale* of 1722, in powder 'snuffed up the nose' causes sneezing, and cleanses the head of 'tough slimy humours'. Left in the garden the double forms – known long before Miller's time – are easy, decorative plants which succeed in the worst conditions. Heavy wet clay holds no terrors for this plant. Two-foot stems carry sprays of pure white buttons, longlasting both in the garden and when cut. 'Perry's White' and 'The Pearl' are named forms on offer. This is a simple cottage garden plant apt to be despised, quite unjustly.

ACONITUM NAPELLUS MONKSHOOD

A poison to which there is no known antidote: can there be any more daunting statement? Can there be any justification for growing a plant to which it applies? Yet this is monkshood, an ornament of cottage gardens since they were in existence, with its tall, imposing spikes of clear blue-hooded flowers towering up beside the currant bushes in summer and autumn.

This potentially lethal herb seems not to have been brought into medicinal use, at least in Britain, until the mid-eighteenth century, when its sedative and pain-killing powers were recognized. Danger of over-dosing was always present and its use declined to 'apply externally only to the affected spot' for sciatica and so on. That it is clearly not to be trifled with is emphasized by common names such as wolfsbane (for *Aconitum vulparia*, a bait-poison) and the knowledge that in ancient times it was an effective arrow-poison in eastern Asia.

However, none of this detracts from its beauty. *Aconitum napellus* itself, though fine enough (especially in cool northern gardens in its pink form 'Carneum'), is also the parent with other species of further good garden plants. These are grouped under the name of *A × bicolor*. They give a range of colours from white to thunder-purple and, just as important, a range of heights from 3 to 6 feet. Different in effect is wolfsbane, for here the narrow hooded flowers are pale horn-yellow.

All monkshoods have elegant divided foliage clothing the stems. Though not flowering until mid or late summer the first leaves push through the still chilly soil in late February. This is the only moment when these true aconites have any visual connection with winter aconite – that tiny golden chalice above its choir-boy ruff of green.

ACORUS CALAMUS SWEET FLAG

A proliferation of vernacular names indicates one of two facts about any plant. It either indicates a wide natural distribution within an area, with regional differences in language providing its many frequently visually descriptive names. Or, though not common in the wild or actually exotic, it may indicate that it has a large number of uses. In the case of *Acorus calamus* the latter is clearly the case: it seems to have originated in eastern Europe and adjoining Asia, being used in various ways, even before those regions obtained their names. Biblical references and those in Egyptian texts demonstrate its antiquity and thus it was well placed, as with so many herbs, to move westward with the progress of civilization.

Sweet flag, sweet sedge, myrtle flag, common calamus, true acorus (as distinct from the less medicinally desirable yellow flag, *Iris pseudacorus*) and, to add John Parkinson's evocative title, calamus of the shops, hint as to its herbal value. Predictable recommendations for 'obstructions of the liver and spleen, for the colick' and so on combine with commendations with which the least herbal-minded can easily concur. Joseph Miller (1722): 'It has a strong smell, not so pleasant while green, but growing more grateful and aromatic as it dries' making it fit as a strewing herb 'against pestilential contagious and corrupt noctious Air . . . and outwardly used in sweet bags and perfumes'.

It will be realized by now that this is an iris-like plant and, as one of the very few herbs happy to grow in (indeed preferring, if not insisting on) an inch or two of water it is an ideal water-edge subject for a herb garden pool. The long narrow leaves attain a couple of feet above their horizontal fleshy rhizomes: though the foliage is distantly aromatic when crushed, the rhizomes, orris-like, have the greatest virtue. For ornamental use the less vigorous variegated form, elegantly striped with green and cream, is by far the best.

In spite of every visual simile being towards irises, sweet flag is in fact a strange member of the arum family. The flower clusters, however, lack the enfolding spathe which is the showy part of most arum lilies and merely emerge from the side of a leaf-like stem (to quote Miller again) 'in shape like the Catkin of the Hazel or like long Pepper'.

A strange and intriguing plant well worth its place: if a pool proper is not available a shallow container will suffice or even moist soil on the shady side of the garden. The spear-like, vertical leaf-pattern of variegated sweet flag makes an excellent foil to the shapes of most herbs.

On a much smaller scale, the related *Acorus gramineus* is useful as a 6-inch high edging to beds of small herbs rather as chives are often used, but here the formality necessary for a bed-edge is more naturally maintained. In moist soil this little acorus accepts full sun but growth is more typical – like a little tussocky grass – in half-shade. The whole plant is distantly fragrant and the fresh or dried roots are used in the Orient (whence it comes) for, amongst other things, stomach pains.

ACTAEA spp BANEBERRY

It is unusual for transatlantic medicinal herbs not to have been translated into European pharmacapoeias, and vice versa, but this seems to be the case with the North American actaeas. It may be that the Indian name 'cohosh' merely preceded by a colour (see also *Cimicifuga*) causes confusion amongst the half dozen plants that bear it: or perhaps the Old World never tamed their undoubtedly dangerous properties.

In spite of this they were well known to the native peoples of what became New England and eastern Canada and this love was adapted by many colonists. One group of the latter, particularly receptive to such traditional knowledge, were the Shakers who had gone to America from England in 1776 'to found a society free of crime, poverty and misery (and) were devoted to living their lives by natural principles' (*Shaker Herbs* by Amy Bess Miller). Herb gathering, and later growing, became one of their major sources of economic wealth.

Several cohosh herbs, with various recommended uses appear in the first printed catalogue, dated 1830. This came from Watervliet, one of the earliest settled communities, and printed on its cover was the evocative couplet:

'Why send to Europe's bloody shores
For plants which grow by our own doors?'

Both *Actaea alba* and *A. rubra* are forest floor plants where, as the sugar maple leaf canopy begins to unfold above, they make elegant plants (the first up to 2 feet or so in height, the other rather less) of ferny leaves topped by a fuzz of white flowers. The effect is short-lived but within a few weeks the berried display develops which is maintained until autumn. As deep woodlanders they are valuable in the shadiest spot in leafy soil a herb garden can provide: the sort of spot which has been the bane of many a herb gardener.

Perhaps it is suitable that baneberry is one of the alternative names for actaea. *A. alba* is also called Noah's ark and necklace weed: at least the latter name is explicable as each pea-sized fruit is held like a pearl set onto a red-enamelled stem; heads hold up to two dozen berries. The effect is quite unique. *Actaea rubra* carries a head of scarlet berries, while *A. spicata* (rather surprisingly a European and rather British native where locally it is known as herb christopher) has privet-black berries.

Though the medicinally used part is the root, it is, of course, the attractive fruits which could be a danger to anyone foolish (or greedy) enough to eat a number of them.

ACTINIDIA CHINENSIS KIWI FRUIT

It is perhaps not surprising that Chinese gooseberry or, as it is now commonly called, kiwi fruit, has no herbal tradition in Britain. By the time it was introduced in 1900 plant-based medication was at an all-time low (it might be noted that the Society of Apothecaries finally gave up its famous and historic Chelsea Physic Garden in the previous year) and new plants were for long unconsidered from this point of view.

However, though seldom fruiting well in Britain it has much to offer as an ornamental, twining up high walls or up trees and making a fine pattern of great hairy leaves. Small scented white flowers appear in summer and, on selected clones, the brown egg-shaped hairy fruits follow; deliciously sharp-flavoured – hence the gooseberry part of its English name. It makes, therefore, a most unusual herb garden resident.

In its native China all parts of the plant are used medicinally in decoction for such diverse ills as gall-stones and cancer of the liver.

ADONIS VERNALIS

Adonis, it will be remembered, was the beautiful youth who, in Greek mythology, was bred by Venus (Aphrodite). He was killed whilst out hunting by a boar and from drops of his blood sprang up the blood red pheasant eye, *Adonis annua* (*A. autumnalis*).

This lovely little annual – a frequent cornfield edge weed in Mediterranean countries – might, by extension, be grown in the herb garden but it is its bigger spring-flowering relation which earns its place medicinally.

Adonis vernalis is also a far more visually important plant. The effect is somewhat like that of *Pulsatilla* (with which it shares similar, highly poisonous glycosides). In early spring fat flower buds cluster at ground level – where they are apt to be prey to greedy and insensitive slugs. Quickly the stems extend and the golden-yellow flowers open, backed by a haze of love-in-a-mist-like bracts. After the display is over the foliage develops more fully and makes a bright foot-high fuzz for the rest of the season: small twigs should be pushed into the soil round the developing leaves to prevent their falling outwards and spoiling the symmetry.

AEGAPODIUM PODAGRARIA GROUND ELDER

To suggest that Bishop's weed or ground elder, one of the most noxious weeds of European gardens, should be consciously cultivated, seems akin to recommending horticultural hara-kiri. Perhaps it should be mentioned in this context that twitchgrass, or couchgrass, *Agropyron repens* also 'has played a long and important role as a medicinal herb' (*Encyclopedia of Herbs and Herbalism*). Certainly no-one would ever plant the typical green-leaved form of either with their questing underground runners.

But, though vigorous, the white-variegated variant of ground elder is a perfectly acceptable garden plant (though one should watch out for a possible reversion to the unacceptable). In North America, especially, it is a frequent edging or ground cover plant planted round the boles of established trees, objecting neither to the shade nor the drought that such a position inevitably implies. There it looks bright and fresh throughout spring and summer.

Its herb garden validity is indicated by another common name, gout weed which merely translates the Latin: *podagra* = gout. Traditionally it was boiled up to make a drink to aid sufferers of that complaint. More simply, ground elder is a pot herb; the young leaves make an acceptable early spring alternative to spinach.

AGASTACHE FOENICULUM GIANT HYSSOP

In Britain the giant hyssops, as *Agastache* is sometimes known, are uncommon. In North American herb gardens they are expected members, and rightly so. All are tall ornamental labiates, rather like their close cousins, the bergamots; but instead of the bergamots distinctly whorled habit of flowering, the agastaches have showy terminal spikes.

The subject of this entry is the most typical and most valuable, as its range of descriptive common names indicates: anise hyssop, blue giant hyssop, fennel hyssop, fragrant giant hyssop. This is a fine, perfectly hardy plant making a strong 3-foot high clump, at its best in late summer. It revels in rich soil. Bees love its flowers and the pale-backed leaves, fresh or dried, are used for flavouring and to make a refreshing tea. Like borage they can be added to summer fruit cups. Surprisingly, neither it nor the similar *A. scrophulariifolia* are mentioned in the literature of Shaker herbs.

Further species, good for herb garden decorative effect, are native to the southern States and Mexico and thus are less hardy. However, with good drainage in a sunny spot *A. cana* (the mosquito plant) which is a two-footer with pink flowers and *A. mexicana*, scarlet, should survive most winters. The first of these is also known as *Cedronella cana* indicating its resemblance to the plant to which the genus Cedronella really belongs – this is *Cedronella canariensis*, a monospecific genus, native, as its name suggests, to the Canary Islands and Madeira. Canary balm (or balm of Gilead, a title attached to several plants) is a wide spreading subshrub up to 5 feet high. The trifoliate hairy leaves, intensely aromatic with a lemony fragrance, are topped by spikes of pink to blue flowers in mid-summer. Canary balm grows well in light soil at the Chelsea

Physic Garden but in the numerous less favoured gardens it would be wise to overwinter rooted cuttings as one would any frost-sensitive exotic used for summer bedding.

AGAVE AMERICANA

Anyone who has holidayed on the Mediterranean coast will have marvelled at the vast 'cactus'-like plants with steel-speared leaves and towering flower spikes. Surprise is often lavished upon plants which, though maintaining the dramatic architectural effect, have been dead for several years. These are 'century plants' which though not literally taking a hundred years to flower are known botanically as monocarpic perennials; plants which take a decade or two to build up a sufficiently strong rosette and then burst upon an unsuspecting world with a 20-foot high fountain of flowers.

Such an effect is perhaps too barbaric for the usual garden scene and indeed the plant is only likely to develop fully in Britain's warmest gardens – such as at Tresco, on the Isles of Scilly or Glendurgan, a National Trust property in southern Cornwall.

But as a pot plant, so long as it can be given light, near frost-free conditions during winter (such as a spare bedroom windowsill – so long as no guest is expected!) it is invaluable to stand out in the herb garden in summer. The succulent leaf-pattern, both in the typical grey-green form and its striped variant, is superb both in general effect and observed closely when the exact imprint of each spiny leaf can be seen moulded upon its inner and outer neighbour.

To appreciate fully agave's herbal connection it is necessary to refer to its Mexican homeland. There it is invaluable: a purgative, an insecticide, to be rubbed on burns (as aloe is in Africa), used like soapwort to wash clothes (it contains a soap-forming ingredient) and, when all is done, the fermented juice produces *pulque*, a traditional Mexican tipple. With so wide a range of uses it will be agreed that *Agave* deserves its trisyllabic pronunciation: *agavos* is Greek for admirable.

AGRIMONIA EUPATORIA AGRIMONY

According to Joseph Miller 'this is the Eupatorium of Dioscorides, Galen and the ancient Greeks ... Some Authors will have this plant call'd *Eupatorium quasi hepatorium*, from its usefulness to the Liver; others will have its Name deriv'd from Mithradates Eupator (once King of Persia), who as Pliny says, first found out its virtue'.

All this sounds very grand in praise of a common roadside plant of our chalk and limestone uplands with its spikes of yellow flowers above strawberry-like leaves but, though those early herbalists used it greatly ('serviceable for all Diseases') it is an unexciting thing in a modern garden. The flowers are fleeting, replaced only too soon by burrs – to the plants' if not the owners' satisfaction.

AILANTHUS ALTISSIMA TREE OF HEAVEN

The number of trees which may legitimately be employed in a herb garden of hardy plants is so small that those available are well worth consideration. Tree of Heaven has two particular virtues. As a quick growing, elegant shade tree it accepts extreme cold and atmospheric pollution with impunity; it may also be pruned to a near-ground level root-stock from which man-high shoots will rocket each spring, carrying pinnate leaves like those of a wonderfully exaggerated walnut. The pattern is superb – both in detail with pink-flushed petioles – and in the mass, especially when its architectural shadows fall against a plain washed wall.

The mature tree will attain full forest-tree size and if there is space for such a plant the female plant should be obtained if at all possible. Rosy heads of fruit (each like an ash 'key') add to the late summer interest: unfortunately the necessary male flower heads smell somewhat foetid.

While one should always be chary of planting trees of this size close to buildings (and never on clay soils) one is always amazed, and delighted, to see huge trees of Heaven in tiny London yards (and other cities across the temperate world) posing no problem to plant nor building. The effect is invariably superb.

Introduced from China to Britain by Peter Collinson in the 1750's, it was a hundred years later in France that the bark was 'discovered' to be of use in the treatment of dysentery, asthma and other ills. Unacceptable side-effects however make it no longer used in the west. Employment in Chinese medicine, especially against chronic dysentery, both predates and extends our own rather transient use.

AJUGA REPTANS BUGLE

Bugle in Britain is not the bugle of North American herb gardens – there the name refers to species of *Lycopus* (gypsyweed). The European expectation is of a low creeping plant making an un-

dulating quilt of shining, ground-covering leaves from which grow
spikes of flowers 6 or more inches high on the typical square stem of
a labiate. Purple-blue dead-nettle flowers appear in whorls, each
whorl supported by a pair of leaf-like bracts carefully placed at right-
angles to the next.

At close quarters bugle has quiet charm but its particular use is
as a foil for other, bigger plants around which it will creep, entirely
hiding the soil (which is excellent; soil is a medium for growing
plants in, seldom an aesthetic experience in its own right). The wild
green form is perfectly acceptable in the garden but the shining,
metallic, 'Atropurpurea' is even better, maintaining its colour best
in full sun. The beautiful 'Variegata' has marbled leaves of grey-
green and white; it is less vigorous and needs at least half-shade if it
is not to bleach. All forms enjoy a reasonably moist soil at all times
of year – as anyone would guess having met the green one in damp
woodland rides.

An early alternative name is mentioned: carpenter's herb, in
reference to its supposed ability to staunch wounds from a slipped
chisel or saw. Internal bleeding was also so treated. 'The juice of this
plant is esteemed good for internal bruises' says Sir John Hill in his
Family Herbal, the words hinting that he had not tried it himself.

AKEBIA TRIFOLIATA

Neither this, nor the very similar *A. quinata* (with three and five
leaflets respectively) appear in European herb books. The latter was
introduced to Britain by Robert Fortune in 1845 while its relation
followed fifty years later: that no common name has developed here
indicates a certain lack of use. But in China, where it is known (in
translation of course) as August melon and, not very pleasantly, as
hog's kidneys, both vegetative growth and the fruit have herbal
application for, amongst other uses, encouraging milk flow in
nursing mothers.

There are so few herb garden climbers that *Akebia* is to be
welcomed. It is a semi-evergreen twiner which will easily reach a
dozen feet in height. Alternatively it makes admirable ground cover,
even in deep shade. Flowers are carried in short spikes opening in
late March or April with the developing new foliage. It will be
observed that male and female flowers share the same stem. But this,
unfortunately, in no way guarantees the appearance of the strange
fruit. These, when they come, are an autumn treat, looking like fat
gherkins that have been pickled in blackberry juice. The white pulp
inside is pleasantly sweet.

ALCEA ROSEA (ALTHAEA ROSEA) HOLLYHOCK

The inevitable association between herbs and cottage gardens where traditional simple and old-fashioned flowers flourish amongst the gooseberry bushes is epitomized by the paintings of Helen Allingham and other members of the late nineteenth-century 'Surrey School'. These somewhat saccharine effusions with pinafored children of improbable cleanliness are almost inevitably framed in hollyhocks. The height and general effect of these is, however, happily correct: the range of colours, the elegant spire-like outline, the open mallow flowers of the singles or the formal rosettes of the doubles make them as desirable in a modern gardener's palette as in any artist's of earlier times.

Hollyhocks were introduced into Europe in the late Middle Ages from Asia Minor but may have originated further east: they are now naturalized over many parts of the world giving a selection varying in flower colour from pale yellow, through pinks and reds to deep vinous purple. The original plant was a shortlived perennial and, if mallow rust can be kept at bay, garden plants may still occasionally behave so. But a biennial habit is more common and strains now available, sown under glass in February, can be treated as annuals. These will only attain half the height of the 10 feet possible of the old types but give valuable strength to a new garden.

Hollyhocks need a well-drained soil in a spot which gets some protection from wind. To see them towering up over old-fashioned roses with pinks and peonies in front, and backed perhaps by a rosy brick or old knapped flint wall is to evoke (however idealistically) summer gardens of times past.

Medicinally the typical mucilage of the roots of many *Malvaccae* was the main constituent of value. The plant still provides a tisane for chest complaints.

ALCHEMILLA spp LADIES MANTLE

'The good women in the North of England apply the leaves to their breasts, to make them recover their form, after they have been swelled with milk. Hence it has got the name of Ladies' Mantle'. So states Sir John Hill who recommends its use also for those frightening 'bloody fluxes' so common in eighteenth-century medical literature. The *Compendious Herbal* at the beginning of the century commends it for even more evocative ills, Traumatick Apozems.

Modern commentators (see *Encyclopedia of Herbs and Herbalism*) suggest that ladies mantle developed a reputation in the

Middle Ages out of proportion to its actual use, although this was increased by the fact that the funnel-shaped folded leaves caught the morning dew (*Alchemilla* = little magical one) which was itself a valuable constituent of many medicines. The lowland *Alchemilla vulgaris* and the upland species, *A. alpina* both with soft downy leaves and heads of greenish flowers are the plants of the herbals and are the ones to be grown if verisimilitude is important.

But from a visual point of view a bigger plant from Asia Minor is the best garden plant. This is the lovely *Alchemilla mollis*, which arrived too late for effective assumption of magical properties. Here the grey-green velvet leaves support a mound of lime-green flowers in early summer. It takes any spot in shade or sun, seeding into cracks of paving and retaining walls. Deadheading may be desirable if it is not to overstay its welcome but spare seedlings are usually welcomed by anyone who sees it. It looks superb billowing about the base of a statuesque clump of angelica.

ALLIUM spp CHIVES, GARLIC, ONIONS ETC.

As pot herbs, vegetables, medicines and garden ornaments the onions have much to offer. Varying in height from a few inches to a few feet the growth pattern is distinctive; linear, often inflated leaves, from which a hollow stem arises to carry a spherical head of small flowers. Many are most beautiful bulbous plants and though this description does not apply to those of most use herbally, as herb associates they are admirable.

Visually, garlic (*Allium sativum*) does not offer much but has the garden advantage of maintaining a link between one year and the next, emphasizing the fact that the seasonal cycle never ceases. Traditionally garlic cloves (the small divisions of the bulb) are planted on the shortest day of the year and harvested on the longest. Certainly late autumn planting gives a far superior crop than if one waits till spring. Rotating the ground, that vacated by garlic (and a square yard is ample for all but the most extravagant alliophiles) is perfect for an August sowing of chervil. In spite of this ease of growth (well-drained soil provided) it is still apt to be thought that garlic from abroad is better, or the only possible. In this context we have not moved far in 250 years. 'Garlick is call'd the Countryman's Treacle', says Joseph Miller, 'though it is not used nigh so much in England as it is in Foreign Parts'. Only in recent years have the British accepted garlic as a valuable flavouring for so many dishes though maybe some atavistically fear that 'If Garlick be applied to the soles of the feet, the breath will stink of it.' (*The Compleat Herbal of Physical Plants* by John Pechey, 1694.)

Like conventional herb garden onions, garlic is not expected to flower; it does so only at the expense of the bulb. Egyptian or tree onions have the strange habit of developing bulbils on their flowering umbels which, as they swell, weigh down the stems so that eventually, meeting the ground, the cluster of bulbils and roots makes a further clump. Nothing, obviously could be easier to propagate. These are little more than amusing oddities, though on occasion useful as flavouring when normal onions are unavailable (April and May are the usual empty months when the stored crop is over – no-one ever grows enough onions – and the new crop, even the Japanese August sown one, is not ready). Much more valuable both in the kitchen and in the garden, are chives, *Allium schoenoprasum*. This charming little tussock makes bright early leaf growth – grist to the scissors of those gathering material for a spring *omelette aux fines herbes*. It is soon replaced and accompanied by copious 9-inch heads of purple flowers which make a show for weeks, especially if the plants are kept moist. Chives form charming semi-formal edging to beds of herbs.

Allium tuberosum is Chinese chives, which has flat leaves and flowers, each white with a black eye. It can be used similarly indoors and out.

All onions when bruised have the typical smell of their tribe, though some of the flowers are charmingly perfumed; and hence, could be used as flavouring but one feels to eat some would be almost akin to gobbling down larks' tongues. Among the most attractive for herb garden use are *A.schubertii* and *A. christophii* with melon-sized spheres of flowers on 2-foot high stems. When the starry flowers open, purple and pink respectively, the effect is of a firework preserved in mid-explosion. They look particularly well with lavenders and santolinas and other grey-leaved shrublets. The smaller *A. narcissiflorum* and *A. pulchellum*, to continue the image, are at the stage when the cascade of stars begins to fall to earth. All these and many other ornamental onions flowers are excellent as part of dried arrangements.

ALNUS GLUTINOSA COMMON ALDER

Common alder (not to be confused with elder) is one of our most beautiful trees. Accepting and enjoying moist soil it is a frequent riverside plant making, in the west and north, considerable stands with individual specimens attaining 70 or 80 feet in height.

Flowering and fruiting is distinctive with long purple-brown male catkins opening and shedding pollen in early spring: the tiny female flowers are carried in cones which, as the seeds mature and ripen, become woody and thimble-sized. The pattern in winter against a low sun is delightful with the cones of one year held against the developing catkins of the next.

In spite of its natural propensity for water alder will take much drier conditions where it makes a small gnarled specimen, not overwhelming in a herb garden position.

Alder, containing tannins, appears in all the early herbals, sometimes confused with alder buckthorn, (*Frangula alnus*) but says Miller, 'It is rarely used'. It is valuable for the range of colours it produces: green catkins; pink fresh wood; yellow young shoots; various red and black bark.

ALOE VERA

There are about 250 species of aloes native to arid areas of southeast and south Africa. Though varying in size from ground-hugging plants to small trees, they all show effective and necessary adaptation to drought, their thick fleshy leaves arranged in rosettes. From these spikes of red and yellow the flowers, rather like a delicately diffuse red hot poker, push up on smooth bare stems.

Only the little *A. aristata* has any chance of surviving a normal English winter, the Isles of Scilly excepted, of course, where in the garden of Tresco Abbey aloes hang out over old stone walls making a fine, if barbaric pattern.

But like *Agave*, a pot of *Aloe vera* (*vera* = true; the true medicinal bitter aloes) makes an excellent focal point standing out from May to October. Though armed, it is not so aggressively eye-gouging as *Agave*. A fine clump can build up over the years without needing repotting; a summer feed or two will maintain health and vigour. Any small rosette taken off will root and such a plant kept on a kitchen window sill is valuable in two ways; to ensure an overwintering stock if the spare-bedroom specimen succumbs, and to be immediately to hand in case of burns. A broken leaf applied at once is extraordinarily comforting.

As a medicinal plant aloes have been used at least since the fourth century BC and they are still commercially grown.

Joseph Miller describes the eighteenth-century method of obtaining the necessary abstract; 'it is made by gently pressing the Leaves pluck'd from the Roots, stroaking them downwards, by which the bitter juice, which is contain'd in particular Veins, drops into Vessels set under, and having stood all Night, the thin Liquor is pour'd off and the Sediment is dry'd and harden'd in the Sun, which is our Aloes'.

It should be emphasized that, apart from the external application of a part of a leaf, aloes are not for home medication.

The famed bitter properties have, of course, passed into many languages as the classical opposite of sweetness. ('La côte d'Adam contient plus d'aloes que de miel' a suitably chauvinist remark from the French.) Pronunciation is apt to cause confusion; the genus *Aloe* has three syllables, the common name spelled the same has two.

ALOYSIA TRIPHYLLA (LIPPIA CITRIODORA) LEMON VERBENA

The specific epithet of the synonym is repeated in the wholly satisfactory common name, lemon verbena. This is a Chilean shrub, not very hardy, coarse in leaf, and when in occasional flower (when it bothers) quite undistinguished – a combination of attributes which might be thought to place it at the bottom of anyone's hundred best herbs. Yet it is near the top. For its rough-textured narrow leaves have one of the most delicious lemon scents available, warm, rich and strong: a few crumbs left to dry in a coat pocket and discovered months later will evoke perfectly the moment and place of their picking.

Lemon verbena needs a light, warm soil (it is very happy on chalk) and, in all but the mildest gardens, a sheltered sunny wall as well. Alternatively it can be grown in a large pot and overwintered indoors. Like old specimen pelargoniums or fuchsias it can be pruned back and almost (but not quite) dried off. Then with lengthening days, spraying the top with warm water will bring it gently into growth ready in a few weeks to be stood out when frosts are over.

The leaves are used to make a tea, pleasant and effective against nausea. They are also obviously invaluable in pot pourri and scented sachets. Lemon verbena is an essential plant in every herb garden which deserves the title.

ALTHAEA OFFICINALIS MARSHMALLOW

Marshmallows, those deliciously squidgy pink and white cubes or cylinders dusted with icing sugar are known to children of every age. One wonders how many still derive from the charming plant which is not given the herb garden place its beauty deserves.

From a strong and almost woody root-stock marshmallow makes a robust 4-foot high clump, softly greyish green and downy in all its parts. Unobtrusive pea sticks pushed in and around the clump when it is only a foot high ensure that it does not break open. Rather small grey-lavender mallow flowers are carried for a long period from early summer on. The whole effect is gentle, making a fine foil for the striking shapes of, say, Madonna lilies or vivid colours of bergamots and giant hyssops.

Both the young shoots and roots can be eaten but its commercial uses – for the sweetmeat and for medicine – are solely from the latter.

AMARANTHUS spp

The most important species medicinally, at least in western medicine, is *A. hypochondriacus*. A rapidly growing annual up to 3 or 4 feet high, it resembles in flower a vertical love-lies-bleeding (*A. caudatus*, a close relative with similar attributes), varying in flower-spike colour from green to a rich red-purple with the texture of a Victorian plush-covered sofa. It was this colour that gave rise to the belief that amaranth would staunch bleeding. Today its mucilage content makes it of use in a gargle for mouth ulcers though in its native Central America its application is much wider. The seeds of this and other species have been important sources of flour cereals in their countries of origin for thousands of years.

For ornament their speed and ease of growth and bulk make them valuable in new gardens. A green tasselled form of *A. caudatus* is particularly attractive. Sown *in situ* in late March they usually come up like mustard and cress: effective thinning is essential. These can be eaten as a spinach substitute though they are pretty bland.

AMPELOPSIS BREVIPEDUNCULATA SNAKE GRAPE

The plant in cultivation under this name is a splendidly rampageous tendril-climber with hop-like leaves. Lush and green during summer they colour well in autumn when, if the season is sufficiently extended, they are then joined by the ripening fruit with exotic effect. For unlike the dark-bloomed berries of most grapes, in this Chinese species they are a brilliant blue. Draping a tree in a warm spot or clothing a wall, the snake or mountain grape closes the season with a flourish.

In China *Ampelopsis* is recommended for the treatment of

abscesses, boils and bruises: fruits, leaves or roots are crushed and a decoction made for external bathing of the wound.

There is a charming variegated form with pink and white splashed leaves: often grown as a house plant it seems hardy enough outside. It is especially attractive when pot grown and put out in a wall urn in summer to cascade down the sides.

ANAGALLIS ARVENSIS SCARLET PIMPERNEL

Scarlet pimpernel is, in detail, one of our most beautiful wild plants. It is a weak annual which in dull weather could be passed over as a poor bit of chickweed. But, come the sun, the warm brick-red flowers open and glisten like rubies amongst the shining leaves, hence the charming names of poor man's weatherglass and shepherd's clock.

This relative of the primulas is very poisonous yet has been used from classical times to the nineteenth century for a wide range of mainly mental disorders: even now its active constituents are not entirely understood. Simpler, but less importantly, pimpernel water was reputed to dispel freckles.

This, the typical plant, will be grown by those whose herb garden is to be fully authentic: a blue-flowered variant of scarlet pimpernel causes only slight confusion. Both can be sown *in situ* in spring. But more visually effective and not stretching authenticity too far is the superb *Anagallis monellii*. Each flower is bright glaring gentian-blue and bigger than a penny piece. Good soil, well drained – such as one would sow carrots in – will give a marvellous summer show in the front of a herb patch.

ANEMONE spp

As a highly ornamental garden genus *Anemone* is difficult to beat, offering as it does such a wide range of form – woodland carpeters for early spring, rarified alpines, robust perennials for the late summer herbaceous border. For convenience the pasque-flowers, often separated into their own genus, *Pulsatilla*, and the *Hepatica*, have been included here. Like so many of the *Ranunculaceae* the anemones contain highly poisonous glycosides and other constituents and should be confined to herb garden decoration.

The earliest to flower is *Hepatica americana (triloba)*. Native to the whole eastern side of North America from Florida in the south to Nova Scotia in the north, its wiry flower stems emerge from woodland leaf-litter often only a few feet from declining snow banks. Usually less than 6 inches high the cup-shaped flowers can be of white, pink or several shades of blue. The mottled three-lobed leaves, purple backed, develop with the declining flowers.

It is this leaf in the shape of a liver which, following the teaching of the medieval Doctrine of Signatures, provides both its name and its major use. The Shakers' common names follow directly: noble liverwort, kidney liver leaf (hedging their bets) and liverleaf. (A similar association, but botanically confusing, is Joseph Miller's adjoining entry, *Hepatica vulgaris*, which he calls common liverwort. This is in fact the moss-related bryophyte, *Pellea*.)

Hepaticas make charming front line plants on decent soil which does not dry out: more striking, though of doubtful herb garden validity is the eastern European *H. transsilvanica*.

The pasque group includes what must be some of the loveliest of all flowers – a pretty tall claim for such short plants. *Pulsatilla vulgaris*, or *Anemone pulsatilla* is a rare British native: legend has it that where it grows the blood of Danes was shed, which must give some connection between blood and chalk. (Were battles against the Norse invader concentrated on the dry grassy chalklands of Newmarket and Royston Heaths, the Ridgeway and Malborough Downs?)

Fortunately the plant does not insist on such esoteric fertilizer in the garden. Though preferring lime, any well-drained spot in full sun will suit it. Its spring growth is a marvellous progression when, sometimes in late February, the brown root-stock seems to burst as a dozen or more spheres, veiled in long hairs which hold the dew and glint in the early morning sun, slowly lift above the soil. In some forms they open at a couple of inches high, though some are taller, to upward facing flowers of considerable substance, rich royal purple petals enclosing a golden boss of stamens. Other colour forms exist: all are lovely but none more beautiful than the type.

When pollination is complete the flowers become nodding, the petals drop and silky seed heads develop, around which the summer-long carroty leaves appear. From seed sown at once young plants will begin to flower in two years. It is hardly possible to have too many – but for ornament only. The fierce glycoside causes violent convulsions.

Anemone vitifolia is a rare plant in gardens but as a part of the delightful 'Japanese anemone' we all know it could hardly be more common nor more useful. The extremely vigorous, typical plant of *A.* × *hybrida* (*A. hupehensis japonica* × *A. vitifolia*) is a vital part of any autumn border, with other herbaceous plants or amongst shrubs. Four feet or so is not uncommon, with a display of great pink saucers from August onward above the vine-like leaves it inherits from its Chinese parent.

Although extremely poisonous, this is the plant used medicinally in China, against malaria and eye ailments. A bit of fresh root applied to the pain is recommended there for toothache.

ANETHUM GRAVEOLENS DILL

Dill is yet another of that race of umbellifers, similar yet distinct, that makes a collection of herbs so interesting. Visually dill is very much like a slender fennel with its filigree of leaves and flat heads of dull yellow flowers. But distinct from fennel's short-lived perennial habit, the annual plant is normally unbranched until the umbels are reached. It needs to be grown therefore as a clump, the seeds sown *in situ* in March or April. Thinned to 6 inches apart each way, they are then robust enough to hold each other up. As a natural weed of Mediterranean cornfields it needs the help its fellows can give.

Dill is still a constituent of gripe-water for young children's use but it is as a common flavouring that the leaves, fresh or dried, and the seeds come into their own: it is quite distinct. Dill-flavoured cucumbers are commonly enjoyed yet it is forgotten that the original combination was less for the taste than for the herb to 'correct their windiness'. Adult gripe-water therefore.

ANGELICA ARCHANGELICA

Angelica is one of the noblest of herbs. Whether at the start of the season when the yard-wide clump of fretted leaves seems to develop by the day, or soon after when the melon-sized spheres of its compound umbels are seen against an early summer sky, the garden effect is of the very first order. Even when by late July the leaves decline and the chartreuse-green of the umbels turns to a sere straw-yellow the pattern is maintained, acting as a backdrop and foil to its fellows.

Angelica looks superb in any position but is particularly good in an association with other plants with striking leaves – hostas, *Acanthus*, *Macleaya* and so on. There is only one disadvantage: angelicas usually behave as biennials so that if a conscious arrangement is planned its regeneration must be carefully contrived.

Not that propagation, as such, is the slightest problem. Each flower stem produces many hundreds of seeds and almost all seem to germinate if sown as soon as ripe: self-sown seedlings are always available from August on – but for full development they must be in their permanent positions by the following spring. Even plants most carefully maintained in pots are apt to fail to reach the statuesque 6 feet of free grown specimens.

As a garden plant therefore (and for dried arrangements indoors) angelica is of great worth and as a herb its diversity is as marked. To those old enough to have known the real thing the scent of a bruised stem or leafstalk is immediately evocative of the pale green candied angelica on the tops of cakes. The bright emerald, apparently plastic, alternative of today cannot compare. Though it cannot be picked out individually from amongst the others used, angelica is an important flavouring agent in liqueurs such as Benedictine. The origin of such cordials was, of course, medicinal so that angelica's use is not surprising. To quote Joseph Miller: 'Angellica cordial, Alexipharmick, of great Use in malignant pestilential Fevers, in all contagious Distempers, and the Plague itself'.

Other species of angelica are recommended: *A. atropurpurea* by the Shakers in North America, and *A. pubescens* and *sylvestris* in China. None, however, are as ornamental as this.

ANTHRISCUS CEREFOLIUM CHERVIL

So popular is parsley in Britain (even to the extent of fabricating a plastic imitation for decorating butchers' slabs) and so apparently vital for almost every dish that it is surprising that the similar chervil is not more commonly grown. In France it is considered invaluable as a delicate flavouring herb, especially for winter use because it is easy to obtain fresh, and as every cook knows (French or otherwise) no dried culinary herb can be compared to its living state. Almost every recipe for a mixture of *fines herbes* includes *cerfeuil*.

Chervil is one of several slender annual 'cow parsleys' (umbellifers). A single plant is a poor thing visually but a scattering of seeds over a couple of square feet gives a bright green ferny heap of leaves topped by flat heads of tiny white flowers. Frequent sowings in good soil will provide leaves for picking at almost any season: sown in August or September seedlings will overwinter for the earliest outdoor supply. This can be preceded by kitchen-window pots.

One clump outside, in a not too obvious spot, should be allowed to ripen seed for next year.

APOCYNUM CANNABINUM INDIAN PHYSIC, INDIAN HEMP

Any hardy plant with a prefix 'Indian' is likely to need a pre-prefix of 'Red' to indicate its North American origin. This plant was introduced to the early settlers and the Shakers employed it for fevers, pneumonia and dropsy: certainly it acts as a powerful heart stimulant. But, as with most of its family, it is also highly poisonous.

Nonetheless Indian physic is an elegant perennial up to 5-feet high with diffuse heads of little white flowers followed by striking seed pods which hang down in pairs like inflated tweezers. An interesting addition to any collection of medicinal or economic plants – the alternative name of Indian hemp refers to its stem fibres being used to fabricate ropes and twine.

Grown from seed (more likely to be available than plants) it will reach flowering size in two years. It has an invasive root.

AQUILEGIA VULGARIS COLUMBINE, GRANNY'S BONNET

This is one of those charming plants which seems to epitomize the true country cottage garden. Quaint spurred flowers in a range of colours from white, through pink to deep purple are held on wiry stems above maiden-hair leaves. However common they are, columbines never cease to be a delight.

Yet in spite of this simple image the plant contains glycosides and alkaloids which are extremely poisonous to man, although it has been used homoeopathically and, quoting Joseph Miller, 'The leaves are used in Gargarisms (gargles) for sore mouths, and inflammations of the mouth and throat'. But as no-one is likely to eat it there need be little concern.

For herb garden ornament aquilegias can be sown *in situ* one year and they will flower the next. A better use of the space, however, is to sow a short nursery row and put them out in their flowering quarters, preferably in semi-shade, in late autumn rather as one would wallflowers or polyanthuses. Immediate deadheading will prolong flowering from May into July and prevent the exuberant seeding which can be a nuisance amongst more delicate things.

ARBUTUS UNEDO STRAWBERRY TREE

When it does well there are few more distinguished evergreens than this: lustrous leaves are held on black branches, but as these age the bark flakes off to reveal rusty-red patches (stretching the herb theme marginally the hybrid between this western European *Arbutus* and its Grecian close cousin, *A. andrachne*, has superb smooth cinnamon-red trunks). The flowers are bunches of creamy-white or pink urns and they open in September to accompany the rosy ripening result of the previous year's flowering. These are the 'strawberries' of the name, a visual resemblance, not unfortunately one of flavour. The *unedo* of the specific epithet reflects this, meaning 'I eat one' – and one is enough: they are in fact bland and rather gritty. All parts of the tree have been used medicinally: decoctions provide an effective antibiotic mouthwash. This is one of the plants, it is suggested, which deserve detailed clinical study.

Arbutuses can reach 20 or 30 feet in height and then the effect of its bark is greater. In a relatively restricted herb collection these large shrubs or trees can take the place of a clipped sweet bay, although, of course, if clipped it will flower and fruit less.

As a relation of heathers and rhododendrons *Arbutus* is unusual in accepting a limy soil without complaint.

ARCTIUM LAPPA BURDOCK

There is little doubt that burdock is a big, coarse weed. Yet, avoiding prejudice and accepting the definition that a weed is just a plant in the wrong place, there is equally little doubt that it is a statuesque and ornamental thing which can look superb in the right place. From a rosette of big white-backed leaves a 4 or 5-foot stem appears, leafy to the head of bristly thistle-flowers. These develop in autumn into the 'burrs' of the name and the plant should be cut down before they begin to be shed, for their hooked bristles are adapted to grasp any passing creature – human or otherwise. One good plant uses a dozen square feet of ground so it is not for restricted spaces.

Like Jerusalem artichoke the roots contain inulin, and are used against skin diseases. It can be eaten as a vegetable: Japanese varieties bred for this are now available in the West. In China the seeds are recommended in decoction for influenza and tonsilitis.

ARCTOSTAPHYLOS UVA-URSI BEARBERRY

Bearberry's bunches of pink and white urns closely resemble those of *Arbutus*. Indeed they are related, being both in the Ericaceae family.

But there the resemblance ends, for here the flowers are carried by a low evergreen carpeter, a plant of northern acid uplands. In spite of its remote habitat, however, bearberry is perfectly easy to grow so long as an acid soil and good drainage is offered. It will even lay out its shining carpet in the shade of other evergreens, though in such a spot flowers will be infrequent. It is invaluable therefore to fill in the 'body' of knot garden beds when full sun is not available. It looks particularly well draping rocks, moulding itself to the contours beneath in the manner of *Cotoneaster dammeri*.

Bearberry seems to have been little used in Europe after the Middle Ages though recent research has discovered effective antiseptic properties. It is those, no doubt, that are reflected in the Shakers' recommendation of bearberry (or mountain-cranberry, as they also called it in North America) for chronic afflictions of the kidneys and bladder.

ARISAEMA TRIPHYLLUM JACK-IN-THE-PULPIT

This is the wild arum native to the North American east coast woodlands, of which the Shaker herbal literature lists various uses under many common names. They are worth listing: wake robin, wild turnip, dragon root, dragon turnip, Jack-in-the-pulpit, pepper turnip, bog onion, marsh onion, Indian turnip. Such names offer a range of associations: early flowering, resemblance to the European Jack-in-the-pulpit, a tuberous root growing in moist places and, of course, through 'Dragon' and 'Indian' suggestions of a poisonous plant used by native peoples.

It is a most distinguished plant, up to 2 feet in height in well grown specimens. From a fleshy shoot trilobed leaves unfurl exposing a central arum 'flower'. The hooded spathe is purplish green striped with white inside. Eventually in late summer the leaves yellow and fall back leaving a bright stem of scarlet berries to catch the sun in the woodland glade.

In China tubers of the related *Arisaema consanguineum* are used for high fevers and convulsions as well as, externally, for boils and abscesses. Here in cultivation it needs a warm spot, good leafy soil and dappled shade. It is a most distinguished plant of which translations of two of its vernacular names indicate: southern star and tiger palm grass. Sometimes 3 feet high, the leaves have usually eight finger-like divisions; the spathe of the florescence is again striped, this time green and brown. The typical scarlet fruit is seldom produced in captivity. Arisaemas are certainly not plants for the hurly-burly of general mixed borders – herbal or otherwise – but in a corner for special plants they will always catch the eye.

ARISTOLOCHIA CLEMATITIS BIRTHWORT

Birthwort is a direct translation of the generic name of this highly distinctive herbaceous perennial and indicates its medicinal application in times past. The same virtues, to ease birth and the subsequent problems were credited to other Mediterranean species such as *A. longa* and *A. rotunda*. But though these are quaint and strange little plants, *A. clematitis* is by far the most ornamental.

Although one sees it as a noxious weed of Mediterranean vineyards, it is only aggressive in light, warm soils, when in a cool northern climate. Four-foot high stems carry waved green leaves – a strange olive-green – with small tubular flowers of horn yellow during high summer which make little effect.

ARMERIA MARITIMA THRIFT

Meeting thrift in the salt marshes of southern England, on the wind torn cliffs of the Outer Hebrides or on high mountain ledges, one can only be amazed that it can be happy in the confines of the garden. What these habitats share, no doubt, is lack of fierce competition from more robust plants and this the gardener ensures as well.

Herbal value is slight – though records exist of dried thrift being employed to reduce obesity – but as a garden plant, in or out of the herb garden, its value is high.

Perhaps one can note that, as thrift was a common herb garden plant of early days, even then herb-associates were an accepted part of the layout: not every plant having to be of actual medicinal or culinary use.

Thrift is an admirable rock garden plant, its evergreen tussocks of short grassy leaves soon forming a complete mat. In late spring and then again irregularly through the summer it becomes starry with the six-inch high heads of white or pink flowers. The mats can be pulled apart as an easy means of increase. In formal knots thrift is one of the best plants to use as a regular edging or as blocks of solid green. While preferring full sun and a light soil, it will do surprisingly well on clay, even in half-shade. A most adaptable little plant.

ARMORACIA RUSTICANA HORSERADISH

Though sounding like one of a pair of well known operas ('Arm and Pag') this is in fact the ubiquitous horseradish. At least it would be ubiquitous if it had its own way. Like a huge green dock, its waved leaves springing from the soil are an inevitable haunt of garden snails and clump once introduced to a collection of more restrained herbs is extremely difficult to get rid of, except on the driest soils which it resents.

Anyone who is not perfectly happy with those admirable little pots of proprietory horseradish sauce to accompany their smoked trout or roast beef would be well advised to grow the plant in a corner of the garden wanted for nothing else. A variegated form is more acceptable.

ARNICA MONTANA MOUNTAIN TOBACCO

Above its flat hairy leaves, its foot-high stems carry fine yellow daisies, rather like a distinguished *Doronicum* that has moved into summer. As its name suggests, *Arnica* is an upland, even alpine plant, a fact repeated in the alternative title of mountain tobacco.

The Shakers of New Lebanon (New York State) recommended it for external application to a number of wounds and they made a salve 'by heating one ounce of flowers with one ounce of lard for a few hours'. It is poisonous if taken internally and even the salve could cause skin irritation if used too freely. It is, however, a highly ornamental plant with a long flowering season. *Arnica* should be placed well towards the front of its bed as it resents crowding and shading from other things. Any soil which is well drained will suit.

ARTEMISIA spp

Few genera of hardy plants have such a range of aromatic properties and hence offer such a variety of uses to the herbalist, to the perfumer or to the gardener who merely enjoys an extension of the senses by crushing a leaf as he passes. Several are invaluable 'ever-greys' for edging or for knot garden filling. Only *Artemesia lactiflora* has much beauty of flower (rather like a white golden rod) but this has no herbal properties. Otherwise the floral effect is in greyish sprays made up of insignificant rayless daisies.

But it is the foliage which is their major garden virtue, in varying shades of grey from the sage green-greys of old man (or lad's love) and *Artemisia pontica* to the near whites of *A. stelleriana, A. canescens* and *A. ludoviciana*. All but the last have deeply divided filigree leaves, lovely in the mass or in undivided stems for flower arrangement use.

As might be expected, such greyness is an indication of adaptation to hot dry places and good drainage is an essential part of their cultivation.

The biggest, *A. arborescens* is a magnificent grey-white subshrub from Crete where, on the limestone cliffs above Souda Bay, it makes great heaps 4 feet high. It grows very quickly in Britain but is only for warm spots: generally it is a good London garden plant maintaining an air of distinction even against the ceaseless traffic at Hyde Park Corner. In the oasis-like air of Chelsea Physic Garden it is superb. Seedlings seem to offer a range of hardiness; some will not survive a first winter – those that do are worth every effort to maintain. The new hybrid 'Powis Castle' is even better.

Close to it in effect, and perfectly hardy are Mrs Fish's selections of *Artemisia absinthium*; 'Lambrook Silver' is for general use – about 3 feet high – with 'Lambrook Giant' when a bigger plant is wanted. Both are lovely and invaluable garden plants. 'Lambrook Silver', with purple flag irises, catmint and *Alchemilla mollis* is a superb association for early summer herb garden effect.

Herbally *Artemisia absinthium* is used for flavouring various cordials, vermouths and, of course, specifically absinthe, that *fin de siècle* brew apparently essential to the Parisian world of *La Bohéme*. Absinthe, of course, makes the heart grow fonder.

Southernwood, *A. abrotanum*, is another highly aromatic member. It makes a 2-foot high bush of woody stems, most of which indeed do survive the winter. A tidier plant is obtained if it is cut back by half each spring and if, also, the insignificant flower sprays are removed as they develop. Grown thus, in light soil and a sunny spot, southernwood makes an admirable low hedge in the manner of *Santolina*. A pair planted each side of a seat, as if they were the supporters on a coat of arms, are well placed for the appreciation of their scent. Pleasant to us, it used to be employed, as a substitute to mothballs, to keep insects out of clothes. Its other country name, lad's love, refers to its optimistic use as an aphrodisiac.

As well as being aromatic the smaller grey artemisias are invaluable for foliage effect in the border. At around 18 inches high they are front row plants, tumbling forward over paving or gravel, a perfect foil to spring or autumn bulbs. Nerines, dwarf cyclamens and colchicums are particularly good associates. *A. stelleriana* has the virtue of remaining evergreen (or grey) in most winters.

It is the principle of this book to omit herbs that are both visually dull and of merely arcane interest. Sometimes, however, beauty being only skin deep, a plant which would never be given house-room aesthetically is essential. Such a one is *Artemisia dracunculus*, French tarragon. The true plant, towards 2 feet high, with narrow pale green leaves and miserable sprays of rayless daisies, possesses an utterly distinct scent queerly compounded of anise and liquorice. Classically used in *poulet à l'estragon*, its flavouring is always of interest, cooked or raw.

Strangely, French tarragon is neither easy to obtain nor to grow. It needs a warm sunny spot and resents being overgrown with other things. Frequent propagation and replanting in new soil seems to help. But a major problem is its almost complete resemblance to a virtually useless relation *A. dracunculoides*, whose scent and flavouring capabilities are almost nil. If one's 'French Tarragon' grows vigorously into an ever-spreading clump of 3-foot high stems then without doubt it is the Russian tarragon. Except in Botanic Gardens whose collections aim at comprehensiveness all herb gardens would do well to dispose of the Russian plant, lest it overwhelms its more delicate cousin from the West.

ARUM MACULATUM LORDS AND LADIES,

Our native lords and ladies, Jack-in-the-pulpit or cuckoopint is an extremely beautiful plant. Rich green spears begin to push through the leaf-litter of its woodland floor home as early as January – a personal testament to the re-emergence of life and the power of spring. By March the leaves have begun to unfurl into their typical araceous arrowheads to support the strange inflorescence within its creamy-white spathe. Its growth cycle is completed in July as the leaves yellow and die and the drumstick of brilliant and poisonous scarlet berries glistens in the summer sun. A strange and intriguing plant indeed.

As so often happens with strange plants, the wild arum accumulated a range of visual or imagined associations in the minds and writings of the early herbalists. Recommended as an aphrodisiac (inevitably), as a purgative, for rheumatic pain, for plague sores, none was more bizarre than Matthiolus's recipe for 'a Poultice of the Roots beaten to Mash, and mix'd with Cow Dung, to be apply'd to ease Pains of the Gout'. At least external use could do little harm, except to the hands of the sixteenth-century laundresses who used a fierce starch made from the roots to crisp the fashionable linen ruffs worn at the time.

In the garden lords and ladies is happy in the deepest shade, its glossy leaves picking up and reflecting back every gleam of light. Even better is *A. italicum*, a very similar plant of more southern distribution, its garden virtue is that its growth pattern is a couple of months ahead than the other and thus, in most years, its full growth leaves, amazingly frost resistant, enrich the winter scene. This is in fact the plant most common on the Isle of Purbeck which was the centre of the seventeenth-century ruff-starch trade. In the case of its narrow-leaved relative 'Pictum', with grey and cream marbling above the green, the effect is superb when grown among hellebores, winter aconites and *Iris foetidissima*. This is a plant association of the first order.

ASARUM spp WILD GINGER

Here are a couple of the most useful ground cover plants for shady spots that we have. Alphabetically at least *A. canadense* comes first. It runs about in dark woodland in its eastern North American home unfolding heart-shaped leaves in early spring which rather resemble coltsfoot but fortunately it lacks that plant's aggression. They continue, soft and pale green, until the first frosts of autumn. The purplish flowers, waxy upward-facing urns, huddle at the ground level in a completely unprepossessing fashion.

This is the wild ginger so prized by early settlers who found the root-stock an acceptable alternative for an expensive spice. The leaves, too, are agreeably aromatic. Wild ginger has a complicated chemistry containing a resin, a volatile oil, and an alkaloid as well as sugars and other principles. The Shakers used it as a digestive: and according to their religious principles they presumably needed to know nothing of the native peoples' use of this wild ginger (or Canadian snakeroot) as a contraceptive. Nor therefore is it so mentioned in their lists.

The Old World plant is *Asarum europaeum*. Here growth is tighter and less wide ranging; clumps of shiny leaves like those of *Cyclamen europaeum* gradually extend outwards hiding similarly inconspicuous flowers. Asarabacca (the odd name is the product of early nomenclatural confusion) is still a most attractive little plant that its violent emetic and purgative properties cause some surprise. Thus John Pechey (1694) writes: 'Tis diuretick also and forces the courses: wherefore wenches use the decoction of it too frequently, when they think they are with child'. And Joseph Miller recommends its use in 'stubborn tertian or Quartan Agnes; against the Dropsie, Gout and Jaundice' etc.

Though these early writers mention the seeds 'that are like the stones of grapes', simple division in spring or autumn is an easy method of propagation. Both asarums associate well in shade with snowdrops and winter aconites.

ASCLEPIAS SPECIOSA PLEURISY ROOT

This is such a common roadside plant in south Canada and New England, growing with wild golden rods and michaelmas daisies, that it is surprising, since the latter have become common English garden plants, that it is not equally valued. Certainly it is a most striking plant. Stout stems carry opposite pairs of waved grey-green leaves, glossy and pale on the underside. Bunches of starry flowers hang out from the leaf-axils for the top third of the stems; their colour is most distinctive – close to that final spoonful of cream after the strawberries have been eaten. At the end of the season the leaves fall and a few horny fruits, like small pears, remain to split and let free a mass of silk-tasselled seeds. Their skeletons survive to be etched by hoar-frost well into winter – if enthusiastic flower arrangers have not already picked them.

In the garden an open position with impeccable drainage is necessary; acid or limy soils seem equally acceptable.

It is, however, its smaller close relative *A. tuberosa* which has the greater reputation for effective medical properties as its name pleurisy root indicates. Less easy to grow than the other, it is native from the Great Lakes down into Mexico. Perhaps new introductions from its northernmost stations would help: certainly its heads of brilliant orange-red are highly ornamental and would do much for any August border or herb bed. Again, a warm soil is required. Propagation from seed is easy enough though the seedlings seem slow in their first year. Nonetheless they should be planted out as soon as possible because under glass they become immediate prey to whitefly.

ASPARAGUS OFFICINALIS

The mystique surrounding the growing of asparagus is such as to prevent many people enjoying both a delicious vegetable and an ornamental foliage plant. Certainly long rows in the great walled garden of a country house are a joy to behold – as is the professional gardener who maintains them. But lacking that space, and assistance, a yard wide clump in the herb garden can provide surprising amounts of magnificent spears for the table. With regular feeding it is possible to cut enough for two twice a week from April to mid June. Beyond that, every spear taken reduces the vigour of the crowns and their power to build up for winter and next season.

Fortunately there is pleasure, too, in the development of asparagus growth from the tight, fleshy spear to the cloud of feathery 'fern'. It makes a charming backdrop to heavier things planted at its foot.

Light, rich soil, full sun and perfect drainage seem essential. A dozen young crowns, seven planted on the circumference of a circle and a quincunx in the middle will soon build up a subterranean tangle of fleshy roots which must not on any account be meddled with: deep hoeing is anathema.

Asparagus contains a volatile oil, a glucoside and other active principles. As a powerful diuretic it was recommended against dropsy: the Shakers were still using it thus over a century after Withering's discovery of the value of *Digitalis*.

ASPERULA ODORATA SWEET WOODRUFF

A healthy spread of sweet woodruff is a quiet but major pleasure of any garden. In leafy soil it makes marvellous summer-long ground cover in shade and half-sun, starred with little white cross-shaped flowers in spring.

The sweetness referred to in the name (the ruff is the little whorl of leaves behind each bunch of flowers) is not immediately appreciable. But cut the plant at, or just before, flowering time and as it dries a pervasive scent of new mown hay develops. Sweet woodruff was used with sweet flag as an important strewing herb in times past. Though this today is redundant, being bound to clog the vacuum-cleaner, woodruff is still valued in perfumery and for pot pourri. The scent is also released when leaves and flowers are steeped in hot water to make a herbal tea: this is made both to relieve stomachache and for the simple pleasure of drinking it.

Woodruff is easily grown from seed and from divisions taking off at almost any time.

ASPHODELUS spp

The tall white spikes of asphodels are a typical sight flowering on the rocky slopes of every Mediterranean littoral, mainland or island alike. That they stand out so dramatically is proof of their poisonous properties, they never seem to be browsed by even the most ravening flock of sheep or goats. Unlike many poisonous plants which have been effectively harnessed, however, even seventeenth-century texts, giving every possible benefit of the doubt, merely suggest that asphodels once were used 'by the Ancients'.

In their homes they are invariably surrounded by a mass of the most typical culinary herbs – sage, savory, thyme and lavender – so to introduce a clump into a modern herb garden or a sunny border of greylings is to evoke momentarily that southern image.

There are several white asphodels of botanical distinctness: any would suitably serve this purpose. *A. albus, A. cerasiferus, A. microcarpus* are all around 3 or 4 feet in height with diffuse spikes of apricot-tinged white starry flowers above strap shaped leaves.

The yellow *Asphodeline luteus* is a shorter (2-foot) alternative. Unbranched spikes come from blue-grey grassy leaves and make a lovely effect in early summer with clary and other soft purple things.

ASPIDISTRA LURIDA

There is always employment for plants with striking leaves to be stood out on focal points in the herb garden. *Agave and Aloe* have been mentioned but without full sun their effect is diminished as is their well-being. *Aspidistra*, epitome of Victorian front-room windows, surviving in an 'art-pot' on a diet of dust and tea-leaves, seems to offer little to herbalism or to the garden. Even Miss Gracie Fields, who, it will be recalled, had the Biggest Aspidistra in the World, would hardly have made such a claim.

Yet Chinese medicine is unaffected by such cultural undertones. Vernacular names, in translation, refer lightly to the rhizome (woody and rather resembling that of Solomon's seal): centipede grass, contented centipede and iron dragon-bone grass. Decoctions of all parts are used to stop bleeding from traumatic injuries, for abdominal cramps and stones in the urinary tract.

Hence its inclusion here is perfectly legitimate. *Aspidistra* is surprisingly hardy and in sheltered shade would succeed in many gardens. But its broad, glossy leaves are long-lasting and hence any damage that results from weather or predators (not slugs here perhaps: aspidistras welcome them as vehicles for pollinating its flowers) is in view for a long time. It is better to have a well-fed specimen to stand out in a shady corner from May to October, where its elegant habit can be fully enjoyed. There is (except to the molluscs mentioned above) no normal enjoyment to be gained from the ground level *Asarum*-like flowers.

ASTRANTIA MAJOR MASTERWORT

Masterwort is a delightful cottage garden plant which Joseph Miller commends heartily for 'use in putrid malignant Fevers, and all contagious pestilential Distempers' etc. Yet it seems not to be included today even in collections of historical herbs.

Coming from Austrian alpine meadows it is utterly hardy and

easy to satisfy. A clump of strawberry-like leaves supports 2-foot high sprays of white flower heads. Each head is in fact an unusual umbel; the florets lie within a starry ruff of green bracts to give the effect of individual flowers. They are extremely long-lasting and put on a good show in half-shade or sun so long as moisture is sufficient.

There are several good garden forms as well as an exquisite pink relation (which could be acceptable by extension) called *Astrantia maxima*. In spite of its name it is no bigger, just different.

ATROPA BELLADONNA DEADLY NIGHTSHADE

The fascinating meanings which lie behind the botanical name have already been discussed, as have the properties reflected in the vernacular, deadly nightshade. The old botanical name of *Solanum lethale* is equally clear.

It is an unusual plant of the British chalklands but extends into eastern Europe and along the Himalayan chain (I have found it in Kashmir). *Atropa* is not listed among Chinese medicinal herbs which indicates that it is not found as far as China. Joseph Miller is very specific: 'it is found in a ditch at the end of Goswell-street in the Road to Islington; in Cuckstone, near Rochester in Kent, all the yards and Back-sides are over-run with it'. To the considerable danger of local children, presumably.

One of the relatively few hardy plants still grown commercially for medicinal use, it is very striking. Usually 3 or 4 feet in height it can exceed this (that referred to so ominously in L. P. Hartley's 'The Go-Between' must have been a monster) with lank oval leaves and bell-shaped flowers. These are very different from the usual nightshade flowers, like those of potato with reflexed petals and a forward-pointing beak of yellow stamens, with which there should never be the slightest confusion. Equally distinct, the black cherry-like fruits, each held in a star of green sepals, are lined along the summer stems.

Atropa is a highly effective narcotic, its alkaloids affecting the central nervous system of the body. The Shakers in North America considered that 'in the hands of skilled herbal physicians this botanical has great virtues, but it is too powerful and dangerous for general home use'.

This sentence of warning should be taken seriously by all who wish to grow a definitive collection of herbs. Certainly *Atropa* should be seen and recognized: in the wild it should be honoured as an uncommon species – never should it be destroyed with hysterical cries about poisonous plants – but its garden cultivation should be likened to a situation such as when someone keen on collecting reptiles naturally considers including an adder or two.

BALLOTA PSEUDODICTAMNUS

That this little shrubby horehound is not usually included in lists of herbs is reasonable enough: it is not medicinal nor culinary, it is not even aromatic. Yet, with its soft grey-white foliage it looks very much as if it should be, and indeed as a Mediterranean compatriot of lavenders and sages one is surprised by the lack. Visually, it fits perfectly with the white garden scene of which so many of those plants form the bones.

Fortunately *Ballota* does have a life-enhancing role, if now one which is largely redundant: the dried calyces, looking like tiny furry spinning-tops, were used as floating wicks in primitive oil lamps. A power failure during a remote Greek island holiday could bring them back into favour.

BAPTISIA TINCTORIA WILD INDIGO

The epithet 'tinctoria' invariably implies that the plant bearing it is, or was, used as a dye-plant. This one is the wild indigo of eastern North America, native from Massachusetts south into Florida. It is a fine upright legume, rather lupin-like, with spikes of yellow pea-flowers in summer. The Shakers recommended it as a wash for all sorts of ulcers especially those in the mouth (one wonders if wild indigo is better than most reputed mouth ulcer cures of which it can usually be said that the ulcers take a week to disappear if treated and seven days if not).

The most frequent *Baptisia* in British gardens is the lovely *B. australis*. Its blue spikes above blue-green foliage make a superb picture in early summer and the foliage remains attractive until frosts turn it charcoal black; then it picks up another kind of beauty. This can legitimately be grown as a herb associate.

A third species is the tall (to 5 feet) white *B. leucantha*. This is the prairie false indigo which is listed as having medicinal properties: coming from beyond their area, however, it seems not to have been employed by the Shakers.

All the baptisias are long lived plants, liking deep soil and, once there, to be left alone.

BEGONIA EVANSIANA

It is heartening to discover that the only *Begonia* listed in *A Barefoot Doctors' Manual* is the only species which can be considered to be a hardy garden plant. Though its top growth is as sensitive to frost as any florist's form, it overwinters both by its tuberous root-stock and by the bulbils which form during summer in the leaf axils. These pea-sized structures make propagation easy and also give the Chinese name: *Yen Yuan tzu*, rockpill.

It is a lovely plant, enjoying half-shade in leaf-mould-rich soil. The leaves have the typical off-centre base of all their tribe, green above with purplish-red undersides, a colour that is picked up by the elegant sprays of flowers above. A white-flowered form also exists. In American (under the name of *B. grandis*) and Chinese texts it is stated to attain 3 feet in height. British gardens are grateful for half that it usually attains here. *Begonia evansiana* is often very slow to get going at the beginning of the season and care must be taken to ensure that the first pink shoots are not overshaded by robust early leaves of for example, hostas, which enjoy similar conditions; nor, while they are at this vulnerable stage that they make a slug's breakfast. It gives no pleasure to know that those wretched beasts might benefit from rockpill's ability to relieve pain and spasms and reduce swellings – unless of course it could reduce them to invisibility.

BERBERIS VULGARIS BARBERRY

The common barberry no longer lives up to its name for the very good reason that, as the winter host of wheat rust, it has been removed from the chalkland hedgerows it once inhabited. Such economic considerations inevitably overrule the less-used virtues for which the plant was widely grown in earlier times. The brilliant yellow roots provided a dye, the sweetly acid fruits provided preserves and the bark mouth washes.

A comprehensive herb collection will still include barberry and, away from wheat-growing areas, could be used as an effective 6-foot high enclosing hedge: it is lethally spiny. But at flowering time in early summer it might be altogether too much of a good thing: in quantity they are close to foetid. A single plant, perhaps, is acceptable and, to build up a particular garden picture with the grey leaves of lavenders and santolinas the purple-leaved form 'Atropurpurea' is admirable. If the picture is more important than herbal truth – or if wheatfields are close – the purple form of *Berberis thunbergii* will do the job just as well.

I   The herb garden at
    Brooklyn Botanic
    Garden

II *Laurus nobilis*
    sweet bay

III   *Rosmarinus officinalis* rosemary

IV *Primula veris*
    cowslip

V   Rues, feverfew and
    agrimony

VI *Saponaria officinalis*
soapwort

VII *Chrysanthemum
parthenium* feverfew

VIII *Iris florentina* orris root

IX *Pelargonium quercifolium* rose geranium

X   *Rosa gallica variegata* 'Versicolor' Rosa Mundi

XI   *Papaver somniferum* (peony flowered) opium poppy

XII *Actaea alba* white baneberry

BETULA PENDULA SILVER BIRCH

Few trees are more beautiful than silver birch: as a garden focal point it can hardly be bettered. But garden ornament is not the same as forestry where strong straight single trunks are required for timber. Silver birch grown as a multi-stemmed clump (three or five young plants put into the same hole) looks, as it matures, infinitely lovelier, with much more silvery trunk area developing. The well-known 'Young's Weeping' is singularly useless for this effect as its solid curtain of branches entirely hides the trunk.

Almost any soil will suit and mature trees may reach 30 or 40 feet: in restricted spaces this is seldom too much as the shade cast is very light but root constriction and careful branch thinning can keep the plant smaller: balanced feeding and watering then becomes necessary in the growing season.

Uses were many. The dried young leaves have antiseptic qualities and had various medicinal applications ('. . . the Dropsy and the Itch. . . .'); the copious spring sap which makes an acceptable country wine ('. . . for the Stone and Gravel and for the Strangury . . .'); even as firewood is 'next to Junipo, prefer'd to burn in times of Pestilence and contagious Distempers'. One senses, reading Joseph Miller here, an air of desperation underlying the apparent Augustan calm of the Age of Reason. Health was not necessarily associated with wealth, nor medical knowledge with cure.

BLETILLA STRIATA

Early European herbals suggest various uses for native early purple and other similar terrestrial orchids, the fleshy tubers set in pairs at the base of the stem, relating easily to imaginative upholders of the Doctrine of Signatures. In the West today only one orchid has any herbal application and that is vanilla; ripe seed pods provide that delicious flavour and scent. But the *Vanilla planifolia* is a tropical epiphyte. It is easy enough to grow in a warm greenhouse but the chances of flowers and fruits are remote.

It is interesting to note therefore that the charming and hardy *Bletilla striata* is in the Chinese list of valuable medicinal herbs; a decoction of its bulbous roots which are crushed into a powder is to be taken to reduce bleeding of gastric and duodenal ulcers. Prepared in decoction they are used externally for cracked skin on hands and feet.

Here the plant needs a sunny spot in light soil. Its growth-habit is much like that of montbretias, with tussocks of pleated leaves and sprays of pretty and obviously orchidaceous flowers each like a little *Cattleya* in late spring. The typical colour is purple but, even in the wild, white forms exist. It is wise to grow *Bletilla* in a pot for the first year after buying it. So often the roots are half dried out and need all the help they can get to re-establish themselves: even worse, weak shoot growth begins in the plastic bags in which they are delivered and care must be given to see these do not damp off before the plant really gets a hold. It is worth every effort.

BORAGO OFFICINALIS BORAGE

Borage is one of the essentials in any arrangement of herbs or old-fashioned cottage garden plants. The slightly cucumbery flavour of its leaves causes it to be enjoyed in summer wine cups (though to be honest cucumber proper does the job better). The clear blue starry flowers floating on the surface add a further pleasurable dimension. Perhaps there is still some belief, strongly held by the ancients, that borage brought happiness; it might not, however, be beyond the bounds of possibility that the drink it decorates creates the greater effect.

Borage is a splendid plant for quick garden decoration: as a biennial its seedlings overwinter and make prodigious spring growth, especially in the fresh soil of new gardens. By June there is a 2-foot stand of fleshy, hollow stems with broad oval leaves. All parts are covered, in stiff hairs, bristly and even on the way to positive prickliness.

The heads of flowers are highly attractive to bees, as is the fine white-flowered form (which must be kept separate from the blue). This is a delightful white-garden plant: it looks well with white variegated honesty.

Once seeds have been formed it is as well to collect as many as necessary and scatter them where next year's borage is required, to ensure at least a token crop rotation: over the years it matters. The old plants can either be taken out and the space filled at once with some summer aromatic such as scented-leaved geraniums waiting in their pots, or they can be cut to the ground when, in some years, further growth results. To ensure late summer borage, however, seed should be sown in spring, though seldom do these big fleshy plants overwinter.

BRYONIA DIOICA WHITE BRYONY

Height in the herb garden, especially quick height, is not easy to achieve, which is why climbers grown on tripods are so valuable to provide the necessary bones of an architectural design. To line a walk or to be the centrepiece of one or more pairs of beds planned as mirror-image, offers suitable positions to such plants as this.

White bryony is a hedgerow vine of European chalk and limestone hills, scrambling up woody shrubs to 10 feet or 15 feet. The leaves are typically ivy-shaped, pale green in colour, amongst which the clusters of flowers, equally green, are effectively hidden. No bright show from these.

As its name suggests *Bryonia* is dioecious, that is with separate male and female plants, and the latter ends the season draped in orange-scarlet berries. These remain bright long after the leaves have declined with autumn frosts. Further vernacular names are devil's turnip and English mandrake referring to the great misshapen root which can weigh 20 lb or so in a large specimen and in times past the poisonous and violently purgative properties caused it to be much used, both by serious physicians and mountebanks.

John Pechey (1694) writes: 'Jugglers and Fortune-tellers make wonderful monsters of this root, which, when they have hid in the sand for some days, they dig up for Mandrakes; and by this imposture these knaves impose on our common people'. Recipes follow of great complexity which are no longer used. It is worth noting however that the glycosides and alkaloids possessed by white bryony are currently being clinically re-examined.

BUXUS SEMPERVIRENS BOX

It is convenient that box, in its dwarf form 'Suffruticosa' provides the archetypal edging in formal herb gardens and delineates the pattern of parterres and knots, because the plant itself has some faint claim to herbal use. It contains alkaloids and the extremely hard wood produces a volatile oil; but even early commentaries such as John Pechey's (1694) state 'tis seldom used in physic. The oil drawn from the wood is much commended for the falling-sickness and pains in the teeth. Tis said', Pechey goes on doubtfully, 'the decocton of the wood cures the French-pox', but 'tis chiefly used by turners'.

Which, of course, 300 years later, the wood from the typical box-tree still is: it is said to be as hard as brass. This form is one of the best evergreens for topiary work, developing the tight growth necessary to maintain such formal shapes. Silver and gold variegated types are available but none is better than the glaucous, rather blueish, one. From this, particularly, seems to come a musky fragrance after rain that is so evocative of old gardens. Delicious though it be to most people, Queen Anne was not so amused. She hated the smell and had the box parterres in St James's Park torn out which had been planted for her predecessors, William and Mary, in the last years of the seventeenth century.

❧❀❧

CALAMINTHA spp CALAMINT

Both this generic name and the fact that the half-dozen species concerned were once included in *Satureia* indicates considerable herbal importance. There are two or three occasionally grown.

C. *nepeta* is mountain mint or mountain balm, a bushy 2-footer with the typical square stems of almost all labiates and sprays of catmint-like flowers, white to pale lilac, above greyish leaves. It has a noticeable pepperminty scent and it is this which comes through in the tea made from the leaves. This, and *C. ascendens* are virtually interchangeable in the garden and prefer a well-drained limy soil: they are plants of limestone uplands.

C. *grandiflora* is rather smaller in height but the flowers, a clear lilac-pink, make more of a show. This is a lovely front row plant to put amongst the grey-leaved herbs that are its natural neighbours in its southern European home. Though it has been with us since Gerard's time it sadly has never become common. These calamints are easily divided in spring or, if a larger stock is required, cuttings of the young shoots can be taken, also in spring.

CALENDULA OFFICINALIS POT MARIGOLD

Few plants are more evocative of old-fashioned cottage gardens than the ever-bright pot marigolds. In light soil especially they seed around abundantly though they never become a nuisance. Plants naturally appear amongst the soft fruit bushes as well as around the flower-plots and provide that barely controlled (but never contrived) miscellany such gardens developed.

As a Mediterranean annual, self-sown seeds normally germinate in autumn and overwinter with just a couple of pairs of leaves. In most winters they survive and flower in June – sometimes even in May – with sweet williams and Canterbury bells. To be certain of continued marigold colour therefore a spring sowing should also be made: these are the high summer flowers. Early thinning, or very restrained sowing, is essential for it is surprising how few plants, really well developed, are necessary to make a fine clump. Deadheading extends the season wonderfully.

While there are many colour selections available, and all beautiful, the typical orange form is best for herb-garden use. 'Radio' is right for colour, if rather bigger than the old sort.

Pot marigolds had, indeed have, wide uses. Medicinally they emphasize its healing properties: marigold, said the Shakers, is unequalled for preventing gangrene. The orange petals have been used as a colouring for butter and cheeses, and as an adulterant in saffron. With more principle they can be cast into salads, to enliven both colour and flavour.

In the garden marigolds look superb against purple flowers or backed with a haze of bronze fennel.

CALLUNA VULGARIS SCOTS HEATHER, LING

As the sole diet of adult grouse the young shoots of Scots heather or ling must clearly be nutrient rich to a surprising degree. Medicinally its oils, resin, acids and glycosides produce an anti-bacterial action and it was widely used for stomach complaints and, externally, against those of the skin.

Heather does not associate happily with the predominantly calcicole herbs from the Mediterranean: however, on an acid soil (its natural medium) and in cold areas when the latter are less than perfectly suited it has definite herb- garden use. The smaller forms, of which there are now dozens – almost all selections from the wild – can be used as low clipped edgings or to fill knots and parterres. Loss of flowering from this treatment is no problem when foliage can be golden, bronze, red, grey or green.

CAMELLIA SINENSIS TEA

The word tea is derived from the Chinese: there it was specific, referring to the beverage made with leaves of the above plant. It has become equally specific throughout the world, alternatives have to be always qualified by their origin: mint tea, oswego tea, even beef tea. It must be one of the herbs in greatest use.

Cultures, attitudes of mind and behavioural patterns have all been built around the production and subsequent drinking of this mild stimulant. Commercially, of course, most tea growing takes place in the temperate uplands of China, India and Ceylon, areas which, climatically, have little in common with Britain. But, not surprisingly, after millennia of cultivation and selection, hardier forms exist and it is possible therefore to grow one's own tea in, for example, London without necessarily popping round the corner to Fortnum's.

Camellia sinensis here makes a tight slow-growing evergreen with rather corrugated leaves and, for a camellia, small single white flowers which make little show. Like the more usual garden hybrids, it needs a lime-free soil: one of these might well accompany it in a warm, half-shaded corner for fascinating comparison.

CAMPSIS GRANDIFLORA TRUMPET VINE

It is interesting that while this beautiful self-clinging climber is used in traditional Chinese medicine, its close (and similar) relative from east North America (*C. radicans*) is not listed by the Shakers.

However, the Chinese cloud vine, to translate one of several vernacular names, adds a highly distinct dimension to a herb garden wall. Though it will reach 20 or more feet up a tree it seldoms ripens wood sufficiently early in the season to flower well and hence is best to be pruned to a framework or a warm wall when its annual shoots carry sprays of flowers in late summer, like those of an orange-red paulownia, if such a thing were possible.

Apart from a sunny spot essential to encourage flowering, *Campsis* is happy anywhere. Soil can be acid or alkaline and the shoots, with their ash-like leaves will be equally robust on either.

CARDAMINE PRATENSIS LADY'S SMOCK

Moist meadows used to be commonly dotted in spring with the pale lilac heads of lady's smock or cuckoo flower: they become an inevitable part of children's wild flower bunches, wilting all too quickly. Efficient drainage and high nutrient fertilizers have made this lovely gentle flower sufficiently uncommon in the wild for it to be now a worthwhile garden plant for a damp, half-shaded spot.

This would, in fact, be coming full circle as lady's smock used to be cultivated as a pot herb, its early growth making it useful to fresh vegetable-starved northern communities. Hence its eighteenth-century recommendation against scurvy. The leaves have a pleasant watercress flavour; it is, indeed, yet another crucifer.

A charming double-flowered form, again around a foot high and of similar colour is available and makes a longer show in the garden, not producing seeds. Propagation obviously is by division and care has to be taken that it is not lost by being overwhelmed by more vigorous sharers of that moist spot.

CARLINA ACAULIS CARLINE THISTLE

Writing at a time when horticulture, no less than medicine, was at an early stage Joseph Miller remarks of the carline thistle that 'it is rarely used in Britain'. Doubtless this was because, though a perfectly hardy plant it was rarely grown. The fulsome dedication of his *Botanicum Officinale* to Sir Hans Sloane refers to 'your late noble present of the Physick Garden at *Chelsea* to the *Apothecaries Company*, on condition of its being kept up to the Improvement of *Botany*.'

Sloane's deed of gift of the freehold (he had become landlord when he bought the Manor of Chelsea) in 1721 preceded Miller's compilation by just a year. Exactly a half-century later what is credited as being the first rock garden in the country was built there – a suitable site for the cultivation of carlina.

As a plant of stony uplands of southern Europe it needs perfect drainage, limy soil, and an open spot to spread out its thistly rosette. In its centre in late summer grows a single white flower, resembling a near-stemless-animated globe artichoke, opening and closing with the weather for a month or more (hence the French name of *baromètre*). It is marvellous, suitably wired, in dried arrangements.

Beneath is the long aromatic tap root which when used in decoction makes an antiseptic wash for skin disorders and as a mouthwash.

In cultivation it looks superb as the dominant plant in an association of houseleeks and creeping thymes.

CARUM CARVI CARAWAY

Like carrot and parsnip, caraway is a typical umbelliferous biennial with a fleshy overwintering tap-root which sends up the 2-foot high flowering stem to flower, fruit and die in its second year. Sown in a tight clump in the herb garden individual plants are thin and fail to make the size of root which made many people, in the eighteenth century, prefer it to parsnips. Doubtless the sort of breeding programmes to which these other vegetables have been subjected would effect similar changes in caraway.

Be that as it may, although young leaves can be used in salads, caraway today means seed and seed only; to those old enough it evokes 'seed-cake' and long-departed maiden aunts who, it seemed at the time, virtually lived on the stuff. One cannot be ambivalent about seed-cake. Beyond this rather national delicacy caraway is used widely as a flavouring in cooking and liqueurs, especially in central Europe where it is grown on a field scale.

Although typically a biennial and succeeding best from a June sowing to make its cow parsley effect twelve months later, an earlier sowing will often produce some flower in the autumn of the first year. Any sunny well-drained spot will suit.

CARYOPTERIS × CLANDONENSIS

The vast majority of grey-felted, often aromatic plants seem to have developed in response to the warm-wet-winter, hot-dry-summer climate which we know as Mediterranean: thus plants from California, South Africa and parts of Australia join those from the classical base.

Caryopteris is one of those exceptions said to prove the rule. The product of two far Asiatic shrubs, it fulfils all the other criteria to perfection, adding to its grey-green scented leaves splendid blue spikes of flower for August and September. The gun-metal tinged calyces remain attractive even where their corollas have fallen. All parts are useful in pot pourri.

Clipped back in spring, plants can be kept to a couple of feet in height and take on the role in late summer which lavender has provided earlier. As a low hedge or filler in a knot pattern few shrubs are more charming. All soils, chalk included, are happily accepted: poor winter drainage, however, is not.

'Kew Blue' and 'Ferndown' are named forms of particularly good colour.

CEANOTHUS AMERICANUS NEW JERSEY TEA

New Jersey tea, wild snowball, red root are three North American vernacular names which, in combination tell us much about this little woodland edge evergreen. Its bark was particularly used by the Shakers in cases of asthma, whooping cough and chronic bronchitis. The leaves provided material for the beverage that was doubtless in especially great demand following that famous occasion in Boston: only a later tea-party at the Mad Hatter's is more universally known.

As a garden plant, with its heads of rather dull white flowers, this *Ceanothus* pales beside its splendid west coast cousins, which are amongst the best blue flowered shrubs we can grow. But, as most British gardeners sadly realized as they picked around the corpses after the 1981/82 winter, many of the latter are not as hardy as might be wished. It is this invaluable attribute which New Jersey tea brings to its hybrid with the Mexican *Ceanothus caeruleus*.

This cross, dating from the mid-nineteenth century (150 years after *C. americanus* appeared) has produced an invaluable group of summer-flowering deciduous ceanothuses which with their background and soft colourings fit beautifully into the herb garden scene emerging from billowing grey foliage of artemesias and santolinas. 'Gloire de Plantières' and 'Henri Desfosse' are dark blue while the best known, 'Gloire de Versailles', carries big heads of soft powder-blue from July through to October. They are usually pruned hard back with the buddleias in spring.

CELASTRUS SCANDENS BITTERSWEET VINE

This is known rather confusingly in North America as bittersweet, where the European bittersweet (*Solanum dulcamara* or woody nightshade) is now a common established alien. *Celastrus* is a much more striking plant which twines to a height of 20 feet or more. It is not particularly attractive in leaf or in flower but in a good year (both male and female plants being on hand) the fruiting is spectacular.

This is the species used by the Shakers against skin cankers and scrofula (one disadvantage of a country's becoming a republic is that there is then no monarch to touch for the King's evil).

In China the closely related and visually similar *Celastrus orbiculatus* takes on the role. Stems and roots are used in decoction for flatulence and stimulating the blood-flow. Its reputation for strengthening the sinews probably related to the strength of its own liana-like growth. The fresh leaves are used externally.

Of the two the latter is by far the better garden plant: the hermaphrodite form especially fruits consistently and it is then that its spindle-bush connection becomes clear. The bunches of pea-sized capsules split open to reveal a bejewelled combination worthy of a Fabergé: the inside walls of the capsules are bright orange and hold scarlet seeds. Against the gold of the autumn leaves the effect is superb.

Celastrus is utterly hardy and happy in all soils but it must be remembered that much space is needed. The oriental species will attain 30 feet or more and deserves a tall open tree to climb into on a suitable prop: on the only too ubiquitous chain-link fencing, if encouraged in the ways of truth and light, it makes a splendid screen.

CENTAUREA CYANUS CORNFLOWER

'It grows every where among the Corn; flowering (sic) in June and July.' Joseph Miller's comment upon cornflowers or, as he called them, small blue-bottles, evokes a pre-agricultural revolution world when corn was still sown, broadcast as in Biblical times. The impossibility of weeding such crops turned arable fields into flower gardens, corncockle, corn marigold and poppy joining the clear blue of cornflowers; visually delightful but a bane to those attempting to wrest a living from the soil.

Sowing in drills, hoeing between them and today's ubiquitous use of herbicides makes such scenes as distant as farthingales and stage-coaches. Nonetheless these plants, individually, are of great garden merit, cornflowers especially having been subject to the breeders' art.

The thin 2 or 3-foot high wild plant is now seldom seen. Seedsmen's packets will produce dwarfer, more floriferous individuals in a colour range varying from white through shades of pink to a true blue even darker than the original. All, sown *in situ* in spring and rigorously thinned, give a splendid display from June onwards. A sunny spot and a light limy soil is preferred.

It was this typical blue colour as much as its actual chemical constituents which made cornflower so famed for use in eye-washes. Today, as the colour is retained well when dried, the flowers are more highly regarded in pot pourri.

Centaurea montana (bluebottle) is a perenial version: 'This is reckon'd among the vulnerary plants; the juice being commended against Bruises and Contusions which come of Falls, though a Vein be broken and the Party spilt Blood; as also to heal any Cut, or green Wound': thus Joseph Miller. Even then, however, the plant was little used. As a cottage garden ornament, however, it has clearly been with us since early times and it still fulfils a useful role in the early part of the season before most border perennials are at their best.

With bearded irises, lupins and catmint the great bluebottle (or 'Blew-bottle' as Gerard had it) is splendid. It makes a clump of divided leaves, pale beneath, above which the big blue flowers are held. Pink and amethyst forms exist as well as a good white one. All are happy in dry spots and are able to take chalk a couple of inches down without a blench. Division is easy at almost any time: a useful, comfortable flower.

CHAENOMELES SPECIOSA JAPANESE QUINCE

The so-called Japanese quinces or 'Japonicas' (actually native to China) have been valued garden plants in Britian since the turn of the eighteenth century. No thought has been given to them in the

West, however, as having medicinal application, though the delicious amber-coloured conserve which can be made from the fruit is admirable with meat and hence can be considered culinarily valid.

It is these fruits, like small, rock hard, near stalkless yellow pears holding tightly on to their branches which the Chinese use very specifically: for cramps associated with cholera and numbness in cases of beri-beri. Fortunately neither of these dire afflictions are likely in the West so that *Chaenomeles* can rest its main claim to garden-worthiness on its floral beauty.

On limy soils especially, where early spring colour is dominated by daffodil-yellows, *Chaenomeles* provides the reds, pinks and scarlets which acid soils, with their rhododendrons and camellias, have in greater abundance. Tight interweaving branches build up wide-spreading shrubs seldom much above 6 feet in height. They make a marvellous hedge, being pruned after flowering to maintain formality.

Many colour forms are available, the semi-double forms having greater substance; amongst the best are 'Phyllis Moore', clear pink, 'Spitfire', dark crimson, and 'Simonii', a dwarf blood-red, perhaps the best of all.

CHAMAEMELUM NOBILE CAMOMILE

Camomile tea is one herbal recipe known to everyone if only through Beatrix Potter. Peter Rabbit, it will be remembered, having had such a horrid experience in Mr MacGregor's garden 'was not very well during the evening. His mother put him to bed, and made some camomile tea; "One table-spoonful to be taken at bedtime!"'

Its effect on humans has an even longer record. Camomile tea is a renowned stomach-settler and appetite-improver, being made of the white and yellow daisy flowers together with the little fern-like leaves, doubtfully apple-scented.

Though not particularly ornamental camomile is an essential herb garden plant. The common conceit of providing a camomile seat (apparently an Elizabethan idea) has the virtue of bringing the plant to a height easily reached and smelled. It also give the well-drained spot the plant requires. As a place to rest in comfort however it leaves a lot to be desired.

As a lawn-plant camomile gets greater credit than the effect normally deserves, influenced by the camomile lawn behind Buckingham Palace. It is worth giving the warning that a camomile lawn is infinitely less easy to keep in good condition than a conventional lawn made up of grass. The latter invariably contains several species which, in combination, make up the sward and cover the ground: a single species cannot easily do that. And then, of course, broadleaved weeds can be got rid of by herbicides. There is no selective herbicide which will preserve camomile and kill the rest, including the weed grasses.

This does not mean that on a light, slightly acid soil camomile will not make good, if not very hardwearing cover: for it will. But it is a hands and knees job to keep it weed free. More sensibly, on the right soil, is to introduce the non-flowering form of camomile, 'Treneague' into existing turf and let them fight it out. A more specific combination is to grow 'Treneague' with creeping thymes. In a slightly raised bed around a central sundial, or in an urn with dwarf crocuses coming through in early spring a delightful focal point is contrived.

CHEIRANTHUS CHEIRI WALLFLOWER

The hybridists' art has carried wallflowers far from the woody yellow flowered perennial of ruined lime-mortar walls and cliff edges. Yet, as with so many highly-bred plants, the delicious scent has not been lost and today the modern hybrids in a range of colours from cream to deepest mahogany-red are the most fragrant of all spring flowers, a fragrance that seems to repeat the velvet texture of the petals themselves.

These flowers were considered of great value in the eighteenth century. An oil was prepared by infusion and used to 'strengthen the nerves and help the Apoplexy and Palsy'. If wallflower's herbal application today has declined to being a part of mixed pot pourri, its garden value is by far the greater.

Conventionally wallflowers are used extensively in spring bedding schemes and in essence this is their herb garden role – to take the place of summer annuals, to flower and in turn to be removed in mid May before the ground is required for the tender plants of the next summer. But small groups can be used almost anywhere, against a clump of developing sweet cicely or lovage, for instance, and the dark mahogany colours are splendid against young shoots of purple fennel. Wallflowers are also excellent for large containers which bring the scent near the appreciative nose.

While the plant is naturally perennial – and old plants in dry spots can go on for years – such is our demand for full use of garden space that they are invariably grown as biennials. Seed is sown outside in a nursery row in late May and the requisite number of young plants is then planted out at about a foot square to make the bushy, compact plants needed to overwinter. Transference to their flowering positions should take place as soon as the ground is ready in autumn.

CHELIDONIUM MAJUS GREATER CELANDINE

The greater celandine is a great plant for the base of crumbling walls, clearly enjoying the decaying lime-mortar and good drainage. Though thus considered a weed, there are many cultivated plants of considerable less charm and garden use.

It makes an open clump of blue-green fingered leaves rather like those of the related plume poppy. Heads of four-petalled golden flowers are followed by long pods. Every part leaks a brilliant orange sap when bruised. Not surprisingly the early herbalists found it 'of great use in curing the Jaundice & Scurvy. Some reckon it cordial', Miller goes on, 'and a good Antidote against the Plague'. It is still used on warts externally and its alkaloids are being further investigated.

In the garden greater celandine takes dry shade happily and is good above spring bulbs to give summer interest when they have gone to rest. Though it seeds itself about, so soft is the growth and weak at the root that there is no trouble in keeping it in order.

Sadly this is not the case with the lesser celandine or pilewort, *Ranunculus ficaria*, which is no relation. This is the shining gold buttercup which lights up hedge banks in earliest spring. It has the herbal attributes combined with great beauty which give it every reason for inclusion in this list. But so easily do the little tubers spread that amongst small plants it can become a major pest, never to be introduced into the cultivated garden.

Interestingly this is another example where the ancient Doctrine of Signatures appears to work: the name refers to the clustered tubers and ointments prepared from the plant which are still used externally for the relief of haemorrhoids.

CHELONE GLABRA TURTLEHEAD

Although a plant of woodland bogs in eastern North America, turtlehead (referring with considerable imagination to the shape of the flowers) seems very happy to be brought out of such obscurity into the garden border so long as it does not dry out. It makes a 3 or 4-foot high clump, rather monarda-like, with its egg-shaped flowers produced in late summer and autumn. Colour forms exist from

white through pale pink to clear rose, making *Chelone* a useful end
of season plant for the herbaceous border and even more so for the
herb garden whose main effect is invariably earlier.

It was used as a tonic by the native peoples of North America
and taken up by the colonists. The Shakers used it for jaundice and
an ointment made from the fresh leaves was recommended for
piles. In the writings of several Shaker communities *Chelone* is
referred to by nine different names, the attractive balmony being
the most general.

In the garden it is as easy to propagate by division in spring or
autumn as any other herbaceous perennial. Closely related species
are *Chelone lyonii* and *C. obliqua*, both shorter in height.

CHIONANTHUS VIRGINICUS FRINGE TREE

The fringe tree is one of the most spectacular ornamentals introduced to Britain by Mark Catesby in the 1730s. In spite of its two-
and-a-half centuries here, however, it has never become common,
perhaps because it needs a lot of space; 10 feet high and almost as
much across is likely before it settles down to flower well. It is well
worth the wait to see the plant virtually covered with a curtain of
white, fragrant flowers. These hang down in huge bunches, the four
narrow petals of each combining to provide the fringe of the name.
Leaves are long, up to 9 inches, and rather coarse.

Chionanthus needs a place in full sun to ensure the good wood
ripening which in turn encourages flower bud formation to earn its
place.

In its home the fresh bark of the trunks and dried bark of the
roots was made into a tonic for use after serious illness.
Surprisingly it was not taken up by the Shaker communities,
perhaps because, though fully hardy in cultivation in their areas
(even in southern Ontario) it only existed in the wild – and hence in
collectable quantities – further south.

CHRYSANTHEMUM spp

Depending on which authorities are followed, up to a couple of
hundred species can be included in the genus *Chrysanthemum*. It
is interesting to note that the originals of the florists 'mums' from
the Orient (which of course had been florists' flowers there for
centuries before they reached the West) are also valued members of
the Chinese druggists' lists. These are specifically *C. indicum* and
C. × morifolium: the whole plant of the former is used externally

against boils while a decoction of the flowers of the latter is employed against headaches and dizziness.

Thus it is perfectly valid to include a wide range of garden chrysanthemums within the extended collection of herbs. Obviously the big show varieties, marvels of both hybridists' and growers' arts alike would not look right, but the dwarfer spray types such as Korean chrysanthemums cannot be bettered for extending the season of floral interest into November. They should be placed in front of the spikes of late-flowering aconitums. In addition to these, however, several European chrysanthemums are conventional herb garden plants of considerable visual value.

Chrysanthemum balsamita: alecost, costmary, English mace and mint geranium offer a range of names to hint at a range of uses in earlier times. This was the predominant flavouring given to beer in the Middle Ages before hops took over. Its leaves can be used in salads and added to soups and stews. 'Mint Geranium' is a horrendous bit of confused nomenclature – the plant has not the slightest connection with either part but it is understandable when once the sweet, spearmint flavour of a crushed leaf is experienced.

Alecost is a fine upstanding herbaceous perennial of 4 feet or so, with upward pointing grey-green leaves, good in cut arrangements. Heads of small, white, yellow-eyed daisies appear in high summer but make little show. It accepts shade but fails to flower there: little is lost. Division is simple in spring and autumn.

Chrysanthemum cinerariifolium: It is comforting to people justifiably chary of many modern insecticides – initially claimed as innocuous to the user but subsequently damned – that the recent developments in pyrethrum-based killers have returned to this historic 'bed bugicide'. Native to a restricted area of Yugoslavia, it is now, as 'Dalmatian Pyrethrum', cultivated widely. The dried flower heads produce the insecticidal pyrethrine. However, in humans prolonged contact is known to cause skin irritations and other allergic symptoms.

In the garden it makes a pleasant tussock of grey divided leaves and gives quite a show of white daisies in early summer: rich, moist soil produces soft, atypical growth and must be avoided.

Chrysanthemum parthenium: Here is another old herb which modern research is demonstrating to have value in treating certain migraines, but the home 'remedy' of feverfew sandwiches should be treated with the greatest caution: the resultant mouth ulcers may be more distressing than the original complaint.

In spite of the name of 'feverfew' it seems not to have any

reputation as a febrifuge (or fever-expeller) but as an aid to digestion and as a general tonic.

In the garden feverfew has many uses and is a most valuable plant. The wild species from southeast Europe makes a heap of divided leaves covered in white daisy heads in early summer: it often flowers itself to death but self-sown seedlings – appearing, as so often, in most felicitous places – are always about. A similar sized (about 18 inches) double flowered form has been in gardens for centuries and is most attractive. So too is the smaller golden-leaved variant and selections from this 'Golden Feather' are commonly used in summer bedding schemes. They are therefore ideal for formal herb garden knots, edgings and parterre fillings. They still possess the spicy aromatic foliage of the original.

CICHORIUM INTYBUS CHICORY

Chicory has, or has had, many uses. In the garden as a border plant its thin leaves and often irregular stems seem to offer little, especially in the latter part of the day. But, in the forenoon, no plant has a more beautiful flower, a clear cerulean, morning-glory blue; the sort of colour which brightens any day on which it is observed.

Medicinally chicory was used as an aid in jaundice: it is interesting that it is suggested that chicory, when used as a well-known coffee substitute or adulterant, protects the human liver from an excess of the real thing. According to Shaker literature a tea made from the roots is valuable in any stomach upset by excess or unfortunate food.

The plant is known more commonly as a delicious winter salad: roots are lifted in autumn and packed tightly together in sand or peat in the dark. Resultant shoot development appears as the 'Belgian endive' of greengrocers' shops.

CIMICIFUGA RACEMOSA BLACK SNAKEROOT

Black snakeroot, black cohosh, rattlehead, squaw root, bugbane – a range of names for a beautiful late flowering herbaceous plant. Though introduced to Europe in the seventeenth century from eastern North America its medicinal reputation never took off fully. In its home, however, the last two names indicate some of its folk uses, as an insecticide and, as squaw root, in various female complaints, notably as a postpartum accelerator. The Shaker literature lists many more. Like all ranunculaceous plants it is potentially poisonous and not to be trifled with.

Though not common in gardens – being slow of increase – it fully deserves to be. It achieves 5 feet or so, but it needs no staking. A clump of elegantly divided foliage can sit tidily towards the front of the border because the flower stems, when they appear, are leafless and slender adding frontal height without bulk. The white fuzzy flower spikes are like multiple croziers off the central stem and maintain this elegance in fruit right into winter.

Other cimicifugas exist and should be snapped up for the garden if seen to be offered. The closely related but bigger and later *C. ramosa* is also North American while there are several Asiatic representatives which get a passing mention in druggists' lists. All are beautiful plants.

CISTUS spp SUNROSE

The lovely Mediterranean sunroses have particular claims to herb garden space; apart from their considerable beauty. Several species produce an aromatic gum, usually called ladanum or labdanum which was an important part of many medicinal inhalations in the past, and in perfumery and incense. Two methods were employed to obtain it; by beating the bushes as Miller describes: in Candy (Crete) 'they make use of a kind of whip, of two Rows of Leather Straps, with which they brush and beat these Shrubs; the Gum, which sweats out from the Leaves, sticking on the Straps, which they scrape off with Knives, when they are sufficiently loaded'. Until quite recently laudanum gave goatherds and shepherds a secondary income as they combed the gum from their flocks after their day of browsing in the *maquis*.

While the Isles of Greece are given the entire credit for production in Miller's account, the actual gum cistus is *C. ladanifer*, a solely western Mediterranean species. In fact, as is realized when pushing through a mixture of species in their native habitat or merely crushing a leaf at home, all have a certain amount of the scent.

Thus, by close association or capability of gum production cistuses are admirable companions for lavenders, santolinas and rosemary to build up in northern gardens something of that omnipresent aromatic quality that is the very essence of hot southern hillsides.

Obviously, as may be guessed from their habitat and countries of origin, most cistuses are at the limit of their possible range with us. But full sun and impeccable drainage helps immeasurably. These provided, several can be pretty certain of giving years of success before succumbing to the 1981/2 type of winter. Even this is but a temporary concern: replacements are quick to grow. Fortunately for herb garden use several natural bi-specific hybrids having the gum cistus as one parent are among the best for general planting. All, it should be mentioned, are evergreen and have wide open flowers, like single roses, that fall soon after lunch; certainly by tea time, which makes them useless for a terrace on which one might normally sit in the evening.

Cistus × cyprius makes a sparse bush up to 6 feet in height and hence is one of the biggest. The dark leaves set off 4-inch wide flowers, each petal having a blood-red basal blotch. *C. 'Pat'* is lower but has even wider flowers while *C.* × *purpureus* is intermediate in size but has bright rose-crimson flowers.

Cistus × corbariensis is ideal where little space is available: it makes a perfectly regular 2-foot high dome of tidy crimped leaves and carries masses of old-penny sized white flowers, surrounded by the pink buds which are tomorrow's open blossoms. In cultivation the lovely pale pink natural hybrid *Cistus* × *skanbergii* seems by far the most aromatic. Narrow, grey-green leaves float out waves of ladanum onto the air, spilling, in the words of that previously mentioned appropriate verse, a 'beaker of the warm south' even on a northern winter's day; an immediate evocation of its home.

CITRUS AURANTIUM ORANGE

There is little doubt that, if invested with god-like powers, and asked to create the ideal plant, one would produce something very close to an orange tree. What could be more perfect: an evergreen with lustrous leaves, aromatic bark, beautiful creamy flowers whose rich scent is utterly enchanting, followed by magnificent edible fruit. So that no moment of the year should lack such beauty it is contrived that there is no gap between flowers and fruits, their seasons miraculously overlapping. A god-like plant indeed.

So much so indeed that *Citrus aurantium* and other species spread in pre-classical times, along the spice route westwards from a citrus epicentre in southern Vietnam, developing regional selections of importance in its various areas of cultivation. This sour, bitter or Seville orange is probably very close to the original species and it is this and the closely related lime which was of such service in the eighteenth century against scurvy.

Herb garden use in northern climes is naturally restricted by the amount of winter protection available. Surprisingly, perhaps, Seville orange trees in tubs survived, with only minimal damage, the severe 1981/82 winter in at least one Chelsea courtyard. The ability to bring such specimens into an unheated greenhouse or even a garage is often enough to be able to reproduce on a gentle scale the lines of citruses brought out from the grand orangeries of earlier times. Even one, in a Chinese pickled egg jar perhaps, makes a marvellous focal point, even if it seldom flowers and never fruits.

Meyer's lemon is perhaps the hardiest proper *Citrus* of all (excluding as only half citrus the 'Citrange', the Seville orange × *Poncirus* hybrid) which with care can even be persuaded to ripen fruit when it is quite small and hence it is easily protectable.

CLERODENDRON BUNGEI

Both this and the other *Clerodendron* we can grow outside in British gardens, *C. trichotomum* (*C. fargesii* is a geographical variant) are listed amongst Chinese medicinal herbs and hence, as highly ornamental plants, earn their place here. Both are used against, among other things, rheumatoid arthritis.

C. bungei is a rather coarse shrub with purplish heart-shaped leaves forming a thicket of suckering stems. In hard winters they may be cut back but this is no concern as they flower late in summer on new wood: fine heads of rose-red flowers. These are deliciously scented, very distinct from the unpleasantly foetid leaves: the former must be predominant in the herbal preparations which the Chinese state as being pleasant to taste.

C. trichotomum is an equally distinctive but visually very different plant. It makes a strong 8-foot dome with sprays of delicate, highly scented white flowers, each held in a purple calyx. When the flower falls each calyx becomes the receptacle for a bright blue berry. This overlapping sequence of surprising events provides interest for weeks in late summer and autumn; and when underplanted with colchicums the effect is delightful. It is a plant that is happy on thin chalk soils, though naturally preferring something better.

COIX LACHRYMA – JOBI JOB'S TEARS

Job's tears is one of the most delightful of ornamental grasses: ornamental that is, in warm Western gardens. In the East it is a cereal, the hard pea-sized seeds are strung as beads and, in decoction, have many applications in Chinese medicine.

With us it must be treated as a half-hardy annual. A few seeds should be potted, germinated in heat and then when all danger of frost is past planted out unseparated in a sunny spot which can be kept moist. The plant's pattern is rather like that of maize though only a couple of feet high and more slender.

Like maize there are separate male and female flowers the latter, of course, developing triplets of ivory, grey or black seeds which hang out with their weight to demonstrate the descriptiveness of both Latin and English names: in translation the Chinese (knowing nothing of Job) refer to mountain or pearl barley.

In late summer when the 'tears' have formed the stems cut whole will dry well for winter decorations indoors.

COLCHICUM AUTUMNALE MEADOW SAFFRON

The autumn crocuses or meadow saffrons are extremely useful garden plants both in the informality of orchard grass or in beds and borders amongst shrubs. There are two periods of particular beauty: in spring when the broad green leaves, as lush as those of hostas later on, unfurl amongst the sere grasses and tired evergreens – and in September and October when, those leaves having gone, clumps of flowers appear unannounced from the bare earth. Such sudden surprise gives other vernacular names: wonder bulb and mysteria. However atypical the foliage, it is the flowers which promote the 'autumn crocus' name – the six stamens (against the three of true crocuses) making one obvious difference.

Several species are highly ornamental. *C. byzantinum* and *C. aggripinum* vie for earliness, an odd flower sometimes appearing at the end of August. Six weeks later come the big forms of *C. speciosum*, the size and shape of half-pint tulip wine glasses which make such fine cut decoration for table centres (the double 'Waterlily' is particularly long-lasting). In mid-season the old *C. autumnale* appears. This has the widest distribution from northern France southwards. All come in shades of pink and lavender and white.

Known to the Greeks as a medicinal herb it has subsequently had a checkered career, being more highly regarded today than ever before, now that its highly poisonous aklaloids can be effectively harnessed. Colchicine is the principal one responsible for pain relief in chronic gout and rheumatism. This same extract has another modern use: as an aid in plant breeding it can be employed to promote mutations in chromosomes – the resultant polyploidy making possible crosses between plants which would be naturally sterile.

In cultivation colchicums are remarkably tolerant of a wide range of soils: only the wettest clays are unsuitable. A reasonably sunny spot is needed for the daily opening of the flowers. Planting should take place in July or August when the bulbs are quite dormant. Those left on seedsmen's shelves can be seen to burst into flower where they lie as if mutely crying for soil.

CONIFERS

One of the inevitable problems of herb garden design is the availability of visually striking woody plants which are also herbs in the broad sense of the word. As has already been discussed, only sweet bay would be of use in temperate areas if a narrow culinary definition were adhered to. Fortunately the early herbals offer a wider choice.

Thus there are a number of formal or semi-formal evergreens which are legitimate herbs for extension of the herb garden palette. Yew is often recommended as a surrounding hedge: more logical is to use *Thuja*. It makes as tight a screen with the advantage of quicker growth and wonderfully aromatic foliage. The great difference between it and the visually similar Lawson's cypress is the fragrance of *Thuja*.

Tsuga also makes a fine hedge and is very accepting of shade: foliage is dark, in ferny sprays. This is the tree known in North America as hemlock which causes confusion with the poisonous umbelliferous herb of that name. Neither its early medicinal uses nor effects are really comparable.

White pine and Scots pine, white fir and Norway spruce (never a good garden plant) are all too big for anything but herb garden backing and framing use. But the narrow spires of *Cupressus sempervirens stricta*, though not for cold areas, is very suitable as an accent plant and adds a further air of the *maquis* to groups of herb shrubs. Good for evergreen furnishing is the dwarf mountain pine mentioned above. Though eventually attaining 10 feet in height and as much wide, it can be kept smaller or replaced when it gets too big. It makes a good support for thin climbers.

Our very natural association of conifers with rugged uplands in the wild and informal schemes in cultivation makes their use restricted in the essentially domestic ambience of the herb garden. Nonetheless their aromatic foliage and these traditional uses give them a perfectly legitimate place.

Though two single plants of any kind seldom grow in exactly the same way, in a relatively large-scale herb garden paired specimens can frame a vista or enclose a seat, ornament or urn. Single specimens make focal points.

The Western tradition in garden design is to leave conifers (except yew, grown as hedges or in topiary shapes) severely alone to develop as they will. In Japanese gardens, by contrast, accentuation of 'natural' form – that which traditional aesthetics deem perfect – leads to 'cloud-pruning' and other forms which train pines such as *Pinus parviflora* into bonsai shapes, not necessarily of diminutive size.

They may be in the open ground or in containers for which nothing is more suitable than the big Oriental pickled cabbage and pickled egg jars which may be bought at Chinese emporia in Soho. Such bonsai provide a strength of form throughout the year which herb gardens frequently lack. This is, of course, merely an extension of the topiary idea (see *Buxus, Taxus*) of high herb garden validity.

'Pine-scented' is a phrase commonly attached to toiletries, cleaners and sprays: there is an expected scent of clean freshness to which we all easily relate. Though today the scent may be synthetic, the plants from which it comes naturally have, not surprisingly, a long history of herbal application. With their antiseptic effects the pine-scented resins and different forms of turpentine were commonly used while pumilio oil from the dwarf mountain pine (*Pinus mugo* var. *pumilio*) remains in several pharmocopaeias in south east Europe for respiratory disorders.

Joseph Miller described how of the silver fir 'The leaves or tops are used in Diet Drinks for the Scurvy, for which they are highly commended by the Inhabitants of the Northern Countries' and how the 'Cones or Nuts' of Mediterranean cypress staunch bleeding and 'fasten loose teeth'. An interesting botanical side-light is that the narrow form was then considered the female tree while the more open form the male. He also refers to several European pines as do both the Shakers and Chinese herbalists to species native in their own countries. Elsewhere are herbal references to *Thuja occidentalis, Tsuga canadensis* and *Cephalotaxus fortuni*, the plum yew.

It was reported that young leafy tops of several conifers were used by the early settlers of northern climes as a remedy against the scurvy (perhaps atavistic memories of 'eat up your greens or you'll never be a big boy' account for a common Scottish aversion today to any vegetables beyond 'tatties' and 'neeps'). But while the eighteenth-century herbalists, such as Joseph Miller, repeat the story, their main concern with the plants, lumped together as fir or firr-tree is the groups' production of balsams or fluid resins. These produce oil of turpentine on distillation which has many medicinal uses.

ABIES spp and PICEA spp

Abies (true firs), *Picea* (spruces – with pendulous instead of upright cones), *Pinus* (true pines), and *Larix* (larch) are all possible sources of turpentine. The first and last produce Strasbourg turpentine and the spruce Venetian turpentine.

Turpentine and resin producers can, by careful and regular pruning (as distinct from clipping) be maintained as elegant columns or cones though without the complete architectural formality that is usually provided by yew. Of the Europeans, though *Abies alba* was the fir still in the London pharmacopoeia until 1788, *A. cephalonica* (Grecian fir) and *A. pinsapo* (Spanish fir) are among the easiest in cultivation, accepting chalky soils happily. The Korean fir (*Abies koreana*) keeps a naturally smaller habit, often producing its striking purple-blue cones when only a few feet in height.

Again, though *Picea abies* is the medicinal spruce, it is a poor garden plant, as anyone knows who grows a Christmas tree. The Colorado spruce (*Picea pungens*) is the best alternative. This has small to medium sized forms such as 'Hoopsii' and 'Moerheimii' which need little pruning to keep in scale. Their glaucous blue foliage is marvellously complementary to the greys of lavender, santolinas and sages.

While yew is the classic encloser of herb gardens it is by no means the only one: indeed, on a boundary the erratically poisonous effect upon stock can never be discounted and here it should never be used. Even inside the garden, though magnificent, it has no scent to commend it. The false cypresses, Lawson's or Leylands's (that overplanted cliché of the 1970s) make good tight hedges as do the fern-leaved hemlocks (*Tsuga* spp) which have the virtue of accepting shade. But Western red cedar, *Thuja plicata* is the best. One of the most deliciously aromatic of all hardy plants – a warm, rich scent emanating from the glaucous-backed green sprays – it makes a tight formal hedge at any height required.

North America's eastern side has its own white cedar or arborvitae, *Thuja occidentalis*. This can take much colder winters and, in its range of forms, replaces *T. plicata* where conditions demand it. In Britain, however, it is generally a less good plant. It is interesting that a young plant was taken from the St Lawrence River area by Jacques Cartier in 1536. This lived for many years at Fontainebleau and according to John Parkinson (in *Paradisus* 1629) was the source of extensive European plantings up to this time.

Parkinson recommended chewing thuja leaves to expel 'thick purulent phlegm'. A century later Miller records, 'It is but rarely used'.

JUNIPERUS spp

Junipers have a clearer herbal connection. To look across chalk downland or upland where juniper still grows wild is to understand at once why so many forms are offered, especially too when it is recalled that this juniper is native all round the northern hemisphere. Vertical, flat, and bushy types – are all present. For garden use, therefore, carpeting ground covers and formal columns are equally available. Of the latter the Irish juniper is by far the best with an outline of a Mediterranean cypress which is unlikely to reach more than 10 feet in height. *J. communis* 'Compressa' is a minute form of this, seldom exceeding a yard high.

Of the carpeters some, such as 'Effusa', remain green throughout the year while others like 'Depressa', a Canadian variant, become bronze during winter. Planted a couple of feet apart these junipers will soon cover wide areas while keeping absolutely flat. For parterre use and ground cover around other plants they are equally useful.

The aromatic oil which can be smelled by merely bruising a leaf or two is especially concentrated in the 'cones' – pea size fleshy berries. In their first year they are green with a blue bloom, then black on ripening in the autumn of the second. It is these which provide the major flavouring agent of Hollands or Geneva (Dutch *jenever* = juniper, and hence its abbreviation to gin). Hill writes; 'With these is also made the true Geneva but the liquor our poor people drink under that name is only malt spirits and oil of turpentine'. A sad reflection on eighteenth-century Gin Lane.

Juniperus sabina is a very poisonous plant employed in Europe (where it is native) in vetinary medicine and even then only externally. The garden forms are mainly broad spreading carpeters; 'Blue Danube' is an excellent low plant, grey-blue in colour while 'Tamariscifolia' eventually makes a wide flat bush like a small trunkless cedar.

The disagreeable smell of these savins distinguish them from the small forms of *J. virginiana* which the Shakers also used, it being an available local plant, as with savin. Again the garden forms vary from large evergreen trees (the species reaches 75 feet in the wild) to flat ground covers. Especially fine is 'Skyrocket' which makes an extremely narrow spire of blue-grey foliage, quicker to make the vertical effect than the Irish juniper.

CONIUM MACULATUM HEMLOCK

Hemlock is well known as the basis of the poison used in classical Athens as an effective method of disposing of recalcitrant philosophers. There is no doubt it would be equally efficient today and hence it is one of the herbs that should only be grown advisedly; it does, however, have no luscious berry like deadly nightshade which could attract children.

In appearance hemlock is a typical biennial umbellifer – a rather coarse cow parsley with distinctive purple-spotted stems reaching 6 to 10 feet in height. Until recently, though not uncommon in the wild, it was not particularly noticeable. Now in the last four or five years vast stands have appeared along several stretches of English motorways.

Hemlock has been exhaustively examined chemically: several aklaloids are present of which coniine provides the principal poison. Medicinally it was used to treat asthma, neurological conditions and chronic rheumatism. As such it has spread to other parts of the temperate world and is now well naturalized in many areas. In North America the Shakers employed hemlock though it was probably established before their herbal role became extensive. It has no connection whatever, either visually, chemically or botanically, with the tall coniferous trees which are known as hemlocks in North America. Originally species of *Tsuga* were called hemlock spruce, referring perhaps to the sprays of fern-like (or hemlock-like) foliage. An unfortunate confusion.

CONVALLARIA MAJALIS LILY OF THE VALLEY

It is to be hoped that the rather excited texts devoted to poisonous plants have never put a single person off growing lily of the valley. No cottage garden plant is better loved; no plant deserves such devotion.

Lily of the valley is familiar to every gardener: purple shoots spearing through the ground in early spring to unfurl pairs of brilliant green leaves. By May wiry stems hold up to a dozen exquisite bells, typically white but a pink form exists, as do other variants. 'Fortin's Giant' is bigger and takes another couple of weeks to come into flower, so extending the season valuably. All possess an incredible fragrance and, though many plants are said to have flowers that look like lily of the valley, none really smell like it – though *Mahonia japonica* gets close on both counts.

Convallaria is a typical woodlander making dense carpets in the wild. In cultivation it can be unpredictable going, like the wind, only where it listeth. Thus one may see it languishing in lovely leafy soil (with which it must be initially tempted) and then romping through a gravel path to demonstrate, cat-like, its independence. Beneath shrubs, where it can be left undisturbed, is probably a good place to try it. Occasionally the scarlet berries occur in sufficient numbers to make something of an autumn eye-catcher: these too are highly poisonous.

Unlike most medicinal plants whose use has declined with the advent of modern medicine, *Convallaria* is employed more. Its cardiac glycosides have a similarly effective action to those of *Digitalis* and are considered safer, but it is not a plant for home medication in any form at all.

CORIANDRUM SATIVUM CORIANDER

It is strange that a plant with something of an unpleasant smell when fresh should develop such a delicious aromatic savour in its ripe fruits. The name coriander derives from the Greek *koris*, a bedbug: fortunately the herb's sweet, cloying smell is as close as one is likely to get to that traditionally distinctive odour.

Coriander is a rather weedy umbelliferous annual. Sown in spring as a hardy annual in a sunny spot it will ripen its distinctive orbicular fruits by late summer. These, on ripening, develop a delightful orange-like scent and are used widely as a spice and a condiment. Both these and the fresh leaves (much more of an acquired taste) have been enjoyed throughout the old world for thousands of years; so much indeed is it a plant of cultivation that it is no longer known in its wild state. In eastern Europe particularly many named selections are available.

Medicinally coriander's volatile oil flavours and corrects the action of other, less agreeabler potions.

CRATAEGUS MONOGYNA HAWTHORN

Though a tree of hawthorn in full flower in May is as splendid a sight as any exotic of similar size that we can grow, it is seldom considered a garden plant: the conventional wisdom concerning familiarity is as valid as usual. Nonetheless, to quote Stuart: 'Medicinally, the herb is very important and is widely used in orthodox Eastern and unorthodox Western medicine for the treatment of hypertension' (*Encyclopedia of Herbs and Herbalism*). Hence a herb garden position is desirable in any collection which makes some attempt to be comprehensive. If the plant is too big in its natural state it makes a valuable and impenetrable herb garden hedge: it can also be used as a subject for topiary whether as a pair of simple obelisks or in such flights of fancy as peafowl or pouter pigeons.

When clipped of course, neither May's foam of flower nor autumnal haws (the source of the hypotensive) will be borne freely.

CROCUS SATIVUS SAFFRON

It is surprising that a plant now so difficult to grow should give its name to a town that was, in the late Middle Ages, the centre of a considerable industry. The architecture of Saffron Walden in Essex testifies to its early prosperity.

Saffron – the flavouring, the drug, and the dye, are the product of the three long blood-red styles which are conspicuous inside the open flower. Large though they are by *Crocus* standards, towards an inch in length, it will be readily realized that a vast number of flowers is necessary to produce even the saltspoon of dried saffron required to flavour and colour a dish of rice.

Saffron has been cultivated in the Middle East and southern Europe – areas to which *Crocus sativus* was once native – since earliest times. It is now not known in the wild but its important areas of commercial growing extend especially into Kashmir. As with other materials of great price and rarity saffron was formerly considered to have aphrodisiac qualities.

Garden cultivation in Britain has two particular difficulties: to obtain stock in the first place and to maintain any once obtained. Turkish saffron corms appear to have more reliance needing a warm sunny spot in reasonably rich soil. As true autumn-flowering crocuses (as distinct from *Colchicum*), corms are planted when dormant in mid-summer. The flowers, typical pale purple fragrant crocuses with their brilliant styles, open in September and leaf growth begins soon after, not fully developing, however, until the following spring. Foliar feed at this time helps to build up strong bulbs: these should be lifted and divided every two or three years to prevent a mere tussock of grassy leaves.

Saffron is beautiful enough and sufficiently significant herbally to lavish such care upon it.

CUCURBITS CUCUMBER ETC

As Joseph Miller states 'the cucumber is a Fruit so well known, that it were Labour lost to say much of it . . .' He then goes on to do so.

Here it is included with other similar members of its family, the Cucurbitaceae, the squashes, pumpkins, marrows and gourds of all types. Early texts refer constantly to the cooling properties of cucumber fruit and its seeds used therefore in 'burning Fevers and Pleurisies'. Chinese medicine and the Shakers recommend seeds of squashes and pumpkins to dispel tapeworms.

In an illustrative herb garden therefore several *Cucurbits* have a legitimate place. They are also highly desirable for their rapid effect. Few plants provide such a splendid summer screen or give immediate height in a new garden when grown up strong tripods. Although all are tendril climbers some initial encouragement is appreciated, and it is also necessary to give support to developing fruits which may, especially in the case of pumpkins, weigh half a hundredweight.

All these *Cucurbits* must be sown in a greenhouse (or on a warm kitchen window-sill): mid April is about right if the seedlings are not to be too big and soft before they are put out at the very end of May. There a sunny spot is needed with copious water and food for dramatic growth. Care must also be given to the fact that such rumbustious growers can overwhelm gentler things.

CYNARA SCOLYMUS GLOBE ARTICHOKE

Few herbaceous plants are more scenically spectactular than globe artichokes. It has a huge heap of *Acanthus*-like grey leaves, a steadily developing flower spike, the buds are smooth as if carved from rarest jade, and the open flowers are great bosses of blue-purple, which even in sere decay maintain an architectural pattern for months.

But such potential provokes considerable confusion: are the buds to be cut as the most delicious of vegetables or allowed to develop their full ornamental effect? Medicinally too *Cynara* is valuable in liver complaints and hence is used for jaundice: the whole plant produces the medicinal extracts.

As an original southern European (no longer known in the wild and possibly a cultivated derivative of *Cynara cardunculus*, the cardoon) it is in Britain on the northern limit of its accepted range. Full sun, therefore, is needed, rich yet well-drained soil and, for cold areas, a heap of bracken or wood chips over the crowns in winter. Important too is to maintain young stock: as growth begins in spring clumps are best reduced to three shoots, and with the suckers removed can then be lined out to give a few late heads for cutting, and eventually to begin new permanent clumps if required.

DAPHNE spp

Daphne mezereum is one of the best loved of early-flowering shrubs – a little bush of 3 feet or so smothered with scented rosy-purple flowers opening first on the bare twigs from late February into April. A taller white-flowering form is equally desirable. In August they put on a good display of red and yellow berries respectively. These last in direct proportion to the local population of green-finches which seem to find mezereon seeds irresistible.

To humans, however, the fruits and indeed the whole plant are highly poisonous. Though still in the homoeopathic list its historic applications for venereal and scrophulous diseases are no longer made.

Hence it can be enjoyed as a lovely garden plant without ominous overtones. As a woodland shrub it likes, except in the north, a half-shaded spot. Lime and a clay soil are both appreciated: even in apparently ideal conditions however it is not long-lived, often being struck down by virus leaf-mottling. Keeping aphides down is a help but occasional renewal from seed is necessary, which germinate easily if sown as soon as ripe, but a branch may need netting. Such a miffy plant should never be planted in formal pairs: the effect is seldom obtained.

Though mezereon is occasionally found wild in Britain, much commoner is *Daphne laureola*, the spurge laurel. A 3-foot shiny evergreen of clay woodlands, it is a most distinguished shrub for a shady spot, green at all times even when in flower in February, for the flowers themselves (erratically fragrant) are also green, enlivened only with a tiny orange eye. It is just as poisonous as mezereon. Berries and leaves were given as a violent purge and, says Joseph Miller, with a hint of grim humour, 'by some adventurous persons given in the Dropsy'. Chinese medicine includes two further daphnes, both very beautiful plants. *Daphne genkwa* was introduced to Britain by Robert Fortune in 1843 but because of its rather erratic behaviour it has never become well known. A good plant, however, it is one of the loveliest of spring flowers: a 3-foot bush with its slender shoots lined with clusters of silvery lilac-blue flowers. When these are over and the leaves appear it looks more like a dwarf willow.

In China it has a great proliferation of common names – if indeed they do relate to this one plant – from (in translation) nine-dragon flower, Szechuan mulberry, fish poison to mouse-flower etc. None describe its appearance as it grows in the West. The root bark and flowers are used in decoction for wounds.

For these, sciatica and various skin diseases, the flowers and stems of *Daphne odora* also are used. One of its vernacular names, flowers-blooming-in-the-snow, reflects the early flowering for which this splendid plant is so valued with us as an ornamental garden plant. It makes a wide low evergreen with clusters of white flowers from purplish buds: they have a marvellous crystalline texture and a rich lemony fragrance. The first flowers open as early as February in good years and continue for at least a couple of months. The form 'Aureo-marginata' with cream-edged leaves is rather hardier though both like some protection in cold areas. Any soil seems to suit, acid or limy, with a little summer shade for preference. This superb shrub is a major addition to the herb garden scene.

DATURA STRAMONIUM THORN APPLE

Thorn apple is one of those plants that, since man first harnessed its narcotic and pain-easing powers, seems to have hitched itself on to his coat-tails. Its origins are confused: reputable authorities categorically state such diverse areas as Asia Minor and North America (the latter is suggested in its other names, Jimson – or Jamestownweed). Tropics of the old world is perhaps as close as can be guessed.

It is now a field-edge and rubbish dump annual weed common through much of the warm temperate world. Even in Britain it appears, occasioning, if noticed, a picture in local newspapers under a banner headline 'Beware this plant: dangerous weed discovered'. Again, unlike *Atropa*, no-one is ever likely to attempt to eat the prickly, unsucculent fruit nor its foetid leaves. Visually, thorn apple is not unattractive; a robust 2 to 3-foot high plant, its dark foliage contrasting well with the white funnel-shaped flowers. Even after a frost the carcase of a well-fruited plant presents a striking picture.

The big shrubby angels' trumpet *Datura* species are now often placed in a separate genus *Brugmansia* which does not therefore belong here. Very close however are *D. inoxia* from Mexico and *D. metel* from southwest China. The former is widely cultivated as an ornamental having 6-inch long pink or lavender trumpets; leading to possible confusion is the name *D. meteloides* for a couple of sub-species of this. All of the group, if available, are more striking garden plants than conventional thorn apple. As they produce similar alkaloids of medicinal importance they could well be chosen, if available, in its stead. They all need a warm sunny spot to develop well: sowing under glass produces a more certain plant.

As medicinal herbs, sources of the alkaloids hyoscine, hyoscyamine and atropine for which they are grown commercially, these daturas have many applications. Traditionally leaves have been smoked to relieve asthma: recent uses are in conditions of epilepsy and Parkinson's disease. None of these narcotic, hallucinogenic plants from the Solanaceae should ever be a part of home medication. A phrase in *Shaker Herbs* makes the point. Of thorn apple, in large doses, we read: 'its victims suffer the most intense agonies and die in maniacal delirium'.

DELPHINIUM CONSOLIDA LARKSPUR

There is considerable botanical confusion over certain annual delphiniums: ought they to move (or revert) to their own genus of *Consolida* and, if they did, how are the species best arranged? More simply, and sufficient for this book is to refer to larkspurs. Like many members of the Ranunculaceae they are very poisonous and violently purgative: Miller states that it 'is said to be of a healing Nature, but is seldom or never used in *England*'. He fails to mention a common European use, that a strong decoction of the seeds disposes of fleas and lice in human hair.

More agreeably larkspurs are delightful garden annuals: breeding and selections have moved far from the diffuse spikes of the species so that some are almost of the size and weight of perennial border delphiniums. These are fine in the cutting garden; for winter use they dry well in a sand bath or silica gel and hold their colours miraculously. The lighter types however are best for border or herb garden decoration – pinks, blues, whites are all available separately or in mixed colours. Height varies from 2 to 4 feet. Larkspurs may be started under glass but are best sown *in situ* in good soil and rigorously thinned.

The early herbals all list a close relative, *Delphinium staphisagria*, a short-lived perennial from southern Europe whose herbal use repeated the insecticidal properties of larkspur. Known as stavesacre it is a stately pyramidal plant of 4 feet or so with large vine-shaped leaves at the base declining upwards until the flower spike is reached. Flowers are a sombre blue-purple and strangely hairy. Stavesacre is sufficiently distinct to be worth growing but one will need, almost certainly, to collect one's own seed on a Mediterranean holiday.

DIANTHUS CARYOPHYLLUS CARNATION

The divide in times past between the different categories in which herbs were put was never definite. Thus the clove carnations or clove gillyflowers are classic herb garden plants without medicinal applications, their role being that of today's definition of a herb – a plant whose qualities enhance life rather than support or preserve it. A tonic cordial can be made from the flowers and petals added to wine cups, pot pourri and scented sachets. This follows the medieval practice of adding clove-scented pinks or gillyflowers (French: *girofle* = clove) to liquor; they became known as sops-in-wine and the phrase later extended to certain types of pinks.

Double selections of the original Mediterranean species (probably no longer in existence) were grown and loved in Elizabethan times and any modern herb garden should grow the old crimson clove, the old salmon clove ('Lord Chatham') and any others that can be found. They retain the classic clove scent to a wonderful degree: sheaves of modern greenhouse carnations without any perfume are an insult to the nose.

The old cloves flower in late July and August and are thus excellent for fronting old-fashioned roses such as 'Rosa Mundi' or the apothecary's rose to extend the season of that part of the garden.

Flowering earlier are the garden pinks, based originally upon *Dianthus plumarius*: over the years carnation blood has been brought into them so that apart from season (and some like the seventeenth-century 'Bat's Red' flower into autumn) and their smaller size they are very similar. The mid-nineteenth-century 'Mrs Sinkins' is well known though the flowers are apt to be messy with an inevitably split calyx out of which the petals tumble. Such a splendid scent, however, forgives all.

Many lovely old pinks and carnations have been lost but specialist nurseries still offer some. Once obtained, new cuttings must be pulled off with a heel every September and firmed into the ground with a little sand at the base (either in a nursery row or where they are to remain). They need a light limy soil and a sunny spot. Pigeons and rabbits enjoy the hummocks of grey leaves, though from a less aesthetic point of view, as much as humans do.

DIGITALIS PURPUREA FOXGLOVE

The story of the physician William Withering, who in the late 1770s was investigating a local herbal tea which had amazing effects upon cases of dropsy, is well known. He was able to isolate foxglove as the vital ingredient and modern research confirms the presence of several glycosides, notably digitalin, which act directly upon the muscles of the heart. Foxglove is grown commercially for production of the drug whose fortuitous discovery was a major medical breakthrough. It is a classic example of treating effective folk recipes with scientific curiosity and seriousness.

Joseph Miller of course, writing half a century earlier can only offer the then conventional wisdom: 'The Plant is rarely used inwardly, being strongly Emetic, and working with Violence both upwards and downwards: though *Parkinson* extols a decoction of it in Ale, with Polypody Roots, as an approved Medicine for the Falling Sickness'.

Foxglove is one of our most beautiful native plants seen most commonly on acid soils – though not insisting upon this in the garden. In the south it makes a great show in woodland glades, magnificent in June with its great one-sided spires 6 feet high. A pilgrimage to the same spot the following year is an inevitable anticlimax: as a biennial last year's plants are dead, and leafy rosettes from their seeds merely indicate next year's promise. In the north and west foxgloves are smaller, hedgebank plants with several spikes and often appearing to be perennial.

In cultivation it is best to grow a row in the kitchen garden putting out clumps in autumn or spring where they are to flower. The clear rose-purple of the species is extended but hardly improved by selections (often with flowers all round the spike) which go as far as apricot. The white form, lovely with grey foliage and other white flowers, must be segregated from the type if it is to remain pure.

Commercial production of digitalin now takes place mainly in southeast Europe with their native species: these are regularly perennial and are also lovely garden plants easily grown from seed and flowering in the second year. *Digitalis lanata* is the most important, its flat rosettes pushing up narrow spires of lightly packed flowers each the shape of a helmet coal-scuttle. Their colour is a strangely attractive mixture of cream and purplish-grey.

D. ferruginea at 4 feet is taller, more reliable in most gardens, with flowers of tawny brown. *D. grandiflora* is much more like the northern forms of our native foxglove in size of plant and shape of flower. These are a soft creamy-yellow. All these exotic foxgloves like sun but will take some summer shade happily: but winter wet is death.

DRIMYS WINTERI WINTER'S BARK

The story is told that by the time they got to Cape Horn, of the five ships that had set out as Francis Drake's fleet in 1577, only two remained. One was his own *Golden Hind* which went on to complete that epic voyage around the world; the other was the *Elizabeth*, commanded by Captain Winter. Parted by one of the great storms for which the area is notorious the two were permanently separated. Drake went on and Winter turned back, but not before he had sent ashore for supplies. Among them was the aromatic bark of a local evergreen tree which became a valuable remedy for scurvy. Over two centuries later it was botanically named (having been collected on Cook's second great voyage) *Drimys winteri*.

Winter's bark has never become common in gardens mainly because its origin and size in the wild encouraged planting only in great mild gardens of the southwest. There is a certain justification in that vast plants 50 feet across and as much high have developed.

But, needing a bit of frost protection up-country, it makes a marvellous west wall plant and is easily kept to size. The attraction lies principally in the leaves which are long and narrow, pale green above and milk white beneath, held on pink-tinged shoots. Every part is deliciously aromatic. The fragrant flowers are carried over many weeks in spring, hanging bunches of ivory-white.

ECBALLIUM ELATERIUM SQUIRTING CUCUMBER

Squirting cucumber is not a plant for small gardens. Its broad clump of bristly leaves takes up a lot of space and the florin-sized yellow flowers make little show. But as one of the classic purging plants any comprehensive collection of herbs will include it. Miller describes it as 'one of the strongest Cathartics we have, carrying off ferous watery Humours, both upwards and downwards, with great Violence – whereby it is of singular use in the Dropsy'. So strong is the effect that elaterium (the preparation made from the fruits) could cause abortions.

Anyone searching for confirmation of the medieval Doctrine of Signatures would light upon this with glad cries as its natural habit is so perfectly reflected in its medicinal effect. In mid-summer the little cucumber fruits soon assume a position at right-angles to their stems; as they grow, each looking like a yellow-green kiwi fruit, their weight causes the angle to become more acute. When fully ripe they fall and the black seeds are ejected with considerable force in a stream of acrid juice for twenty feet or so; its aim to passers-by sometimes seems more than fortuitous! It is an irresistible toy for children of all ages but to the gardener seed collection is a positively hazardous operation.

In well-drained spots squirting cucumber is perennial: it can alternatively be treated like any other cucurbit. Sown under glass and then planted out in April it will perform its act perfectly well by August.

ECHINACEA ANGUSTIFOLIA CONEFLOWER

The specific epithet refers to similarly narrow leaves. In this case they are on one of the North American coneflowers whose central, hard boss of disc-florets, surrounded by a ring of drooping petals or ray-florets gives the vernacular name.

It is surprising, although the United States Dispensatory recommended its use over a century ago, that the Shakers, more usual receptors of folk tradition, omit it. Purple coneflower helps to resist infection and is effective against boils, abscesses and other skin eruptions.

Visually it is a rather sparse, though distinctive purple-flowered daisy a couple of feet high. Bigger – sometimes twice that – and altogether a more spectacular garden plant is *Echinacea purpurea*. It shares the same common name. The fine daisy-flowers stand stiff as soldiers and visually they are in reversed profile the shape of *Dodecatheon* or shooting stars.

The cone is orange-brown, while the corona of 'petals' is a strangely lovely pinkish mauve. Each flower lasts for several weeks and makes a fine pattern in the garden. Coneflowers need sun in reasonably rich soil.

ELAEAGNUS PUNGENS

Chinese medicine recommends the stems and leaves of this common garden evergreen shrub, native to China and Japan, to be used in decoction to relieve asthma and control diarrhoea. It therefore becomes a legitimate herb garden addition as a hedge, clipped into shapes in a formal situation or, where space permits, allowed to develop its full growth potential. Eight feet high and as much across is not uncommon.

While the wavy leaves with their brown-dotted silvery undersides are distinctive in their own right, the range of golden or cream variegated forms ('Dicksonii', 'Maculata' etc) make brilliant winter effect, bright as forsythias which cannot compete until spring. To use such a dominating plant therefore is to raise the herb garden into an area of year-long interest: around it the lesser winter-flowering plants can cluster.

Elaeagnus pungens flowers late: unless one looks hard nothing will be seen until suddenly in October, when a whiff of clove carnations comes clear and strong. A search will lead to little white tubular flowers clustering beneath the leaves. In Britain the edible scarlet barries, silver and brown when young, are seldom produced: the variegated types seem not to flower at all.

ELSHOLTZIA STAUNTONII MINTBUSH

Mintbush is a title usually kept for the Australian genus *Prostanthera*. It is just as valid for this useful shrub from northern China. Unlike the other mint bushes there is little difficulty with frost damage as shoots always regenerate from the base.

Pruned to 18 inches or so each spring, *Elsholtzia* (not to be confused with *Eschscholzia*, the Californian poppy) then puts out 2 feet of growth with narrow aromatic leaves which can be collected, dried and used in pot pourri. Untouched shoots produce a fine show of lilac-pink spikes from August until early October. This mintbush associates particularly well with *Caryopteris*, flowering as it does at the same time and providing suitably soft autumnal michaelmas daisy colours without the mildew.

Elsholtzia is happy in any decent soil in full sun but summer drought produces a plant too mean to be worth growing.

EPILOBIUM ANGUSTIFOLIUM ROSEBAY WILLOW

Less than a century ago rosebay willow herb was quite a rare plant and such is its beauty that people made expeditions to see it in flower. The Second World War caused it to have what can only be described as a population explosion: its other name of fireweed indicates the habit of colonizing burnt-over sites, and bombed cities provided perfect positions for expansion. It is no exaggeration to state that for ten years buddleia and rosebay did more to hide London's bomb-scars than cohorts of planners.

It appears in the list of Shaker herbs as an astringent used in dysentery.

Not surprisingly rosebay must be used with some care in the garden. The 4 or 5-foot high clumps with their beautiful spires of deep rose flowers are invasive at the root and prodigious producers of fluffy, windborne seeds. Less aggressive is the equally lovely white form which has to be propagated by division. Both flower for weeks from July onwards.

EPIMEDIUM GRANDIFLORUM

There are few more beautiful ground cover plants than these little, mainly Asiatic, berberis relations. Foliage and flowers are both of great elegance. Only one has any reputation as a herb, and this, also listed as *E. macranthum*, is from Japan. It is reputed to act on impotency, the leaves being steeped in white wine.

Visually its effect is very much clearer. The sequence of growth in epimediums has particular charm. Towards the end of March thin hairy stems, like unfurling maidenhair fronds, appear from the rhizomes and at about a foot high they produce a swarm of flowers like little aquilegias. Meanwhile leaf stems have been slowly catching up and, just when the flowers go over, as if to prevent a moment of disappointment, unfold their leaves, prettily veined and tinted with pink. These remain all summer and even when killed by frost maintain a warm rusty brown. To enjoy next year's progression dead foliage should be cut off just before new growth begins. 'Rose Queen' and 'White Queen' are fine selections of this species.

All epimediums like a leafy soil and part shade: clumps are easily divided in autumn or spring.

ERIOBOTRYA JAPONICA LOQUAT

It might be thought that the delicious fruit, like hairy yellow plums, would be the part of the plant used medicinally. Perhaps it is like the bunch of grapes brought by the visitor but kept just out of reach of the hospital patient who is fed only on prescribed drugs. Here, Chinese medicine recommends a decoction made of the leaves for chronic coughs.

As a garden ornamental loquat has great potential. Hardy in London and to the south and west it eventually makes a high bush with foot-long corrugated evergreen leaves. Heads of dull-white flowers, hawthorn-scented, open in autumn and should naturally develop for the next few months to ripen into clusters of fruit at Easter time. Not surprisingly the British climate does not permit this. It is a marvellous courtyard plant where it succeeds, offering to limy soils the sort of foliage normally only seen in big rhododendron gardens.

It can however be easily treated as a tub plant and, like *Citrus*, can be stood out for all but the coldest months: winter light and minimal frost-protection is all that is needed. Though, like sowing the pips of any fruit tree, it takes some years for wood to reach fruiting stage, in the case of loquat early growth is quick and apparently mature. Exotic fruiterers usually offer the source in spring: a single ripe loquat provides up to four large viable seeds.

ERUCA SATIVA ROCQUETTE

Rocquette or rocket-salad. This is not a particularly ornamental plant but one which is valuable to have continuously and conveniently for salad use. Common in the Mediterranean countries, it is there usually sown in autumn to ensure winter leaves: in Britain it is best sown *in situ* in August and again in April, for in some years it may not overwinter. Late spring sowings are apt to run quickly to seed.

The hummock of dark green, divided leaves is what is required; if not sufficiently picked, thin stems of cabbagy flowers arise with conventional cross-shaped flowers of pale yellow etched with purple veins. Only in recent years has it returned to the English herb garden, travellers having met it whilst on holiday and liking its rather oily texture and hot taste.

The early texts offer several medicinal uses: mixed with cumin seed, it is 'a mighty preserver against an Apoplexy'; boiled with sugar it provides a cough syrup. But Joseph Miller begins with a warning, however unsubstantiated: 'It has a Name of a Provocative and Exciter to Venery'.

ERYNGIUM MARITIMUM SEA HOLLY

Though not nearly as common as it used to be, sea holly is one of our most distinctive native plants especially when seen emerging from pure sand within sound of the waves. It makes a clump of hand-like leaves with intensely prickly fingers of a strange bluish-white, much brighter than grey. Each teazel-like flower cluster is supported by a star of prick-ended bracts, palest metallic blue.

Once eaten candied as a sweetmeat and as a restorative, the roots strike deeply down through the sand and gravel to moisture beneath. To succeed in the garden, therefore, it requires good drainage: a perfect plant for a poor, hot place. Medicinally the early authorities refer to sea holly's use to help diseases of what Miller calls rather coyly 'the Parts of Generation'.

By extension other eryngiums can be given a place in a herb garden, though none makes the solid dome of mixed foliage and flower which is so distinctive a trademark of sea holly proper. Of these *E. alpinum* and *E. tripartitum* with some hybrids are the best perennials for garden decoration. The biennial *E. giganteum* is just as good: eventually repeating the blue-white colour of sea holly, in its first year it makes an unremarkable rosette of leaves from which in a year or two a ghost-white stem of flowers springs up. This is a lovely cottage garden plant often known now as Miss Willmott's Ghost: that famous but daunting Edwardian gardener was reputed to scatter its seeds on her visits and thus, one or two years later, her passing presence was recalled.

EUCALYPTUS GLOBULUS GUM TREE

Eucalyptus oil must be one plant product which is known to everybody: the words are virtually synonymous with 'common cold'. The oil is expressed from the foliage of which a single leaf is enough, fresh or dried immediately, to evoke the product and the condition that made it required.

There are well over 500 species of gum trees from Australia and Tasmania. Almost all are aromatic to a greater or lesser degree; the timber is extremely valuable and eucalyptus honey is an important product. Most exhibit foliage polymorphy with distinctly different juvenile and adult leaves.

This is particularly noticeable in *E. globulus*, the blue gum. A native tree has a beautiful cream trunk and branches where the bark has sloughed off, and long narrow leaves hanging vertically from the twigs. In the first 3 or 4 years from seed, however, foliage is sessile and of a brilliant sea holly blue-white. It is thus that we usually see it because blue gum is not amongst the hardiest of its genus for British gardens and though huge trees exist in the west they can be badly injured even there.

For herb garden and decorative use it is better to raise it as an annual from seed (cuttings seem to be impossible) and put out young plants which can make 6 feet in their first season. They will produce quite enough leaves for a daily passing sniff or even an extended summer cold. Far hardier are *E. niphophila* and *E. gunnii*, the snow and cider gums respectively.

EUONYMUS EUROPAEUS SPINDLE

The lovely spindle-bush of our chalk or limestone hedgerows has much to answer for as the winter host of black bean aphis or 'black fly'. It is a very beautiful plant, as the leaves turn in autumn, the green stems are hung with pink fruits which open to reveal brilliant orange seeds. Such a colour combination would be almost inconceivable to contrive. In the garden a selected form 'Red Cascade' is even brighter and more certain in its display.

Herbally, spindle is a dangerous purgative but is still used externally to rid the body of skin parasites. The Shakers listed a North American spindle, *Euonymus atropurpureus*, not to be confused with the purple-leaved cultivar of the European plant. There too it was clearly not for home medication.

While the American is probably not in cultivation in British gardens the species used in Chinese medicine certainly is. This is *Euonymus alatus*, one of the best of all shrubs for autumn colour. The specific name refers to the corky 'wings' all the way down the stems: these are referred to in one of their vernacular names: *szu-pa tao* or fourknives. The stems are used for gynaecological troubles.

As a garden plant, apart from requiring full sun to encourage the fullest possible autumn tints, it will take any position. The form 'Compactus' is ideal for small gardens.

EUPATORIUM PURPUREUM JOE PYE WEED

Though our own hemp agrimony (*Eupatorium cannabinum*) gets a passing mention in the old texts, it is a coarse plant and both garden and herbal interest is concentrated more upon a couple of North American species.

Joe pye weed is a most imposing plant reaching up to 10 feet in rich soil in the wild and as such is probably one of the biggest self-supporting herbaceous perennials: the top of this giant opens into a great purple plate of rayless daisies on purple stalks. It then takes on a further local and fully justified name: queen of the meadow.

Fortunately it fails to become such a monster with us but still attains 6 or 7 feet with ease and is obviously a back-of-the-border plant.

The Shakers used joe pye in all urinary troubles, as another name, stonebreak, indicates. They found a closely related plant,

Eupatorium perfoliatum, of even greater use. In the wild they are seen together: this one white, only two thirds the height and bearing the distinctive pairs of leaves, like those of teazel, which provide the Latin epithet.

Shaker vernacular names emphasize their interests: feverwort, thoroughwort, ague weed, sweating plant, vegetable antimony, boneset. It was made into ointments and syrups: 'a strong tea of Boneset sweetened with honey will break up an ordinary head cold' – apparently as effective as a good hot lemon drink and, in colonial times, a great deal easier to obtain.

FERNS

As many ferns resemble one another in appearance and cultivation it seems sensible to deal together with the half dozen or so which appear in the early European texts, in the Shaker literature and Chinese lists.

To the early writers ferns were mysterious plants, without normal flowers, though the dust-like spores usually produced from underneath the fronds were thought to be seeds. Those plants with separate spore-bearing fronds or parts of fronds, such as osmunda, were considered 'flowering' ferns. Any hint of the strange and primitive alternation of generations, sexual and asexual by turn, by which ferns reproduce was quite unknown. Fortunately, as now, propagation of garden ferns by vegetative division was simple enough. All, too, were collected from the wild.

Herbally most ferns were accounted effective expellers of tapeworms from the human body. The male fern, *Dryopteris filix-mas* was most commonly used in Britain while *D. spinulosa*, which is native both to Europe and North America and employed by the Shakers, is twice as strong. These people used maidenhair fern (*Adiantum pedatum*) freely for asthma, pleurisy and influenza. These last ailments are taken up by Chinese herbalism which recommends *Cyrtomium falcatum*: it is also said to aid infective hepatitis. That several ferns are known commonly as spleenwort indicates a further application.

In the herb garden ferns are extremely valuable as they enjoy, indeed need, the moisture and shade which most other herbs reject. Thus for the north-facing beds of any formal design they will be chosen from the range of lovely plants available.

For garden use one can list these in ascending order of size. No more than a foot in height, but capable of developing wide mats of evergreen leaves is our native polypody (*Polypodium vulgare*). Though liking atmospheric moisture it will accept surprising dryness at the root as proved by its ability to grow epiphytically upon branches of trees, especially in moist climates.

About the same height but much more delicate in effect and constitution are the decidious maidenhairs, lovely in development, maturity and decline.

Making one of the strongest patterns is hartstongue (*Asplenium scolopendrium*). The shuttlecock of broad, shining, evergreen leaves are barred by rows of spores on the reverse like a mackerel's back.

All the species of *Dryopteris* are good, male ferns and buckler ferns alike: they associate splendidly with foxgloves to provide an association which is herbally, ecologically and aesthetically right. While the magnificent Himalayan *D. wallichiana* will reach 5 feet it is a difficult plant to obtain but the size can be attained more easily with *Osmunda regalis*, the royal fern. This really does need moisture, even a pond edge to reach its full size and visual potential.

FICUS CARICA FIG

Ripe figs, to the *cognoscenti*, are one of the most delicious of all fruit, rich and sweet like nothing else. Similarly their constituency and morphology which causes it is quite unique. It was clearly something of a mystery in the early eighteenth century for 'it beareth no visible Flowers, and they are therefore supposed to be hid in the Fruit'.

This is in fact true; the fruit is a fleshy receptacle like the 'plug' of a raspberry, but turned inside out thus protecting, as well as bearing, the individual seeds. The small hole at the top of the young fig permits pollination by little gall wasps in those types that need it. Delicious as the fruit is, it is only as a childhood laxative medicine that many northerners know it: 'Syrup of Figs' was traditionally doled out on Saturday nights regardless of need.

The fig's origin is probably Asia Minor whence it spread into the classical world in early times; several colour forms now exist and two crops annually are enjoyed, in June and autumn. In Britain, unfortunately, though the plant is relatively hardy and makes a fine foliage wallcovering right into Scotland, fruiting is restricted. Only incipient figs which overwinter about the size of peas are likely to provide a crop the following summer. Two cultivars are generally recommended: 'Brown Turkey' and 'White Ischia', the former being the hardier.

Even with the imponderability of regular crops a fig is a fine herb garden wall plant making a grand pattern against brick or stone, wood or stucco. An approximate fan pattern is to be preferred and, on rich soils, some root constriction is necessary to promote harder growth. The young plant can be put into a big sunken container (drainage holes are essential) and roots escaping over the rim can be controlled as necessary. Alternatively a deep hole can be taken out and half filled with brick rubble before replacing soil and planting the fig. Figs also make good terrace or patio plants, for, being deciduous, they do not require winter light in their over-wintering quarters. The back of a garage is quite satisfactory.

FILIPENDULA ULMARIA MEADOWSWEET

The foam of meadowsweet in waterside pastures and moist upland fields is a major pleasure of the summer scene. It is not surprising that it was also known in earlier times as *Regina Prati*, queen of the meadows, which was applied to a much taller American species.

Its connection with medicine makes a marvellous bridge be-tween the past and the present. Early recommendations for in-fusions of the flowers and roots for use in fevers and urinary troubles move into the research done upon the plant in the 1830's which first isolated salicylic acid. This, as is well known, was the chemical base from which aspirin was subsequently synthesized. Today home medication could hardly exist without it.

Still, as Stuart points out, the flowers of meadowsweet are valuable in the control of peptic ulcers and gastritis for 'they are probably the most effective of all plant remedies for the treatment of hyperacidity and heartburn'.

In the garden meadowsweet needs too much space – its forte is the flowery mead – but the golden-leaved form 'Aurea' is extremely valuable for bright foliage effect early in the year, making a lovely hummock of pure yellow which turns to pale green as the seasons move on. Flowers are the typical cream fuzz and if green seedlings are not to appear and swamp the stems must be taken out the moment flowering is over.

Filipendula ulmaria must have a moist spot: its close cousin *F. hexapetala* comes from dry chalk uplands, a polarization of which Mr and Mrs Jack Sprat would have approved. Dropwort is a delight-ful little plant with a rosette of carroty leaves and 2-foot stems of meadowsweet flowers, which in its double form make a good show. It associates in every way with the usual wide range of Mediterranean herbs.

Early medicinal uses of the root refer to those alarming-sounding ailments which are so much a part of seventeenth- and eighteenth-century texts. 'The Powder is commended by Mr Ray to stop violent Floodings and the Whites' and 'Prevotins likewise commends it from his own Experience agains the Bloody-flux'. It is a relief to enjoy dropwort as a simple cottage garden plant without thought of such things.

FOENICULUM VULGARE FENNEL

Fennel is a perfect herb. It is beautiful at all stages of its growth, its medicinal uses are well documented and its culinary virtues are diverse. Hence it can hardly be too highly praised.

In the garden different conditions produce very different results. A hot dry spot causes the sort of plant one meets on Mediterranean roadsides, a clump of 4 to 5-foot high sticks with vestigial leaves so mean as to be virtually invisible (yet sufficient to be the food-plant there of swallowtail butterfly larvae) and typical yellow umbels of flowers. By mid-summer such a plant is sere and dry, the seeds are collected for flavouring and the stalks make fuel for a fire on which fish are grilled: no flavour is more distinctive.

In decent garden soil fennel has a very different appearance, from a distance like a huge dome of green candyfloss. The purple-leaved form is just, or even more, attractive depending upon its associates (with bergamots and rose-coloured opium poppies it looks very fine). Both seed themselves around and it is good to use several sites – a danger of herb gardens is to attempt rigidly to keep to the original plan when, like vegetables, all short-lived herbs succeed best in rotation. Though fennel is a perennial, after three years any clump is past its best and must be replaced.

In southern Europe selections of fennel have traditionally taken on the northern role of celery as a crisp salad or cooked vegetable. Selections and breeding have developed delicious Florence fennel (*Finnocchio*) with its swollen leaf bases building up a sort of bulb sitting on the ground. One or two varieties are now suitable for English gardens but their season is short, in late summer.

Examples of fennel's adaptability in cooking are given in the recipe section. Medicinally its volatile oil has an emollient use and early texts suggest it was of use to 'increase Milk in Nurses and lessen Fat, and procure Leanness of Body'.

Closely related are the giant fennels (*Ferula* spp.). These are marvellously architectural plants with spreading, much divided leaves, usually monocarpic and taking two or three years to build up a root-stock, and when sufficiently established sending up a vast head of dull-white or yellow umbels: its pattern is superb. The mature plant can be 4 feet across and twice that in height. It needs therefore carefully siting and the realization that a big hole is left when it dies, as it will, after seeding. Several species have gum-resins (*Asafoetida, Galbanum*) but with us they are purely decorative plants needing a sunny spot and perfect drainage.

FORSYTHIA SUSPENSA

At first it appears strange to Western ears to hear that the well-loved *Forsythia suspensa* has an honoured place in Chinese medicine. The fruits are used in decoction for ailments as far apart as poliomyelitis and strokes. The first introduction to Europe was by Robert Fortune (from whose original plant offspring are still at the Chelsea Physic Garden) in 1833 and though it has been overtaken commonly by the big-flowered × *intermedia* types, it is still, with its long sprays of soft yellow, amongst the most beautiful.

Left alone it makes a 10-foot high bush, a cascade of shoots; but it is also good on a wall, accepting any exposure happily. Any soil suits. After flowering it can be pruned back quite hard and its framework used as a support for light-growing summer annuals. Morning glory would be admirable if the shrub is grown on a south wall.

FRAGARIA VESCA STRAWBERRY

This is the original wild wood strawberry and selections of it obtained their place in the early herbals. Obviously the fruit then, as now, was considered delicious and 'grateful to the stomach', but the texts go much further. Gargles and mouthwashes for sore gums and mouth ulcers were made from the leaves; if dried they make an acceptable tea-substitute for those who prefer to avoid caffeine, and the roots make a bitter tonic.

For herb garden use today obviously the modern big fruited, hybrid strawberries could be used, but the sort of cultivation and care they need is out of place. It is better to concentrate upon the wild plant, and its excellent white-fruited variant. This last has the virtue that birds, which are apt to reach ripe strawberries before their planter, here just sit around waiting for the fruit to turn red.

This type is a small but robust carpeter, good therefore, under shrubs: it needs some care amongst other herbaceous species. Propagation is easy from seed which, sown under glass in spring, will give a first small crop that autumn to bushy plants able to produce. The following year fruit will ripen from July to October.

The form 'Baron Solemacher' is a selection which does not have runners and is increased by divison; it can be used to fill knots or to act as a bushy edging to beds, thus doing two jobs in one. Only heavy clays which lie wet in winter are unacceptable.

GALANTHUS NIVALIS SNOWDROP

The poisonous alkaloids present in snowdrop bulbs are only now being researched as having possible medicinal application, and this predominantly in eastern Europe. Not only are the dozen species centred upon southeast Europe and Asia Minor, but, perhaps, those areas are less far removed from a folk culture and look more favourably upon a herbal basis for cures.

From the point therefore of *Herbs in the Garden* it means that a well-loved and very beautiful range of winter and early spring flowering bulbs are permissible to a herb garden. Our common snowdrop is available in a number of forms, varying in size and amount of green on the petals; some are distinguishable only by galanthomaniacs with remarkable eyesight. It is a woodland plant and normal garden soil should be enriched with leaf mould.

Of those from farther south and east, *Galanthus elwesii*, a gorgeous giant 8 inches high, is the easiest to grow and needs a more open position than the shade-loving *G. nivalis*. And any of the others which can be obtained, or afforded, are as highly desirable.

All snowdrops are best moved and divided either in flower or as they are just going over. This adds marvellously to their distribution by generous gardeners for they are unlike most plants which have to wait (and often be forgotten) till dormancy, months after their admiration and consequent offer of a place.

GALEGA OFFICINALIS GOAT'S RUE

Goat's rue is a fine upstanding plant for the mid-summer border. At the beginning of this century, in particular, several colour-form selections were made of hybrid origin of which two or three are still available. The original species makes a 4 to 5-foot high clump of divided vetch-like leaves and carries masses of pointed spikes of tiny pea-flowers, pink or white.

So long as it is given a bit of brushwood support before it reaches its full height (otherwise the clump falls out and engulfs anything near) goat's rue earns its keep in any sunny spot.

An infusion of the fresh plant is able to increase milk flow in animals, and indeed humans, to a surprising degree – Stuart states by up to 50 per cent. Of this proven use Miller, by comparison, makes no mention, merely going through the usual list of 'pestilential Distempers, Bites of venemous Creatures' etc. In turn this repeats Pechey (1694) who remarks that goat's rue was incorporated in a preparation known as 'The London Plague-water'.

GAULTHERIA PROCUMBENS WINTERGREEN

On an acid, woodsy soil, few ground covers are more attractive than the North American wintergreen or checkerberry, but unlike the related bearberry, wintergreen is not happy in open areas where the soil may become dry. It makes a carpet of dark green leaves amongst which in summer the pink flowers – typical ericaceous urns – appear. Much more distinctive are the pea-sized scarlet fruits which last well into winter. A single crushed leaf immediately recalls the taste of various gargles which one has met in the past.

Almost certainly the 'Wintergreen Oil' used in such preparations would have been a synthesized methyl salicylate, of which the plant's natural volatile oil is mainly composed. Tea-berry plant and mountain tea are two North American names which reflect its folk use: a few leaves in a cup of boiling water produce a marvellous aroma.

GENISTA TINCTORIA

Dyers' greenweed is a valuable small summer flowering shrub – a 3 or 4-foot high broom with bright green branches and equally bright yellow pea-flowers for much of the summer. 'Royal Gold' is a selection which is particularly floriferous while 'Plena', semi-prostrate in habit, covers itself with double flowers.

As its vernacular name suggests it is a dye-plant. Of some antiquity, it was especially used, combined with woad (itself a blue dye) to give a fine green. It is still of importance in home dyeing. Chemically, dyers' greenweed contains alkaloids which have an action upon the heart: formerly it was used as a diuretic and a

purgative. Joseph Miller's culinary recommendation is worth a trial:
'The Flowers, before they are grown to any bigness, are pickled with
salt and vinegar, and eaten for Sauce, like Capers, and are esteemed
by many as wholesome to the stomach'.

Like its close relation, the common broom, dyers' greenweed is
naturally a plant of heaths and dry places. In the garden it merely
needs some approximation of this: good drainage and an open spot. It
seems to be equally happy on limy or acid soil. Quite often branches
get cut back in winter and it is sensible each spring to prune all soft
twiggy growth back to a 2-foot high framework; from this the
current year's flowering wood will develop anew.

GENTIANA LUTEA GENTIAN

Nothing could be more unlike our normal conception of a gentian.
Instead of sky-blue trumpets at ground level here there are stout
stems 3 or 4 feet high, the top half of which carry whorls of horn-
yellow tubular flowers. These emerge from fine sheaves of pleated
leaves looking very much like those of a *Veratrum*. In spite of this
dissimilarity from its own relations, the plant has been known since
early times as the great gentian or great felwort and to have a
reputation of equal greatness for dealing with almost every dire
distemper from dropsy (of course) to 'the Bites of noxious and
venemous Animals, particularly that of a mad Dog, the Powder
being mix'd with Venice-Treacle and applied to the Wound' (Miller).

Yellow gentian's role in improving appetite, discussed for
hundreds of years, remains entirely valid and it is an extension of
this which has made it a part of so many European liqueurs and
cordials. The fermented root provides a bitter principle.

The plant is a native of limestone uplands of Europe, eastwards
into the Balkans and Asia Minor in areas which do not dry out badly.
Such knowledge, as always, gives us a lead in growing the plant
successfully in cultivation. When happy a plant will remain in
gradually increasing health and vigour for decades rather like old
garden peonies.

If a plant can be bought, so much the better, for it is difficult to
germinate and not easy to bring through infancy. It is best to sow
seed as soon as ripe (or available), in moist compost and keep the pot
covered at the bottom of the refrigerator until the turn of the year.
Only after such chilling should it be brought into a cool greenhouse
and germination expected.

Certainly the great yellow gentian is worth every trouble both
for its herbal history and for its most distinct effect in the garden.

GERANIUM spp

Several hardy herbaceous geraniums, as distinct from the tender South African *Pelargonium*, get honourable mentions in the old texts. The dove's foot (*G. columbinum*) is a softly downy annual, charming in the wild but hardly a garden plant. The latter remark could well be said, especially by tidy gardeners whose definition of a weed is anything they themselves did not plant, of *Geranium robertianum*.

For herb robert, or, to use an earlier name, *Gratia Dei* (this name is also given to *Gratiola*, hedge hyssop, a poisonous foxglove relation) is also an annual, quick to grow and make its hummock of deeply divided chervil-like leaves. In shade the plant is soft and green, in sun it is smaller and crimson-tinged: autumn colours in high summer, with which the little pink flowers combine. Sometimes a white-flowered form occurs and could be selected. But though an annual, herb robert seeds around vigorously, and its rootstock is so small and shallow that it never becomes the slightest bother and hence makes valuable summer ground cover above spring flowering bulbs when they are out of sight.

Herbally it is another of those plants which should have come into the ascendant with the rise of republicanism as being, according to Miller, 'particularly commended for the King's Evil, and all scropulous Swellings'.

Of wider use was the North American *G. maculatum*. The Shakers found it a powerful astringent with several applications: for instance as a gargle and for diarrhoea.

In the garden it is one of the best of its race. Flowering as it does from the end of May it is admirable to cover the so-called 'June Gap', that pause for breath between spring and summer. A 2-foot high hummock of elegantly divided downy leaves it produces its show of lilac-rose, inch-wide flowers for many weeks. A white form of this exists also. It is happy on any but the wettest soils on which it may not overwinter. Propagation is normally by division, in early spring, of its rather woody root-stocks.

GINKGO BILOBA

It was long thought that this strange and primitive conifer-relative was extinct in the wild but it is now known from a remote province of eastern China. Frequent in the gardens of oriental monasteries, its highly distinct leaves and yellow plum-like fruit are listed as exerting an astringent effect upon pulmonary energy, and hence used in cases of tuberculosis. More certain is that the nuts inside the fruit are delicious when pan-fried: even simpler they can be bought in tins from Japan.

A tree which attains heights (in a couple of hundred years or so) of 100 feet and beyond might not be thought to be herb garden material. But two or three opportunities occur. A fully established tree makes a fine and logical base around which to establish a herb garden of size. The highly typical vertical shape of ginkgo, for its first century, offers possibilities for an entrance pair of trees. Even when small an effect is immediate. Thirdly a small courtyard collection of oriental herbs can be centred upon a large container with the pruned, bonsai-like ginkgo providing an interesting focal point.

It should be emphasized that the fruit, produced of course only on female trees is unlikely to appear in much less than forty or fifty years (the much-publicized foetid smell from the seed coat is greatly exaggerated) but the leaf pattern and its clear golden autumn colour is a continued pleasure.

GLYCYRRHIZA GLABRA LIQUORICE

Though certainly not a showy plant *Glycyrrhiza* makes an attractive pattern and, as the source of commercial liquorice, is bound to be grown in a collection of herbs. Medicinally it has been used for coughs and bronchitic complaints for centuries and equally long employed as a sweetener and flavouring agent.

Liquorice is added to many tobaccos, and it flavours Guinness beer but the extraordinary imagination of sweet manufacturers who made liquorice confections seems less exercised than twenty years ago. The liquorice pipes, liquorice skipping ropes, liquorice shoe-laces, liquorice comfits and, of course, Pontefract cakes seem to fill the shelves: a nostalgic thought for those that liked the stuff and are today rather deprived.

Beginning in the fifteenth century liquorice is now grown commercially in many parts of the world. In Britain, Pontefract in Yorkshire is classically associated with its cultivation, which was introduced there by the Dominican order of Black Friars. It must have been of considerable economic value that the whole of the huge cobbled courtyard of medieval Pontefract castle, razed after the Civil War, was covered by 4 feet of topsoil for this very crop. It was grown there until the area was turned into a public park in the 1880s.

Above the long snake-like root growth is that of a tall, self-supporting vetch. Long pinnate leaves carry spikes of small bluish pea-flowers in their axils during mid to late summer. Rusty brown seed pods follow. It will grow in almost any conditions, but for the required thick roots of commerce the classic horticultural desideratum is needed: a deep rich loam, well drained yet retentive of moisture.

HAMAMELIS VIRGINIANA WITCH HAZEL

The lovely garden witch hazels without which no considered winter garden can be complete, are orientals. *Hamamelis mollis* and its superb form 'Pallida', the bigger *H. arborea* and the hybrids between them can only have relevance here by association. For the source of the witch hazel that is a part of so many liniments (essential to football changing rooms) for applying to bruises and abrasions is *Hamamelis virginiana*.

In leaf it is a similar plant to the others, a broad spreading shrub, to 10 or 15 feet in height, looking very much like hazel proper. But flowering is in late autumn, the twisted yellow petals unrolling as the leaves themselves take on their golden autumn colour. It is native right down the eastern side of North America, and in Ontario particularly selections are being made from the wild of large and late flowering forms. Scent, unlike the sweetness of *H. mollis*, is somewhat foetid.

Witch hazel is cultivated commercially in England on a small scale specifically by drug firms who produce distilled witch hazel from the volatile oil in the flowering shoots: it is this which goes into the liniments and ointments used for the relief of haemorrhoids. Warnings are given, however, against the extremely astringent properties of home-produced tinctures made from leaves or the bark. These are best avoided.

In cultivation any normal garden soil suits it: when really happy old plants may develop into small but wide trees. Though not often chosen in Britain as a garden plant it is grown more commonly than is realized as an understock for the orientals; occasionally it takes over from basal suckers and becomes the whole plant, to the disappointment of its owner who was led to expect something better.

HEDERA HELIX IVY

The forms of ivy are valuable garden plants and it is most fortunate that they may be included in a comprehensive list of herbs. Though

today, because the plant is so poisonous, it is only used externally
as poultices for skin disorders (an early use was to try to remove
freckles) the seventeenth century was less restrictive; "Mr Boyle,
in his *Usefulness of Experimental Philosophy* commends a large
dose of the full-ripe berries, as a 'Remedy against the Plague'."
(Joseph Miller). Such a treatment, one feels, merely anticipated the
effect of the disease by a short head and may well have been
preferable to the patient.

As only one or two of the biggest-leaved species are not derivatives of common ivy (ie. of *Hedera colchica* and *H. canariensis*
and even these are acceptable by association) the great majority
may be legitimately grown in a herb collection. Variegation may
reduce but not eliminate the basic chemical constituents which
anyway, in this instance, are *not* for general use.

Thus green, white-edged, gold or golden-splashed ivies can be
used as wall climbers or as ground cover. 'Gold Heart' for example
is superb to lighten the darkness of a shady corner. The robust Irish
ivy is an especially good ground cover – though it will climb if it
meets a suitable vertical surface. The self-clinging habit is particularly valuable and it is always worth emphasizing that, in spite of
dire warnings from phytophobes, ivy does no harm to masonry in
good condition: indeed it can help protect it.

Where a formal effect is required ivy can be used as a clipped
edging to parterre beds while a different form can fill such beds.
Small-leaved types are good, either as permanent inhabitants of
ornamental containers or to give winter interest when tender
summer things have been taken inside. There is nothing better
than ivy to 'soften' urns when a bit of plant growth is required that
cannot be conveniently watered: so long as a reasonable amount of
soil is there a plant will often last years with no attention at all.
Equally, growth in tubs of bay (*Laurus nobilis*) provides sprays that
can be trained down to cover the sides of the container. Such
florists' uses are endless and one has only to look at illustrations in
a Victorian gardening book to realize how many possibilities are no
longer considered.

HELIANTHUS ANNUUS SUNFLOWER

One feels that, though it does not start from such small beginnings,
the annual sunflower would have been a better illustration for the
parable of the mustard-seed than the original. But, of course, being
a North American plant, it was not available in Israel until recent
times for either figurative or actual use.

But certainly from a May-sown seed it is extraordinary that a great woody stem up to 2 inches diameter can grow 10 or more feet high and bear one or more dinner-plate-sized flowers all within the space of four or five months. Very much of a size that 'the fowls of the air may roost therein', to complete the simile.

Sunflowers were once considered proof against plague, if grown near to the house, and there are still homoeopathic uses. But it is as a source of a valuable oil that sunflowers are a major farm crop in areas with a summer hot enough to promote its rapid growth effectively. In Britain it would be a doubtful agricultural proposition but as a garden plant in a sunny spot success can always be expected. It is always a great pleasure.

It is important that the spot from which the magnificent flowers are to be enjoyed is to their sunny side. Otherwise they turn their heads away in the rudest fashion. It might be mentioned that grey squirrels can be a major predator of ripening sunflower heads and often take every seed before they can be collected. A few may be saved for next year, the rest make a pleasant though untidy alternative to peanuts.

HELICHRYSUM ANGUSTIFOLIUM

Though the nomenclature of this plant is somewhat confused (*H. italicum* usually results in the same thing) there is no doubt as to its distinctiveness in the garden. It is one of the whitest-leaved shrubs we have. It makes a 2-foot high bush, wider than that across, of hard woody branches clothed with narrow leaves, silver-white all over. Long stalked heads of bright yellow rayless daisies occur in summer but, like those of *Santolina*, merely detract from the foliage effect.

Sadly, while apparently suitable for the same sorts of roles and positions as santolinas, this *Helichrysum* resents being clipped and shows its disapproval of being cut back into old wood by excising branches so affronted. It considers, presumably, that its own tidy habit should be sufficient for even the keenest gardener.

The scent from a single leaf is enough to provide a vernacular name – curry plant. Why a single shrublet should be able to encapsulate a smell which is the product of a dozen spices and herbs in combination is a mystery. A small sprig stuffed into the cavity of a roasting chicken makes an interesting variant on *poulet à l'estragon*. Some other helichrysums have the smell but not the looks.

H. petiolatum on the other hand has the looks but not the smell. This is a tender, wide-spreading shrub known in America as liquorice plant (it has no connection with *Glycyrrhiza*) quickly spreading over a square yard of ground before being killed in winter. As a South African it is only in the warmest gardens (and often London window boxes) that it survives. Thus rooted cuttings have to be overwintered indoors.

Liquorice plant, with its heart-shaped woolly grey leaves and elegant habit is one of the most valuable things to use in containers, planted with more upright scented-leaved geraniums or round a bay-tree. Pale straw-yellow flower heads in summer are pleasant if not striking.

HELLEBORUS NIGER CHRISTMAS ROSE

To see a fine plant of Christmas rose in flower at the year's very end is one of the miracles of the turning seasons. Above the leathery, dark green fingered leaves thick stalks arise and carry one or two flowers of purest white, set off by a central boss of golden stamens. In good forms such as 'Potter's Wheel' the flower may be as much as 5 inches across and the whole effect is extraordinarily sculptural – a sculpture in finest porcelain.

As the flowers age they take on a pink tinge which darkens eventually to greenish purple surrounding the cluster of seed pods that by now have developed. It is thus clear that what appears to be petals makes up the permanent calyx, while the true petals existed as the circle of green nectaries at the base of the stamens. Such flowers are inevitably prey to slugs and to weather; though proof against frost their perfection can be sullied by mud splash.

A spot providing summer shade without drying out seems to offer the best chance of success, for Christmas rose can be erratic in behaviour: often an apparently unregarded clump in the corner of a cottage garden does better than a cherished, spoilt specimen in a specialist collection. Seed germinates well if sown as soon as ripe in early summer and to have a number of plants strewn around is the best way to find a site that suits.

Though still employed in homoeopathy *Helleborus niger* is no longer of herbal use. Even Joseph Miller uses the past tense: 'Black Hellebore was a Plant of great Use among the Ancients, and particularly for Melancholy and Madness . . .' By his time its very poisonous nature had presumably been realized. Miller's direct translation of the Latin name refers to the roots of the plant which are indeed black, however incongruous it seems when admiring the pure white flowers. In his day hellebore referred also to *Veratrum* and other plants.

The other true *Helleborus* species such as the splendid *H.*

corsicus and the Lenten rose, *H. orientalis*, in all its colour forms could be included here by association. Although they have had no herbal use they are marvellous and easy garden plants.

HUMULUS LUPULUS HOPS

The role of hops as a flavouring in brewing and as something of a preservative in beer is well known. Less well realized are its herbal and culinary overtones, though the life-enhancer definition of a herb is sufficiently demonstrated by the beer connection to give the plant validity here.

The hop is a strong-growing perennial twiner, capable of reaching 15 to 20 feet annually from its herbaceous root-stock. The size and strength of the poles and wires erected in commercial hop gardens – especially in Kent, the Farnham district of Hampshire and parts of Worcestershire where conical oast houses or hop-kilns are a feature of the local architecture – shows how it grows. So too does the old method of harvesting the crop as pickers move along the rows precariously balanced on high stilts. Here the valued parts are the little female flowers which are arranged in bunches of soft scaly cones, expressly evolved and designed, it would seem, for decorating the church pulpit at country harvest festivals. The flowers on the male plants by comparison make inconspicuous open sprays.

The growth of the bristly climbing shoots in spring and un-folding of the vinous leaves is extremely rapid. These may be the conventional green or a fine golden form. These, in the garden situation, need thinning and encouragement to twine where required rather than where they choose. Support can vary from an old orchard tree, trellis on a wall or a robust tripod to give height, to a bed of herbaceous things. Hops disguises chain-like fence wonderfully and can thus hide a tennis court with great effect. At the start of their growth is the time when the soft tips can be lightly boiled and eaten as asparagus: their earliness really does make this worthwhile. The characteristic strong oily scent does not develop until the plant attains near-maturity. Perhaps it is this which is reputed to encourage drowsiness: small pillows stuffed with the dried female flowers are still sold to combat insomnia.

A final obvious use of hops for any garden close to a brewery is to obtain an annual load of the spent hops after they have done their flavouring job. Few materials are better as a mulch and layers in a compost heap help the final job immeasurably.

HYOSCYAMUS NIGER HENBANE

Henbane is all a traditional herb should be, strange to look at, mysterious in reputation and highly poisonous in fact. It is one of that visually very diverse, but closely related group of solanaceous plants of which thorn apple and deadly nightshade are best known, containing alkaloids which provide the herbal value: dangerously narcotic in large doses yet a useful sedative under careful control.

Henbane's production of atropine, hyoscine and hyoscyamine is no longer generally harnessed, except in homoeopathic tinctures. Not only the observed effects of its internal use but also its appearance and texture encouraged the henbane myth where it was supposed to be an ingredient of magical potions and witches' brews. Added to this, as a wild plant it almost only appears in places of old habitation. It enjoys turned soil and decayed mortar rubble and if these are provided by haunted castle walls or historical ruins of ill repute so much the better for the myth.

'The Roots are considered Narcotic, and are but rarely used inwardly; they are frequently hung about Children's Necks, being cut into Pieces, and strung like Beads to prevent Fits, and cause an early Breeding of their Teeth'. Thus Miller, in the Age of Reason.

In dry soil henbane may only reach 1 or 2 feet in height which it can double if well fed and also if a plant behaves as a biennial, which it may. But only the scale differs dramatically. A woody stem holds pairs of opposite leaves, peculiarly clammy to the touch and offensively foetid. The top half develops into a long arching flower spike, each tubular flower suitably sick-yellow in colour with ominous purple veins. It has a strange beauty and this is enhanced as the seed capsules develop, flagon shaped as if drawn in some heraldic design. It sounds almost like bathos to suggest that they are charming dried for winter arrangements indoors.

Henbane is extremely easy to grow from seeds sown *in situ* on well-drained soil. Early thinning is essential. Occasionally other species such as *H. mutabilis* and *H. albus* are offered and are worth growing as slight variants from the type. The perennial golden henbane, *H. aureus* from the eastern Mediterranean (see it on old walls in Crete and Rhodes) is more difficult to suit.

HYPERICUM spp ST JOHN'S WORT

The shrubby St John's worts have taken on a major decorative role in our summer gardens with their golden bowl-like flowers opening for week after week and holding central brushes of stamens. Happy in sun or shade *Hypericum patulum* and its close forms and relations make symmetrical domes of shining leaves and bright gold flowers. This group varies in height from about 2 feet in *H.* × *moseranum* to 'Hidicote' which will reach three times that height. *H. forrestii* and 'Gold Cup' are intermediate. As vigorous ground cover, where nothing else is required to grow, *H. calycinum*, the rose of sharon cannot be bettered, even on the thinnest chalk soils. All of these are acceptable as herb garden associates: they follow on well from old-fashioned roses which are past their best by mid July.

But there are two St John's worts which are in all the herbal literature, both attractive European – and British – natives. The shrubby representative makes this clear in its vernacular name of tutsan, a corruption of the French *toutsain* (all-heal) which was accounted a good wound-herb.

This 2 or 3-foot high shrublet is one of the best plants for tree shade. The heads of small yellow flowers are succeeded by red fleshy capsules soon turning black and dry in which state they hold on for many weeks. The tutsan is one parent of *H.* × *inodorum* 'Elstead' 'an altogether brighter and more desirable plant. Here the fruits do not blacken but remain vividly pink. The succession of bloom is such that fruit and flower appear together in a positively fairground miscellany'. (*Plants for Shade*, Paterson, Dent).

H. perforatum is a plant of dry limy soils in open downland situations. It has a folklore reputation long pre-dating its obvious Christian name. The crushed petals turn red-blood-like and its balsamic smell when crushed was reputed to dispel evil spirits. This scent comes from the oil held in the glands which, when the leaves are held up to the light, appear transparent, hence perforated.

The list of folk uses for St John's wort's is impressive, so too is the fact that it contains, according to Stuart, 'an antibiotic which has been patented as a possible food preservative' (*Encyclopedia of Herbs and Herbalism*). It is one of those plants whose herbal connection with man's interests extends from pre-historic times to the present and, as is suggested above, well into the future.

HYSSOPUS OFFICINALIS HYSSOP

'Purge me with Hyssop and I shall be clean', cries the Scripture, and indeed into the eighteenth century hyssop was considered 'open and attenuating, good to cleanse the Lungs of Tartarous humours'. More interesting, perhaps, is the claim that 'the bruised Herb, applied outwardly, is famous for taking away black and blue Marks out of the Skin'. Was it applied, one wonders, to the protagonists after the horrendous prize-fights so popular later in the century?

Hyssop is one of the classic herb garden residents. A low subshrub, seldom reaching more than 2 feet in height, it makes a charming hummock of scented foliage or equally is effective as an internal hedge. A labiate, it makes a good floral display in July and August, the top 9 inches of each shoot holding the little two-lipped flowers. The typical colour is mid-blue but pink, purple and white forms occur and may be easily selected for particular associations.

As a southern European, hyssop does need the sort of well-drained spot which we give to lavenders and rosemary and of course full sun if it is to keep a compact habit. This can be helped by reducing top growth by a few inches at the end of the season and a little more the following spring so that plants do not rock about in the wind.

ILEX AQUIFOLIUM HOLLY

Holly's traditional association with Christmas is pre-dated by its use in pagan ceremonies concerned with the turning of the year at the winter solstice. Yet the Christian symbolism is particularly apt: holly's permanence and the bearing of sharp-pointed leaves and brilliant red berries suggesting the instruments of the Passion.

'The Holly bears a prickle as sharp as any thorn . . .

The Holly bears a berry as red as any blood. . . .'

Such lines are the basis of innumerable carols. Religious connections are apt to wash over into herbalism but with holly, though the attempt was made it met with little success. While the berries are purgative they are also toxic; with their mild tonic and diuretic action the leaves have been used in herbal teas and to treat fevers. But Joseph Miller, for example, in his 'Account of all such Plants as are now used in the Practice of Physick' makes no mention of it.

Holly's value as a garden plant needs no recommendation, except that of an encouragement to plant it. Though apparently slow to make a good specimen, once holly is established, it goes ahead by leaps and bounds (if accompanied by secateur restraint at Christmas time). While a seedling selection is perfectly suitable for hedge-making, as a specimen one is bound to choose from the fifty or more variants of common holly on offer. Size of plant, prickliness and colour of leaf, colour of berry, all vary. So, of course, does their sex: obviously only female trees will produce berries and, equally obviously, only if there is a male (staminate) plant to hand at flowering time.

Holly is particularly at home in moist woodlands and seems to like some protection in its early years. Later it will accept even seaside exposure. In the wild in Britain it is on the northern limit of its natural range.

In other cultures other species of *Ilex* – there are some 400 to choose from – are employed herbally but these are generally not used as garden plants with us. In China *Ilex rotunda* is listed and in South America *I. paraguariensis* is the source, via its dried leaves, of the widely drunk *maté* tea.

North America has *I. verticillata*, an unusual member of the genus, being deciduous. An 8 to 10-foot high, open shrub with narrow leaves it carries a marvellous show of scarlet berries on bare branches well into winter. Another plant of moist woodland, it is less tolerant of open sites than common holly; equally it will not accept lime. Medicinally a tonic, promoting both appetite and digestion, is made from the fresh bark.

INULA HELENIUM ELECAMPANE

Elecampane is one of the traditional denizens of early gardens stretching back into monastic times. The uses from its dried root-stock were wide – to flavour wines and liqueurs, to be eaten candied, to be a part of preparations to treat bronchitic conditions, to treat skin troubles (hence a second less attractive name: scabwort). Elecampane possesses an essential oil, a resin, and a camphor *inter alia*. The root, according to Shaker literature, was gathered in its second year in the autumn.

It is a tall robust perennial from southeast Europe, extending into Asia, with woody stems up to 6 feet high. The downy foxglove-shaped leaves, huge at the base, lessen as they reach the summer head of yellow daisies and the whole builds up a splendid pattern. If a large clump can be permitted it looks particularly well against purple filbert, purple fennel and other coppery-leaved things.

Inula magnifica is a very close relation which if anything is even grander in effect. Though excellent when used in the same way as elecampane itself, it is one of those few perennials which can stand alone with great success, rising out of orchard grass.

IRIS spp

Though all are obvious irises, the three important species in herbal literature are extraordinarily dissimilar plants from a cultivational point of view – which adds greatly to their herb garden value. We

have with *Iris florentina, I. foetidissima* and *I. versicolor* highly
ornamental plants for dry sunny spots, for shade both dry or moist,
and sunny moist positions respectively.

Although there are taxonomic doubts as to the validity of its
specific epithet, the Florentine iris is perfectly distinct enough for
anyone to be sure of obtaining the true plant. It is in fact a bearded
iris of very particular virtues: an ideal white-garden plant carrying
above its greyish leaves spikes of dead-white, sweet-scented flowers.
Flowering time is around the end of May, just three weeks of cool
beauty but, if kept tidy and not too dry the foliage remains respect-
able throughout summer. Unlike so many of the grand modern
bearded irises the Florentine, only 2 feet high, never needs a stake.

Its herbal fame is equally definite. The dried rhizomes are the
orris root of commerce providing a violet-scented powder (Miller
says 'somewhat like Raspberries') used as a base in perfumery and at
home in pot pourri, the aromas of which it helps to 'fix'. As a fierce
purgative the fresh root was inevitably recommended medicinally in
the eighteenth century.

Iris florentina is a southern European, so obviously good drainage in Britian essential and indeed it will take drought with impunity: a rather richer spot will encourage finer rhizomes.

Though the Florentine and its close cousin the blue *Iris
germanica* are sometimes found apparently wild they are with us
just garden escapes. A true native is the gladdon or gladwyn,
pleasanter names than a direct translation of *Iris foetidissima* which
really is a calumny. Only the leaves, if bruised, are at all foetid and
even this must be liked by some for it also is known as roast beef
plant. Appreciation of scent is a very personal decision.

Gladdon is one of the best ground covers for shade that we have.
It makes fine clumps of evergreen leaves which are always with us.
The dusky buff-purple flowers can pass in summer almost without
being noticed but, as if to make up for this, they develop into sprays
of heavy pods which open to show off brilliant spindle berry-orange
seeds. This display lasts for months so long as flower arrangers can
be fended off.

'Citrina' is bigger in all its parts with paler, showier flowers.
'Variegata', lovely to make a bright winter splash with ivies and
snowdrops and Christmas roses is also worth searching out. Sadly it
hardly ever flowers and hence more importantly fails to fruit. These
spendid plants take moist or dry shade right up to the boles of trees.

Iris versicolor is different again; a plant of open boggy sites in
east North America where it grows with pitcher plants (*Sarracenia*)
and several orchids. In cultivation it also needs a rich, moist soil but

given this it is perfectly easy to grow. It makes a 2-foot clump of rather lax leaves with good sprays of flattish iris flowers. Typically blue-purple, both 'Rosea' and 'Kermesina' (a fine deep claret colour) are worthwhile variants. This blue flag or poison flag was in use by the native peoples before North America was colonized and is still employed in folk medicine to purify the blood in eruptive skin complaints.

A fourth plant to be included here is listed in the early texts as 'the Hermodactyl Plant'. Typically, Joseph Miller is honest: 'This is a Root that is brought to use from Turkey, but what Plant it is the Root of, we have no certain knowledge, some taking it to be the Root of a Colchicum, or a Dens Caninus; others of a tuberous Iris; and others of a Species of Cyclamen'. Sir John Hill, equally typically, makes broad statements describing something he has obviously also never seen, but does not like to admit it, sure in the knowledge that he will not be corrected.

Miller's 'tuberous Iris' hits the mark and it was as *Iris tuberosa* that it became known, having now moved on, or back, to *Hermodactylus tuberosus*. While we can reject recommendations for its treatment of gout it would be sad to neglect real garden virtues of the snakeshead or widow iris. From the tuberous roots the leaf growth – like that of *Iris reticulata* – begins in January and depending on site and season can open its strange flowers by the end of February. These are a unique combination of avocado-green with black-blotched falls. The effect is fleeting but intriguing. This little foot-high iris needs full sun and good drainage: soon going back to rest it fits well under a dwarf lavender or rosemary.

ISATIS TINCTORIA WOAD

Woad is an historic dye-plant which only in our own century ceased to be grown as a commercial crop. But as production of the blue dye from a fermentation process of the leaves is sufficiently complicated one can only be surprised by the oft-repeated tale that (to quote Miller) 'The ancient Britons used to stain their Bodies with it, to make themselves appear terrible'. Stuart offers the additional thought that as woad is an effective styptic the painting helped to staunch the wounds of battle. Home dyers still use woad, rejecting its tropical supplanter and even more the aniline dyes which now replace both.

Hill expounds upon woad's herbal use to remove 'obstructions of the liver and spleen . . .; this infusion must be continued a considerable time: these are disorders that come on slowly and are to be slowly removed'. In fact the plant is highly poisonous.

Woad is a biennial crucifer like so many of its *Brassica* relations. From seed a clump of blue-green leaves is built up in the first season which overwinters thus. The following spring yard-high leafy stems arise to display a cloud of tiny yellow flowers. These are quickly replaced by flat seed capsules, rather like small ash 'keys'; first green and then turning black. Thus for some weeks woad makes an interesting pattern and is well worth growing. Naturally a plant of the chalk it is happy in any well-drained spot.

JASMINUM OFFICINALE JASMINE

Few plants better evoke the lanquid warmth of a summer evening – unfortunately rare in Britain – spent on the terrace as the twilight dims and the moon comes up. Then all-white flowers shine with a lambency they lack in the day time and those with scent seem to pour it out with greater freedom. Our white summer jasmine, or as it is called more charmingly in America, poet's jasmine, is one such plant.

A strong twiner, it can reach 20 feet or more on a wall with suitable support, but its best herb garden use is to grow it over an arch or arbour where the scent is most likely to be appreciated, although it can only be grown away from a warm wall in mild districts. The sprays of white flowers, heavily fragrant, are carried from June through to September: the form 'Affine' has bigger individual flowers which are flushed with pink on the reverse of the petals and hence seen in bud. Attractive too but less floriferous is a fine variegated-leaved form.

It is these that are used in perfumery by the distillation of the essential oil. Hill offers a simple and attractive recipe for cough-linctus: 'pour a pint of boiling water upon six ounces of the fresh gathered and clean-picked flowers of jessamin; let it stand twelve hours, then pour it off; add enough honey to make the liquor into a thin syrup.' It sounds almost worth getting a cough for this!

Other jasmines are used in perfumery but lack hardiness. By association, however, herb gardens could well offer homes for the lovely pink *Jasminum* × *stephanense* (which has the poet's jasmine as one parent) and in warm spots, *J. polyanthum*. This exquisite plant is often grown as a house plant: having outgrown their pots numbers of these are flourishing on walls in London.

JUGLANS REGIA WALNUT

While it is quite unnecessary to describe a walnut tree a mistake would be made by omitting it on this account. Though ultimately a fine broad-headed tree and hardly therefore an inhabitant of a herb garden, it makes a logical backdrop to one. The fact that it is one of the latest trees to come into leaf in spring and one of the first to lose its foliage in autumn adds to this, and to its use close to the house which will be only thickly shaded in high summer.

In times past the bark of walnuts, its leaves, the green peel of the unripe fruit, the nuts and even their shells had specific uses. Today pickled walnuts, and the ripe nuts are still rightly esteemed; and walnut oil traditionally takes the place of olive oil in the cuisine of soutwest France – or did until it became too expensive for general use.

It is enough justification to plant a walnut merely with the intention of developing a lovely shade-tree. Any well-drained soil, limy or not, is suitable but known frost-pockets should be avoided as the young growth is very susceptible to a late spring night-frost. However, like any tree-fruit of which a seed can germinate and grow into adulthood, rapid fruit is only likely from grafted plants of named varieties. These are well worth searching out.

LAURUS NOBILIS SWEETBAY

Sweetbay, bay, or bay laurel is in many ways the archetypal herb garden plant, so it is apt that it should be chosen as a central plant in a formal herb garden plan. In spite of still being highly esteemed, however, the bay has fallen sadly from its social eminence of classical times. Whereas now the leaves are used as part of a bouquet garni, to flavour stews and rice puddings, they once were sacred to Apollo, crowned the *Victor Ludorum* and were worn by emperors as a protection from lightning. As proof of their efficacy in this last respect not one crowned head is recorded as ever having been struck while so adorned.

Sweetbay is a typical evergreen member of the Mediterranean forest zone with its thick leathery leaves. Inevitably therefore it is sensitive to extreme cold and in Britain can get cut to the ground in really bad winters. In spite of this, fine 10-foot high bushes can be seen as far north as Dundee, and beyond, given courtyard protection. Conversely, in what might be thought to be much warmer areas, tub-grown bays are killed in droves every winter: root exposure to frost is much resented and this, in addition to leaf dessication accompanying the lack of water that follows freezing of the root-ball, is the main cause.

The visual value of bays in containers (as well as the price of replacements) makes some winter protection wise: the containers can be lagged as one would treat exposed plumbing, or they can be moved to protected places, even into an unheated shed or garage for short periods (if numbers of containerized plants are moved about annually a strong board on castors is worth constructing). Bays that have been trained into topiary shapes deserve the added care of a swathe of sacking over their tops in the severest weather: the old 'a stitch in time' maxim is never more true.

Apart from this natural sensitivity bays are the easiest thing to grow in all but wet soils, acidity or liminess having no effect; they take sun or shade with equal effect. When happy, huge multi-stemmed bushes 20 or 30 feet in height can result with enough leaves to fulfil a nation's need for bouquets garni. On unpruned plants the yellow, rather fuzzy, flowers are carried in sufficient quantity to make quite a display in spring and the black fruits self-sow the plant around. In mild areas there is no more suitable plant to make a hedge around an area of herbs or Mediterranean plants.

Laurus nobilis has a charming form with longer, waved leaves listed as 'Angustifolia' or 'Salicifolia', rather lighter in effect. But the so-called golden bay ('Aurea') is apt merely to look chlorotic especially on a chalky soil which is blamed at once for such an effect, however intentional the choice of plant.

Of interest, worth growing, and with even more strongly aromatic leaves are the Chilean laurel, *Laurelia serrata* and the Californian laurel, *Umbellularia californica* of which (to indicate its hardiness) there used to be a fine tree at the Cambridge Botanic Garden. A crushed leaf from the latter is reputed to send even daunting dowagers off into a dead faint. Personal experimentation has proved this to be greatly exaggerated: they barely sway. The leaves are often sold in Paris shops in place of true bay.

LAVANDULA spp LAVENDER

Though it has no direct culinary application, a herb garden without lavender is like a boiled egg without salt: the scent from a crushed leaf, even more from a flower spike, immediately evokes an idealized Helen Allingham type of cottage garden with great bushes of Old English lavender tumbling forward over grey flagstones amongst a riot of colour, the whole being pensively admired by a pre-Raphaelite peasant girl of quite remarkable charm.

This role of lavender is still perfectly valid even in less picturesque positions; eventually a shrub 3 feet high and as much through, this type (of which 'Grappenhall' and 'Vera' are the most robust) associates marvellously with the cottage garden miscellany of old-fashioned roses, peonies and pinks – a perfect early July scene. All lavenders like full sun, a limy soil and good winter drainage.

Smaller lavenders such as 'Twickel Purple', 'Munstead' or 'Hidcote', all a couple of feet high, make fine interior hedges, fillings for large parterres or for lining a terrace edge. As well as flowering in various shades of 'lavender', useful white and pale pink cultivars exist. It is almost impossible to have too many; never do they pall. Though old plants with arm-sized trunks will develop, frequent repropagation is wise for most positions. Fortunately this is simple: seed from the cultivars breeds more or less true, cuttings root easily and old plants can often be pulled apart to increase the stock. This last method is assisted by choosing a couple of stock plants and replanting them deeply in sandy soil in spring: this causes rooting up the stems, each one of which gives a new plant when the whole is divided a year later.

Lavender the herb with its natural volatile oil produces commercial oil of lavender, so important in perfumery: folk medicine puts it to various uses where a gentle sedative is required. Dried flowers are a vital part of pot pourri; scented sachets are moth-repellant; and it is pleasant also to have it in bowls about the house to be fingered as one passes. Traditionally a covered dish of dried lavender was brought to the fire on winter evenings: uncovered the warmth brought out the scent and a half-handful was thrown upon the flames to add to this celebration of summer.

The genus *Lavandula* offers several species of interest and charm which are well worth growing: they are, however, less frost-hardy and some must be considered mainly as specimens to be put out in the summer – bunched together in pots to increase their effect.

L. lanata makes a foot-high dome of white-woolly leaves which triples itself in height when in late summer the long-stemmed dark purple flower spikes develop. This has a typical lavender scent. The next two, however, have a cloying smell which is, to most noses, much less agreeable.

L. stoechas is French lavender (though with a wide Mediterranean distribution). Here the flower spikes are topped by wavy bracts, as if lavender had been crossed (a genetic impossibility) with annual clary. These two will survive our mildest winters.

L. dentata, with the same perfume, makes a green bush of indented leaves and good purple spikes. Very different are *L. multifida* and *L. pinnata* which look, out of flower, much more like artemisias with their grey fern-like leaves. Only the gentle scent and flower spikes proclaim them to be lavenders. Seed of these unusual plants can sometimes be found in specialist's lists. Once germinated, plants can be vegetatively propagated: they make a most interesting addition to the usual types.

LEDUM GROENLANDICUM LABRADOR TEA

As its specific epithet indicates, this is a plant of the far north, not only of Greenland itself but along the arctic fringe of Canada: one sees it on Baffin Island flowering in July with the cassiopes and dwarf rhododendrons to which it is related. With us it makes a tidy 2-foot high bush and carries attractive heads of white flowers with long protruding stamens and provides quite a show in May and June. In spite of its chilly home *Ledum* is perfectly happy to have a more comfortable life so long as it is given acid soil.

Its tannin, essential oil and resin have made it used to treat diarrhoea and, by the Shakers, skin diseases. A vernacular name, Labrador tea, reflects its use as a table tea especially during the American War of Independence when the blockade made the real thing almost unobtainable.

LEONURUS CARDIACA MOTHERWORT

'This Plant is called Cardiaca, from its supposed Virtue to relieve Disorders of the Heart, to cure the palpitation thereof, and to prevent swooning'. Thus Joseph Miller in 1722. Later commentators quote its sedative effects and use in anxiety, delirium and sleeplessness. It is still used homoeopathically. Surprisingly, although its vernacular name is motherwort, no text makes much of its effects on childbirth or 'women's disorders', except to allay anxiety.

In the garden this European (naturalized now in North America) makes no great splash of colour but develops into a quietly dignified clump, 3 or 4 feet high. Straight stems carry three-lobed leaves to their tips supporting, during the last foot, whorls of small pale purple dead-nettle flowers. The distinguished growth pattern is maintained into winter even when this top growth is sere and dead.

Very spectacular is a South African cousin, *Leonotis leonurus*: with both names referring to lion's tails and lion's ears respectively and with its spikes of tawny orange flowers this is a leonine plant indeed. Likely to survive only our mildest winters, it is easily overwintered as a pot plant when kept almost dry, and then stood or planted out in a sunny spot for the summer; all as one would care for a large fuchsia.

LEVISTICUM OFFICINALE LOVAGE

Lovage is one of the essential culinary herbs for temperate gardens: though reminiscent of celery, its flavouring is very distinct. The fresh leaves make a marvellous soup, they may be added to *fines herbes* for omelettes, thrown into salads and combined in a bouquet garni. All these may be enjoyed in the distant hope that, as the name suggests, it is also something of an aphrodisiac. The younger the leaves used the more delicate the flavour and though, as a perennial, foliage is available from April to October, for the last couple of months it becomes coarse and strong-flavoured. If, therefore, three clumps are grown and one is cut back in late June and another in August (rotationally, each year) if watered well they will still have time to provide spring-fresh leaves throughout the season. Finally, seed may be collected and stored dry to be used as celery-seed for winter soups.

Though lovage has innumerable umbelliferous friends and relations in the herb garden, very few are such long-lived perennials. Lovage will go on for years building up as big a clump as can be wished, or permitted. A fountain of olive-green leaves, rather like an exaggerated maidenhair fern, develops with flower stalks (statuesque but of little floral beauty) towering to 6 feet high. The typical flat heads of tiny yellow flowers are not particularly ornamental.

A closely related plant, though shorter and white flowered, is *Ligusticum scoticum* which also is sometimes called lovage. It can be used culinarily in similar ways but it lack the other plant's flavour; visually it is much less distinguished and thus is only worth growing in herb gardens which attempt a comprehensive collection.

LIATRIS SPICATA BLAZING STAR

From moist grasslands in much of North America comes this highly ornamental herbaceous plant. It is known there variously as button snakeroot, gayfeather and blazing star. It is an excellent plant for bringing height towards the front of the border with its clumps of grassy leaves and upright bottle-brush spikes of brilliant pinkish mauve. These spikes have the odd distinction of starting from the top and working down, instead of the other way up which is almost invariable with other plants. In the wild blazing star reaches 4 feet in height but is seldom more than half as high with us: a couple of other species are sometimes available (there are about forty altogether) and are equally good garden plants needing similar treatment. They like full sun and good living in summer but resent lying wet in winter: their position should be marked because they can very easily be forked out by mistake when dormant.

Liatris spicata had wide use in Shaker medicine, the roots used against scofula and 'in Bright's disease, combined with bugle and unicorn' – a splendid medieval sounding prescription (but 'unicorn' here is no mythical beast but the starwort, *Chamaelirium*). Research has shown other species to possess anti-cancer agents.

The scent of the powdered roots, though much less distinct than orris, provides a use in sachets and pot pourri.

LIGUSTRUM LUCIDUM PRIVET

Though the Shakers used leaves of the common privet (*L. vulgare*) as a mouthwash, it has little to recommend it as a garden plant. Much more valuable is the shining privet or waxtree, as it is generally known in China. There its seeds, prepared in decoction, are believed *inter alia*, to strengthen muscles and bones, improve both hearing and sight and encourage the kidneys. In Britain it flowers so late in summer – indeed often well into September – that the fruit seldom, if ever, ripens.

It can be grown simply as a beautiful small, evergreen tree which makes a splendid focal point even in restricted spaces. Occasionally reaching 30 feet or more in height it can be encouraged to develop tree form by early selection of a strong central stem.

Seldom reaching this size are a couple of lovely variegated forms, mottled or edged with white, and these provide cut foliage which is always in demand to the limit of what the plant can offer without being denuded. The white panicles of flower stand out well against the glossy leaves and, blessedly, lack the cloying heavy scent of many privets.

LINUM USITATISSIMUM FLAX

Linnaeus' tongue-twisting Latin superlative reflects the wide range of uses to which flax has been put over the centuries. Linen cloth made from the stem fibres dates back to the dawn of recorded history and its manufacture continued through all the major Western cultures to the present day. It is still most highly regarded. The oil (linseed oil of commerce) has medical, veterinary and culinary uses and its value in paints is well known. The seed detritus from which it has been expressed then becomes a part of cattle feed. No part of this paragon seems to be wasted.

Seen as a single plant with its slender stem, thin and distant leaves and ethereal blue flowers one can only register surprise that flax has such hidden virtues. Seen on a field scale in June when the flowers seem to merge with the horizon the surprise is heightened that such beauty combines with economy. The effect, however, is sadly ephemeral and thus as a garden plant it offers little but cerebral interest. For herb garden ornament two other flaxes are far more suitable.

Also an annual is the scarlet flax, *Linum grandiflorum*, easily raised from seeds sown *in situ* in late March or April. More gorgeous in colour is the perennial *Linum narbonnense*. From a wiry, almost twiggy plant a display of florin-sized flowers, of a blue unsurpassed by even gentians or morning glory, continues throughout summer. As a Mediterranean it needs a light soil and a warm spot and thus associates perfectly in cultivation and in looks with grey-leaved herbs.

LIQUIDAMBAR STYRACIFLUA SWEET GUM, LIQUIDAMBER

The sweet gums are marvellous, maple-like trees grown especially for their autumn colour. Though this attribute has always something of the fortuitous about it – soil, season and aspect seeming to affect things differently in different years – the sweet gums are as certain performers as any can be, developing a deep rich red and lasting well.

Liquidambar styraciflua is another of those east North Americans which came to Britain in one of the direct exchanges made by the Pilgrim Fathers and their successors in the seventeenth century. Though it never gained a herbal reputation in Britain the immigrants in America learnt from the native peoples that the bark could be used in cough linctus and 'an ointment to rub on sore throats'.

This is the species which does best with us, though not attaining the 120 feet possible in the wild. Indeed such a possibility would put it out of court for most gardens but, unlike many trees it exhibits all its desirable attributes when still small and takes decades to exceed its space.

The very similar Formosan sweet gum is slightly less hardy in Britain but has the advantage in that the spring growth is also attractively tinted. This is used in Chinese medicine internally against certain forms of urticaria. Smaller with us, usually seen as a large rounded bush, is *L. orientalis* which is the source of so-called levant styrax, an aromatic gum.

In spite of resembling maples in habit and leaf shape (though note alternate, not opposite, leaves) they are in fact related to witch hazels and, like them, are not happy on thin chalky soils.

LIRIODENDRON TULIPIFERA TULIP TREE

The lovely tulip tree is another of those small genera with a disjointed distribution in North America and the Orient. The Chinese plant is rare in cultivation but the American has been a favourite tree since its introduction in the seventeenth century. Like liquidambar, with which it grows in mixed woodland, it has only developed a herbal reputation in its home. The bark was listed by the Shakers as a tonic and a stimulant and used against intermittent fevers and when the patient was considered 'low'.

In the wild tulip tree (a name to be avoided for magnolias proper, though this species is related) makes a magnificent specimen up to 200 feet in height, with the first 100 feet often being a perfectly straight and uninterrupted trunk hardly appearing to narrow as it ascends. Its timber value as tulip poplar or whitewood has long been prized. With us, it frequently stops at about a quarter of its potential, which for garden use is a good thing. Then, its utterly unique leaf shape – like a three lobed maple with the centre lobe bitten off – makes a fine pattern at all stages of growth from tender unfolding to rich yellow autumn tints. Flowering comes late in life but is worth the wait: tulip-shaped and tulip-sized flowers, horn yellow with orange markings inside are followed by narrow cone-like fruits. A superb specimen tree.

LOBELIA CARDINALIS CARDINAL FLOWER

It would be difficult to find a plant more visually different from the usual expectation of the ubiquitous *Lobelia* than this. Instead of the little blue annual of every bedding scheme here is a stately 3-foot high perennial with spikes of glowing scarlet flowers with a reputation as a vermifuge. Unfortunately this lovely plant is not easy to succeed with in Britain as its eastern Canadian origin would suggest. It is a plant of moist ground and stream-sides where it goes into an enforced rest when all freeezes up from December to March: in Britain it is enticed out prematurely by the erratic mildness of winter and gets bashed by the next cold spell.

From further south comes *Lobelia syphilitica*, its name indicating the diseases for which it was thought efficaceous (as well, in Shaker medicine, for dropsy and dysentery). This is a similar, easier and blue-flowered plant from which a range of true hybrids now exist between it and the cardinal flower. These are purple, blue, red or white and all are very beautiful for mid-summer flowering in good garden soil: a mulch of leaves over their crowns helps to ensure they survive the winter. Propagation is easy by division and a box-full could always be overwintered in a cold frame.

Both these species contain poisonous alkaloids and a narcotic latex not unlike that of opium poppy. These dangerous properties exist in greater quantities in the North American indian tobacco, *Lobelia inflata*, a thin 2-foot high annual. The vernacular name refers to its being smoked by the native peoples as a relief from asthma: its use was greatly extended by the settlers internally and externally as a poultice for sprains and bruises and the effects of poison ivy. It is hardly worth cultivation for herb garden ornament, except in a comprehensive collection.

LONICERA PERICLYMENUM HONEYSUCKLE

Here is yet another example of a classic cottage garden plant being right by both association and traditional use for herb garden planting. But it is clear from Miller's comments that by the early eighteenth century its presumed values were being doubted if not yet quite discounted. 'The Leaves, which are the only part used, are sometimes put into Gargarisms (gargles) for sore Throats; though others affirm, they are not so proper for that Purpose. . . . Some commend a decoction of them for a cough . . .' etc. The only recommendation that remains to us today is for external use for skin troubles. The berries are actually poisonous.

However none of this detracts from honeysuckle as a lovely and well-loved twiner whose long-tubed flowers have one of the garden's most delicious perfumes. As a native woodlander it can be seen coming into growth as early as the turn of the year and its first flowers open in June: even in the wild colour varies from a creamy-yellow to purplish. Forms listed as 'Early Dutch' and 'Late Dutch' really seem to have very little difference between them. Both are purple-red outside the tube with yellow interiors and flower off and on from June to October. Honeysuckles are usually given wall space but they can be put up trees or be trained as charming mop-headed standards (if carefully staked) on 3 or 4-foot high stems. Used thus they are highly effective in the herb garden at Cranborne Manor as formal accents.

Other European species such as *Lonicera caprifolium*, the perfoliate honeysuckle, and *L. etrusca* are equally desirable: these enjoy hotter walls than our own native. The semi-evergreen *L. japonica* with its fragrant flowers carried in leaf axils (rather than terminally) is also suitable, being still used in Chinese medicine today. In the garden it is apt to build up an enormous tangle of shoots and is best allowed to clamber over a tree stump or low roof. Attempts to train it tidily are a lost cause. Long flower sprays are available for indoor decoration from June until Christmas. None of these honeysuckles is particular as to soil and take lime very happily.

LYTHRUM SALICARIA PURPLE LOOSESTRIFE

Purple loosestrife is one of our most spectacular waterside plants. Four or 5-foot high spires of brilliant magenta-pink last for weeks in summer. Eventually, when this display is over and autumn comes, the foliage takes on the orange and flame tints which are the usual prerogative of Japanese maples. At the water's edge both effects are doubled by reflection but the plant is equally happy, if not quite so lush, in much drier situations. A named form, 'Robert' is a clearer safer pink, less likely to scream at its neighbours. Both look well in front of the grey-green leaves of plume poppy.

Stuart states that purple loosestrife is anti-bacterial: the whole plant, both fresh and dried can be made into a gargle, used as wound cleanser as it rapidly staunches blood and can be taken to combat the effects of food poisoning. It is interesting to note such modern eulogies of the plant: Miller was decidedly cool about it while reporting that a century earlier John Parkinson 'highly commends a Water distill'd from it for Wounds'.

MACLEAYA CORDATA PLUME POPPY

It is, from the point of view of herb garden decoration, most heartening to discover plume poppy to be highly commended in Chinese medicine. One of the most beautiful and statuesque of foliage plants, it acts as a superb foil to brighter things throughout the summer, at the back of the border or amongst shrubs.

Its lobed leaves, sometimes almost a foot across are grey-green above, the undersides flashing with white when caught by the wind. Above these, 6 or 7 feet up, are feathery clouds of tiny petal-less flowers which make it very difficult to believe that the plant really is a poppy. But the copious yellow sap instantly recalls *Chelidonium* (greater celandine) of which it might be considered a giant edition.

The true plant makes a robust clump but is not invasive which is the most obvious difference between it and *M. microcarpa* (this, confusingly, was known as *Bocconia cordata*), also a very lovely herbaceous perennial.

Roots, stems and leaves are used medicinally in decoction in China for an extraordinary range of conditions from hook worm disease, through skin diseases to osteomyelitis. There seems to be no such interest in the West.

MAGNOLIA LILIIFLORA

It will gladden anyone who wishes to extend the range of hardy plants that may legitimately be classed as herbs to discover that this lovely plant (parent of the famous × *soulangiana* group) has medicinal uses in China. These are humble: the buds are ground up and used in decoction for headaches. For a running nose a physical control is suggested, the offending organ is literally plugged with pulverized magnolia.

In translation two of the local names are woody lotus and spring welcoming flower, both of which would be entirely satisfactory wherever magnolias are grown.

M. liliiflora is one of the best for small gardens here, seldom exceeding 10 feet in height. It also has the virtue, especially valuable if only one magnolia can be grown, of continuing to flower off and on, after the main spring flush, well into summer. The darker form 'Nigra' with deep purple outside petals keeps on even longer. Flowers are waxy and sit upright upon the branches.

By extension it is perfectly valid to plant any of the lovely (but eventually very big) × *soulangiana* types, which vary in colour from purest white, through shades of pink to reddish purple. All have the exquisite magnolia perfume, strangely fruit-salad like.

By further extension *Magnolia salicifolia* is possible, because of its deliciously lemon-scented bark and twigs. This is a Japanese species which makes an elegant little tree with white flowers – rather like those of the star magnolia – in April before the leaves unfold. It deserves more frequent planting because, unlike many of the tree magnolias, it does start to flower when comparatively young.

Magnolia officinalis is used medicinally in its native central China and is listed in *A Barefoot Doctor's Manual*. Traditionally the bark of young trees twenty to thirty years old is used for respiratory congestion. Recent research has shown the extract to have anti-bacterial actions, particularly useful against salmonella poisoning. It is especially fine as a foliage plant in the garden, reaching small tree size; flowers are the size of breakfast cups, white and fragrant.

Only really thin limy soils are resented, otherwise apart from giving wind protection these lush plants are happy almost anywhere.

MAHONIA AQUIFOLIUM OREGON GRAPE

Oregon grape is one of our most valuable and consistently beautiful shrubs. Throughout the year the whorls of divided leaves, holly-like but not holly-armed, reflect every gleam of sun. As the weather gets colder in late autumn they often take on bronze tints; the form 'Atropurpurea' does this particularly well. By early March the ends of every shoot carry tight heads of fine yellow flowers. And then these are followed by glossy grape-bloomed berries in thick clusters; a plant could hardly offer more.

The fact that it is happy in any soil, in shade or sun, and hence needs no care in cultivation makes Oregon grape less considered than if it were rare and difficult. Since its introduction by David Douglas from western North America in the 1820s it has become a part, not only of our gardens but also woodlands where it has been planted as pheasant cover. In any sophisticated position it is important to cut out shoots from the base which are not perfect in form: this will emphasize the plant's beauty.

Though a conserve can be made of the ripe berries it is the dried root-stock which, containing several alkaloids, has uses in skin complaints.

In China the yellow roots and stems of two other mahonias are used, both well-known garden plants with us; decoctions are used for backache and knee pains. These are *Mahonia bealei* and the far more desirable *M. japonica* (at last we seem to have grown out of the nomenclatural confusion which dogged them for years).

As a garden plant *Mahonia japonica* really does have everything: magnificent evergreen leaves in great shining whorls, long sprays of scented flowers carried throughout the dullest months of the year and a strikingly architectural habit. It is seen at its best as the dominant plant of a carefully composed association. A position in half-shade seems to suit it best in any soil but the driest; this is a plant to build any garden around.

MANDRAGORA OFFICINARUM MANDRAKE

Though never a showy plant mandrake is sufficiently strange both in reputation and in looks to make it well worth growing in any collection of herbs where interest is of greater importance than mere colour.

As is well known, mandrake is the archetypal mystery plant capable of uttering such a shriek when its man-shaped root is pulled from the soil that anyone hearing it falls lifeless to the ground. Such remarkable stories were, of course, put about by early herb gatherers to safeguard their supplies. That it possessed very real narcotic, hallucinogenic, and anaesthetic powers added to its mystic reputation; these, until relatively recently, defied explanation. John Donne put it into context:

> 'Go, and catch a falling star,
> Get with child a mandrake root,
> Tell me, where all past years are,
> Or who cleft the Devil's foot.'

Mandrake's properties are derived from a number of the alkaloids, atropine, hyoscyamine, scopolamine that are also found in its equally poisonous relatives, deadly nightshade and henbane (which make up the perfect trio for a classic witches' brew).

Plants are seldom, if ever, offered in nurseries but seed is occasionally available. It must be sown as soon as ripe, or obtained. Seedling growth is very slow and they may take three to five years to flower: having reached maturity a plant will last in a warm spot on light soil for decades.

Its mature aspect and behaviour suit its reputation. Growth begins usually in late February: shoot growth pushing from the ground like the tip of a chicory chicon. This reluctantly unfurls and at once an array of upward facing hare-bell-like flowers, bluish or yellowish, open. As they go over the leaves continue to develop until they form, by late spring, a flat rosette up to 2 feet across. In their centre, if it had earlier been warm enough to encourage pollination, a clutch of pullet-egg-sized fruit gradually turn from green to yellow. These, like a deserted pheasant's nest, remain when, in late July the leaves shrivel and go to rest.

The site must be marked with cane lest a careless hoe takes off next year's buds.

MARRUBIUM VULGARE HOREHOUND

Though found wild on the chalk in Britain there is some doubt as to whether it might have escaped from cultivation in times past when white horehound was an important folk remedy in respiratory ailments. It is still extensively used in cough medicines in Europe and North America. White horehound is indeed one of the whitest of plants. It makes a wide clump, a couple of feet high of twiggy white square stems, with pairs of white leaves and whorls of white flowers towards the top. Even when these are over the pattern and paleness remains to the very year's end.

Any well-drained sunny spot will suit *Marrubium* which will gradually extend its clump. It looks extremely well with colchicums and nerines, though these latter lack herbal validity.

MELISSA OFFICINALIS LEMON BALM

Lemon-scented plants never pall, thus it is lucky that amongst the relatively few available to us in Northern areas this, at least, is extremely easy to grow in all but the driest positions. Though lemon balm is a visually undistinguished plant: a 2½-foot high dead-nettle with inconspicuous pale purple flowers, at every moment from its first leafing in spring to the final dessication of its dry stems in winter a piece can be crushed to give that citrus smell. This comes from the plant's essential oil which, with tannins, makes it valuable in flavouring several well-known liqueurs, for a tisane, and in cooking.

Though the lemon scent is not as lasting as might be desired, when the leaves are dried lemon balm is a useful base for pot pourri. Plenty of material is always easily available.

Unless, as in the case of pot pourri, a lot of the plant is required, its golden-leaved form is by far the better garden plant. This makes a fine clump of colour throughout the season. Unfortunately its seedlings (which are no less frequent as from the type) revert to green: it is thus best to cut the plant's tops off before seeds are shed.

MENTHA spp MINT

Though the French are apt to suggest that mint sauce with lamb is a barbaric custom of an island race that knows no better and is unlikely to learn, there is no doubt that it is one of the few herb uses which everyone knows.

Though literally hundreds of mints have been named, modern taxonomists suggest that there are only about twenty-five distinct species of *Mentha*. Most of these interbreed in an uninhibited fashion amongst themselves and then again almost incestuously so that tri- and tetra-specific hybrids exist. In the garden therefore mints are available in a range of sizes, colours and, of course, flavours. Their selection is very much affected by availability and then by personal choice. One person's favourite for mint-sauce may be quite unconsidered by another.

For culinary use there are three main types. Spearmint (*M. spicata*), has smooth, rather long, narrow leaves and a characteristic sweet 'chewing-gum' scent. Its hybrid with water mint is *Mentha × piperita*, peppermint, that invaluable flavour for sweets, toothpastes, liqueurs and so on. Rather between the two are the hairy leaved types often known as horsemints. One of these, *M. × alopecurioides*, is an enormous plant sometimes 5 feet high.

More ornamental in leaf colour and texture is eau de cologne mint; this name most effectively describes its intense and delicious scent (other titles are orange, bergamot and lemon mints). Leaves are rounded with dark purple undersides and stems. It is too strong for most culinary uses but is superb in sachets and for pot pourri.

Ginger mint is a name which refers to the colour not the flavour of *M. × gentilis* 'Variegata'. A splendid mint no more than 1½ feet in height with a netted golden variegation which is especially good on the young growth. It flowers late more ornamentally than most and accepts dry conditions without fuss. Apple mint (*M. rotundifolia*), with a very mild flavour, also has a variegated form with hairy white-blotched leaves. This is the least robust of all the culinary mints and is the best for really small herb beds or even window boxes. Watch has to be kept for reverting green stems.

As is well known, most mints are highly invasive in good garden soil with underground runners travelling busily in all directions and some form of restriction is usually necessary, especially if several types are grown. Rings of robust polythene a foot deep are ideal – a fertilizer sack will provide these – and runners clambering over the top can be headed off before they are out of sight. It is wise to replant elsewhere at least every three years to maintain a good stock and avoid the build-up of mint rust, that unpleasant fungus which dessicates top growth long before spring lamb has become mutton.

Rather different from these big culinary mints is pennyroyal, *Mentha pulegium*. This makes good leaf and aromatic ground cover from which interrupted spikes of flowers towards a foot high make a decent show. It used to be considered an effective and efficient aborti-facient, now realized as being so only in toxic quantities.

Corsican mint (*M. requienii*) is quite the most surprising of its genus – so long as it is not completely overlooked. It naturally grows in cracks of rocks and hence in gardens seems to have been created especially for the interstices of paving flags. It has virtually no height, and on this mossy carpet (table-mat is a better metaphor) tiny purple flowers can just be discerned. From this faint filigree an authentic mint-scent rises up fresh and strong. This is a plant to be cherished and put around the garden in several positions to ensure continuity in at least one place: it is worth every care.

MENYANTHES TRIFOLIATA BOGBEAN

Buckbean or bogbean is one of our most ornamental aquatic plants; rooting in the mud beneath shallow water where it can develop considerable rafts of shining trifoliate leaves and, standing up above them, spikes of flowers in June. From a distance the effect is charming, and close up the pale violet flowers have a particular elegance. Each is made up of five petals which are fringed as if edged with finest lace.

Stuart states that *Menyanthes* root is accepted as a substitute for *Gentiana lutea* and has similar tonic- and appetite-promoting properties. The leaves are stated as making a tea as well as having been dried for a tobacco substitute.

While, as stated above, bogbean can cover wide areas, in a small garden pool it is happy when planted in a container just submerged in the water. Space is economically used if the pot contains, say, *Iris versicolor* to rise above the water and the *Menyanthes* to travel out from it. This makes an interesting combination of vertical and horizontal lines.

MESPILUS GERMANICA MEDLAR

'Medlars are cooling, drying, and binding, especially before they are ripe, and are useful in all kinds of Fluxes'; Miller goes on ominously, 'The ripe fruit, eaten too freely, is apt to tye up the stomach and cause the Cholic.'

No current thought is given to medlars as a medicinal aid, but it has much to commend it as a picturesque, old-fashioned specimen tree for the garden. Eventually making a broad small tree – rather like a gnarled apple – the dog-rose flowers in May make a good show, set amongst long leathery leaves. These turn a fine russet colour in autumn as the fruits, like flattened golf balls in size, mature.

To eat them, of course, they have to be 'bletted', in other words kept until they begin to rot. If Miller's cholic is feared they may be used to make the delicious preserve known as medlar cheese or medlar fool.

MITCHELLA REPENS SQUAWBERRY, CHECKERBERRY

The checkerberry or partridgeberry of east North American woods is another of those charming little evergreen carpeters such as *Arctostaphylos uva-ursi* and *Gaultheria procumbens*. Though surprisingly it is related to the bed-straws it resembles and needs similar conditions to those ericoids. Hence it is a plant for humus-rich acid soil and shade: given these it will make good ground cover under trees – even under evergreens – and light up in September with its pea-sized scarlet berries.

In Shaker literature checkerberry is stated to be a powerful uterine tonic. A further name, squawberry, suggests that the fruits were collected as food by the Indians: the flavour is good but the berries lack juice.

MONARDA DIDYMA BERGAMOT

Bee balm, horsemint, wild bergamot, Oswego tea are just some of the names given to this lovely North American perennial. The latter title refers to a role it took on particularly strongly after 1773: historians will recall this as the date of the Boston Tea Party.

Boiling water poured upon bee balm leaves makes a still perfectly palatable drink and its deliciously aromatic properties make it suitable for a wide range of uses: dried leaves in sachets and for pot pourri, the vapour is inhaled to assist in colds and so on.

As a garden plant it is one of the most ornamental of aromatics. It makes a strong upright clump 3 or 4 feet in height with the typical opposite leaf-pairs on square stems of most labiates. The final pair sits below a fine head of hooded sage-flowers, white, pink, purple, or scarlet which lasts for a long time from mid-summer onwards. *Monarda didyma* grows best in a rich and moist garden soil: for drier spots the similar *M. fistulosa* and its forms are a better choice. These are in softer colours of pinks and lavenders: the leaves are similarly scented. Both are easy to propagate by division.

MORUS NIGRA MULBERRY

Like medlar and quince, the black mulberry is one of those trees considered, rightly indeed, to associate with old houses and traditional 'old-fashioned' gardens. They are often positioned in association with herbs or herb gardens. All, too, have their own herbal properties and the fact that in maturity they take on a gnarled and venerable appearance adds to the effect. Fortunately, with mulberries especially, this air is attained when quite young. This accounts for the endless stories of King James I having planted this or that particularly bent specimen. King James did indeed encourage the planting of mulberries in the hope of setting up a silk industry in Britain; unfortunately many imported were this, the black mulberry, not the necessary *Morus alba* beloved of silk worms.

Bark from the root as well as the leaves had medicinal uses but the fruit then, as now, was of the greatest use, as is apparent to anyone today making the delicious wine (a perfect rosé), jams (apple and mulberry is particularly good) and ice-creams.

While it is possible to train mulberry up as a conventional standard tree this is a mistake: branches become enormously heavy and invariably break when full of fruit and foliage; a lot of space is required in growing this as a wide-spreading plant, propping it as necessary or required.

The black mulberry is happy on any well-drained soil – chalk not excluded – and good feeding in the early years can bring a plant into productive fruiting in less than a decade. There is no beauty of flower: separate male and female flower clusters with the most vestigial of petals line the young branches in May. The fruit, the colour and shape of a ripe loganberry, ripens from the end of July until well into September (starlings and wood pigeons permitting) giving a most usefully protracted crop. Only one word of warning: this is not a tree for taking tea under while the fruit is ripe – it stains the clothes irrevocably.

Both the white and red mulberries are also listed in various pharmocopeias but neither is so useful a garden plant, at least not in Britain.

MYRICA GALE BOG MYRTLE

Bog myrtle is one of the continual surprises of upland bogs of intensely acid soil. A tight yard-high twiggy bush, its leaves are amazingly aromatic as are the little brownish flower clusters which appear, on separately sexed bushes, in April and May. The general appearance, as well as a certain expectation of what ought to grow in such sites, has provoked a further name, sweet willow.

A leaf or two can be added to soups or stews (preferably cooked on a camp fire in the near-wilderness where it can be plucked fresh) and these leaves used to form the basis of gale beer.

As garden plants on other than very acid soils a couple of eastern North American relatives are better. *Myrica cerifera* is the wax myrtle which reaches 30 feet or more in height. Only a quarter the height and taking dry soils is *M. pensylvanica*, bayberry or candleberry – it is a plant of maritime sands and thus is greatly employed for roadside planting in areas which are affected by salt-spray in winter. Like northern bog myrtle the flowers are nothing spectacular but the berry clusters are like peas stuck together with blue-white wax.

This wax is still employed in making decidedly expensive aromatic candles and soaps.

MYRRHIS ODORATA SWEET CICELY

Sweet cicely is a most valuable garden herb: it develops its mound of fern-like cow parsley leaves very early in spring which become topped with typical white umbel-heads in June. Most distinctive are the black inch-long fruits which take their place. If seed is not wanted, either to reproduce the plant or for winter flavouring, the whole plant should be cut to the ground immediately after flowering when a new batch of spring-fresh leaves will soon develop. Gertrude Jekyll recommends this plan to enliven the often tired foliage of other border plants in high summer, planted ahead of irises, perhaps, and peonies.

Myrrhis is a British native seen especially on northern hedgebanks with the big *Campanula latifolia*, an association which is well worth repeating in half-shade in the garden. Texture, size and colour are all highly complementary.

As Joseph Miller remarks 'This is more a Sallad (sic) Herb than an Officinal one, being much in the Nature of Chervil'. Indeed, great chervil was one of its names and the leaves are used in just the same way possessing something of a similar anise flavour.

MYRTUS COMMUNIS MYRTLE

It is strange that this plant, type genus of a huge group of 3000 or so trees and shrubs, should be its only European member; the pre-Linnean name, it seems, was just waiting for the Antipodes to be discovered.

Myrtle is an essential plant in every herb garden for its beauty, its scent and its classical associations. Wreathes of shining myrtle leaves were used to garland magistrates, athletes and poets, an unlikely trio for a plant sacred to Venus.

In Britain the plant is on the edge of its hardiness range: even 15-foot high shrubs against a south of England wall can get badly seared or even cut to the ground in really bad winter. Fortunately it usually springs again from the base and initial replacement shoots are pretty quick. They will, however, take a couple of years to settle down to flower again, an occasion to be anticipated with pleasure one September when the little spherical buds finally cast off their protective sepals. Five pure white petals are then seen to support a fuzz of creamy stamens: these flowers are like tiny eucryphias or, more conventionally, white St John's worts. They are followed by black flask-shaped berries which are also intensely aromatic. These, dried, are a possible alternative spice to peppercorns; unfortunately, though the flavour is pleasant, they do seem to clog the mill.

Myrtle has several garden forms, as would be expected from a shrub with centuries of cultivation behind it. An old double-flowered form is no improvement but a couple – especially *M. tarentina*, small in all its parts, is delightful. So too is the variegated one with pink-tinged leaves splashed with cream: this appears less hardy and is perhaps best grown as a large pot plant for standing out in summer. Only the most basic winter protection is needed under glass.

NARCISSUS PSEUDO NARCISSUS DAFFODIL

It is to be presumed that as they were easily available native plants in Europe but unrecorded in the herbal lists, daffodils were considered to be of no herbal significance. Yet one Shaker community recommends them. Union Village was one of the biggest of Shaker communities which flourished for almost a hundred years from 1805 near Cincinatti in Ohio, at one stage with 600 members in six 'families'.

Here daffodil bulbs were dried, powdered and used as an emetic, the secondary effect as a purge. While this one reference does not turn *Narcissus* into an important herb it does make it possible to include Lent-lilies in a collection of historic medicinals. Planted with colchicums, for instance, they make full use of a piece of ground with their complementary life-cycles: one up and one down.

NEPETA CATARIA CATMINT, CATNEP

It is probably best to keep the name catnep for this, the most 'herbal' of its group. This is the plant that cats will savage in a feline fashion finding the smell almost irresistible. They do also nibble at the young tips, finding perhaps the stomach-settling action for which catnep tea was once used, especially by children. The aromatic volatile oil is appreciated by merely brushing the leaves.

The plant makes a grey-green hummock 2 or 3 feet high and the same across but the purple-spotted white flowers, like small dead-nettles, make little effect. Better in the garden is catmint, *Nepeta* × *faassenii*. A smaller plant, it is covered for weeks with sprays of lavender blue: it makes a marvellous edging to tumble out of raised beds or soften hard edges of stone flags. It looks particularly well fronting old-fashioned roses and peonies. When the main flowering is over it should be cut back hard to encourage a second crop. Excessively enthusiastic cats sometimes fall for this too.

Catmint is a plant for well-drained soils, with or without lime. What it cannot abide is winter wet. Less choosy is a much bigger plant usually available as *Nepeta gigantea*. Still very beautiful, at 3 feet high it is hardly an edger, however.

NICOTIANA RUSTICA TOBACCO

This original tobacco was cultivated by the native peoples of Mexico and eastern North America: this is the plant that first reached Europe in the sixteenth century. It is smaller, 2 to 3 feet in height, and less frost-tender than the cultigen which has developed from it and been accorded specific status as *Nicotiana tabacum*. Selections of this can reach 10 feet. Whatever the size, tobacco makes a similar pattern: a single strong stem with soft, broad dock-like leaves decreasing in size as they reach the head of pink tubular flowers. The plant is interesting, rather than particularly ornamental, as having developed within 500 years from restricted tribal use in the New World, to one of man's major plant crops, yet one which is of little real 'value' to him.

However, eighteenth century accounts, such as Joseph Miller's, report not just the current 'every packet carries a Government Health Warning' but the broader applications real and assumed. It is interesting that an alternative name was *Hyoscyamus peruvianus*, correctly indicating both botanical and medicinal relationships. It was, and is, chewed, made into snuff 'as well as smoak'd in a Pipe, in which vast quantities are consum'd, the greater part by way of Amusement, though some commend it as a Helper of Digestion. . . . The dust destroys Fleas, Lice and other troublesome Vermine, the Dealers in Tobacco being seldom disturb'd with them'.

This insecticidal use remains an important one: nicotine sprays and smokes, though having to be treated with great care by the operator, are amongst the most effective destroyers of horticultural pests.

Tobacco flowers, selections of *Nicotiana × sanderae*, are well-loved as providers of delicious summer scents. The habit of the original species of looking half-dead during the day, opening to pour forth their scent at night, has been bred out, but only, one feels at the expense of some of the scent: dissemination as against concentration. A further fine tobacco flower is *N. sylvestris*, the size of tobacco proper with long narrow white tubes, very sweetly scented.

All *Nicotiana* must be treated as half-hardy annuals. Sown in March under glass they can only be put out after all danger of frost is past: however, sometimes the fleshy roots overwinter.

NIGELLA SATIVA LOVE-IN-A-MIST

Under various names such as black cumin and Roman coriander the seeds of this white love-in-a-mist are occasionally used as seasoning. Ground to a snuff they were once employed to recover the lost sense of smell – perhaps the resultant sneeze did the trick.

But it is unlikely that this species is much in cultivation, being less ornamental than the bigger, brighter *Nigella damascena*, the true love-in-a-mist or devil-in-a-bush. This has the most 'mist', the cloud of intensely divided fennel-fine bracts which support the clear blue petals. A further lovely species is *Nigella hispanica*, thunder-cloud blue.

Nigella is a charming hardy annual which, once established, seeds itself about from year to year in a suitably random cottage garden manner. Occasional thinning will produce bigger and better plants for the summer as well as stronger stems to support the inflated seed capsules (which are round in *N. damascena*, longer and beaked in the Spaniard) to be kept for dried winter arrangements.

NYMPHAEA ALBA WATER LILY

Plants like our lovely native white water lily and the great pink Indian *Lotus* caused men to wonder that such perfection of form and purity of colour could arise from the stinking mud at the bottom of ponds. Modern understanding of plant physiology and genetics in no way disperses that wonder.

It is not, perhaps, entirely unrelated that these plants developed a reputation as anti-aphrodisiacs: in Miller's words 'rendring Persons less disposed to Venery'. However the reputation is, if anything, being supported by modern research. The rhizome contains alkaloids and acts as an antiseptic and an astringent; its mucilage made it an occasional substitute for soap.

The white water lily needs no description: as a wild plant it is especially frequent in acid lakes and bogs in the north, including Scotland, and the west, flowering superbly from July until the frosts. It needs a couple of feet of still water to do well. For garden pools there are less robust hybrids in a range of colours from white, through cream, yellow and pink to deep crimson, still with sufficient *Nymphaea alba* in them to make their herbal planting valid. It is worthwhile noting that M. Marliac's original hybridizing work on *Nymphaea* in France was suitably in time for Monet to develop his garden at Giverny and paint that extraordinary range of water lily pictures: reproduction of one of these in fact is not an ignoble aim. For really small pools or even large tubs it is still possible to enjoy the beauty of these plants: *N. pygmaea* and its hybrids need only a foot of water and never exceed 2 feet across in spread. Water lilies must never be planted within range of a fountain: not surprisingly thinking it to be raining, they just close up.

❧

OCIMUM BASILICUM BASIL

There is no herb we can grow which possesses quite such a rich and utterly distinct aroma as basil, a strange, warm combination of unknown fruits and spices blended with newly ground pepper. Strangely enough the essential oil which produces it is estragol, found in tarragon with which it has not the slightest connection, botanical, visual or nasal.

As a fresh herb basil associates particularly well with tomatoes – a simple salad of cooled, skinned fresh tomatoes with oil, vinegar and basil is one of the indications that summer is here – or that one is on holiday with the Mediterranean not far away. It is there that so many people made its first acquaintance. On sunny front steps, in back yards close to the kitchen door one sees containers – tins, pots, old saucepans and elegant urns alike – holding the vivid green domes of bush basil, ready to be plucked and cast into the cooking.

In the north it is not so easy. The basils are truly tropical plants and not only blacken at the first breath of autumn frost but sulk most dreadfully if put out too soon. Mid June usually is quite soon enough. But then in a warm spot in light but reasonably rich soil one can expect three months of growth and fresh leaves (an excess can, of course, be dried but the result is as close as dried figs are to those sun-ripened off the tree).

All culinary basils are forms of *Ocimum basilicum*. The typical broad-leaved type is known as sweet basil and leaf size can go up to 'lettuce-leaved' and down to bush basil. Fine purple-leaved variants with a metallic cast add interest to a summer bed of basils; their flower spikes are also predictably purple, as distinct from the usual white, but the flowers of neither are showy. The so-called lemon-scented basil seems not to live up to its name. Sweet basil has various medicinal uses for stomach complaints (it allays excessive vomiting) and its oil is abstracted for use in perfumery.

Many other species exist and are grown in the tropics: in India *Ocimum sanctum* has a high reputation, even in cancer cases. This and *O. canum*, the hoary basil, are also possible summer annuals with us. Their scents are quite different from the culinary types and are grown, if at all, in Botanic Garden collections.

OENOTHERA BIENNIS EVENING PRIMROSE

Evening primrose is a decidedly coarse plant making a wide rosette one year and sending up a flower-spike in the second to a height of 4 feet or so. Two or three flowers open at a time and during the day look rather tatty: but as the sun goes down they seem suddenly to take an interest in life, they widen their petals and glow in the twilight like distant lamps. They fully earn their keep in a rough place or in the herb garden behind angelica, which leaves a big hole early in the season.

This is a North American native which has gone wild in dry places throughout southern and eastern England. Medicinally evening primrose has been used for coughs and, in ointments, on abrasions and there has been a recent revival of interest in its healing powers. It is also a pot herb with roots, stems and leaves and even flower buds being eaten.

Other *Oenothera* though without herbal pretensions, are of greater garden value, especially *O. tetragona*, a dwarf bushy plant which covers itself with vivid golden flowers throughout the summer. This is a highly satisfactory perennial in any sunny spot: it does not shut up shop in the daytime.

ORIGANUM VULGARE ORIGANO

Origano is immediately evocative of the warm south and the culinary arts of Italy in particular. That it was seldom used in English kitchens until relatively recently merely indicates the lack of importance given to all but a very few herbs: the surprise here is simply that it is not an uncommon plant over much of the British Isles on limestone hills and chalk downs and is as easy to collect here as it is on the Continent. It seems that the home-grown plant is less strongly aromatic which may account for some neglect.

It is a perfectly easy garden plant, making an evergreen ground cover of tight leaves from which the summer bush of upright stems develops. The whorls of small purple flowers are pleasant without being remarkable. Much more useful is the little golden leaved form 'Aureum'. This makes a perfect dome of gold throughout the summer. Its placing however requires some care: too much sun and the young leaves burn, too little and the gold fades while the dome breaks out to reveal an untidy middle.

The dried plant has many uses, in medical preparations for stomach and respiratory troubles, in cosmetics and, of course, in numbers of culinary dishes: it is especially good with meat.

Two southern Europeans, from east and west respectively are *O. heracleoticum* and *O. virens*. Both are closely related to common origano and could be considered as little more than geographical variants of it. They do, however, seem even more aromatic. In their native countries these origanos are collected and dried for use regardless of botanical nicety. If stock can be obtained they should be tried in the garden for visual and culinary comparison.

Much more highly scented, rather than tartly aromatic is *Origanum onites* or pot marjoram. It is an eastern form of the rather similar and more widely cultivated sweet or knotted marjoram, *O. marjorana*. This is also confusingly and incorrectly known as annual marjoram because being rather tender it is often treated as a half-hardy annual. A 9-inch high bush whose branches root where they touch the earth (so it is perfectly easy to bring a bit inside for the winter), it carries its infinitesimal dead-nettle flowers in little swollen heads which give the 'knotted' effect of the name. A charming plant to have and in cooking a little goes a long way.

There are other marjorams of greater or lesser aromatic quality, all delightful plants in their different ways. A collection in a raised bed makes a marvellous conversation piece; not least because scent, being such a fleeting and individual sense, is seldom appreciated by two people in quite the same way. Specialist nurseries which concentrate upon alpine plants are a likely source for the Mediterranean uplanders such as *Origanum dictamnus*, the famed dittany of Crete. A tea made from its little woolly leaves is considered there almost a panacea and consequently the plant is becoming rare: what the flocks do not browse off, their shepherds gather to sell in the markets of Chania and Heraklion.

PAEONIA OFFICINALIS PEONY

There is no grander cottage garden flower than the old double red peony which has been with us certainly since the sixteenth century, its huge blood-red globes opening as early as the beginning of May. Pre-Linnaean texts call this the female peony and refer to a single red form as its opposite, *Paeonia mas*. The tuberous roots, the flowers and the seeds were all considered valuable for 'the Epilepsy, Apoplexy, and all kinds of convulsions and nervous Affections, both in young and old'. In fact peonies are extremely poisonous and one fears for the patients.

Nonetheless the Chinese peony, *P. lactiflora* and the Moutan, *P. suffruticosa* are both listed as being used today in Chinese medicine for a wide range of complaints. Traditional uses of the latter are to reduce fever and dispel blood clots: recent investigation has indicated anti-bacterial properties.

From the point of view of the garden it is fortunate that, though many marvellous species are omitted, the three with the most diverse forms and colours are legitimate herbs. However it would be a mistake to introduce into the gentle palette of the herb garden raucous colours and unnatural shapes. The early forms are quite sufficiently sophisticated, especially in the Chinese species.

Paeonia lactiflora is a most elegant plant, tall and slender by comparison with our cottage garden double red. Here, flowering in June, is a 3-foot high plant with bronze stems and leaf-stalks and a dark cast to the leaves which perfectly set off the flowers of great, white, gold-centred bowls. This is the plant the Chinese had bred and selected from for a thousand years before it reached the West at the turn of the eighteenth and nineteenth centuries; neither their work nor that which has come after it surpasses the original.

The same can be said of *Paeonia suffruticosa*, parent of innumerable and often amazing tree-peonies. For here there is the perfection of milk-white flowers, each petal purple-blotched, against grey-green leaves.

PAPAVER SOMNIFERUM OPIUM POPPY

As morphine, the opium poppy brings for man's use the most important plant-based pain-killer, still not effectively synthesized. As opium it brings, by his misuse of it, one of the major drug scourges of all time. This simple, beautiful annual poppy has been the cause of nations and fortunes being made and broken, of untold pains eased and of innumerable addicts dying in delirium. It is at once both black and white, devil and god.

Seed sown *in situ* in spring soon produces a 3-foot high plant with elegant grey-green glaucous leaves; terminal flowers are large, pale violet with dark petal blotches around the stamens and incipient seed capsule. A whole kaleidoscope of colour variants with single, semi-double and double flowers will occur from a seedsman's mixed packet.

The seed capsule continues to swell until it is towards an inch across. Commercially this is incized with a special sharp tool and the white latex which issues from the wound solidifies and is gathered and pressed into resinous lumps. This is raw opium which contains, it is suggested, at least twenty-five distinct alkaloids.

Surprisingly the ripe seed from within the capsule lacks the narcotic properties of the latex and is used to top breads and cakes. It is also ground up to produce an oil used in cooking. These same roles are filled by seed of our native poppy, the scarlet *Papaver rhoeus*, and its flowers are used to colour medicines and wines.

Modern farming methods have reduced the blood-red tinge which swathes of this poppy commonly gave to corn fields, but country road-works, uncovering seed that has lain dormant for decades, still often provides a show. The diverse soft colours of Shirley poppies are selections from mutant colours of this wild plant.

As a herb garden plant the field poppy is better replaced by a close relative from southeast Europe, *Papaver commutatum*. This is a little bigger, flowers are an even deeper blood-red accentuated by a black blotch on each petal-base – all much like the special flowers rather grand people used to display on their motor cars for

Poppy Day. Spring sown seed gives a marvellous mid-summer display.

PELARGONIUM GRAVEOLENS ROSE GERANIUM

Rose geranium is the best known of a group of marvellously aromatic herb garden plants which should be used more. All are sub-shrubby South Africans and thus cannot sensibly be considered hardy in the English climate, any more than are their cousins, the brightly coloured bedding 'geraniums' (derivations of *Pelargonium zonale*). Yet in coastal gardens of the southwest all survive for years; they will also survive up-country in warm spots on light soil. This is the case particularly in London. At the Chelsea Physic Garden a number of scented-leaved species maintained much of their top growth through several winters; others, though cut to ground level, sprouted from below and produced better plants by the mid-summer following than did young plants newly set out.

While we none of us know what the next winter will bring it is sensible, having rooted a few cuttings in early autumn to keep indoors, to consider keeping the stock plants as well if the ground is needed for nothing else. In about mid November the soft tops – by now looking rather resentful – are cut off and the whole plant heaped over with bark chips or dry leaves (the latter held together with a bit of wire-netting). This mulch can be opened up in early April to reveal – perhaps a corpse. This is now cut back, hopefully to living tissue, or to the ground and still growth may appear; the indoor insurance policies can be set out in late May. Alternatively they may be kept in pots and grouped together, as at Jenkyn Place, in Hampshire, around an old sundial.

Though, obviously, all of this group do flower, these are generally small and attractive only in detail. Their claim to herb garden cultivation lies in diversity of shape, texture and scent of the leaves. Specialist nurseries must be visited to discover the range of delights.

Pelargonium tomentosum has leaves cut out of moss green velvet that has been steeped in peppermint; *P. crispum*, on an upright little 'tree' has small lemon-scented crimped leaves. A variegated form is even more choice. Other names are tantalizingly suggestive: *P. myrrhifolium, odoratissimum, fragrans, mellissimum* and so on.

But rose geranium remains the basis of the group. By far the easiest to cultivate, it is the main commercial source of the volatile oil of geranium used in perfumery, or dried. A couple of fresh leaves in various sweets are delicious as are the dried leaves for pot pourri and in sachets.

PEROVSKIA ATRIPLICIFOLIA

This is a subshrub from the western Himalayas which has never been formally embraced by the herb garden but fulfils every condition for entry as a herb associate or pot pourri ingredient.

From a permanent woody base white 3-foot high stems of grey, highly aromatic leaves gradually pass into elegant spikes of small blue dead-nettle flowers. This progression takes the whole season, with the flower display being at its best in August and September. 'Blue Spire' is a splendid selection with more deeply cut leaves and bigger flowers of a lavender blue cast. It is equally, and deliciously, scented.

Unlike the majority of grey-leaved plants which are Mediterraneans and which are tight and compact in habit, *Perovskia* is light and diffuse. Colours blend perfectly while the texture makes a perfect contrast. Similar garden conditions are required: sun and decent drainage. It can be pruned back by half in spring to prevent a floppy plant developing.

PETROSELINUM CRISPUM PARSLEY

Of all herbs parsley must be the best known and presumably the most desirable, or why would a secondary industry have developed to manufacture plastic parsley for the decoration of butchers' windows? This, of course, is a dreadful diminution of the herbal role: certainly the visual appeal of a dish is important and garnishing is not to be neglected but parsley's beauty is not just skin- (or epidermis) deep. In fact its essential oil provides a surprisingly unique flavour, when one considers the number of its umbellifer herb relatives.

Though old medicinal recommendations are no longer considered, the fresh leaves are used in innumerable culinary recipes and they may be made into a soothing tea as well as a very palatable wine; this develops the rich gold colour of old Sauternes.

All of which indicates that it is almost impossible to grow too much parsley. Fortunately it is, in full growth, a highly ornamental plant and is admirable for the edgings of paths or in parterre blocks. It usually behaves as a biennial and hence one or two sowings a year are necessary, depending on the expected amount of use.

A first sowing is made in April and a second in August. Fresh seed is important – all umbellifer seed loses viability quickly if kept over the years. Even then germination is slow – old folk tales of parsley growing down to the Devil before it comes up to the light are well known.

Pouring boiling water into the drill after sowing does sometimes seem to help. But good fresh seed is probably the key as witnessed by the ease with which parsley seeds itself about if happy with the site; keeping a couple of plants especially for seed is a good plan.

Though capable of growing almost anywhere the best results are obtained in good garden soil which does not dry out. Half-shade is acceptable which promotes the high humidity it enjoys. Parsley which dries out is invariably prey to aphides.

The plant generally grown in continental Europe is closer to the original species with flat sprays of celery-like leaves: in Britain breeding has concentrated upon intensely curled leaves, prettier but not better (some would say worse) for flavouring. Hamburg parsley is a form bred for its swollen roots, looking rather like small parsnips and it is cultivated similarly for winter use. The leaves are still perfectly usable as flavouring parsley so that a dual role is achieved: yet in spite of such sensible economy Hamburg parsley is common only on the Continent.

PHLOMIS FRUTICOSA   JERUSALEM SAGE

Jerusalem sage is one of the joys and standbys of gardens on dry soils. It makes a fine mound of grey furred leaves which is proof against all but our most severe winters even up into Scotland. Flower spikes in summer carry well-separated whorls of yellow, hooded flowers which, gradually opening further up the stem, give colour for a long period.

With judicious pruning *Phlomis* can be kept to a regular 3-foot high dome but given the space it can exceed this considerably. On the great south terrace of Pusey House in Oxfordshire a pair of huge plants got 10 feet or so across, looking superb in leaf and flower against the pale tawny stone of the house.

Though listed amongst neither medicinal nor culinary herbs the leaves are pleasantly aromatic: one sees dried bunches of this and related species, having been collected on the hillsides, hung up for sale in Greek markets. The leaves are made into a tea.

PHYSALIS ALKEKENGI   CHINESE LANTERN

The fruit of the common old Chinese lantern has been used as a diuretic since early times both in the East and West and hence strongly recommended for dropsy and for 'the stone'. This we might conveniently forget as well as eating them for food – time and voyages of discovery have brought better members of the Solanaceae. But it (as well as its bigger Japanese cousin *P. franchetii*) is still of great value as a late autumn garden plant and subsequently in dried decorations indoors using the papery lanterns, bright orange in colour. In translation a Chinese name is heavenly bubbles.

For the rest of the year it deserves no more than an unconsidered corner. A running root puts up 3-foot high stems with full, rather foetid leaves; in their axils lurk little white potato flowers with no hint of their potential.

If the indoor arrangements are most important *Physalis* might as well go next into the compost heap out of sight to gather strength from nutrient seepage. If, on the other hand, an autumn brightener is required it should go behind some tall herbaceous plant, elecampane, fennel or some such which will take the eye until the season has come for the lanterns to light up. Grown with *Iris foetidissima*, these two display almost identical colours in fruit; the final flame of the year.

PHYTOLACCA AMERICANA POKEWEED

Pokeweed or Indian poke is one of a small group of often huge herbs native to East and West. They are nomenclaturally confusing but this one may be taken as the type. From a woody root-stock thick fleshy stems arise to a height of 5 or 6 feet and spread similarly. In the upper axils of the dock-like leaves grow 6-inch spikes of tightly packed flowers. As those at the top of the spike eventually open, pollinated flowers at the bottom are turning into fleshy purple-black berries. Soon this is the full pattern all over the plant, very effective where sufficient space is available, especially in early autumn when the yellowing leaves contrast with the glistening fruit-spikes.

Various texts suggest that the young boiled shoots make a pleasant vegetable. With some forms this may be so, but such is their confusion and such is the toxicity of others that it is wiser to go and cut a cabbage.

Pokeweed is one of the North American plants used by the native peoples and taken up by colonists. In our own time it has been the subject of much pharmacological enquiry and this has begun to unravel a highly complex chemistry: Stuart shows that its constituents are used in modern immunology as well as a molluscicide which may control bilharzia in tropical Africa.

PODOPHYLLUM PELTATUM AMERICAN MANDRAKE

The herbaceous members of the Berberidaceae are, without exception, interesting and rather strange plants. The *Podophyllum* is no exception. This species is the May-apple of eastern North American woodlands. Because of its diverse, and sometimes dangerous, applications in medicine it also has the name of American mandrake. It is an extremely fierce purgative but has none of the narcotic qualities of *Mandragora*. A current commercial use is in preparations to dispel worts and verucas.

As a garden plant it has great beauty throughout its life. From a slender underground rhizome single leaves push through the soil looking rather like ink-cap mushrooms. The drooping folds then raise themselves into a foot-high umbrella making complete ground cover. Occasional paired leaves carry between them a single exquisite flower, like a small cream peony. This is succeeded by a juicy fruit, the size and shape of a yellow plum. It is aromatic and pleasant to eat; collected in the wild it is made into May-apple jam.

From northern India comes the similar *Podophyllum hexandrum* with brown-banded leaves, blush pink flowers and rosy fruit; it is just as beautiful. They both enjoy leafy woodland soil in shade but are happy with a much more conventional garden site.

POLEMONIUM COERULEUM JACOB'S LADDER

This is a lovely cottage garden short-lived perennial which it is somehow rather surprising to find listed as a medicinal herb. Stuart states that it remained in some European pharmacopaeias into the nineteenth century, being considered useful in the treatment of rabies and syphilis.

The vernacular names have a charm to match the plant; Jacob's ladder is most usual but Greek valerian and charity also occur. It makes a clump of pinnate, somewhat vetch-like leaves and 2-foot high spires of, typically, lavender blue flowers in June and July, giving the effect of a delicate campanula. White and variously blue forms exist; any named forms will of course be propagated by division but the species seeds around happily. Jacob's ladder is not particular as to site or soil. The clear blue forms look wonderful against purple foliage.

A much smaller plant is *Polemonium reptans* which makes a 9-inch clump, still with the typical ladder leaves but heads of nodding lavender flowers. An excellent front of border plant it is one of the earliest perennials, coming out with *Doronicum* and flowering on and off throughout the year as well. The Shakers called it abscess, but used it, confusingly, for pleurisy and fevers.

POLYGONATUM MULTIFLORUM SOLOMON'S SEAL

Solomon's seal is one of the glories of our woods, if sadly an uncommon one. An arching stem of smooth paired leaves comes up from a fleshy rhizome and hanging from the stem is a row of little waxy white bells; the whole is obviously the original of Edward Lear's well-known 'Nonsense Botany' plant *Manypeoplia upsidedownia*.

Solomon's seal flowers with bluebells make a natural association that no artist could better. There is a bigger garden form *Polygonatum × hybridum* which gets to 3 feet and is equally lovely, so too is the rather rare variegated one.

Miller suggests that a poultice of the rhizome reduces the marks of bruises as an alternative, no doubt, to the other traditional remedy of a lump of raw beef similarly applied to the afflicted spot. Most of the Shaker communities used it against a wide range of disorders from female debility to piles and as a wash after contact with poison ivy.

As a natural woodlander, it is quite obvious where Solomon's seal does best, but in cultivation it can take almost anything except full, hot sun – even the dry shade under evergreens if the soil can be built up with added humus. In autumn the leaves turn a clear yellow and sometimes as they fall a few round black berries are seen to have been hiding there. Propagation by division, however, is both easier and quicker.

POLYGONUM BISTORTA BISTORT

Within this genus there are some lovely garden plants as well as some pestilential weeds. Herbal texts describe one plant from each of these categories: in the latter is the common knotgrass, an unpleasant little annual so difficult to hoe up that it appears almost made of wire. Bistort, however, is in the other group, a useful long-flowering perennial especially happy in moist spots and in half-shade. The basal leaf clump is bluish-green with white undersides and from this comes 2½-foot high wands each carrying flower spikes rather like ears of wheat. The colour is a soft, clear pink, even better in the form 'Superbum'.

The twisting rhizome provides an alternative name, snakeroot, and it is this, dried, which is the source of its medicinal properties. This rhizome contains several tannins which produce a strong astringent action; powdered, it is used as a styptic. Miller considered it 'binding and drying, in Service in all Kinds of Fluxes and Haemorrhages', which indicates a similar effect.

PONCIRUS TRIFOLIATA HARDY ORANGE

The use of a decoction of the unripe fruit of the hardy orange in China as an aid in pulmonary congestion, indigestion and constipation brings another fine plant into the herb garden orbit even if one would prefer to go to the local chemist if suffering from any of these complaints.

Though lemons have ripened outside in London, and oranges in Devonshire, this is the only species (sufficiently closely related to have been once classified as *Citrus trifoliata*) with claims to real hardiness in the normal British climate. A cross between it and Seville orange, known as the 'Citrange' grows well but seems not to settle down easily to flower or to fruit.

Not so *Poncirus*. Though slow to reach the 10 feet or so that is possible it flowers when young if vegetatively propagated: seed would take for ever. The big wide-open orange-blossom flowers, well scented, but not so ravishingly as the real thing, are carried in enough quantity in spring on thorny green twigs to make a good show. They go over as the aromatic leaves unfold which hide the developing fruit, so exactly the same dark green as the branches, that they are apt to be overlooked until the leaves fall. Suddenly then, it seems, they ripen and one has a crop of small, rock-hard tangerine-like fruit.

From these a rather nasty marmalade may be made by those who cannot sit still: those who can should quietly admire the effect against a dull November sky and leave it at that.

Full sun produces better flowering and a well-drained soil a better plant: it is very happy on chalk. Pruning to obtain the required shape is important: though if there is plenty of space a big domed bush with a tangle of branches is acceptable, but in any more sophisticated spot it should be taken up as a low half-standard. It then makes a good support for a thin annual climber such as morning glory.

POPULUS CANDICANS BALSAM POPLAR

In the corner of the herb garden at Chelsea Physic Garden stands a big specimen of this balm of Gilead poplar. Its questing roots and cast shade make it not the ideal tree under which a collection of Mediterranean sun-lovers is to flourish, yet even on that thin silty soil things do remarkably well, so long as a reasonable humus content can be maintained.

On the plus side is that the air for a hundred yards radius of the tree is so aromatically scented that, on mild, moist, spring mornings it is like walking into an apothecary's shop. Even before they unfold the pointed sticky buds crushed in the hand are intensely perfumed and a few twigs cut to unfold in water bring it into the house in winter. It is these buds which, fresh or dried, can be employed in respiratory troubles and in ointments for cuts and bruises.

The title of balm of Gilead (though originally belonging to a Middle Eastern shrub no longer available) is apt to spread to several other scented poplars – notably *P. balsamifera* – with similar properties. For small gardens the variegated 'Aurora' is a good choice: it is naturally weaker with the reduction of green photosynethetic tissue and can also be easily pruned back – its cream, pink-tinged leaves flash in the wind and give the appearance from a distance of a narrow small tree in full flower.

PORTULACCA OLERACEA PURSLANE

The little, flat, fleshy-leaved species native to Greece and eastwards into China used to be extensively employed against scurvy. That scourge of sea voyagers having been satisfactorily dealt with, the wild purslane is not commonly grown in the herb garden. But it does have a use: being only a couple of inches high, with a very thin root system it can be satisfactorily scattered amongst other upright annual or biennial herbs – like coriander, dill or caraway, to act as a herbal ground cover.

The whole young plant or shoot tips can be cast into salads (in moderation) or cooked as spinach. If enjoyed to the extent that too little purslane is produced by this method then a clump of the garden form (var. *Sativa*) can be sown in spring. This is upright and gets to 1½ feet tall. Still very fleshy in stem and leaf it makes much greater bulk as a pot herb than the prostrate species. Bunches of purslane are often on sale in the vegetable markets in Italy and France. There is no beauty of flower which anyway is reduced by cutting the plant over for use. Three or four cuts per season can be expected if the clump is kept well-watered and reasonably fed.

POTERIUM SANGUISORBA SALAD BURNET

Salad burnet is an unlikely member of the rose family: it has pinnate leaves like a potentilla and little globular heads of petalless flowers which just offer a fuzz of reddish stamens. In Britain it is a plant of chalk: this is a very convenient fact that the first Director of Cambridge Botanic Garden, Humphrey Gilbert-Carter, used to tell his students when on the Gog Magog hills, because you did not need to bring cucumber sandwiches for lunch, you could just add leaves of salad burnet to whatever you had.

Certainly they have an authentic cucumber flavour and are said to aid digestion. They can also be used, instead of borage, in fruit cups. Medicinally a decoction of the woody root can be used on cuts to stop bleeding.

In the herb garden salad burnet makes a pleasant little tussock of leaves and has been used as edgings.

PRIMULA VERIS COWSLIP

The time when it was possible for country folk to go out every year to collect bushels of cowslip flowers to make wine is sadly past, a casualty of improved farming methods which do not permit long-lasting pastures to settle down to develop a perennial flora.

Fortunately, however, the cowslip is still a known and well-loved plant. Its natural distribution leads it especially to the limy well-drained soils of East Anglia where it retains the old alternative name of paigle (pronounced peggle): there, of course, farming regimes have changed more than anywhere and its loss has been the greater. However, wide-banked motorway edges in chalk and limestone areas which do not go in for foolish herbicidal sprays, are being colonized.

Rosettes of soft leaves support heads of nodding flowers – the deep yellow petals just showing outside the slightly inflated yellow-green calyx tube. The orange forms that exist are something of a disappointment. The scent is exquisite, so typical that other things, such as species of *Corylopsis*, are said to be 'cowslip-scented' but fail quite to attain it. In a dryish warm spot in the garden a clump of cowslips should easily be established and start to seed themselves around – even in paving cracks. Like *Polyanthus* (which has cowslip in its parentage) germination from bought seed is both slow and erratic while one's own fresh seed comes up like cress if sown at once.

PRIMULA VULGARIS PRIMROSE

Primroses flourish well in lime-rich woodland clays in the south and in acid hillsides in the north: one of the great floral sights in Britain is to see, in the Outer Hebrides, ground rising from the sea, turned soft yellow – primrose-yellow indeed – by myriads of this lovely flower. What it obviously needs is atmospheric humidity, without this then shade is essential.

And it is as a shade plant that it is most valued as a garden plant. As so often happens, modern selection and breeding has produced 'primroses' (the inverted commas are deserved) in a wide range of colours but what they gain in brightness and size they lack in grace and scent. 'You pays your money and you takes your choice.' Such a decision is less pronounced with the delicate pink *Primula sibthorpii* from Greece which can be naturalized with the normal primrose around the boles of trees, even in thin grass to be mown over.

Like cowslips, primroses have a number of country uses: flowers can be candied for cake decoration, cast into salads and made into a tea. In herbal medicine the root-stock is used as an expectorant.

PROSTANTHERA ROTUNDIFOLIA MINTBRUSH

This is the mintbush native to southeast Australia and Tasmania, one of the most beautiful plants from an area renowned for its wild flora. It makes a bushy small-leaved evergreen which is utterly transformed when in late spring, and after a mild winter, it becomes covered in sprays of rich purple flowers.

Throughout the year, however, the foliage has a strong and delicious mint savour. Unfortunately this and other delightful pros-tantheras are on the very edge of frost-hardiness with us. Plants have reached 10 feet high and lasted that number of years in Cornwall before succumbing. Further up-country half that size and period is commendable if attained and well worth attempting if not. Cuttings will root easily so an insurance-plant is easily kept.

A warm corner and lime-free soil is required.

PRUNELLA VULGARIS SELF HEAL

All-heal, self-heal, carpenters' herb, all give the expectation that this little labiate could come to the aid of wounds. Indeed this is so: it has been used as a styptic on external cuts and in mouth washes and gargles for mouth ulcers and sore throats.

It is typically a plant of moist woodland rides where its 9-inch high spikes of clear purple make a pleasant show. In the garden, however, especially on moist soil, it can develop into something of a pest; anything else competing for the space is apt to lose. Around and in the shade of shrubs, however, it is entirely acceptable.

Better is the closely allied *Prunella grandiflora*; especially in the forms 'Alba', 'Rosea' and 'Carminea'. These little plants excite a certain amount of taxonomic confusion and appear in lists also under *P. vulgaris* and *P.* × *webbiana*. 'Loveliness' and 'White Loveliness' exist as further cultivar names. All make excellent ground cover for moist shade and put up a long succession of pink spikes. Deadheading is essential, however, if the stock is not gradually to degenerate with the insinuation of inferior seedlings.

PRUNUS spp

A number of *Prunus* species are listed in the various pharmocopaeias or in texts on folk medicine which offer delightful and usually small, flowering and fruiting trees for herb garden associations.

The dried fruit stalks of our wild cherry or gean are still used as a diuretic: cherry laurel leaves (chopped up by small boys to make an insect killing bottle) were once made into a preparation to treat nausea. Miller states that sloes, the fruit of blackthorn (*Prunus spinosa*), can produce a useful gargle which will even 'fasten loose teeth'. Sufficient sloe gin causes loose teeth, and most other ailments, to be forgotten, at least temporarily. The inner bark of the North American choke cherry (*Prunus serotina*) were made by the Shakers into a valued tonic. And in China fruit of *Prunus mume*, known as Japanese apricot, though in fact a mainland plant, is used in decoction as a vermifuge and to treat dysentery.

Nearer home the common almond, one of the loveliest of all spring-flowering trees in Britain, has a history of economic use with almond oil being a valued base to many preparations in medicines, confectionery and perfumery.

These six plants span the diversity of a genus invaluable to man – his plums, peaches, apricots, nectarines and cherries. As a garden tree *Prunus avium* may be considered too big and its flower too fleeting but it is light in effect and autumn colour is splendid: the double-flowered form is superb in its spring moment but makes a heavier-looking tree.

Nothing is more heartening to see the first blackthorn break into its snow-white flower: again perhaps not a garden plant except in its excellent purple-leaved form which deserves much more use. A crop of sloes may still be produced for that best of home-made liqueurs.

Prunus serotina is one of the bird cherries with long spikes of white flowers and good yellow autumn colour. The Japanese apricot by comparison is closer to our general expectation of *Prunus* – that is, a flowering cherry. It is one of the most charming of small trees whose different forms have white or pink flowers, single or semi-double opening in earliest spring, with a wonderful fragrance.

Cherry laurel is one of the surprises of the prunuses with its long, leathery, evergreen leaves and spikes of white flowers in April. Encouraged to develop trunks it makes a magnificent low tree but of such strength and visual weight as to be impossible for all but large gardens. Dwarf forms such as 'Otto Luyken' make marvellous evergreen ground cover even under trees, and still flower well. Finally narrow-leaved types such as 'Angustifolia' make admirable tub plants and take rather more cold than sweet bay, for whom they can substitute in the garden but emphatically not in the kitchen. What kills insects is apt to make men at least unwell.

PTELEA TRIFOLIATA HOP TREE

Hillier's manual makes the point that the little known hop tree is 'probably the most fragrant of any hardy tree, being equal to those of the best scented honeysuckle'. With such a perfume it would be too much to expect a spectacular show as well; indeed the heads of little yellowish flowers are rather like those of the spindle-bush and cluster amongst the leaves. However, they are followed interestingly by dry fruits composed of a central seed surrounded by a green membranous 'wing', new penny-sized, very much like those of wych elm, rather than hops as the name might suggest. 'Tree', too, is something of an exaggeration: with us it is seldom more than a large bush.

Its North America names are rather more descriptive: wingseed, wafer ash, shrubby trefoil. It is a plant of open woodland, seeding itself liberally around to the consternation of ramblers for, at ground level, the three-lobed leaves look ominously like poison-ivy. The Shakers of Mount Lebanon in Ohio used the root bark for fevers, asthma and indigestion. In Britain any light, well-drained soil suits it.

PULMONARIA OFFICINALIS LUNGWORT

Linnaeus' binomial which picks up and legitimizes earlier names is at once a pointer to medicinal use for pulmonary troubles. Lungwort, says Miller, 'is accounted a pectoral balsamic Plant, and good for Coughs, Consumptions, Spitting of Blood, and the like Disorders of the Lungs'. Perhaps 'is accounted' indicates early eighteenth-century doubt for it was greatly overrated but, as one of those plants supported by the Doctrine of Signatures it maintained a reputation into recent times. The leaves are grey-spotted and the flower colour changes from pink to blue. The lungworts are amongst the most valuable of early-flowering perennials, a virtue which combines with good ground cover attributes throughout the summer.

P. officinalis itself is the type lungwort making a 1½-foot wide clump of slightly bristly borage leaves; its March flowers pass from pink to blue before the corollas fall. Others are very close and are perfectly acceptable in a shady herb garden border: any soil suits.

Pulmonaria picta (P. saccharata) is more vigorous with grey-green leaves, white spotted, and carries a due sequence of colour from flowers at all stages through their colour change. *P. rubra* is equally robust but has no claim to the alternative name of soldiers and sailors: it begins (as early as January) a military plant and stays there, its clear coral-red heads are unique in the open garden at that time of year. *P. mollis* maintains the naval connection.

PUNICA GRANATUM POMEGRANATE

There is probably very little chance of ever eating a ripe pomegranate from a British outdoor plant, not, to many people, a major disappointment. But established bushes usually flower well throughout the summer on a warm wall and their splashes of orange-vermilion amongst the shiny leaves always catch the eye.

Punica is the only genus in its own family and has only two species; *P. granatum* is the one cultivated today as it has grown for millenia in Asia Minor and the Mediterranean region. It makes a dense, twiggy bush: two aged plants, one with single flowers and one with double, have gone above the 9-foot high herb garden wall of the Chelsea Physic Garden. Even in that favoured spot, across the path from the famous olive tree which does fruit, they seem determined not to.

Stuart makes an interesting point about the pomegranate's medicinal history: 'although various parts of the plant – such as the fruit rind – can be traced in the writings of the apothecaries and druggists, the valuable root bark apparently fell into disuse until the nineteenth century'. This latter use is the expelling of tapeworms in man and his domestic animals. The fruit rind is a strong astringent while leaves have an anti-bacterial effect upon open sores.

PYRACANTHA FORTUNEANA FIRETHORN

Though far less common in cultivation than other firethorns this oriental species is listed as being useful – both the leaves and berries – in decoction to apply to abscesses and boils. The Chinese name, in translation, is emergency soldier's ration, which indicates that the fruits are also edible, if only as a last resort.

The closest available species is the fine *Pyracantha atalantioides*, another Chinese plant which E.H. Wilson introduced in 1907. It has dark, shining, evergreen foliage, which makes an admirable foil to both the creamy white flowers in early June and the superb scarlet berry display which lasts from September well into the New Year. In areas where birds have developed a taste for them the yellow-fruited form makes a good alternative. As with white strawberries the birds are apt to wait around for the expected colour of ripeness. Hopefully they lose patience and fly off elsewhere.

Like all the firethorns this is a fine robust shrub where there is plenty of space. It also makes a spendid wall shrub, even in dense shade. Here alternatives are offered: it can be trained to give a complete wall covering or, where architectural effect is important it can, with careful pruning, be made into an espalier. Flowers and fruit lining the horizontal branches look particularly well.

RHEUM PALMATUM RHUBARB

This is the most ornamental rhubarb, a wonderfully architectural plant in all its stages from when the first warmth of spring encourages great fleshy buds to push away the black scales of the root-stock. Huge palmate leaves with pointed lobes eventually frame a flower stem which has rocketed to 6 or 7 feet high. In the selection which E.A. Bowles made and which bears his name the red pigment is maintained on the undersides of the leaves and is taken up into the flower spike to make a most spectacular picture.

As the plant has a spread equal to its height it is not for small spaces. Nor either is the common garden rhubarb which, looked at with an aesthetic rather than a culinary eye, is also a magnificent plant. In cultivation these plants will take almost anything but summer drought causes small leaves which go to rest prematurely. A decent moist garden soil in full sun produces wonders.

The medicinal rhubarb, *Rheum officinalis*, of which the dried rhizomes have been imported to the West since before the birth of Christ, does look rather similar. This is still employed as a mild purgative, in Miller's early eighteenth-century account it is given much space and was clearly considered one of the most valuable of purges: 'It is said to grow in the great Tartary, and the Northern parts of China, from whence it is brought by Caravans to Aleppo. We have not yet attained to the certain Knowledge of the Plant; many Botanic Writers believing it to be the Rhaponticum of the Antients . . .'

RIBES SATIVUM RED CURRANT

The usual expectation of the traditional cottage garden is of a miscellany of plants – herbaceous perennials, old-fashioned roses, self-sown annuals and simple herbs all growing together amongst soft fruit bushes with the gnarled limbs of an aged apple tree framing the picture. To contrive such a scene is nearly impossible, yet such a juxtaposition of plant types is just what this list of herbs (in the widest sense) includes.

The bushes which are botanically *Ribes* make the soft fruit component – red, white and black currants (of which the white is merely a distinctive form) and Miller recommends that 'a jelly made with the juice and sugar is cooling and grateful in Fevers'. Fortunately illness is not obligatory before red currant jelly can be appreciated; roast leg of lamb will do just as well.

The delicious fruits of red and white currants (*Ribes sativum*) are so well known as to need no description but every year they appear less often in the shops and it becomes essential to grow one's own. The cottage garden has much to teach us, not least that these plants can be most ornamental. They flower and fruit on spurs on old wood, like many apples and pears, and hence can be trained into similar, though smaller, shapes. Free-standing vase-patterns are used as central features in formal beds too small to take an apple; walls can be used for multiple cordons: thus they can reach 8 feet. What, of course, is being described is a potager, that sophisticated, formal French version of a cottage garden where every inch of space is made to be productive but at the same time to look well. Both red and white currants grown like this are extremely beautiful when hung with their strings of translucent berries. The only trouble is that harvesting ruins the display, and a decision must be made as to what sense is to appreciate them the longer.

Black currants, *Ribes nigrum*, cannot be grown in the same way for new wood from the base must continually replace that which has fruited. The plant therefore is less ornamental. Nonetheless they deserve to appear because in addition to the delicious and distinctive fruit with its high vitamin C content, black currant leaves (also very distinctive in scent) are also used in an infusion to treat stomach upsets.

The two species from which our garden currants are derived are both British natives, coming especially from northern woodland edges. Hence a good moist soil, or one enriched by lots of organic matter, is desirable in the garden and half-shade is accepted happily. This last is a valuable trait as most crops which require a fruit to ripen demand full sun.

RICINUS COMMUNIS CASTOR OIL

To a modern generation of youth the words castor oil do not evoke the hideous connotations that their parents recall: castor oil, that most beastly of laxatives forced down unwilling throats by the well-meaning. So popular was its use in the early nineteenth century that specially designed spoons, often elegantly made in silver, became a part of the ritual. Though still available, its traditional use has declined in medicine but there are further important economic applications for the oil in the manufacture of soaps, paints and varnishes.

As a garden plant *Ricinus* has much to offer. Although naturally a 40 to 50-foot high tree from tropical Africa its growth from seed is so rapid as to make statuesque plants in six months. Seeds are sown in heat in March and planted out like any half-hardy annual when frosts have passed. A stout stem carries fine palmate leaves – green, bronze, or dark purple according to the cultivar chosen – and reaches 5 or 6 feet within the season. In most years it culminates in a spike of reddish flowers which turn into prickly fruits rather like small horse chestnuts. The ripe seeds inside are extraordinarily beautiful, the size and shape of ancient Egyptian scarabs marbled like a yellow-hammer's egg.

The evergreen sold as a house plant with similar shaped leaves and called 'Castor Oil Plant' is *Fatsia japonica*: it is a valuable hardy shrub but has nothing to do with *Ricinus*.

ROSA spp

Flos florum, the flower of flowers sacred to medieval cult of the Virgin Mary called Mariolatry, the rose inevitably becomes one of those plants whose virtues hover between the mystical and the medicinal. Though there are over 100 wild rose species strewn around the northern hemisphere the majority have had no part in the development of the thousands of garden roses that have been put on the market in ever increasing numbers over the last 200 years. Even less have they had any effect on those roses which claim a place in the herb garden. But from these half-dozen some of the loveliest roses of all time have been derived, old-fashioned garden roses of fascinating form and exquisite scent.

None have the brilliant colours of the modern hybrid teas or floribundas, neither, in most cases, are they so remarkably re-montant – flowering continually from early summer to autumn. Roses to grow with herbs are essentially conventional shrubs with their short season of June and early July flowering but followed often by a fine display of fruits.

The base-plant is *Rosa gallica*, the European red rose which at some time in the depths of history produced a variant that became the basis of an important medieval industry – the making of conserves and medicines found especially in the French town of Provins. This is *Rosa gallica officinalis*, the rose of Provins, the apothecary's rose. It makes a 4-foot high, suckering bush with soft light green leaves above which the flat semi-double flowers look outward as if brightly welcoming the viewer. For such an old rose the colour is clear and strong, a vivid cerise-red: the texture is also surprising, with two layers of firm petals. The scent is delicious, rich and penetrating.

All but the colour is repeated with the fascinating sport of the apothecary's rose which occurred, in the early 1600s. It was given the name 'Rosa Mundi' for clearly up to that time nothing so spectacular had been seen, its petals striped red and white. Con-nections with King Henry II's mistress, the fair Rosamund, are to be discounted as also is any confusion with the York and Lancaster rose whose colours are much less striking.

The next herb-rose is the famous provider of attar (or otto) of roses, *Rosa damascena trigintipetala*, grown by the acre in Bulgaria. Each morning, while the dew is still on them, the pale pink flowers are plucked: pounds of petals make the concentrated base of so many perfumes and scented preparations.

Round the fields of the damask rose are high hedges of *Rosa alba semi-plena*. This gives a certain amount of attar and is thus a productive as well as a protective screen. In northern gardens it is a more useful plant. Whereas the damask is a rather weak, tumbling plant (best within an outward-leaning tripod of stakes joined by a trio of top rails), the white rose of York is a robust touch of elegant grey-green foliage starred with semi-double, intensely fragrant flowers. A good crop of hips follows in late summer.

The gallicas, damasks, albas and another historic group, the cabbage roses, all have numbers of eighteenth- and nineteenth-century cultivars which were the mainstay of gardens until the 1850s: they are close to their originals and are thus entirely valid in the herb garden scene, variation in colour making interesting associations possible.

A further strange group are the moss roses, derivatives especially of the cabbage roses whose flowers, often well-scented in a conventional way, have their calyces covered with sticky glandular growths – the moss. This is intensely aromatic and adds another dimension to roses in the herb garden: the original pink common moss, dating back to the early 1700s, is still the best of these.

While the actual moss has to be touched for the scent to be appreciated, the scent from the leaf-glands of sweet briar, *Rosa eglanteria*, drifts out onto the air, especially after a shower of summer rain. It is altogether delicious, slightly apple-like. The little circular herb garden at Jenkyn Place in Hampshire is enclosed by a hedge of sweet briar: the scent comes and goes throughout the season; a gentle show of dog roses appears at the beginning and it closes with a fine crop of red and orange hips. These, like those from *Rosa canina* – the usual source – can be made into a purée rich in vitamin C.

For size of fruit the Japanese *Rosa rugosa* far exceeds our native briars. They are like small tomatoes, full of flesh and follow a long season of wide open flowers of red, white or pink, though it should be remembered that the splendid doubles such as 'Roseraie de l'Haÿ' do not set hips. With their corrugated foliage, complete disease resistance, ability to take extreme exposure (they even make low hedges in the Western Isles) and delicious perfume they are highly to be recommended.

A selection of these various roses can give strength and weight to a herb garden or, conversely, because of their traditional associations with catmint, peonies and others, an area of these old-fashioned roses can be inter- and under-planted with herbs. Each legitimately supports the other.

Domestic use of roses lies in the conserve made from the hips, already mentioned, and the collection of rose-petals for drying and incorporation in pot pourri. Simple rose-water is also possible but attar, perhaps, is best left to the Bulgarians.

ROSMARINUS OFFICINALIS ROSEMARY

Joseph Miller's opening sentence can well serve today: 'This is a Plant very well known, growing almost in every garden'. His description of its virtues and uses, however, are of times past. 'Rosemary is a Plant of great Service in Affections of the Head and Nerves, helping the Apoplexy, Palsy and all kinds of Convulsions. . . . It strengthens the Sight and the Memory.' This last is the reference Ophelia makes: 'There's Rosemary, that's for remberance; pray love, remember: and there is pansies, that's for thought'.

If it were possible to grow only one aromatic plant the choice, for many people, would fall on rosemary. The scent from one crushed leaf is sufficient to evoke the traditional expectation of the ideal herb garden as well as the stony slopes in the warm south from which it comes.

Certainly rosemary has been in recorded cultivation in Britain for 500 years and it seems very likely to have been grown here by the Romans and by their native British imitators. Though not able to take our coldest winters in fully open positions (especially on soil that lies wet in winter) it is remarkably hardy and old sprawling bushes with trunks as thick as one's arm are sometimes seen. The whole bush has a greyish cast with its narrow, inch-long evergreen leaves – paler on the underside – and small clustering grey-blue flowers in April and May.

Selections found in the wild have been chosen for tidiness of habit, such as 'Miss Jessup' which grows in a much more upright fashion, and for brighter flower colour: 'Severn Seas' and 'Majorca' are two of these. 'Miss Jessup' is the best for a hedge (a tight wire or two strung within it helps the definitive role) while the others, like the type, should be allowed to tumble where they will. When falling over a low wall or out on to flagstones close to a path where a leaf can be plucked as one passes, nothing is more delightful. When some pruning becomes necessary the twigs should be dried and stored to be thrown onto winter fires: the scent is delicious.

RUMEX ACETOSA SORREL

Though not a particularly ornamental plant, sorrel's clumps of fresh spring leaves, one of the first plants to 'move' when winter is hardly over, is always welcome. They are equally welcomed by wood pigeons who find the luscious young growth an admirable addition to their usual diet: netting may be necessary.

Sorrel is a common wild plant and in this form is just as delicious for gooseberry-tasting sauces or as sorrel soup: but one word of warning is wise. In the moist hedgebanks in the south and west the arrow-shaped leaves are remarkably like those of wild *Arum*; they often grow together. The important difference is that the *Arum* is poisonous.

No such confusion can occur with the much bigger garden sorrel, which anyway provides a much greater crop. In moist soil, and happily in half-shade, sorrel makes a fine bright edging. For this use the reddish flower-spikes should be cut out as they appear. Nothing much is lost; the individual flowers are quite insignificant.

French sorrel is a very different but useful plant: *Rumex scutatus* is much more able to take dry conditions and makes a wide-spreading mat of small grey-green shield-shaped (hence *scutatus*) leaves. They are just as agreeably acid as the bigger relation: equally, they can be chopped up for salads.

RUSCUS ACULEATUS BUTCHER'S BROOM

Butcher's broom is one of our strangest native plants. An unlikely member of the Liliaceae, it makes 18-inch high clumps of wire-hard, dark green stems with equally stiff myrtle-like leaves, each armed with a fierce prickle. This, for much of the year, is all the plant may seem to do until in the late autumn it ripens, apparently suddenly, a crop of scarlet marble-sized berries. Each appears to sit on a leaf.

At this point the thoughtful observer will start to doubt his eyesight: berries do not grow on leaves and, anyway, what happened to the flower which presumably preceeded them? A New Year's resolution will be made to follow it through more carefully (or to turn to a book). In fact these 'leaves' are flattened stems or cladodes – the true leaves are the vestigial scales beneath them – on which the tiny purple and white starry flowers occur, so small as to be easily overlooked, especially on male plants which, of course, never fruit.

Gardeners must look out for the hermaphrodite form: as the plant accepts full shade even under trees it is valuable planted with gladdon (*Iris foetidissima*) to add to its winter brilliance.

The early texts refer to preparations of its rhizome being used as a diuretic and to disperse kidney stones. Until very recently it was being sold from door to door by gypsies as Christmas decorations: often the berries were of improbable size and turned out to be crab-apples painted and impaled upon the prickles. Very soon indoors they began ominously to rot.

RUTA GRAVEOLEN RUE

The herb o' grace o' Sundays is the charming name for a low Mediterranean shrub whose scent is apt to excite strong reactions – it is enjoyed or hated: few sit on this particular fence. As the type genus of its own family, the Rutaceae contains many plants with strong aromatic oils – the citruses and burning bush amongst them.

Visually there is no doubt as to its value – the little round bushes of blue-green leaves look tidy throughout the year. Heads of horn-yellow flowers with fringed petals are followed by interesting seed capsules. The lovely garden form 'Jackman's Blue' does not flower much but its billowing heaps of elegant blue foliage makes it even more desirable than if it did. A variegated rue also exists: interesting rather than striking. Rue, like lavender and *Santolina*, makes an admirable internal hedge and, like them, needs full sun and a well-drained soil. It should be cut back by half in spring to keep its compactness.

While the pungent perfume makes it unsuitable for culinary use (in spite of some recommendations), rue has a wide range of medicinal applications. Historically they ranged from Miller's curing 'the Bites of venomous Creatures, and of mad Dogs' to employment 'against infections, pestilential Diseases, and the Plague itself'. Stuart suggests that rue deserves modern investigation but warns against its poisonous properties if taken carelessly.

SALVIA OFFICINALIS SAGE

Culinary sage is, if anything, even more useful in the garden than in the kitchen. Yet another Mediterranean aromatic shrub, it can be used as low hedges, to make solid blocks of colour or to offer contrast of leaf texture and shape to mixed plantings. Like all its compatriots it enjoys full sun but is apt to be mean and weedy in really dry positions. The Vale of Evesham, with its rich market-garden soils, is (or was) the main area for commercial sage growing in Britain: in such conditions growth is full and luxuriant though not softly lush.

Sage has been in cultivation for centuries, a vital part of

stuffings, sausages and herb mixtures: sage tea was greatly prized and the essential oil with its antiseptic properties still has medicinal and culinary application.

Several garden forms are available. The typical foliage is (of course) sage-green, with greyer, narrower variants – these are often hardier and can take a shadier position. Purple sage is *S. officinalis* 'Purpurascens', one of the best of all dwarf shrubs – the fact that the leaves are also perfectly good to use in sage and onion stuffing is a fortuitous bonus because it would certainly be grown anyway.

It makes a regular 2-foot high dome; the foliage is a splendid downy purple especially when young. This causes a great dilemma. By early June the first flush of new growth has settled down and flower spikes start to appear. If the bush is clipped over at this stage, more leaves develop and the pattern is set for the season. If, however, it is left alone it becomes covered with fine sprays of purple hooded flowers which make a splendid show for weeks. Eventually, however, exhaustion sets in and though pruned back it is too late to expect much foliage to develop. Used formally in a regular number of beds those in mirror image can be treated equally in pairs to flower in alternate years.

Fortunately there is no such worry with the splendid gold-variegated form 'Icterina' which virtually never flowers. This is as vigorous as the purple but the charming *S. officinalis* 'Tricolor' is apt to be very weak. Nonetheless for its white, grey-green and pink splashed leaves it is worth perseverance and it is good in a herb window box where the others would be too big. All of these shrubby sages can be increased by soft tip cuttings in summer or whole shoots pulled off with a heel in spring and sunk at least half way down in sandy soil outside. A shaded cloche accelerates rooting.

Altogether there are about 750 species of *Salvia* strewn about the world as annuals, perennials and shrubs. Many in the latter category are from sub-tropical South America, which precludes their being hardy plants with us; this is why *Salvia splendens* is cultivated as an annual. For herb association *Salvia rutilans* is a must. Though not very distinctive in leaf and often not attempting to open flowers until so late in the season that in cold areas frost beats them to it, the leaf scent is so distinctive that as pineapple sage it is always enjoyable. Old plants may survive the winter but insurance cuttings are easily rooted and maintained, even on a window sill.

The oil from clary, *Salvia sclarea*, is also used like that from culinary sage. Similarly, boiling water poured upon the leaves makes an effective gargle for sore throats and coughs. The whole plant has a strange (non-admirers say cat-like) aromatic scent, but visually there is no doubt as to clary's complete acceptability.

A striking biennial, it creates a broad foxglove-like rosette in its first year and this is followed in the next year by a 3-foot high, widely branched flower spike. Each whorl of white, typically lipped labiate flowers is supported by pinkish bracts. They last well if picked for dried winter decoration. The geographical form *turkestanica* is apt to behave more regularly as a perennial, and this trait is maintained by the Grecian *Salvia haematodes* which, by only slightly stretching the rules of herb-ness, should certainly be included. A cloud of lavender-blue flowers is carried above flat dark green rosettes and looks superb with peonies in early summer.

SAMBUCUS NIGRA ELDER

If elder were a rare exotic and difficult to grow, it would be cherished with care by the *cognoscenti*. As it is, it is apt to be treated as a weed to be grubbed out at the earliest opportunity and usually replaced by something dull – and certainly less useful. Every part of the plant, flowers, fruit, leaves, root bark and the distinctive stem-pith have roles in herbal medicine. Elderberries are used to make a very acceptable red table wine and elderflower champagne (see p. 139) is one of the major pleasures of summer.

Elder makes a wide bush or even a small tree with ash-like leaves and a marvellous show of flat heads of creamy flowers – when newly open they produce a most delicious scent. They are followed by great bunches of shining purple-black berries which bow down the branches with their weight. Garden forms exist with white and yellow variegated leaves, or fully golden, plus finely dissected foliage and are all useful, easy plants. Elder takes shade or sun and any soil, even the thinnest chalk; but here the golden forms are best avoided, looking, in such a place, unhealthily chlorotic.

Sambucus racemosa is another easy and ornamental shrub although it is less often seen, except in the north where having been planted as game covert, it has sometimes gone feral. It has pointed heads of green passing to cream (rather like *Viburnum plicatum*) standing out on bare branches and then a good midsummer show of red berries. This too has a splendid golden cutleaved version.

In North America *S. canadensis* picks up most of the European medicinal roles, Shaker literature listing numbers of uses for its berries, bark, leaves and flowers. This makes a plant as big as our common elder but, especially if pruned back in spring as for buddleias, produces gargantuan flat flower heads well over a foot across. A form offered as 'Maxima' lives up to its name. Flowering is usually in July, with September fruits.

Sambucus ebulus is *danewort*, a strange herbaceous plant which makes a broad 3-foot high clump topped with typical elderflowers and elderberries. Though it has medicinal uses it is so fiercely purgative that of all elders this should be considered as poisonous. Nonetheless it is most ornamental with equally robust perennials.

SANGUINARIA CANADENSIS BLOODROOT

One of the joys of northeastern American woodlands, bloodroot spells the fact that an apparently interminable winter really has ended. From a fleshy rhizome pairs of grey-green lobed leaves arise, carrying between them a single, elegant pure white flower like a small terrestrial waterlily. It is sadly fleeting, with but a week of extraordinary beauty. The leaves continue to develop, becoming almost hand-sized and resembling those of macleaya: this and the vivid orange-red sap give clues to the poppy relationship that bloodroot claims.

Though Shaker references to its use in a whole range of ailments exist, from 'typhoid pneumonia' to ringworm, bloodroot is extremely poisonous and hence in no way a home medicament.

A delightful double-flowered garden form is available: not setting seed, it has a slightly longer season in flower. With us bloodroot (or Indian paint or red puccoon) needs a woodland equivalent; a leafy soil and summer shade. It is thus good under shrubs with other early flowering things such as hellebores and anemones.

SANTOLINA spp LAVENDER COTTON

Though most obviously 'herbs' from every observational point of view the lavender cottons seem to have been no particular use either in the kitchen or in the apothecary shop of the past. Yet their delightful aromatic scent, elegant year-round filigree foliage (grey or green) and compact habit makes them ideal herb garden shrubs, especially for interior hedges. Nothing is better for etching the convolutions of a *parterre de broderie*, nor for filling its broader sweeps. As Mediterraneans they are surprisingly frost-hardy, surviving even an eastern Canadian winter, so long as soils are well drained.

The commonest, and perhaps most generally useful, is *Santolina chamecyparissus*. No more than 2 feet in height (half that in 'Nana') it can be kept clipped without looking particularly artificial. Two annual sallies with the shears are necessary, just as the flower heads begin to form, and again in August. The lack of the flowers is no great loss: button-like rayless daisies of a brassy yellow spoil the general whiteness of the bush.

This is more serious in the lavender cotton known as 'Edward Bowles'. The foliage is grey-green and the flowers creamy-white, a delightful combination yet, as with purple sage, the dread decision has to be made – to flower or not to flower? *That* is the question.

It is an equal problem with the pale-flowered *Santolina virens*, which has feathery foliage of dark rich green to broaden the base of the lavender cotton range. Combinations of these little shrubs make marvellous patterns on the ground.

SAPONARIA OFFICINALIS SOAPWORT

The two vernacular names by which this pleasant, but rather coarse, perennial is known are both suitably descriptive. Bouncing bet must come from its irrepressible, indeed invasive, habit while the second, soapwort, refers to its use as a soap substitute since early times. This latter fact has been brought back from the realms of quaint folk belief by soapwort's use in the cleaning and revitalizing of historic fabrics, notably at Uppark in Sussex: a visit to this splendid late seventeenth-century house, now in the care of the National Trust, gives proof of this. The juice produces a lather with water due to the high percentage of natural saponin.

Soapwort looks rather like a spreading, floppy campion with heads of (usually) pale pink on 18-inch stems in early summer. A double form makes more show but it remains an undistinguished plant. Native to continental Europe it is well established in many parts of Britain, especially on poor gravelly soils and coastal shingle. A rich garden soil makes its already undisciplined habit impossible to stake.

A smaller but non-herb relation is *Saponaria ocymoides*, a low, mat-forming perennial which makes a first-rate front row plant to flower with old-fashioned roses and peonies. 'Rubra' is the best form with larger flowers of deep rose-pink.

SAROTHAMNUS SCOPARIUS BROOM

Common broom is still perhaps better known as *Cytisus*; no matter, this brilliant yellow leafless shrub is one of our most spectacular native plants – as bright as gorse without the spines. It is found on most soils except the extremes of alkalinity and acidity and hence, in full sun, is an easy garden plant. Over the years variations in flower colour have been selected from the wild: dark crimson, soft cream, and orange-yellow have occurred and these, carefully crossed, have produced a marvellous range of colour for May display. Named forms can be planted for instant effect or a packet of mixed hybrid seeds sown for flowering in three years can be tried. The results may be just as magnificent but they must, however, be put out from pots after one year, as they resent root disturbance more than most.

Broom had many uses in times past: an alternative to withies for baskets, seeds as a coffee substitute, a green dye from the roots in tanning, as a diuretic and, of course, there is always the use suggested in the name. On the principle of waste not, want not, Joseph Miller's suggestion might be tried today: 'The Flowers, before they are grown to any Bigness, are pickled with Salt and Vinegar, and are eaten for Sauce, like Capers, and are esteemed by many . . .'

SATUREIA spp SAVORY

The two savories commonly grown are extraordinarily different plants. Summer savory is a little twiggy annual about a foot high with tiny leaves and tinier flowers which makes the rich aromatic scent seem out of proportion to the plant itself, rather as with Corsican mint. This is what makes it worth growing and sown *in situ* in mid April it soon builds up its tussock.

In herbal medicine this *Satureia hortensis* is recommended to settle disturbed stomachs and to stimulate the appetite. Culinarily, though easily overdone, it is a useful flavouring in soups and stews and seems to maintain its savour when dried better than most herbs. The whole plant is pulled up and hung up to dry; nothing could be simpler. Summer savory is also known as beanherb as, at least with some stomachs, it reduces what Miller invariably refers to as the 'windiness' of broad beans. The younger the beans the less necessary the beanherb, however.

Satureia montana is winter savory, a little evergreen shrub seldom exceeding a foot or so in height. It makes a good floral display in summer with spikes of pale lavender flowers. Its evergreen nature makes it valuable because, like sages, rosemary and thymes, it is available fresh throughout the year. As yet another

Mediterranean plant, conditions for cultivation depend only upon effective winter drainage and full sun.

Both the savories are important flavourings for preserved meats and sausages, and because they are so compact should be grown where space is limited: they are admirable window box plants.

A third savory is *Satureia thymbra*, a twiggy, almost spiny, shrublet from dry, eastern Mediterranean hillsides. It is one of the most aromatic of all the Cretan herbs and, in June, makes a brave show of pink thyme-like spikes just as most of the rest of the flora is turning summer brown. It needs the warmest spot possible with us but is worthy of every care.

SAXIFRAGA STOLONIFERA MOTHER OF THOUSANDS

It is surprising to learn that this common and charming little greenhouse plant – mother of thousands – should have medicinal application in China. The whole plant is squeezed for the juice which is used externally to reduce boils and abscesses.

In the West, however, it has been merely a well-loved cool-greenhouse pot plant since its introduction (under the name of *S. sarmentosa*) in the year of Waterloo. Other vernacular names add to the visual picture: roving sailor, strawberry geranium, strawberry begonia and others. All point to a little stoloniferous plant with roundish, hairy leaves. The airy spike carries strange pink-tinged flowers with three vestigial petals and two long ones: thus, depending on which way up they are held, one sees rabbit's ears, or the forked beards of feudal barons.

In half-shade mother of thousands is generally hardy and makes excellent summer-interest ground cover above snowdrops and other small spring bulbs that have gone to rest. The coloured leaved form 'Tricolor' is unlikely to survive outside in most gardens but is a delightful pot plant which can stand out in summer.

SCHIZANDRA CHINENSIS MAGNOLIA VINE

In chronic bronchitis Chinese herbal medicine identifies different types of cough with varying symptoms: concoctions of up to nine different herbs are prescribed. In two of these *Schizandra chinensis* is used: known as magnolia vine in America (now in its own family, the genus was once placed in Magnoliaceae), it has considerable garden value.

It is a vigorous deciduous twiner with fine oval leaves and waxy cup-shaped flowers which hang out on long stalks in spring. Fleshy berries follow, bright scarlet in contrast with the palest pink of the petals.

This and other rather similar schizandras are good wall plants (needing wires to twine round) or for going up a thin tree. They seem unconcerned about soil type so long as it is not extremely thin and chalky.

SCHIZOPHRAGMA INTEGRIFOLIUM CLIMBING HYDRANGEA

Another fine Chinese climber becomes, through its use in Chinese medicine, grist to our mill. Its application there, through a reputation for strengthening both muscle and bone tissue, is for aching joints and rheumatism. Roots and stems are made into a decoction.

As a garden plant is has much to offer. It is one of the 'climbing hydrangeas' of which *Hydrangea petiolaris* is the best known. *Schizophragma* is similar in the way it climbs by means of aerial roots, as does ivy. But it lacks the immediate, initial impetus of *H. petiolaris*, often sulkily sitting at the base of the wall chosen for it for several years before putting out roving shoots and showing its potential.

However, once the decision has been made, growth is rapid and it will reach 20 or 30 feet given the chance and suitable encouragement. The floral effect is dramatic, foot-wide heads of small sterile flowers with an outer fringe of creamy white bracts giving the impression of enormous, erratic daisies.

Any aspect seems to suit, but flowering is better in full sun. A very similar, but rather less huge, species is the Japanese *S. hydrangeoides*: it seems to be hardier in North America with its more extreme winter.

SCROPHULARIA NODOSA FIGWORT

Knotted figwort is hardly an ornamental plant with its coarse leaves and insignificant, brown flowers like minute coal-scuttles. But with its knobbly rhizomes it was taken up by the early herbalists as Miller records, though with, perhaps, a hint of doubt: 'This Plant, from the signature of the Root, is accounted good for scrophulous Tumours, or the King's Evil in any Part of the Body . . .'

As a foxglove relation it possesses cardiac glycosides and hence might one day offer more specific medicinal use.

A similar plant, rather bigger, is *S. aquatica*, which Miller says may be similarly used. It lacks the knotted root of the other and prefers wetter ground. This is the species which in 'Variegata' offers a fine garden form, well worth growing in half-shade. A clump of basal leaves is maintained throughout the year brilliantly striped with white, and 4-foot high stems clothed with equally bright pairs of leaves arise in summer. The flowers are predictably dull and must be removed before seeding. This is a plant which lights up a dark corner wonderfully.

SEDUM spp STONECROPS

The little yellow biting stonecrop makes bright mats of fleshy leaves and starry flowers on old roofs, walls and seaside shingle. *Acre*, pronounced phonetically, not like the measure, means acrid. Introduced onto the edges of gravel paths which get little wear it adds an ornamental dimension to an otherwise arid area. A golden-leaved form, still the same 2 inches in height, provides its colour throughout the year.

Biting stonecrop (or wall-pepper) has had a chequered career medicinally, with recommendations and warnings being equally given: the latter depend upon the presence of poisonous alkaloids, the former being now restricted to external applications of the juice on warts.

Chinese medicine uses one of the many oriental stonecrops, *Sedum spectabile* (the last syllables have no medicinal overtones). It is one of our most useful front-of-border plants: throughout late spring and summer it gradually builds up 18-inch clumps of fleshy grey-green leaves which become topped in September by flat plates of puce-pink starry flowers. The effect, already effective, is made dramatic by the addition, in good butterfly years, of the tortoiseshells and painted ladies which find the nectar irresistible.

Darker pink selections exist such as 'September Glow' and 'Meteor', both fine plants.

The hybrid 'Autumn Joy' (*S. spectabile* × *S. telephium*) is also applicable to our use because the latter parent is orpine, a foot-high native stonecrop which is listed in the early texts for uses similar to *Sedum acre*. 'Autumn Joy' is a lovely plant to add to *Caryopteris*, with perhaps *Colchicum* in front. The foliage is similar to *S. spectabile* but the flower heads are bigger: they begin deep pink and gradually turn bronze. Even when the leaves have dropped the pattern remains good throughout winter.

These big sedums need sun but are not particular as to soil: frequent division is desirable.

SEMPERVIVUM TECTORUM HOUSELEEK

The rosettes of fleshy leaves provide one name, houseleek; the custom of growing clumps on the tiles of cottage porches gives another, welcome-home-husband-however-drunk-you-be. It is not necessary to be an inebriated cottager, however, to find this an agreeable little plant.

Happy with very little soil, or indeed virtually none, houseleeks are perfect for growing in shallow stone troughs and similar containers. The succulent rosettes maintain their pattern throughout the year and carry stems of starry pink flowers in summer. Disregarding ominous early suggestions that it be used against St Anthony's fire and to stop the bloody flux, houseleek is best left to fulfil a purely ornamental function. A wide bowl of it, supported on animal-like legs, makes the centre piece to the herb garden at Sissinghurst Castle.

SILYBUM MARIANUM OUR LADY'S MILK THISTLE

Our Lady's milk thistle combines religious myth with the Doctrine of Signatures: not only did the white spots on the shining, spiny leaves look like spots of milk but it was very special milk, that from the Virgin Mary herself. Not surprisingly, therefore, its use in encouraging lactation was inevitable although, sadly, there seems no attestable evidence for its effectiveness.

Fortunately, other curative properties are more easily demonstrated, the plant being an effective tonic and appetite stimulant. The powdered seeds are taken in emulsion (Stuart) to prevent travel sickness, a disorder more in line with our modern age.

As a garden plant, *Silybum* is an obvious thistle, but one of considerable presence. Where it overwinters it is best treated as a biennial: it behaves thus in its southern European home. Seeds germinating in late summer make a wide rosette and from this next spring the 4-foot high prickly stem topped with its purple thistles arises. Alternatively seeds sown under glass – little heat is needed – in early spring will mature if planted out in May.

In addition to medicinal uses *Silybum* has a pot herb role. Young shoots and leaves can be cooked as spinach, and the bud plus some inches of stem beneath it make small alternatives to globe artichokes: botanically the two plants are close.

Full sun and a well-drained soil is required but otherwise *Silybum* is the easiest of plants to grow.

SMYRNIUM OLUSATRUM ALEXANDERS

Yet another umbellifer, alexanders hovers between its historic roles as medicament and pot herb. The latter could well be resurrected today as, unlike most vegetables, it remains, at least in the southwest, lush and green throughout the winter months. It is in those areas, near the sea, that alexanders is especially to be found in Britain (actually naturalized, it is a true native of southwest Europe). Along the undercliff around Ventnor in the Isle of Wight, for example, it maintains brilliant shiny foliage, putting up its yellowish, cow parsley heads, 2 feet high in late spring. The aromatic black seeds become available by July.

The plant combines, though in an undeveloped form, umbelliferous vegetable roles of celery (blanched stems), parsnip (root), aniseed (condiment) and fennel (flavouring). As an addition to the herb garden for use or ornament alexanders is happy in most spots but likes at least half-shade; drought reduces its vigour, decent soil ensures the lush shiny growth which makes it worth growing. Here is a plant worth working on.

SOLIDAGO VIRGAUREA GOLDENROD

Goldenrod (the direct translation of the Latin specific epithet) is a useful group of late autumn flowering perennials. Our big garden forms are derived from species from northeast North America where they are considered more than a little weedy (North American visitors seeing them cultivated in Europe are apt to fall about in hoots of derision). Only one of those species, *S. odora*, has herbal use and seems not to be commonly in cultivation.

The only generally known European in the genus, however, *S. virgaurea* has an honoured tradition of medicinal use in external appliations to assist wound healing and for asthma and rheumatic complaints. Suggestions that is can reduce chloresterol levels (surely a modern concern) remain so.

Goldenrod is a plant of woodland edges and on moorland, especially in the north and west. A pleasant, but not striking, 18-inch high plant with narrow spikes of yellow, it is visually better replaced in late summer by its lovely hybrids. The best has airy sprays of soft mimosa-yellow which provoked the entirely suitable name 'Goldenmosa' under which it can be found in catalogues.

STACHYS OFFICINALIS BETONY

Wood betony is an ornamental native making a mat of corrugated leaves from which it sends up fine summer spikes of purple dead-nettle flowers. Now only used in herbal tobaccos and snuffs, it was still considered of enormous use in the eighteenth century for more diverse afflictions from headaches to the drawing out of splinters. Before listing his own recommendations, Miller says that it was 'of so great Esteem among the Ancients, that Antonius Musa Physician to Augustus Caesar, wrote a whole Treatise concerning it'.

Betony varies slightly in colour and pinker forms exist: a good simple plant for half-shade. Similar is *Stachys macrantha*, smaller in height but bigger in flower, happy in sun or shade.

Though also without herbal application *Stachys olympica* deserves inclusion as a fine herb associate. Known as lamb's ears or flannel feet, its carpets of grey furred leaves are superb front line material. Emphasis has recently been placed upon the non-flowering form 'Silver Carpet' which is excellent for knots, but the type with equally soft and downy foot-high spikes and tiny pink flowers peering out from the fur, like a Yorkshire terrier after a heavy night out, are equally desirable. It looks marvellous with pinks and fronting the apothecary's rose. Full sun is essential.

STYRAX OFFICINALIS GUM STORAX

Incisions made in the branches of this small tree cause a gummy exudation and this is traditionally used as an ingredient in incense. As a native of the Mediterranean ranging from southern France to Palestine it is thus ideally placed to enliven the Roman and Orthodox church services which still regularly employ it. There is a further religious connection in that the hard, bead-like seeds are strung as rosaries. Gum storax is also used in perfumery and, in the past, in cough linctuses.

In Britain *Styrax officinalis* is seldom seen out of botanic garden collections, but in a sheltered spot on a well-drained soil (an enclosed herb garden is the ideal spot) it has considerable charm. With us it is unlikely to exceed large shrub size. The general appearance is like that of a delicate quince-tree with smaller leaves, pale green above, almost white beneath. In May and June little bunches of white, bell-shaped flowers appear, scented and charming, though fleeting.

By extension other styrax species might be grown. *S. japonica* is the most dependable with masses of white, yellow-centred flowers in June. A lovely little tree for a lime-free soil.

SYMPHYTUM OFFICINALE COMFREY

Comfrey has caused considerable flutters in herbal dovecotes in recent years. Having moved with surprising speed from the barely remembered knitbone to a highly recommended vegetable and near-panacea, it is now damned as deeply as it was formerly highly praised for containing dangerous cancer-producing agents. Doubtless this is no final statement and work will continue to be done upon it as a known source of protein and of vitamin B.

As a garden plant comfreys are too coarse, in their unimproved wild forms, for small areas. Our native plant is usually seen by watersides, a 4-foot high bristly borage with small crozier-heads of tubular flowers from white through dusky pink to night-purple. Crossed with *Symphytum asperum* it has produced the lovely *S.* × *uplandicum*. Here, above the pale foliage, pink buds open in May to reveal clear blue flowers.

Graham Stuart Thomas especially recommends *S. asperum* with yellow azaleas and as *Rhododendron molle* (*Azalea mollis*) is listed as being of use in Chinese medicine, it is an association that is acceptable in the herbal context.

SYMPLOCARPUS FOETIDUS SKUNK CABBAGE

In their eastern North American home in wet soil, often in woodland, the tight leaf spears of skunk cabbage begin to elongate in late autumn. Thus they manage to exist without harm through winter temperatures of 40° to 50° of frost. In earliest spring, before this foliage moves further forward, the flowers push through newly thawed ground: waxy, pear-shaped arum spathes, dusky purple mottled with greenish-yellow with a less than pleasant smell. No beauty here, but the final foliage of summer is up to hosta standards and for shady bog garden conditions it is well worthwhile: though it will grow in drought and sun the result is not good. Bruised leaves are also foetid.

Skunk cabbage (polecat weed, meadow cabbage, skunk weed) was quickly taken up by American colonists and it was listed by no less than eight Shaker communities for use (the dried and ground rhizome) in whooping cough and asthma and as an antispasmodic. The name skunk cabbage is also used for the much more dramatic aroid from western North America, *Lysichitum americanum*. This with its foot-high golden yellow spathes and subsequent paddle-sized leaves is a superb waterside plant. It enters these pages legitimately because of its use as a food plant, never to be carelessly imitated with any available aroid: cooking methods learnt over centuries are needed to dispel poisonous properties. A further use is closer, perhaps, to this book's definition of a herb as being a life-enhancer rather than life-supporter. As with banana leaves in the tropics these huge leaves have been used to wrap whole salmon for cooking in the ashes of a fire.

TANACETUM VULGARE TANSY

Tansy cakes and tansy pancakes were once Lenten fare, suitably bitter as gall, to remind the faithful of the approaching time of Christ's Passion. Tansy has a more than seasonal use, however, being a vermifuge (the flowers alone were recommended for children), an aperient and reputedly helping jaundice. Today it is restricted to scented sachets; all parts being intensely aromatic.

Tansy is a somewhat weedy invasive perennial, 4-foot high with heads of button-like yellow daisy-flowers without the rays. Any position suits it, except in the wettest soils, which makes it a simple plant for the back of the herb-border.

With rather more presence is the form 'Crispa'; here the leaves are like dark moss against which the yellow button-flowers stand out dramatically.

TEUCRIUM CHAMAEDRYS GERMANDER

While the patterns of knots and parterres are almost infinite the same unfortunately cannot be said of the number of plants suitable for making them. Thus another is very welcome.

Wall germander is a foot-high tussocky subshrub with tight, dark green aromatic foliage and, if they are not clipped off in the cause of art, little thyme-like heads of flowers. Easily propagated by cuttings, division or seed, it can be quickly and conveniently bulked up for use: it is also hardier than *Santolina* and the other grey-leaved Mediterraneans. Wall germander is native to continental Europe, frequent on limestone uplands. Any reasonably drained soil in sun is suitable.

Though suggested by early writers as a specific against dropsy and the gout, herbal use today is restricted to the flavouring of liqueurs and vermouth. An infusion of the leaves provides a simple tonic tea.

THYMUS spp THYME

Strewn across Europe and then eastwards along the Himalayan chain are three or four hundred species of thymes. Such extraordinary prolificity may be more in the minds of botanical taxonomists than in the garden of even the most thymophile collector, and that comforting abbreviation 'agg' following a name is sufficient for most of us to know that it may include an aggregate of species whose minute differences should only be of interest to other thymes obsessed with genealogy.

For visual convenience it is wise to separate thymes into two main groups, those which make little upright bushes a foot high of strong twiggy growth and those which grow as a prostrate mat of foliage. The first group cluster around *T. vulgaris*, the most important from a culinary point of view. This has the rich aromatic flavour which comes from a high essential oil content, here mainly in the form of thymol. In addition to its kitchen value it is widely used in perfumery, cosmetics and pharmaceutical preparations.

Though typical of the rock-strewn *garigue* of southern France, where the scent seems particularly strong it has been cultivated for centuries and succeeds – so long as winter drainage is effective – anywhere in sunny spots. Like *Teucrium chamaedrys* it makes an admirable formal edging to knots and parterre patterns – a grey-green miniature hedge 9 inches high. There are charming variegated-leaved forms, and one 'Roseus' with brighter pink flowers which are not seen, of course, if clipped. There is also a pretty white-variegated form.

The opposing group centres on wild thyme, *Thymus serphyllum*. It is also known agreeably as mother of thyme. This is the perfect mat-maker for thyme lawns, for filling up cracks in paving, and for clothing dry walls. Though less pungent than common thyme it is still perfectly usable in similar ways. Flower colours vary from white through to deep rose and can be selected by rooting cuttings to obtain a pure stand of the favoured shade.

A delightful textural variation can be obtained by using the grey, downy *T. lanuginosus*, one of the hairy-leaved thymes.

Hybrids between the two major herbal species are known as *T. × citriodorus*. These are the lemon and orange thymes. Intermediate in size and shrubbiness these are invaluable . golden-and cream-splashed and variegated forms which look as charming in pots as in the garden. Frequent propagation is a good rule to maintain; cuttings are a cinch.

Any European holiday, to southern shores or northern hills will turn up thymes of various sorts: cuttings of all are worthy of collection and are, of course, ideally sized for that modern version of the famed Wardian Case – the sponge bag.

TILIA CORDATA LIME, LINDEN

As a vernacular name lime causes confusion to all but the English: elsewhere the word produces expectations of a small, sour citrus fruit. For this tree, therefore, the alternative name of linden has much to commend it.

Whatever the name, however, the small-leaved linden is an admirable herb garden addition. Though this species is typically a fine forest-sized tree it is one of the best for pleaching, that ancient method of contriving a hedge on stilts to enclose a garden on high while making lower views possible. Young trees are planted in a single or double row a couple of yards apart and, while the trunks are kept clean to a height of 5 or 6 feet, branches above are trained along the row to make, eventually, a continuous green wall. Pleaching is an ideal way of raising the effective height of a low garden wall or fence. In past times complicated frames were erected to vary the shape.

Inevitably, such rigorous pruning as is needed greatly reduces the trees' flowering: it hardly matters with hornbean and wych elm (other favourite trees for pleaching) but not to have the delicious, dreamy scent of linden flowers in July is a major disadvantage. The tisane made from fresh or dried flowers is highly appreciated as it relieves headaches caused especially by 'heavy' thundery weather. One can easily make one's own, or elegantly packeted one-cup sachets labelled tilleul can be found in grand grocers.

TRACHELOSPERMUM JASMINOIDES

To read that this delightful evergreen twiner is also a medicinal herb is a fine example of gardening serendipity. It has no vernacular name with us – perhaps one of the several in Chinese, *Feng-t'eng*, or in translation, wind vine, might be adopted to popularize such a lovely plant.

It needs a protected wall, and is not a plant for cold areas, but is reasonably safe in much of Britain. It makes a complete evergreen wall cover, polished and reflective to a height of 15 feet or so, given the chance. Amongst this half-inch-wide, fragrant flowers cluster in mid-summer, with rotate corollas (much like periwinkle) which open white and gradually darken to chamois-leather cream.

The wind vine was introduced to Europe from Shanghai by Robert Fortune in 1844 just after he had given up the curatorship of the Chelsea Physic Garden to collect plants in the Orient. There is no record that he knew of a medical connection: stems of wind vine are used there in decoction for rheumatoid arthritis and, variously, for boils and abscesses.

This is one of the few self-clinging climbers which makes it particularly valuable in the garden. By slight extension its Japanese relation, which is rather hardier, could be planted, this is *Trachelospermum asiaticum*.

TRACHYCARPUS FORTUNEI PALM

This is the only palm which is hardy throughout southern Britain, reaching 20 or 30 feet and bearing a crown of broad palm-fan leaves. From amongst the leaves heavy yellow flower sprays (rather like upside down rhubarb flowers) hang down in suitable summers. Most strange is the trunk which is thickly covered with the dense fibrous remains of old leaf-bases: several growing together, as at Minterne in Dorset, look like the legs of a mammoth raised from the dead.

Obviously so exotic a creature is not a plant for every garden: it also looks very tatty in cold and exposed spots. But as a centre-piece, perhaps of a group of oriental herbs in a courtyard, it can look very fine. It is not particular as to soil, and chalk or acid soil seem equally acceptable.

The medicinal applications appear, to Western minds, as strange as its appearance: ashes from the burnt fibre acts as a hemostatic whilst the fruits (like small black grapes, seldom produced here) and roots in decoction have a contraceptive effect.

TRAGOPOGON PORRIFOLIUM SALSIFY

There is much to be said (though it is seldom done) for growing those plants which double as pot herbs, or vegetables, and herbs proper in both places; kitchen garden and herb garden. But the time scale is often wrong and what is eaten as vegetable must remain to produce what is needed as herb or in order for it to be seen through to flowers. Several such plants are biennials – carrot, parsnip, leek and, here salsify.

The best way to have one's herb and eat it is to sow the requisite row or rows as a perfectly normal vegetable in late spring. Growth and root development proceeds until by early winter the delicious salsify roots are available to live up to their name of vegetable oyster. These are considered an appetite-stimulant and hence good as a 'starter'. At the same time a half dozen roots, perhaps those that have forked and will be hell to peel, are moved into a clump amongst the permanent herbs.

The second year's growth begins with the extension of the long, narrow grey-green leaves (*porrifolium* = leek-leaved) and 18-inch flower stems carrying long pointed buds. These open for only a short time each day into starry purple daisies. The last act of this elongated vegetable drama is the most spectacular: production of superb spherical dandelion 'clocks' up to 6 inches in diameter composed of inch-wide parachutes. As they fly off the curtain comes down for another year.

TRIGONELLA FOENUM – GRAECUM FENUGREEK

This is an Asiatic fodder crop which has been naturalized in the classical world for untold centuries as the direct translation (Greek hay) of the specific epithet indicates. Medicinally it was particularly employed on the southern shores of the Mediterranean.

Today fenugreek enjoys something of a renaissance: Indian uses of both the seeds and the leaves in curries have moved to the west and sprouted seeds are one of those recommended by those who wish to grow vegetables on the kitchen window sill.

Visually in the garden the plant is rather dull, an obvious legume in leaf, 2 feet high, with tiny cream pea-flowers which are followed by long sickle-shaped pods like those of horned poppy.

It is treated as a simple hardy annual.

TRILLIUM spp TRILLIUMS

Any one of the thirty or so wakerobins seen thriving in gardens is an excitement for keen plantsmen. To see the woodland floor in their native North America as thick with them as an English wood is with bluebells is mind-boggling. We might note that for North Americans the reverse is true: as always we covet the difficult to obtain.

Much of the charm of trilliums lies in the fact that they are so very different in form from most other plants. The generic name suggests a trinity which is fully demonstrated. In early spring fleshy stems push through the woodland leaf-litter to unfold a trio of deeply veined leaves: in their centre a green bud is held. Its three sepals peel back and three petals follow to expose two stamen whorls of three and a triple-celled ovary: the whole process is strangely ritualistic. It is also very beautiful.

The North American Indians used the white *Trillium grandiflorum* (the easiest to grow and the most beautiful) for various female complaints and the early settlers, adopting the plant, called it squawroot. Later more sophisticated collectors restricted use to *T. erectum*, a dark blood-red colour: the Shakers employed the roots of this in a poultice to aid insect bites and used the leaves, boiled in lard, for skin troubles.

Trillium needs moist semi-shade: a humus-rich soil above clay seems to be ideal.

TROPAEOLUM MAJUS NASTURTIUM

It is as well for summer herb garden brightness that the well-loved nasturtium is entirely valid, all parts of the plant having been used. Medicinally it contains an antibiotic-producing glycoside, the seeds are used as caper-substitutes and both leaves and flowers are eaten in salads. Their hot, peppery taste has given the botanically muddling vernacular name: easily confused with *Nasturtium officinale* which is watercress, and indeed the taste is remarkably close.

The tropaeolums are all from Andean South America, where *T. tuberosum* is an important vegetable crop. The annual species are rapid scramblers and this original type of *T. majus* is splendid for giving quick herb garden height. A tripod or two provides brilliant lush greenery after the early maturing Mediterraneans have turned brown. Amongst this verdure the bright flowers, yellow, scarlet and vermilion, glow like the brilliant humming birds which pollinate them in their high mountain homes.

Dwarf selections and double forms are also valuable garden annuals, the smaller types being fine for containers and window boxes. Nasturtiums can be sown *in situ* from mid April or started earlier under glass, three to a pot and planted out without disturbance after frosts (to which they are highly susceptible). They are also liable to be devoured by caterpillars of cabbage-white butterflies, for which a watch should be kept in the early stages and when finger and thumb are, in combination, the most efficient insecticide.

T. peregrinum is canary creeper with smaller, divided leaves and prettily fringed yellow flowers: it gives a lighter effect than the others but may be similarly used. *Tropaeolum speciosum* may be stretching things a bit: this is the lovely perennial flame-flower which comes up from fleshy roots each year and scrambles marvellously through shady yew or box hedges. It is a plant for acid soil and areas of high humidity. It loves Scotland, and is known as Scotch flame flower.

VALERIANA OFFICINALIS VALERIAN

The dried rhizome of valerian (also called garden heliotrope) is still listed in several pharmacopoeias and used, from classical times, to treat nervous disorders, migraine and insomnia. Miller, describing the finger-thin rhizome with its questing roots, likens valerian to a large 'Catapillar with many long Feet, of a very strong Smell, especially when dry'. He goes on to report that it had 'come much into Use of late in Diseases of the Head and all nervous Afflictions'. That fragrant root, like orris, is also used to scent linen and for pot pourri.

In the garden, needing decent moist soil and accepting half-shade happily, it makes a fine foliage plant – William Robinson considered it one of the best available – with a hummock of deeply cut heart-shaped leaves. From this 4-foot high hollow stems of flowers arise, looking decidedly umbelliferous from a distance. It is typically white to palest pink but named forms 'Coccinea' and 'Rubra' darken the range. All are deliciously fragrant and make a good, if gentle, late summer show.

VERATRUM ALBUM FALSE HELLEBORE

The veratrums, tall statuesque perennials, are another group which confusingly share the name of hellebore. The only possible connection between such visually dissimilar plants as this, Christmas rose and certain terrestrial orchids is that it was an ancient word used by the classical writers to denote plants which supposedly cured madness. Certainly the veratrums have the ultimate solution because their alkaloids are able to slow down the heart to the point at which it stops. They are highly poisonous and hence were employed until recent times in decoction as effective insecticides.

Fortunately, for they are magnificent garden plants, there are no fleshy tubers or colourful berries likely to encourage uninformed sampling. Like other Liliaceous plants such as asparagus, they make strong root-stocks, with thimble-sized buds which just show at soil surface in winter. These extend into fine rosettes of pleated leaves almost like bromeliads. In well nourished plants each rosette throws up a great flower spike 4 or even 5 feet in height. These are crowded with star-like flowers, palest avocado-green in *Veratrum album*, a definite green in the American *V. viride* and an extraordinary burnished maroon in *V. nigrum*. They all provide a marvellous sight for several weeks as the flowers open up the stem and remain striking as the seed capsules develop. Veratrums like moist semi-shade; once happy a clump can be left alone for years.

VERBASCUM THAPSUS MULLEIN

This is the common mullein, often seen on roadside embankments, specially on chalk, either in flower in early summer or as a statuesque corpse for months afterwards. The yellow flowers are set close together on the hoary stem, striking from a distance but coarse in the garden. As a medicinal herb it was widely used for respiratory disorders: taken to North America by European settlers it has become widely naturalized there. Shaker literature cites its availability and application as a poultice for mumps and sore throats and internally for coughs and catarrh.

In southern Europe *Verbascum phlomoides* and *V. speciosum* are commoner and had similar herbal uses. Also biennials, these make great steeples of greyish leaves and pale yellow flowers. Even greyer as to be almost white is the splendid first year rosette and subsequent second year flower spikes of *V. bombyciferum* from Asia Minor.

All these mulleins need perfect winter drainage and full sun. Other species and some lovely selections of *V. phoeniceum* could also be used, extending the herbal brief ever so slightly.

VERONICASTRUM VIRGINICA VERONICA

Culver's root, bowman's root, physic root, are all local names for this North American which had been in medical use long before the Europeans settled the land. The dried root became one of the constituents of the famed Shaker digestive cordial which included several uncommon plants such as this, gentian and blue flag.

It is an easy perennial in any decent soil growing up to a height of 5 or 6 feet. But it is so light in texture that it is never too strong for a place amongst smaller things. Wand-like stems carry wide-spaced whorls of finger-shaped leaves and are topped by slender spires of pale blue or white speedwell flowers. The season is not long but distinguished and the splendid vertical shape is maintained into fruit.

Like most herbaceous perennials it is very simply propagated by division in early spring or late autumn.

VIBURNUM OPULUS GUELDER ROSE

The dried bark from the stem and root of two North American viburnums is used there as a sedative: these are *Viburnum prunifolium*, the American sloe – from the size of its fruit – and *V. lentago*, the nannyberry. Though both are fine ornamental shrubs they are not frequently encountered in cultivation.

Not so our own *Viburnum opulus*, the well-loved guelder rose, which has been similarly used. Naturally a plant of moist woodland edges it makes a wide open bush 10 to 15 feet high with three lobed leaves reminiscent of a maple and having a similar capability of putting on superb autumn colour. In combination with the bunches of brilliantly glossy red currant fruit the effect is one of the best late autumn sights. Yellow fruited forms are also available. The fruits are inedible when fresh. The flowers that precede them in June are like small lace-cap hydrangeas sprinkling the bush.

Frequently, however, the name guelder rose is reserved for the beautiful form listed variously as 'Sterile' or 'Roseum'. Here, again like many hydrangeas the fertile flowers have given up their viability and the whole head is now a sphere of palest green gradually turning to creamy white. Their weight causes the stems to bow graciously to form a fountain of soft colour. Needless to say such beauty has its price: there is no autumn fruit. It is not, fortunately, required for propagation: hardwood cuttings inserted into sandy soil outside in late autumn give a good percentage of young rooted plants.

VINCA MAJOR PERIWINKLE

Greater periwinkle is a cottage garden plant which has been in cultivation for years out of number. Now naturalized in hedgebanks, its elegant evergreen trails are particularly fine in winter when the bushes above are leafless. In the rush of developing cow parsley and all the other local herbaceous spring growth, all but the earliest of the lovely 2-inch blue flowers of periwinkle are apt to be lost: they open from March to June.

In the garden competition is less and the plant makes superb ground cover on banks too steep to mow, or under trees. It is too vigorous for small cultivated areas but two variegated forms, one with a central bar of yellow, the other with a broad cream edge to the leaves, are more suitable; at least they are so distinctive that aggression is quickly seen. Variegated *Vinca* can be clipped to make an edging or central filling for large knots or other formal beds in sun or shade.

The chemistry of *Vinca* is complicated, possessing alkaloids and tannins and numbers of other constituents. The range of medicinal uses has been as extensive, from employment as a haemostatic to reducing blood pressure and treating diabetes. Similar uses, though proportionately less, came from *Vinca minor*, the lesser periwinkle.

With its smaller leaves and flowers in a number of soft colours from white to plum-purple, both single and double, it is another charming ground cover for use on banks or under mature trees and shrubs. It should not be planted with other young things as it will romp all over them in an unacceptably boisterous way. This too is a continental European long naturalized in Britain.

A close relation, the Madagascar periwinkle, first named *Vinca rosea* by Linnaeus but now removed to its own genus *Catharanthus*, is one of the most important of medicinal herbs today. Its alkaloids provide the most effective plant-based anti-cancer agents known. It is commonly seen as a house plant – a little bush with pink or white (or pink *and* white) periwinkle flowers. In warm years it succeeds well if planted out after all danger of frost is past.

VIOLA ODORATA VIOLET

Perfumes made from flowers of sweet violet, aided and adulterated by the violet-scented roots of orris, have been made for centuries. The last half of the nineteenth century saw a period of intense interest in the plant and acres were grown, also for the cut flower market: no lady, it would seem, would venture out without wearing a bunch of violets.

Viola odorata is not the only scented violet by any means, but only a half dozen out of the 500 species which exist have been brought into the commercial cut-flower and perfume-producing types. Of these our native *V. odorata*, the sweet violet, has been the precursor but in the inevitable search for flower size associated species have been hybridized to produce parma violets, in a range of rich colours, with single or double flowers. After a half century of neglect, a search is now being made for these once popular plants in remote gardens and gradually some of them are being offered again by specialist nurseries.

Violets are naturally flowers of the very early spring and selection has extended this well into winter. Planting takes place in the previous spring in rich leafy soil to build up good clumps for the following year's flowering. A common custom in the huge kitchen gardens of country houses at the turn of the century was to move the best clumps in late autumn into cold frames, from which a summer crop of melons had been taken, to provide flowers for Christmas. Some such less grand system, or even putting a couple of plants into pots is still well worthwhile: violets are propagated by division after flowering is finished.

In addition to its floral charm the sweet violet has therapeutic uses of long standing which are fully validated: it also shows that to do good medicines do not *have* to be nasty. All parts of the plant have been used but the leaves and flowers are the major constituents of catarrh and bronchitis remedies. A gargle is made for sore throats. In America the Shakers adapted a local native species, *Viola pedata* for the same ailments.

Also selected for medicinal use was the heartsease, *Viola tricolor*, with a number of uses ranging from an aid in rheumatism to indigestion. As a garden plant it has been of even greater significance than the violet because, principally with *V. lutea* and *V. altaica*, it has produced the incredible diversity of garden pansies, and from these the modern garden violas with backcrossing. Thus, from the little Johnny-jump-ups, which happily seed themselves, to highly sophisticated large-flowered hybrids bred true to colour and season, the herb garden can employ an extremely wide group of lovely plants. No month of the year need be without them.

VITEX AGNUS CASTUS CHASTE TREE

The usual vernacular name, chaste tree, actually does relate to its traditional use as an anaphrodisiac for men. Research has confirmed the presence of hormone-like substances in the seed which also have medicinal applications for women with hormonal imbalance problems. These same seeds have also been used as a condiment.

They possess the aromatic scent shared by the leaves of this elegant shrub. Native to the Mediterranean region eastwards into Asia Minor it needs a warm wall in Britain to give of its best. There it makes a fringe of fingered foilage and carries autumn spikes of pale lavender, reminiscent of a fragrant *Veronica*. The foliage is much like that of *Cannabis* – a plant which might well be included in this list for its properties but is definitely not for gardens.

Planting Charts

Key		Propagation	
A	Annual	C	Cutting
B	Biennial	C	Cutting
P	Perennial	D	Division
AS	Accepts Shade	G	Grafting
spp	species	R	Root cutting
E	Evergreen	S	Seed
D	Deciduous		

ARVM   Pfaffenbone.

LORDS AND LADIES (Fuchs, 1542)

GENERAL LIST OF CULINARY HERBS. MOST ALSO HAVE MEDICAL ATTRIBUTES.

Herb & Country of Origin	Family & Botanical Name	Height and Spread in Feet	Type & Brief Description	Annual Biennial Perennial	Flower: Colour & Season	Accepts Shade	Propagation	Soil Dry → Moist
ALECOST *Europe, W. Asia*	Compositae *Chrysanthemum balsamita*	4 × 2	Smooth grey-leaves. Scented spearmint	P	Sprays of small white and yellow daisies *Summer*		D	x x x
ALEXANDERS *Europe*	Umbelliferae *Smyrnium olusatrum*	2½ × 2	Evergreen. Good glossy leaves throughout winter in warm spots	P	Greenish yellow *Spring*	AS	S	x
ANGELICA *Europe*	Umbelliferae *Angelica archangelica*	5-6 × 3	Statuesque. Seeds itself around	B	Spherical heads. Lime-green *Early summer*	AS	S	x x
ANISE, ANISEED *S.E. Europe*	Umbelliferae *Pimpinella anisum*	2 × 1	A thin cow parsley	A	White *Early summer*		S	x
BASIL *Old World Tropics*	Labiatae *Ocium basilicum*	1 × 1	Tender, pepper-scented	A	Purple *Summer*		S	x
Bush Basil	*O. minimum*		Purple-leaved forms available		Flower insignificant *Summer*		S	x
BORAGE *S. Europe*	Boraginaceae *Borago officinalis*	2 × 1	Bristly leaves	A/B	Blue or white *Summer*		S	x x
CARAWAY *Europe*	Umbelliferae *Carum carvi*	2 × ½	Conventional umbellifer	B	White	S		x x

CHERVIL *Europe*	Umbelliferae *Anthriscus cerefolium*	2 × ½	Useful for autumn sowing to give winter greenness	A	White *Spring, summer*	AS	S	x	x	x
CHIVES *Europe*	Liliaceae *Allium schoenoprasum*	½ - ¾ × ½	Tuft forming onion. Good for edging. Evergreen	P	Purple *Late spring*	AS	S/D	x	x	x
CORIANDER *S. Europe*	Umbelliferae *Coriandrum sativum*	1½ × ½	Another small umbellifer. Distinctive, orange-scented fruits	A	Whitish pink *Summer*		S		x	x
DILL *S. W. Asia*	Umbelliferae *Anethum graveolens*	2-3 × 1	Like delicate small fennel	A	Yellowish *Summer*		S		x	x
FENNEL *Europe*	Umbelliferae *Foeniculum vulgare*	4-6 × 2	Clouds of delicate leaves. Green or bronze	P	Yellowish *Summer*		S	x	x	x
FENUGREEK *S. Europe*	Leguminosae *Trigonella foenumgraecum*	1½ × 1	Clover-like with long seed pods	A	Pale yellow *Summer*		S		x	x
GARLIC *Asia*	Liliaceae *Allium sativum*	2 × ½	Bulb	P	White onion heads. Seldom flowers *Mid summer*		D		x	x
HORSERADISH *Europe*	Cruciferae *Armoracia rusticana*	3 × 3	Rampant coarse-leaved. Only the white-variegated form suitable for small gardens	P	White *Summer*	AS	D	x	x	x
JUNIPER *Europe*	Cupressaceae *Juniperus communis*	5 × 5	Evergreen conifer. Various forms available	P	Pea-sized black berries		C		x	

Herb & Country of Origin	Family & Botanical Name	Height and Spread in Feet	Type & Brief Description	Annual Biennial Perennial	Flower: Colour & Season	Accepts Shade	Propa- gation	Soil Dry → Moist	
LOVAGE Europe	Umbelliferae Levisticum officinale	5 × 3	Robust growth	P	Greenish heads Early summer	AS	S		x
MARJORAMS POT MARJORAM S. E. Europe	Labiatae Origanum onites	1½ × 1	Greyish leaves. Doubtfully hardy in Britain. Treated as annual	P	White or pink Summer		S	x	
SWEET MARJORAM S. W. Asia	O. marjorana	1½ × 1	Subshrub lacking hardiness. Hence often grown as annual	P	White in small gobular heads Summer		S	x	
WILD OREGANO Europe	O. vulgare	1½–2 × 1	The hardiest marjoram. A fine golden-leaved form exists which does not flower	P	Pink-purple heads Early summer	AS	D/S	x	x
MINTS Europe	Labiatae Menta spp	1½ × 1	All except Corsican are robust and invasive	P	Pale purple flowers Summer	AS	D		x
APPLEMINT	M. rotundifolium	2½ × 1	Soft round leaves. Variegated form exists	P	Pinkish flowers Summer	AS	D		x
CORSICAN	Mentha requienii	½″ × 6″	Tiny, rock-crack denizen	P	Minute purple flowers Summer	AS	D		
EAU DE COLOGNE MINT	M. piperita var	1½ × 1	Purplish leaves on dark stems. Spicy scent	P	Pale purple flower Summer	AS	D		x
GINGERMINT	M. x gentilis	1½ × 1	Fine golden variegation	P	Pale purple Summer	AS	D		x
PENNYROYAL	M. pulegium	1 × ½	Low creeping habit	P	Narrow flower spikes Summer	AS	D/S		x

Common name / origin	Botanical name	Size	Notes	A/B/P	Flower / season					
PEPPERMINT	M.x piperita	1½ × 1	Bright green foliage	P	Pale purple flowers / *Summer*	AS	D			x
SPEARMINT	M. spicata	1½ × 1	Pale green leaves	P	Pale purple / *Summer*	AS	S		x	x
NASTURTIUM *Peru*	Tropaeolaceae / *Tropaeolum majus*	1 × 1 / 6 × 8	Flowers and leaves used in salads. Climbing forms useful for quick height	A	Brilliant orange, red, yellow / *Summer*	AS	D		x	x
ONIONS *Asia*	Liliaceae	1 × 1	Welsh onion makes clumps of leafy growth.	P	White	AS	D		x	x
	Allium cepa forms	2 × 1	Egyptian or tree onion produces bulblets at the top of flowering shoots	P		AS	D		x	x
PARSLEY *Europe*	Umbelliferae / *Petroselinum crispum*	1½ × 1	Bright green biennial. Smooth (French) and curled English forms: Good for edgings	B	Green-yellow / *Summer*	AS	S			x
PURSLANE *India*	Portulaccaceae / *Portulacca oleracea*	½ × 1	Fleshy leaves	A	Flower insignificant		S	x		
ROCQUETTE *S. Europe*	Cruciferae / *Eruca sativa*	2 × 1	Oily green-leaved salad	A	Yellow, mustard like		S	x	x	
ROSEMARY *S. Europe*	Labiatae / *Rosmarinus officinalis* / Various cvs: 'Miss Jessup' (upright) 'Severn Seas' (clear blue)	3-4 × 4	Dark green shrub with narrow leaves. Prostrate forms less hardy. Golden variegated form rare	P	Pale blue / *Spring and early summer*		C	x		

Herb & Country of Origin	Family & Botanical Name	Height and Spread in Feet	Type & Brief Description	Annual Biennial Perennial	Flower: Colour & Season	Accepts Shade	Propa- gation	Soil Dry	→ Moist
SAFFRON *S. Europe*	Iridaceae *Crocus sativus*	½ × ½	A true crocus, flowering in autumn. Leaves follow and die down in summer	P	Purple petals with bright orange stigmata *Autumn*		D	x	
SAGE *Europe*	Labiatae		Downy, low subshrub with several variants:	P	Purple pink or white spikes *Summer*				x
	Salvia officinalis	2 × 2	The typical grey type		*Early summer*		C/S		x
	S. o. 'Purpurascens'		Fine purple-leaved form		*Early summer*		C		x
	S. o. 'Icterina'		Gold-variegated form		Non-flowering		C		x
	S. o. 'Tricolor'		Less robust: white, pink and green leaves		Non-flowering		C		x
SALAD BURNET *Europe*	Rosaceae *Poterium sanguisorba*	1-2 × 1	Elegant pinnate leaves. Flowers insignificant and best removed to encourage leaf and longevity	P	Reddish *Early summer*		D	x	
SAVORY *Mediterranean Region* SUMMER	Labiatae *Satureja hortensis*	1 × ½	Thin, twiggy and aromatic	A	Pale purple *Summer*		S	x	
WINTER	*S. montana*	1½ × 1-1½	Evergreen subshrub, available for winter use	P	Pinkish *Summer*		D/C	x	

Name / Region	Family / Botanical name	Size	Description	Type	Flowers / Season					
SORREL / *Europe*	Polygonaceae / *Rumex acetosa*	2 × 1-2	Profuse shining leaves beginning in very early spring	P	Reddish spikes / *Early summer*	AS	D	x	x	x
SORREL FRENCH / *Europe*	*Rumex scutatus*		Smaller greyish shield-shaped leaves trailing habit	P	Small pinkish spikes / *Mid summer*		D	x	x	
SWEETBAY / *Mediterranean region*	Lauraceae / *Laurus nobilis*	20 × 10	Dense evergreen, dramatic shrub	P	Yellow / *Late spring*	C/S	AS	x	x	x
SWEET CICELY / *N. Europe*	Umbelliferae / *Myrrhis odorata*	2 × 2	Robust perennial. Uninvasive. Distinctive long fruits. Bright ferny foliage.	P	White / *Early summer*	AS	S	x	x	x
TARRAGON / *S. Europe*	Compositae / *Artemisia dracunculus*	2 × 1	Bushy cloud of narrow leaves	P	Greenish, insignificant / *Early summer*		D/C	x	x	
THYMES / *Europe*	Labiatae		Small-leaved subshrubs	P	All pink-purple			x		
COMMON THYMES	*Thymus vulgaris*	1 × 1	Bushy: good as clipped edging		*Summer*		D/C/S	x		
LEMON	*T. x citriodorus*	¾ × 1	Golden and white variegated forms		*Summer*		C	x		
WILD	*T. serpyllum*	¼ × 1	One of many creeping thymes for ground cover		*Summer*		D/S	x		
WOOLLY	*T. lanuginosus*	¼ × 1	Grey leaved species		*Summer*		D/S	x		

GENERAL LIST OF TRADITIONAL OFFICINAL HERBS FROM EUROPE, THE ORIENT & NORTH AMERICA.
PLANTS LISTED HAVE ORNAMENTAL VALUE IN ADDITION TO MEDICINAL ATTRIBUTES.

Herb & Country of Origin	Family & Botanical Name	Height and Spread in Feet	Type & Brief Description	Annual Biennial Perennial	Flower: Colour & Season	Accepts Shade	Propa-gation	Soil Dry → Moist	
ABSINTHE Europe	Compositae Artemisia absinthium	3 × 3	Grey-leaved. Aromatic in all parts. 'Lambrook Silver' best form	P	Flowers insignificant		S/C/D	x	x
ADONIS Europe	Ranunculaceae Adonis vernalis	1 × 1	Fern-like foliage extends after flowering	P	Yellow *Spring*	AS	D		x
AGAVE Mexico	Agavaceae Agave spp	5 × 5	Tender robust monocarpic succulent. Good variegated form	P	Huge (15ft) flower spike only after many years		D	x	x
AGRIMONY Europe	Rosaceae Agrimonia eupatoria	2 × 1	Rosette of leaves	P	Yellow spike *Summer*	AS	S		x
ALOE S. Africa	Liliaceae Aloe vera	2 × 2	Tender South African succulent	P	Scarlet spikes	AS	D	x	x
ANEMONE Nepal	Ranunculaceae Anemone vitifolia	4 × 2	Good summer foliage	P	Excellent white and pink flowers *Late summer*	AS	D		x
ARNICA Europe	Compositae Arnica montana	1 × 1	Alpine daisy	P	Yellow *Spring*	AS	D/S		x

ARTICHOKE *S. Europe*	Compositae *Cynara scolymus*	5 × 4	Statuesque, grey-leaved. Cardoon is similar in effect	P	Blue 'thistles' *Summer*		D/S	x	x	
ASAFOETIDA *Mediterranean Region*	Umbelliferae *Ferula asafoetida*	4 × 2	Robust, fennel-like	P	Yellow heads *Summer*		S/D	x		
ASARABACCA *Europe*	Aristolochiaceae *Asarum europaeum*	½ × 1	Glossy heart-shaped leaves at ground level. Cyclamen-like	P	Insignificant flower, purple	AS	D	x	x	x
ASPARAGUS *Europe*	Liliaceae *Asparagus officinalis*	4 × 4	Clouds of feathery foliage. Long-lived	P	Flowers insignificant. Red berries follow		S/D	x	x	
ASPHODEL *S. Europe*	Liliaceae *Asphodelus albus*	3 × 1	Grey spear-like leaves	P	Tall white spikes *Late spring*		S/D	x		
BANEBERRY *E. North America*	Ranunculaceae *Actaea alba* *A. rubra*	2 × 1	Heads of spectacular fruits. White and red respectively	P	Spikes of fluffy flowers *Spring*	AS	S/D	x	x	
BEAR'S BREECH *S. Europe*	Acanthaceae *Acanthus mollis*	4 × 3	Fine, broad leaves and tall spikes of flowers. Other species also good	P	White and purple *Summer*	AS	S/D	x		
BEGONIA *China, Japan*	Begoniaceae *Begonia evansiana*	1½ × 1½	The only hardy species. A typical begonia	P	Pink *Summer*	AS	D	x		x
BERGAMOT *E. North America*	Labiatae *Monarda didyma*	3 × 1	Aromatic perennial. Several cultivars available	P	Red, pink, white, whorls of flowers up stems *Summer*		D	x		x

Herb & Country of Origin	Family & Botanical Name	Height and Spread in Feet	Type & Brief Description	Annual Biennial Perennial	Flower: Colour & Season	Accepts Shade	Propagation	Soil Dry → Moist	
BETONY *Europe*	Labiatae *Stachys officinalis*	1½ × 1	Waved leaves. Ground cover	P	Pink *Early summer*	AS	D		x
BIRTHWORT *S. Europe*	Aristolochiaceae *Aristolochia clematitis*	3 × 2	Invasive perennial. Stems of elegant heart-shaped leaves	P	Pale yellow *Summer*		D	x	
BISTORT *Europe*	Polygonaceae *Polygonum bistorta*	2 × 1	Sorrel-like leaves, white on reverse. Clump forming	P	Fine pink spikes *Early summer*		D		x
BLOODROOT *E. North America*	Papaveraceae *Sanguinaria canadensis*	½ × 1	Elegant grey leaves develop after flowering	P	White *Early spring*	AS	D		x
BLUEBOTTLE *Europe*	Compositae *Centaurea montana*	1½ × 1	Perennial cornflower	P	Blue *Spring*	AS	D	x	
BOGBEAN *Europe*	Menyanthaceae *Menyanthes trifoliata*	1 × 3	Aquatic or marsh plant. Shiny leaves	P	White flowers. Fringed petals *Summer*		D		x
BRYONY *Europe*	Cucurbitaceae *Bryonia diocia*	10 × 4	Tendril climber	P	Greenish *Summer*	AS	S	x	
BUGLE *Europe*	Labiatae *Ajuga reptans*	½ × 1	Creeping plant for ground cover. Purple, variegated and tricolour forms available	P	Purple spikes *Spring*	AS	D		x

Common name / Region	Family & Species	Size	Description	B/P	Flower / Season					
Europe	*Arctium lappa*	5 × 3	Bristly rhubarb-like plant. White backed leaves	B/P	Purple *Summer*	AS	S			x
BUTCHER'S BROOM *Europe*	Liliaceae *Ruscus aculeatus*	2 × 2	Spiny evergreen subshrub. Hermaphrodite form best	P	Flowers insignificant. Fine red berries	AS	D			
CALAMINT *Europe*	Labiatae *Calamintha grandiflora*	1 × 1	Aromatic, mint-like	P	Pink *Early summer*		D	x		
CARDINAL FLOWER *E. North America*	Lobeliaceae *Lobelia cardinalis*	2½ × 2	Dark narrow leaves	P	Scarlet spikes *Summer*		S	x		x
CARLINE THISTLE *Europe*	Compositae *Carlina acaulis*	¼ × 1	Wide flat rosette	P	Large, thistle-like at ground level *Late summer*		S	x		
CELANDINE *Europe*	Papaveraceae *Chelidonium majus*	1½ × 1½	Soft blue-green foliage, orange sap	B/P	Small poppy flower heads *Summer*	AS	S		x	
CHAMOMILE *Europe*	Compositae *Chamaemelum nobile*	½ × 1	Creeping, aromatic leaves	P	White daisies *Summer*		S/D	x		
CHICORY *Europe*	Compositae *Cichorium intybus*	2½ × 1	Dandelion-like leaves	B	Spikes of sky-blue *Summer*		S	x		
CHINESE LANTERN *Europe*	Solanaceae *Physalis alkekengi*	2 × 2	Coarse plant. Brilliant autumn fruit capsules	P	Flower insignificant	AS	D		x	x

Herb & Country of Origin	Family & Botanical Name	Height and Spread in Feet	Type & Brief Description	Annual Biennial Perennial	Flower: Colour & Season	Accepts Shade	Propagation	Soil Dry → Moist
CHRISTMAS ROSE *Europe*	Ranunculaceae *Helleborus niger*	½ × 1	Leathery palmate leaves	P	Exquisite white 'roses' *Winter*	AS	S/D	x
CHRYSANTHEMUM *China, Japan*	Compositae *Chrysanthemum indicum*	2-3 × 2	Florist 'chrysanth'. Hardy forms. Aromatic leaves	P	White, bronze, pink etc. *Autumn*		D	x
COLUMBINE *Europe*	Ranunculaceae *Aquilegia vulgaris*	2 × 1	'Granny's Bonnet'. Elegant leaves	P	Blue, white, pink *Early summer*	AS	S	x
COMFREY *Europe*	Boraginaceae *Symphytum spp*	2-4 × 3	Bristly borages	P	White, pink, purple *Early summer*	AS	D	x x
CONEFLOWER *E. North America*	Compositae *Echinacea purpurea*	4 × 2	Elegant border plant	P	Pink-bronze *Summer*		S/D	x
CORNFLOWER *Europe*	Compositae *Centaurea cyanus*	2 × ½	Thin plant	A	Blue, pink, white *Early summer*		S	x x
COWSLIP *Europe*	Primulaceae *Primula veris*	1 × ½	Rosette-forming	P	Fragrant, yellow *Early summer*		S/D	
CUCUMBER *S. Asia*	Cucurbitaceae *Cucumis sativa*	8 × 6	Tendril climber	A	Flower insignificant		S	x
DAFFODIL *Europe*	Amaryllidaceae *Narcissus spp*	1½ × 1½	Wide range of forms. Old cultivars most	P	White, yellow *Spring*	AS	D	x

Europe	*Sambucus ebulus*	4 × 3	Sub-shrubby elder	P	Wide white heads *Summer*	AS	D	x	x
DOGBANE *N. America*	Apocynaceae *Apocynum cannabinum*	2 × 1	Willowy growth. Interesting fruit	P	Small, white *Summer*		S/D	x	x
DROPWORT *Europe*	Rosaceae *Filipendula vulgaris*	1 × ½	Meadowsweet of chalklands	P	White froth *Summer*		D	x	
EPIMEDIUM *E. Europe-Asia*	Berberidaceae *Epimedium grandiflorum*	1 × 1	Spreading, wiry plant. Elegant leaves	P	Yellow, pink *Early spring*	AS	D	x	x
EVENING PRIMROSE *E. North America*	Onagraceae *Oenothera biennis*	4 × 1	Coarse plant. Other spp suitable by association	B	Lambent yellow flowers open at night *Summer*		S		x
FALSE HELLEBORES *N. Hemisphere*	Liliaceae *Veratrum spp*	4 × 2	Dramatic pleated leaves	P	White, green, black spikes *Summer*	AS	S/D	x	x
FERNS *N. Hemisphere*	SEVERAL GENERA & SPECIES: SEE A–Z CATALOGUE UNDER FERNS		Fine leaves, sporebearing	P	Flowerless	AS	D		
FEVERFEW *Europe*	Compositae *Chrysanthemum parthenium*	1½ × 1	Feathery, short-lived perennials. Seeds itself around. Golden form (golden feather) is excellent	P	White and yellow *Spring-autumn*	AS	S	x	x

Herb & Country of Origin	Family & Botanical Name	Height and Spread in Feet	Type & Brief Description	Annual Biennial Perennial	Flower: Colour & Season	Accepts Shade	Propagation	Soil Dry → Moist	
								Dry	Moist
FIGWORT *Europe*	Scrophulariaceae *Scrophularia nodosa*	4 × 2	Coarse plant but variegated form valuable	P	Brownish *Summer*	AS	D		x
FLAG IRIS *E. North America*	Iridaceae *Iris versicolor*	3 × 2	Waterside plant	P	Blue *Early summer*		D		x
FLAX *Europe*	Linaceae *Linum usitatissimum*	1½ × ½	Delicate thin plant. *Linum narbonnense* is brighter and bigger	A P	Blue *Early summer*	AS	S		
GAYFEATHER *N. America*	Compositae *Liatris spicata*	2½ × 1	Fine border plant	P	Bright pink-purple spikes *Late summer*	AS	S/D	x	
GENTIAN *Europe*	Gentianaceae *Gentiana lutea*	3 × 1	The herbal gentian. A tall statuesque plant	P	Yellow spikes *Summer*	AS	D		x
GERMANDER *S. Europe*	Labiatae *Teucrium chamaedrys*	1 × 1	Tight subshrub for dwarf hedges	P	Pink *Summer*		D	x	
GIANT HYSSOP *N. America*	Labiatae *Agastache foeniculum*	3 × 2	Aromatic border plant, mint-like	P	Pink spikes *Summer*		D/S	x	
GOAT'S BEARD *Europe*	Compositae *Tragopogon porrifolium*	1½ × 1	Narrow-leaved. Grey effect.	B	Purple star-like. Morning opening		S	x	

Name / Origin	Botanical name	Size	Description	Dur.	Flower / Season					
Europe	*Galega officinalis*	4 × 3	Widely branched. Delicate pinnate leaves	P	Purple, pink, white pea-flower spikes *Summer*		S			x
GOLDEN ROD *Europe*	Compositae *Solidago virgaurea*	1½ × 1	A small golden-rod. Other species to 6 feet	P	Yellow *Late summer*	AS	D		x	x
HEARTSEASE	SEE VIOLETS									
HEMLOCK *Europe*	Umbelliferae *Conium maculatum*	5-8 × 2	Tall cow parsley. Stems purple-spotted. Very poisonous	B	White *Early summer*	AS	S			x
HERB ROBERT *Europe*	Geraniaceae *Geranium robertianum*	1 × 1	Delicate divided leaves	A	Pink, white *Spring*	AS	S			x
HOLLYHOCK *S. Europe*	Malvaceae *Alcea rosea*	6-10 × 1	Towering spires	B/P	White, yellow, pink, purple *Summer*		S	x		x
HOREHOUND *Europe*	Labiatae *Marrubium vulgare*	2 × 2	White-felted leaves. Twiggy effect	P	Flower insignificant		S/D	x		
HOPS *Europe*	Cannabaceae *Humulus lupulus*	15 × 10	Robust twiner. Golden-leaved form available	P	Flower insignificant. Female 'cones' decorative *Autumn*		D			x
HOUSELEEK *Europe*	Crassulaceae *Sempervivum tectorum*	¼ × ½	Spiky succulent rosettes	P	Starry pink *Summer*		S/D/C	x		

Herb & Country of Origin	Family & Botanical Name	Height and Spread in Feet	Type & Brief Description	Annual Biennial Perennial	Flower: Colour & Season	Accepts Shade	Propagation	Soil Dry → Moist		
JACK-IN-THE-PULPIT *E. North America*	Araceae *Arisaema triphyllum*	1½ × 1	Fine arrow-leaves	P	Green-striped, hooded flowers *Late spring*	AS				x
Temperate E. Asia	*A. consanguinem*	1 × 1	Narrow leaves	P	Brown-purple veined	AS	D			x
JOB'S TEARS *S. E. Asia*	Gramineae *Coix lachryma-jobi*	2 × 1	Broad-leaved grass	A	Hanging sprays of heavy seeds	AS	S		x	
JOE PYE WEED *E. North America*	Compositae *Eupatorium purpureum*	8-10 × 2	Enormous herb. Foot long vanilla-scented leaves	P	Rounded heads, purple *Late summer*	AS	D			x
LADY'S MANTLE *Europe*	Rosaceae *Alchemilla spp*	1-2 × 1-2	Elegant foliage. Green or grey	P	Sprays of lime-green *Summer*	AS	D/S		x	x
LADY'S SMOCK *Europe*	Cruciferae *Cardamine pratensis*	1 × ½	Delicate. A double-flowered form is less fleeting	P	Pale lavender *Spring*	AS	D/S			x
LARKSPUR *Europe*	Ranunculaceae *Delphinium consolida*	2-3 × 1	Thin and branching. Delphinium-like	A	White, blue, purple *Early summer*	AS	S	x		
LEMON BALM *Europe*	Labiatae *Melissa officinalis*	2½ × 2	Coarse but strong lemon scent.	P	Insignificant	AS	D/S	x	x	x

Name / Origin	Family / Botanical name	Size	Characteristics		Flower / Season				
Europe	*Glycyrrhiza glabra*	3–5 × 3	Strong with elegant foliage	P	Pink, insignificant *Summer*	AS	S		x
LORDS AND LADIES *Europe*	Araceae *Arum maculatum*	1 × 1	Glossy arrow-leaves unfold in winter	P	Green hooded flowers *Spring*		D/S	x	x
LOVE-IN-A-MIST *Europe*	Ranunculaceae *Nigella* spp	1½ × 1	Ferny growth. Good seed-heads	A	Blue in cloud of green bracts *Early summer*		S	x	
LOVE LIES BLEEDING *Tropics*	Amaranthaceae *Amaranthus caudatus*	3 × 1	Rapid growth from seed	A	Crimson, dangling spikes *Summer*		S	x	
LUNGWORT *Europe*	Boraginaceae *Pulmonaria* spp	1 × 1	Spotted leaves. Ground cover	P	Red, pink, blue *Early Spring*	AS	D	x	x
MANDRAKE *S. Europe*	Solanaceae *Mandragora officinarum*	½ × 1½	Wide leaf rosette. Fruit egg-shaped	P	Bluish *Early spring*		S	x	
MARIGOLD *S. Europe*	Compositae *Calendula officinalis*	1 × ½	Bright daisies in a range of colours. All parts aromatic	A	Yellow/orange *Early summer onwards*		S	x	
MARSH MALLOW *S. Europe*	Malvaceae *Althaea officinalis*	4 × 2	Elegant grey leaves	P	Pale lavender *Summer*		D/S		x

Herb & Country of Origin	Family & Botanical Name	Height and Spread in Feet	Type & Brief Description	Annual Biennial Perennial	Flower: Colour & Season	Accepts Shade	Propagation	Soil Dry →	Moist
MEADOWSWEET *Europe*	Rosaceae *Filipendula ulmaria*	2-3 × 1	Elegant plant. Gold variegated form available	P	White fluffy heads *Early summer*	AS	D		x
MEADOW SAFFRON	SEE AUTUMN CROCUS								
MONKSHOOD *Europe*	Ranunculaceae *Aconitum napellus* and other spp	4-6 × 1	Delphinium-like spikes. Poisonous	P	Purple, white, blue *Late summer/autumn*	AS	D/S	x	x
MOTHER OF THOUSANDS *E. Asia*	Saxifragaceae *Saxifraga stolonifera*	1 × 1	Round and hairy leaves. Spreads by stolons	P	Pink in airy spikes *Spring*	AS	D		x
MOTHERWORT *E. North America*	Labiatae *Leonurus cardiaca*	4 × 1	Erect, nettle like. Good in seed	P	Pink *Summer*	AS	D/S	x	
MULLEIN *Europe*	Scrophulariaceae *Verbascum thapsus*	4-6 × 2	Softly downy. Broad rosettes	B	Yellow spikes *Summer*		S/D	x	
ORCHID *China, Japan*	Orchidaceae *Bletilla striata*	1½ × 1	Wide pleated leaves. Rather frost-tender	P	Purple spikes *Summer*	AS	D	x	
ORRIS ROOT	SEE PURPLE FLAG								
OUR LADY'S MILK THISTLE *S. Europe*	Compositae *Silybum marianum*	4 × 2	Prickly white spotted leaves	A	Purple thistles *Summer*		S	x	
PASQUE FLOWER *N. Europe*	Ranunculaceae *Anemone pulsatilla*	1 × 1	Elegant divided foliage	P	Velvet-like petals, purple, mauve		S/D		x

PEONY *Europe*	Paeoniaceae *Paeonia officinalis*	2 × 2	Fine foliage colours in autumn	P	Wide single or double flowers. Pink, red *Early summer*	AS	D/S	x
PERIWINKLE *Europe*	Apocynaceae *Vinca major* *V. minor*	½ × 3	Evergreen ground cover	P	Blue, white, purple *Spring*		D	x x
PLEURISY ROOT *N. America*	Asclepiadaceae *Asclepias* spp	2-4 × 2	Robust growth. Fine autumn fruits	P	Orange, pinkish *Summer*	AS	D/S	x
PLUME POPPY *China, Japan*	Papaveraceae *Macleaya cordata*	6-8 × 3	Elegant leaves, milk-white reverse	P	Diffuse cream spikes *Summer*		D	x
POKEWEED *N. America*	Phytolaccaceae *Phytolacca americana*	6 × 4	Enormous clumps	P	Pink spikes followed by purple berries *Summer – autumn*	AS	S/D	x
POPPY *Europe*	Papaveraceae *Papaver rhoeas*	1½ × 1	Field poppy. Shirley strain extends colour range	A	Scarlet in typical form *Summer*		S	x
PRIMROSE *Europe*	Primulaceae *Primula vulgaris*	½ × ½	Common primrose and colour forms	P	Pale yellow *Early spring*	AS	S/D	x x
PURPLE LOOSE-STRIFE *Europe*	Lythraceae *Lythrum salicaria*	5 × 2	Spectacular spikes. Pink forms available. Dead seed heads distinctive	P	Magenta *Summer*	AS	S/D	x

Herb & Country of Origin	Family & Botanical Name	Height and Spread in Feet	Type & Brief Description	Annual Biennial Perennial	Flower: Colour & Season	Accepts Shade	Propagation	Soil Dry → Moist	
PURPLE FLAG IRIS *S. Europe*	Iridaceae *Iris germanica*	2-3 × 1	Common flag iris	P	Typically purple. Now all colours except scarlet *Early summer*		D	x	x
	I. germanica 'Florentina'	2 × 1	Orris root		White *Early summer*				
RHUBARB *E. Asia*	Polygonaceae *Rheum spp*	6 × 4	Culinary and ornamental rhubarbs	P	Great white spikes *Early summer*		D	x	x
ROSEBAY *Europe*	Onagraceae *Epilobium (Chamaenerion) angustifolium*	5 × 2	Invasive plant. Wind-borne seeds	P	Fine pink spikes *Summer*		S/D	x	x
RUE *S. Europe*	Rutaceae *Ruta graveolens*	2 × 2	Good blue-grey foliage. Subshrub	P	Horn-yellow *Late summer*		S/C	x	
SCARLET PIMPERNEL *Europe*	Primulaceae *Anagallis arvensis*	½ × ½	Beautiful morning-opening weed	A	Typically scarlet. Also azure *Summer*		S	x	x
SEA HOLLY *Europe*	Umbelliferae *Eryngium maritimum*	1½ × 1	Grey-white prickly foliage	P	Metallic heads *Summer*		D/S	x	
SELF HEAL *Europe*	Labiatae *Prunella vulgaris*	1 × 1	Carpeter with vertical flower spikes	P	Purple *Summer*	AS	D		x

		Size	Description	Type	Flower / Season	AS	D/S		
SKUNK CABBAGE W. North America	Araceae Lysichitum americanum	3 × 2	Both foetid-scented bog plants with huge summer leaves	P	Yellow, spectacular. Purplish *Early Spring*	AS	D/S		x
E. North America	Symplocarpus foetidus	2 × 2							
BLACK SNAKEROOT N. America E. Asia	Ranunculaceae Cimicifuga spp	4-6 × 2	Elegant late-flowering border plants	P	Creamy white *Autumn*	AS	D	x	x
SNOWDROP Europe W. Asia	Amaryllidaceae Galanthus spp	½ × ½	Well-known spring bulbs	P	White and green *Early spring*	AS	D	x	x
SOUTHERNWOOD S. Europe	Compositae Artemisia abrotanum	2 × 2	Aromatic subshrub. Grey-green leaves	P	Insignificant		C	x	
SQUIRTING CUCUMBER S. Europe	Cucurbitaceae Ecballium elaterium	1 × 5	Spreading bristly plant. Explosive fruits	A	Yellow insignificant *Summer*		S	x	x
STARVEACRE S. Europe	Ranunculaceae Delphinium staphisagria	3 × 1	Hairy palmate leaves	P	Deep purple spikes *Summer*		S	x	x
STRAWBERRY Europe	Rosaceae Fragaria vesca	1 × 3	Roving wild forms. Red and white fruits	P	White *Late spring*	AS	D/S		x
STINKING IRIS Europe	Iridaceae Iris foetidissima	1½ × 2	Evergreen tussocks. Brilliant seed pods	P	Dull purple	AS	D/S	x	x
SUNFLOWER N. America	Compositae Helianthus annuus	6-10 × 2	Enormous plant	A	Yellow cartwheel daisies *Summer*		S	x	

Herb & Country of Origin	Family & Botanical Name	Height and Spread in Feet	Type & Brief Description	Annual Biennial Perennial	Flower: Colour & Season	Accepts Shade	Propagation	Soil Dry → Moist	
SWEET FLAG *Europe*	Araceae *Acorus calamus*	2 × 1	Aromatic, iris-like leaves	P	Insignificant		D		x
TANSY *Europe*	Compositae *Tanacetum vulgare*	3 × 2	Invasive aromatic herb	P	Heads of yellow 'buttons' *Summer*		D	x	x
THOROUGHWORT *E. North America*	Compositae *Eupatorium perfoliatum*	4 × 2	Robust border plant	P	Flat heads of small daisies *Summer*		D		x
THRIFT *Europe*	Plumbaginaceae *Armeria maritima*	½ × ½	Tight green tussocks	P	Pink globular heads *Early summer*		D/S	x	x
TOBACCO *N. Andes*	Solanaceae *Nicotiana rustica*	4 × 2	Wide green leaves	A	Pink tubular flowers *Autumn*		S	x	
	N. x sanderae	3 × 1	Range of scented 'tobacco flowers'	A	White, pink *Summer*		S	x	
TRILLIUMS *N. America*	Trilliaceae *Trillium* spp	1 × 1	Distinctive three-leaved woodlanders	P	White, yellow, blood-red *Late spring*	AS	D		x

		Size	Notes		Flower / Season		Type		
TURTLEHEAD E. North America	Scrophulariaceae *Chelone glabra*	3-4 × 2	Unusual border plants	P	Pink and white *Summer*		D		x
VERONICA E. North America	Scrophulariaceae *Veronicastrum virginicum*	4 × 1	Narrow spires. Good also in seed	P	White, blue *Summer*		C		x
VIOLETS Temperate N. Hemisphere	Violaceae *Viola spp*	½ × ½	Range of well-known violets. Not all are scented	P	Purple, mauve, white *Early spring*	AS	D/S		x
WALLFLOWER Europe	Cruciferae *Cheiranthus cheiri*	1 × 1	Scented subshrub. Often grown as annual	P	Yellow, bronze etc *Spring*		S/C	x	x
WATER LILY Europe	Nymphaceae *Nymphaea alba*	- × 3	Floating-leaved aquatic	P	White scented stars *Summer*		D		x
WIDOW IRIS S. Europe	Iridaceae *Hermodactylus tuberosus*	1½ × 1	Thin iris growth	P	Green and black *Early spring*		D	x	x
WILD GINGER E. North America	Aristolochiaceae *Asarum canadensis*	½ × 2	Spreading ground cover soft heart-shaped leaves. Aromatic	P	Flower insignificant	AS	D	x	x
YELLOW ASPHODEL Mediterranean Region	Liliaceae *Asphodeline lutea*	2 × 1	Grassy grey green tussocks	P	Yellow spikes *Early summer*		D/S	x	x

MODERN DRUG PLANTS, EXTRACTS OF WHICH ARE USED TODAY IN ORTHODOX MEDICINE. *All are poisonous.*

Herb & Country of Origin	Family & Botanical Name	Height & Spread in Feet	Type & Brief Description	Annual Biennial Perennial	Flower: Colour & Season	Accepts Shade	Propagation	Soil Dry → Moist	
AMERICAN MANDRAKE E. North America	Berberidaceae *Podophyllum peltatum*	1½ × 1½	Elegant umbrella-like leaves. Bantam-egg sized fruit in autumn – 'May Apple'	P	Pink. Fleeting *Summer*	AS	D	x	x
AUTUMN CROCUS *Europe*	Liliaceae *Colchicum autumnale*	1 × 1½	Bulbous, wide glossy spring foliage	P	Purple or white *Autumn*	AS	D	x	x
CASTOR OIL *Tropical Africa*	Euphorbiaceae *Ricinus communis*	4–6 × 3	Tender subshrub foliage. Red and purple leaved forms available	P	Pink/white spikes *Summer*	AS	S	x	x
DEADLY NIGHT-SHADE *Europe, Asia*	Solanaceae *Atropa belladonna*	4–5 × 3	Robust growth. Shining black berries follow flowers	P	Purple, bell-shaped *Summer*	AS	S	x	x
FOXGLOVES *Europe*	Scrophulariaceae *Digitalis purpurea*	4–6 × 2	Ornamental spikes	B	White, pink, purple *Summer*	AS	S		x
	D. lanata	3 × 1	Woolly foxglove	B	Narrow spikes. Buff-yellow flowers *Summer*	AS	S		x

HENBANE *Europe*	Solanaceae *Hyoscyamus niger*	2 × 1	Clammy leaves. Striking seed capsules follow	A	Pale yellow, purple veined		S		x
INDIAN TOBACCO *E. North America*	Lobeliaceae *Lobelia inflata*	1½ × ½	Thin, weedy growth	A	Blue *Summer*		S	x	
LILY OF THE VALLEY *Europe*	Liliaceae *Convallaria majalis*	½ × –	Creeping habit. Pairs of shining leaves	P	White *Late spring*	AS	D		x x
MADAGASCAR PERIWINKLE *Madagascar*	Apocynaceae *Catharanthus roseus (Vinca rosea)*	1½ × 1½	Tender subshrub for summer planting	P	Pink/white All year under glass	AS	S/C		x x
OPIUM POPPY *S.E. Europe W. Asia*	Papaveraceae *Papaver somniferum*	3 × 1	Glaucous leaves. Single and double flowers. Fine seed capsules	A	White, purple, red *Late spring, summer*		S	x	
THORN APPLE *N. America*	Solanaceae *Datura strumonium*	2½ × 2	Woody growth. Prickly seed capsules follow flower	A	White trumpets *Summer*		S		x

BEST HERBS FOR POT POURRIS AND SCENTED SACHETS.

Herb & Country of Origin	Family & Botanical Name	Height & Spread in Feet	Type & Brief Description	Annual Biennial Perennial	Flower: Colour & Season	Accepts Shade	Propagation	Soil Dry → Moist
CITRUS S.E. Asia	Rutaceae Citrus spp	5-20 × 5 – 15	Orange/lemon trees. Size determined only by size of winter space	P	White Spring		C/S	x
CLARY S.E. Europe	Labiatae Salvia sclarea	3 × 2	Fine hairy-leaved spikes	B	Blue flowers and pink bracts Summer		S	x
GUM TREE Victoria, Tasmania	Myrtaceae Eucalyptus globulus	6 × 2 in one year	Blue-leaved gum, highly aromatic foliage	P	White, only when mature		S	x
	E. citriodora		Lemon-gum. Both tender trees but grown as annuals					
JASMINE W. China	Oleaceae Jasminum officinale	6-15	Vigorous twiner. Best on south or southwest wall. Variegated form exists	P	White, highly scented Summer		C	x

LAVENDER S. Europe	Labiatae *Lavandula angustifolia*	1½-3 × 2-3	Grey-leaved shrub. Range of cultivars, eg. 'Munstead', 'Hidcote' (dwarf) 'Old English' (robust)	P	Purple, pink, white		C/S	x	x
	L. dentata and other spp		Tender types for summer use	P	Purple *Summer*		C/S	x	
LEMON VERBENA Argentina, Chile	Verbenaceae *Lippia citriodora*	4-8 × 5	Deciduous aromatic shrub. Rather tender	P	Flower insignificant		C	x	
ROSE Asia Minor	Rosaceae *Rosa damascena trigintipetala*	5-6 × 5	Shrub rose. Source of attar of roses. Needs warm position	P	Flat pale pink double flowers		C		x
	R. gallica officinalis	3 × 3	Apothecary's rose	P	Bright cerise		C/D		x
ROSE GERANIUM S. Africa	Geraniaceae *Pelargonium tomentosum, P. quercifolium* and other spp	2 × 2	Range of aromatic subshrubs. None reliably frost hardy in Britain	P	Pink *Summer*		C		x
ORRIS ROOT S. Europe	Iridaceae *Iris florentina*	2 × 1	Rhizomatous perennial flag iris	P	White *Early summer*		D		x
SWEET WOODRUFF Europe	Rubiaceae *Asperula odorata*	¾ × 2	Elegant ground cover	P	White *Summer*	AS	D/C	x	x

DYE PLANTS. USED WITH A SUITABLE MORDANT, MANY PLANTS WILL DYE CLOTH. THE FOLLOWING ARE HISTORICALLY RENOWNED. CLOTH-CLEANING SOAPWORT INCLUDED HERE.

Herb & Country of Origin	Family & Botanical Name	Height & Spread in Feet	Type & Brief Description	Annual Biennial Perennial	Flower: Colour & Season	Accepts Shade	Propagation	Soil Dry → Moist	
DYERS' ALKANET S. Europe	Boraginaceae *Alkanna tinctoria*	2-3 × 2	A bristly borage	B	Attractive blue flowers *Summer*		S	x	
DYERS' GREENWEED Europe	Leguminosae *Genista tinctoria*	4-5 × 4	Elegant shrub. Wand-like growth with pea-shaped flowers. Double form less fleeting	P	Yellow *Early summer*		C/S	x	
LADY'S BEDSTRAW Europe	Rubiaceae *Galium verum*	1 × 2	Tussocks of tiny leaves and flowers	P	Yellow *Summer*		D/S	x	x
MADDER S. Europe	Rubiaceae *Rubia tinctoria*	6 × 3	Bristly scrambler. Best grown on tripod	P	Greenish, insignificant		D/C	x	x
SOAPWORT Europe	Caryophyllaceae *Saponaria officinalis*	2 × 2	Invasive. Double flowered form available	P	Pink *Summer*		D		x
WOAD Europe	Cruciferae *Isatis tinctoria*	3-4 × 2	Glaucous leaves. Showers of black seed-capsules in late summer	P	Tiny, yellow *Early summer*		S	x	

TREES AND SHRUBS WITH HERBAL ATTRIBUTES (EXCLUDING CONVENTIONAL 'HERB-SHRUBS').

Herb & Country of Origin	Family & Botanical Name	Height & Spread in Feet	Type & Brief Description	Deciduous or Evergreen	Flower: Colour & Season	Accepts Shade	Propagation	Soil: Dry		→ Moist
AKEBIA China, Japan	Lardizabalaceae *Akebia trifoliata*	15 × 10	Twiner. Elegant foliage	D	Small purple sprays *Spring*	AS	C	x		x
ALDER Europe	Betulaceae *Alnus glutinosa*	70 × 20	Tree. Remains small in dry soil	D	Male catkins in spring. Female 'cones' follow		S			x
BALSAM POPLAR N. America	Salicaceae *Populus candicans*	100 × 30	Rapid-growing tree unfolding buds, strongly aromatic	D	Catkins *Summer*		C		x	x
	P. balsamifera 'Aurora'	40 × 20	Brightly variegated form. Can be kept pruned back	D		AS	C		x	x
BARBERRY Europe	Berberidaceae *Berberis vulgaris*	8 × 6	Prickly shrubs	D	Yellow sprays, foetid scent	AS	S/C	x		
Japan	*B. thunbergii*	6 × 4	Good autumn colour. Purple-leaved forms	D	Yellow sprays	AS	S/C	x		
BEARBERRY N. circumpolar	Ericaceae *Arctostaphylos uva-ursi*	¾ × 6	Widespreading carpeter for acid soils	E	Pink *Early summer*	AS	C		x	x
BIRD CHERRY Europe	Rosaceae *Prunus avium* See A–Z for further spp	70 × 30	Narrow tree. Good autumn colour	D	White *Early summer*		S/G		x	

Herb & Country of Origin	Family & Botanical Name	Height & Spread in Feet	Type & Brief Description	Deciduous or Evergreen	Flower: Colour & Season	Accepts Shade	Propagation	Soil Dry → Moist
BITTERSWEET VINE *N. America*	Celastraceae *Celastrus scandens*	25 × 25	Rampant climber. Spectacular autumn fruit	D	Greenish *Summer*	AS	C/S	x
BLACKTHORN (SLOE) *Europe*	Rosaceae *Prunus spinosa*	15 × 10	Prickly shrub. Purple fruit	D	White *Early spring*		S/D	x
BOG MYRTLE *N. Hemisphere Circumpolar*	Myricaceae *Myrica gale*	3 × 2	Aromatic shrub for acid soils	D	Brownish *Early summer*		D/C	x
BOX (BOXWOOD) *Europe*	Buxaceae *Buxus sempervirens*	15 × 10	Blue-green foliage. Good for hedging and topiary	E	Greenish	AS	C/D	x
	B. sempervirens 'Suffruticosa'	2 × 1	Dwarf form for edging	E		AS	C/D	x
BROOM *Europe*	Leguminosae *Sarathamnus scoparius*	6 × 5	Leafless shrub stems. Evergreen effect	E	Bright yellow pea-flowers *Summer*	AS	S/C	x
CALIFORNIAN LAUREL *California*	Lauraceae *Umbellularia californica*	20 × 20	Small busy tree. Heavy aromatic scent	E	Greenish	AS	C/S	x
CHASTE TREE *S. Europe*	Verbenaceae *Vitex agnus-castus*	15 × 10	Aromatic leaves. Useful wall shrub	D	Airy sprays. Pale purple *Autumn*		C	x

CHERRY LAUREL S. Europe	Rosaceae *Prunus laurocerasus*	20 × 15	Broad glossy leaves	E	White spikes *Early summer*	AS	C	x
	'Otto Luyken'	5 × 5	Dwarf form			AS		
CLERODENDRON China	Verbenaceae *Clerodendrum bungei*	8 × 4	Suckering shrub. Foetid leaves	D	Fragrant heads of pink flowers *Autumn*	AS		x
CONIFERS	RANGE OF EVERGREENS FOR HEDGES & ARCHITECTURAL USE SEE A–Z			E				
CURRANT Europe	Ribesaceae *Ribes sativum*	5 × 4	Redcurrant. Brilliant fruit. Good on walls	D	Greenish *Spring*	AS	C	x
	R. nigrum	4 × 4	Blackcurrant. Aromatic leaves			AS	C	x
DAPHNE China	Thymelaeaceae *Daphne genkwa*	4 × 3	Delicate shrub	D	Lavender blue *Late winter*	AS	C	x
	D. odora	3 × 3	Early flowering shrub	E	White, pink flushed *Early spring*	AS	C	x
	D. odora aureo-marginata		Hardier variegated form		Intensely fragrant *Early spring*	AS	C	x
ELDER Europe	Caprifoliaceae *Sambucus niger*	15 × 10	Soft, pithy shrub. Fine black fruit	D	Wide heads, white and fragrant *Early summer*	AS	C/S	x
	S. racemosa	10 × 8	Bright red fruit in August		Green heads of flower *Early spring*	AS	C/S	x x

Herb & Country of Origin	Family & Botanical Name	Height & Spread in Feet	Type & Brief Description	Deciduous or Evergreen	Flower: Colour & Season	Accepts Shade	Propagation	Soil Dry → Moist
ELAEAGNUS *China, Japan*	Elaeagnaceae *Elaeagnus pungens*	8 × 8	Robust shrub. Bright variegated form available	E	Small, white and fragrant *Autumn*	AS	C	x
FIG *Mediterranean Region*	Moraceae *Ficus carica*	15 × 10	Striking palmate leaves. Good on walls	D	Flower insignificant		C	x
FIRETHORN *China*	Rosaceae *Pyracantha*	8 × 8	Prickly wall-shrubs. Brilliant autumn fruit	E	White *Early summer*	AS	C	x
FRINGE TREE *E. North America*	Oleaceae *Chionanthus virginicus*	10 × 8	Distinctive long leaves	D	White *Early summer*		C	x
GUM STORAX *S. Europe*	Styracaceae *Styrax officinalis*	10 × 8	Soft-leaved shrub. Good for walls	D	White, scented bells *Early summer*		C	x
HARDY ORANGE *N. and Central China*	Rutaceae *Poncirus trifoliata*	15 × 12	Gaunt prickly shrub. Aromatic. Small bitter oranges produced	D	White *Spring*		C/S	x
HAWTHORN *Europe*	Rosaceae *Crataegus monogyna*	20 × 15	Prickly small tree. Good hedging. Red fruit (haws) in autumn	D	White or pink *Early summer*		S	x

		Size	Notes	E/D	Flower / Season	AS	C/S		
Europe W. Asia	*Ilex aquifolium*	30 × 15	English holly. Prickly leaves. Fine winter fruit on female trees	E	White *Early summer*	AS		x	
Europe and S. Central America	*I. verticillata*	10 × 8	Good autumn display	D	White *Early summer*	AS	S		x
HONEYSUCKLE Europe E. Asia — Caprifoliaceae	*Lonicera periclymenum*	10 × 8	Twiner	D	Pink and cream *Early summer*	AS	C	x	
	L. japonica	15 × 10	Rampant climber	E	Intensely fragrant. Cream *Summer-autumn*	AS	C	x	
HOP TREE E. and S. Central America — Rutaceae	*Ptelea trifoliata*	15 × 10	Distinctive tri-lobed leaves	D	Greenish. Fragrant *Summer*		S/G	x	
HYDRANGEA, CLIMBING Japan — Saxifragaceae	*Hydrangea petiolaris*	15 × 15	Robust self-clinging climber	D	White *Summer*	AS	C		
GUELDER ROSE Europe — Caprifoliaceae	*Viburnum opulus*	15 × 10	Soft shrub. Brilliant red fruit. Sterile form more distinctive in flower	D	White *Early summer*	AS	C		x
IVY Europe — Araliaceae	*Hedera helix*	20 × 20	Invaluable self-clinging climbers. Also good ground cover in knot-gardens	E	Greenish only on non-climbing branches *Autumn*	AS	C	x	

Herb & Country of Origin	Family & Botanical Name	Height & Spread in Feet	Type & Brief Description	Deciduous or Evergreen	Flower: Colour & Season	Accepts Shade	Propagation	Soil Dry → Moist
JAPANESE QUINCE China	Rosaceae Chaenomeles speciosa	8 × 6	Prickly shrub. Good on walls. Fine yellow fruit	D	White, pink, red Early spring	AS	C/S	x
JASMINE W. China	Oleaceae Jasminum officinale	15 × 10	Strong twiner	D	Fragrant, white Mid-summer		C	x
KIWI FRUIT China, Taiwan	Actinidiaceae Actinidia chinensis	15 × 15	Robust twiner. Hairy stems and leaves	D	Insignificant Summer		C	x
LABRADOR TEA N. North America, Greenland	Ericaceae Ledum groenlandicum	2 × 2	Dwarf shrub for acid soils	E	White heads Summer		C/S	x x
LIME, LINDEN	Tiliaceae Tilia cordata	60 × 30	Fine tree. Accepts pleaching	D	Green-white scented flowers Summer			x
LIQUIDAMBAR S.E. North America	Hamamelidaceae Liquidambar styraciflua	50 × 30	Maple-like tree, fine autumn colour	D	Insignificant		S	x
LOQUAT Central China S. Japan	Rosaceae Eriobotrya japonica	15 × 10	Long, leathery leaves	E	White flower spikes Autumn		S/G	x
MAGNOLIA China	Magnoliaceae Magnolia liliiflora (Other spp in A–Z)	15 × 10	One of the best spring-shrubs	D	White, fragrant Spring		C/S	x

Common name / Origin	Family / Botanical name	Size	Notes	E/D	Flowers	AS	C		
MAHONIA China	Mahonia japonica	8 × 8	Magnificent whorls of leaves	E	Yellow, fragrant *October – April*	AS	C		x
MAIDENHAIR TREE China	Ginkgoaceae *Ginkgo biloba*	80 × 20	Columnar tree. Distinctive leaf-pattern. Golden fruit on female trees	D	Insignificant		S/G		x
MEDLAR Europe Asia Minor	Rosaceae *Mespilus germanica*	20 × 20	Broad tree. Brown apple-like fruit	D	White. Dog-rose-like *Spring*		S/G		x
MINTBUSH S. Australia	Labiatae *Prostanthera rotundifolia*	10 × 8	Wall-shrub for mild gardens. Scented leaves	E	Rich purple sprays *Spring*		C		x
MULBERRY W. Asia	Moraceae *Morus nigra*	30 × 30	Gnarled tree. Delicious purple-black fruit	D	Insignificant		C		x
Central China	*M. alba*	40 × 30	Silkworm mulberry. Fruit less useful	D	Insignificant		C		x
MYRTLE Mediterranean Region	Myrtaceae *Myrtus communis*	6-8 × 5	Aromatic in all its parts. Variegated form less hardy	E	White *Late summer*		C/S	x	
	M. communis var. tarentina	3 × 2	Attractive dwarf form	E					
NEW JERSEY TEA E. North America	Rhamnaceae *Ceanothus americanus*	5 × 4	Low shrub from east U.S.A. Brighter west coast spp	D	White *Summer*	AS	S/C		x
OREGON GRAPE W. North America	Berberidaceae *Mahonia aquifolium*	4 × 4	Glossy leaves. Purple fruit	E	Bright yellow *Spring*	AS	C/D		x

Herb & Country of Origin	Family & Botanical Name	Height & Spread in Feet	Type & Brief Description	Deciduous or Evergreen	Flower: Colour & Season	Accepts Shade	Propagation	Soil Dry → Moist
PALM *China, N. Burma*	Palmeae *Trachycarpus fortunei*	30 × 10	The only reliably hardy palm	E	Yellow, on mature plants		S	x (Moist)
POMEGRANATE *S.E. Europe*	Punicaceae *Punica granatum*	10 × 6	Wall shrub with reddish young shoots. Fruit seldom produced	D	Vermilion *Spring*		C	x (Dry)
SUNROSE *S. Europe*	Cistaceae *Cistus ladanifer* and other spp	4 × 3	Aromatic shrubs	E	White, pink *Early summer*		C/S	x (Dry)
ST JOHN'S WORT *China*	Hypericaceae *Hypericum patulum*	3 × 3	Low shrubs for summer display	D	Yellow *Summer*		C	x (Moist)
SCOTS HEATHER, LING *Europe*	Ericaceae *Calluna vulgaris*	1½ × 1½	Low spreading shrub. Wide range of forms for acid soils	E	White, pink, purple *Autumn*		C	x (Moist)
SILVER BIRCH *Europe*	Betulaceae *Betula pendula*	50 × 15	Elegant tree, white bark	D	Catkins *Spring*	AS	S/G	x (Moist)
SPINDLEBUSH *Europe, W. Asia*	Celastraceae *Euonymus europaea*	10 × 8	Open shrub, brilliant pink and orange fruit	D	Greenish *Summer*		C/S	x (Moist)
Temperate E. Asia	*E. alata* (winged spindle)	8 × 8	Distinctive. Corky stems	D	Greenish *Summer*			x (Moist)
SPURGE LAUREL *Europe*	Thymelaeaceae *Daphne laureola*	4 × 3	Dark green bush	E	Green, orange eye *Early spring*	AS	C/S	x (Moist)

Common name / Origin	Family / Species	Size	Description	Type	Flowers / Season		Prop.		
SQUAWBERRY, E. North America	Rubiaceae, *Mitchella repens*	½ × 3	Creeping subshrub. Red berries	E	White, *Early summer*	AS	C		x
STAR JASMINE, China	Oleaceae, *Trachelospermum jasminoides*	20 × 15	Robust twiner	E	White scented flowers, *Summer*		C		x
STRAWBERRY TREE, W. and S. Europe	Ericaceae, *Arbutus unedo*	20 × 15	Gnarled tree, orange fruits	E	White or pink, *Autumn*		C		x
TEA, China	Theaceae, *Camellia sinensis*	6 × 5	Source of commercial tea	E	Small, white camellia-flowers, *Early summer*	AS	C		x
TREE OF HEAVEN, China	Simarubaceae, *Ailanthus altissima*	80 × 40	Tall tree. Accepts stooling for huge leaves	D	Greenish	AS	S	x	
TREE PEONY, China, Tibet	Paeoniaceae, *Paeonia suffruticosa*	5 × 4	Fine foliage	D	Huge white flowers, dark petal blotch, *Late spring*		C/S		x
TRUMPET VINE, China	Bignoniaceae, *Campsis grandiflora*	20 × 15	Self-clinging climber	D	Fine orange trumpet-flowers, *Mid summer*		C		x
TULIP TREE, E. North America	Magnoliaceae, *Liriodendron tulipifera*	100 × 30	Fine tree, distinctive foliage. Autumn colour	D	Orange and green, tulip-like, *Summer*		S/G		x

Herb & Country of Origin	Family & Botanical Name	Height & Spread in Feet	Type & Brief Description	Deciduous or Ever-green	Flower: Colour & Season	Accepts Shade	Propagation	Soil Dry → Moist
WALNUT S.E. Europe W. Asia	Juglandaceae *Juglans regia*	80 × 60	Fine tree, late leafing	D	Insignificant		S/G	x
WAXBERRY E. North America	Myricaceae *Myrica pensylvanica*	6 × 4	Aromatic shrub. Blue-bloomed berries	D	Brownish *Early summer*		C	x
WINTERGREEN N.E. North America	Ericaceae *Gaultheria procumbens*	½ × 3	Creeping aromatic subshrub	E	White *Summer*	AS	C	x
WINTER'S BARK Chile	Winteraceae *Drimys winteri*	30 × 20	White-backed aromatic	E	Cream *Spring*	AS	C	x
WITCH HAZEL E. North America	Hamamelidaceae *Hamamelis virginiana*	15 × 15	Hazel-like shrub	D	Yellow *Autumn*	AS	C	x
W. China	*H. mollis*		More distinctive in flower		Yellow *Winter*	AS	C/G	x

HERB GARDEN ASSOCIATES: Of little or no herbal value but visually compatible.

Herb & Country of Origin	Family & Botanical Name	Height and Spread in Feet	Type & Brief Description	Annual Biennial Perennial	Flower: Colour & Season	Accepts Shade	Propagation	Soil Dry → Moist
BALLOTA Mediterranean Region	Labiatae Ballota pseudodictamnus	2 × 2	White woolly subshrub	P	Insignificant		C	x
CARDOON S. Europe	Compositae Cynara cardunculus	6 × 3	Short-lived but statuesque. Fountain of grey leaves	P	Blue, thistle-like *Late summer*		S	x x
CARNATIONS Europe	Caryophyllaceae Dianthus cvs	1½ × 1	The ancient gillyflowers; pinks and carnations. Grey foliage	P	White, yellow, pink, purple, scarlet		C/S	x x
CARYOPTERIS Garden origin	Verbenaceae Caryopteris x clandonensis	2 × 2	Grey-leaved aromatic subshrub. Fine show of blue spikes	P	Blue-lavender *Late summer*		C/RC	x
JERUSALEM SAGE Mediterranean Region	Labiatae Phlomis fruticosa	4 × 4	Grey-woolly shrub for sunny spot	P	Whorls of hooded yellow flowers *Early summer*		C/S	x
LAMB'S EARS S.E. Europe	Stachys olympica (lanata)	2 × 2	White felted leaves. 'Silver Carpet' is non-flowering form	P	Woolly spikes, pink *Early summer*		D	x x
LAVENDER COTTON S. Europe	Compositae Santolina chamaecyparissus	2 × 3	Grey-white aromatic shrub	P	Hardy yellow flowers *Midsummer*		C/D	x
	S. 'Edward Bowles'	2 × 3	Grey-white aromatic shrub	P	Cream flowers, the best flowering form *Summer*		C/D	x

Herb & Country of Origin	Family & Botanical Name	Height and Spread in Feet	Type & Brief Description	Annual Biennial Perennial	Flower: Colour & Season	Accepts Shade	Propagation	Soil Dry → Moist
LAVENDER C (cont.)	*Santolina virens*	2 × 2	Ferny green-leaved species	P	*Midsummer*		C/D	x
LION'S MANE S. Africa	Labiatae *Leonotis leonurus*	4 × 2	Phlomis-like tender subshrub	P	Whorled spikes of vivid tawny orange *Late summer*		C/S	x
MISS WILMOTT'S GHOST Caucasus	Umbelliferae *Eryngium giganteum*	3 × 1	White-bloomed biennial, prickly leaves	B	Metallic blue-silver heads *Summer*		S	x x
ORNAMENTAL ONIONS Europe, Asia	Lilaceae *Allium caeruleum A. christophii A. karataviense A. moly A. neapolitanum*	1-3 × ½	Range of bulbous perennials	P	White, yellow, purple, in spherical heads *Summer*		D/S	x x
PANSY Europe	Violaceae *Viola cvs*	½ × ½	Old-fashioned bedding perennial grown as annual	A/P	Various *Winter Early spring Summer*		S/C	x
PEROVSKIA W. Pakistan	Labiatae *Perovskia atriplicifolia*	4 × 3	Aromatic grey-leaved subshrub	P	Spikes of soft blue *Late summer*		C	x
PINEAPPLE SAGE Mexico	Labiatae *Salvia rutilans*	4 × 2	Scented-leaved tender subshrub	P	Thin scarlet spikes *Autumn*		C	x
WHITE WORMWOOD Europe, Asia	Compositae *Artemisia arborescens* and other spp	4 × 3	Aromatic white-leaved subshrub. Rather tender	P	Insignificant		D/C/S	x

Appendix I: some herb gardens to visit

Places that are primarily farms and nurseries denoted F and N respectively.
This list does not claim to be exhaustive.

LONDON

Chelsea Physic Garden
Fulham Palace
The Museum of Garden
  History
Westminster Abbey Herb
  Garden
Culpeper the Herbalist,
  21 Bruton St. W1
  (Retail herbalists found in
  London and in the
  university, cathedral and
  spa towns)

THE SOUTH EAST

Bateman's (Burwash)
Eyhorne Manor
  (Hollingbourne)
N   Foliage, Scented and Herb
  Plants (Dorking)
N   Foxhollow Nursery
  (Wallington)
Iden Croft Herbs
  (Staplehurst)
Kew Gardens (Richmond)
Knole (Sevenoaks)
Marle Place Plants
  (Brenchley)
Michelham Priory
  (Hailsham)
Scotney Castle
  (Lamberhurst)
Sissinghurst (Cranbrook)
The Old Rectory Herb Garden
  (Ightham)
N   Wells and Winter
  (Mereworth)
Wisley (Ripley)

THE SOUTH

Beaulieu
Claverton Manor (Bath)

Cranborne Manor
Hollington Nurseries
  (Newbury)
Sutton Manor
The Dower House
  (Badminton)
The Old Rectory (Burghfield)
The Roman Palace and
  Museum (Fishbourne)
Tudor Museum,
  Southampton

THE SOUTH WEST

F   Arne Herbs (Somerton)
Castle Drogo (Chagford)
Dartington Hall (Totnes)
Gaulden Manor (Tolland)
Lackham College of
  Agriculture (Lacock)
Lytes Cary Manor (Ilchester)
Polsue Cottage Herbs (Truro)
St Michael's Mount
  (Penzance)
The Old Barn (Fremington)

EAST ANGLIA

Cambridge Botanic Garden
Coney Weston Hall
  (Bury St Edmunds)
N   Daphne Ffiske Herb
  Nursery (Brundall)
Emmanuel College
  (Cambridge)
Felbrigg Hall
Gunby Hall
  (Burgh-le-Marsh)
Netherfield Herbs
  (Rougham)
Norfolk Lavender
  (King's Lynn)
Oxburgh Hall
Peterborough Cathedral

NF Suffolk Herbs (Sudbury)
Thornham Herbs
(Thornham Magna)
Whittlesea Museum

THE MIDLANDS

Abbey Dore Court
Alderley Grange
Barnsley House (Cirencester)
Capel Manor
Chenies Manor House
(Amersham)
N Greenwrys Herb Farm
(Kington)
Hardwick Hall
(Chesterfield)
Hatfield House
Holme Pierrepont Hall
(Nottingham)
Izaak Walton Cottage
(Shugborough)
Knebworth House
Lathbury Park
(Newport Pagnell)
Lincoln Cathedral
N Mary Webb Herbs
(Shrewsbury)
Mawley Hall
(Cleobury Mortimer)
Moseley Old Hall
(Wolverhampton)
Oak Cottage Herb Farm
(Nesscliffe, Shrewsbury)
Oxford Botanic Garden
Selsley Herb and Goat Farm
Stoke Lacey Herb Garden
(Bromyard)
Stone Cottage (Oakham)
Stratford –
Shakespeare's Birthplace
Garden
New Place
Hall's Croft
Anne Hathaway's Cottage
Thornby Herbs
N Thornbury Herbs (Bromyard)
FN Valeswood Herb Farm
(Shrewsbury)
N Wilton Park Nursery
(Old Beaconsfield)

THE NORTH

Abbey House Museum
(Kirkstall)
Acorn Bank Garden
(Temple Sowerby)
Arley Hall and Gardens
(Northwick)
Elly Hill Herbs (Barmpton)
Little Moreton Hall
(Congleton)
Ness Gardens (Ness Neston)
Robin Pottery, Craft and
Herb Centre
(Thorpe-in-Balne)
Stockeld Park (Wetherby)
York Gate (Adel)
F Yorkshire Herbs (Richmond)

NORTHERN IRELAND

Barbara Pilcher Herbs
(Saintfield, Co. Down)
Braidjule (Broughshane,
Ballymena)
Farm Hill Herbs (Farmhill
Road, Co. Down)
Mount Stewart Gardens
(Newtonards, Co. Down)
Springhill (Moneymore,
Co. Londonderry)

SCOTLAND

Findhorn Foundation
(Forres)
Glasgow Botanic Gardens
Hopetoun House   (South
Queensferry)
Netherbyres
Old Semeil Herb Garden
(Strathdon)
Priorwood Garden (Melrose)
Royal Botanic Garden,
Edinburgh
Threave Garden
(Castle Douglas)

WALES
Welsh Folk Museum
(St Fagans Castle Cardiff)

Appendix II
List of metric equivalents
(approximate figures)

1	in	2.5 cm
1½	ins	4.0 cm
2	ins	5.0 cm
2½	ins	6.0 cm
3	ins	7.5 cm
6	ins	15.0 cm
10	ins	25.5 cm
12	ins (1 ft)	30.0 cm
18	ins	45.0 cm
2	ft	60.0 cm
3	ft	100.0 cm (1 metre)
4	ft	1.2 m
5	ft	1.5 m
10	ft	3.0 m
15	ft	4.5 m
20	ft	6.0 m
30	ft	9.0 m
40	ft	12.0 m
50	ft	15.0 m
100	ft	30.0 m

International Measures

U.K.	U.S.A.	Australia	New Zealand	Canada
20 fl. oz.	1 pint	20 fl. oz.	20 fl. oz.	20 fl. oz.
10 fl. oz.	1 cup	8 fl. oz.	8 fl. oz.	8 fl. oz.
⅝ fl. oz.	1 tablespoon	½ fl. oz.	½ fl. oz.	½ fl. oz.
⅖ fl. oz.	1 dessertspoon	no official measure	—	—
⅕ fl. oz.	1 teaspoon	⅛ fl. oz.	⅙ fl. oz.	⅙ fl. oz.

Select Bibliography

Botanicum Officinale Joseph Miller 1722

The Gardener's Kalendar Philip Miller 1732

The Gardener's Dictionary Philip Miller 1768

Encyclopaedie Diderot 1751

The American Gardener William Cobbett 1821

A Barefoot Doctor's Manual Revolutionary Health Committee of Hanan
  Province   Douglas & McIntyre 1977

Oxford Gardens Mavis Batey   Avebury 1982

Medicinal Plants and Home Remedies of Appalachia Judith Bolyard
  C C Thomas, Springfield, Illinois 1981

The Dry Garden Beth Chatto   Dent 1978

Excursion Flora of the British Isles Clapham, Tutin & Warburg
  Cambridge 1968

Spices, Salts and Aromatics in the English Kitchen Elizabeth David
  Penguin 1970

Mediterranean Food Elizabeth David   Penguin 1955

A Modern Herbal M Grieve   Penguin 1980

A History of British Gardening Miles Hadfield   Hamlyn 1969

Medieval Gardens John Harvey   Batsford 1981

Hortus III Bailey Hortorium   Macmillan 1977

Flowers of the Mediterranean Huxley & Polunin   Chatto & Windus 1961

Italian Gardens Georgina Masson   Thames & Hudson 1961

Medieval English Gardens Teresa McLean   Collins 1981

Shaker Herbs Amy Bess Miller   Porter 1976

Plants for Shade Allen Paterson   Dent 1981

The Education of a Gardener Russell Page   Collins 1962

Flowers of Greece and the Balkans Oleg Polunin   Oxford 1980

Rose Recipes from Olden Times E S Rohde   Dover Pubns 1974

Gardens of Herbs E S Rohde   Dover Pubns 1969

Old English Herbals E S Rohde   Peter Smith

Old English Gardening Books E S Rohde

Leaves from Our Tuscan Kitchen Janet Ross & Michael Waterfield
  Penguin 1977

Encyclopedia of Herbs and Herbalism ed M Stuart   Orbis 1979

The Home Book of Greek Cookery Joyce Stubbs   Faber 1963

Perennial Garden Plants G S Thomas   Dent 1984 ed

A Select Herb and Medical Glossary

Antispasmodic – Relieves spasms or convulsions
Anodyne – Allays pain; soothing
Antiseptic – Opposes sepsis, putrefaction, or decay
Aperient – Mild purgative or laxative
Aromatic – Fragrant or spicy
Astringent – Contracts the tissues of the body, checking discharges of blood, mucus, etc.

Carminative – Allays pain by expelling gases from the stomach
Cathartic – Cleanses the bowels
Caustic – Destroy or eat away by chemical action
Chronic – Continuing as a fixed condition

Diuretic – Increases the secretion of urine

Emetic – Induces vomiting
Emollient – Softening application, which allays irritations of the skin
Expectorant – Promotes discharge of mucus from the lungs

Infusion – Steeping or soaking in water or another substance to extract the virtues of a material

Narcotic – Drug that dulls the senses, relieves pain, and induces sleep

Sedative – Tending to calm, allaying irritability and pain

Styptic – Produces contraction of the blood vessels, stopping bleeding

Vulnerary – Useful in healing wounds

INDEX